The Perennial Philosophy

Series

About this Book

"Thought-provoking, comprehensive, and foundational.... This brings to the mind the great intellectual contributions of Sufis through history."

—**Islam Online**, the most frequented Internet site by Muslims in the English language

"Anyone, whether he or she be a Muslim, a follower of another religion, or more generally anyone who is seriously interested in the relation between Islam and the West and Islam in the West, cannot but be attracted to this volume, which is the fruit of the thought of some of the best minds of the younger generation of Muslim scholars, who are at the same time part of Western society, bearing upon some of the most momentous issues of the day. These are issues which affect the lives of everyone, young and old, issues which everyone in the Islamic world and the West who has the necessary capability and vision must seek to address and solve for the sake of all of God's creatures wherever they might be, for as the Qur´an asserts, to God belong both the East and the West."

—**Seyyed Hossein Nasr**, the George Washington University, author of *The Heart of Islam: Enduring Values for Humanity*

"This book is of critical importance in clearing away the confusion and media-induced misconception that fundamentalists—be they contemporary *Wahhābīs* or violent extremists who have hijacked the word '*jihād*'—represent traditional or orthodox Islam. They do not now and never have, any more than that rebel and regicide Oliver Cromwell represented traditional Christianity."

—**Abdallah Schleifer**, the American University in Cairo, and former NBC News Cairo Bureau Chief

"This anthology illuminates a subject all too often obscured by misunderstanding, prejudice, political opportunism, and downright ignorance—namely, the problematic relations between traditional Islam, various strains of politico-religious 'fundamentalism,' and the modern West. These thoughtful essays will prove invaluable to those seeking to understand the deep-seated forces at work, the true nature of Islam, and the malignant role of the secular ideologies of modernity. It is a work of the most timely urgency, addressed to people of good will, whatever their political and religious affiliations and wherever they may be found."

—**Harry Oldmeadow**, La Trobe University, Bendigo, author of *Journeys East: 20th Century Western Encounters with Eastern Religious Traditions*

"Significant numbers of Muslims, especially among the young, the inexperienced, and the disenfranchised see modernity, globalization, and the preponderance of the West as gravely threatening to their culture and Tradition, and in this respect their perceptions are correct. Some of them believe they are defenders of God's works but, like their Western confreres, they lack profound understanding not only of human nature but also of their own Tradition. Both sides operate from false premises and are driven by ignorance and a 'zeal not according to knowledge.' Truth, Justice, and Peace are found on the side of the Eternal, not with erroneous and concupiscent interests, whether Eastern or Western. The essays in this collection will help the serious reader understand the real underlying issues."

—**Alvin Moore, Jr.**, co-editor of *Selected Letters of Ananda K. Coomaraswamy*

World Wisdom
The Library of Perennial Philosophy

The Library of Perennial Philosophy is dedicated to the exposition of the timeless Truth underlying the diverse religions. This Truth, often referred to as the *Sophia Perennis*—or Perennial Wisdom—finds its expression in the revealed Scriptures as well as the writings of the great sages and the artistic creations of the traditional worlds.

The Perennial Philosophy provides the intellectual principles capable of explaining both the formal contradictions and the transcendent unity of the great religions.

Ranging from the writings of the great sages of the past, to the perennialist authors of our time, each series of our Library has a different focus. As a whole, they express the inner unanimity, transforming radiance, and irreplaceable values of the great spiritual traditions.

Islam, Fundamentalism, and the Betrayal of Tradition: Essays by Western Muslim Scholars appears as one of our selections in the Perennial Philosophy series.

The Perennial Philosophy Series

In the beginning of the Twentieth Century, a school of thought arose which has focused on the enunciation and explanation of the Perennial Philosophy. Deeply rooted in the sense of the sacred, the writings of its leading exponents establish an indispensable foundation for understanding the timeless Truth and spiritual practices which live in the heart of all religions. Some of these titles are companion volumes to the Treasures of the World's Religions series, which allows a comparison of the writings of the great sages of the past with the perennialist authors of our time.

Islam, Fundamentalism, and the Betrayal of Tradition

Essays by Western Muslim Scholars

Edited by

Joseph E. B. Lumbard

Foreword by

Seyyed Hossein Nasr

World Wisdom

Islam, Fundamentalism, and the Betrayal of Tradition: Essays by Western Muslim Scholars

Library of Congress Cataloging-in-Publication Data

Islam, fundamentalism, and the betrayal of tradition : essays by Western Muslim scholars / edited by Joseph E.B. Lumbard ; foreword by Seyyed Hossein Nasr.
p. cm. -- (The perennial philosophy series)
Includes bibliographical references and index.
ISBN 0-941532-60-7 (pbk. : alk. paper)
1. Islamic fundamentalism. 2. Islam and world politics. 3. September 11 Terrorist Attacks, 2001. I. Lumbard, Joseph E. B., 1969- II. Series.

BP60.I7848 2004
297'.09'051--dc22

2004007930

Printed on acid-free paper in Canada.

For information address World Wisdom, Inc.
P.O. Box 2682, Bloomington, Indiana 47402-2682

Table of Contents

Foreword

The stream of books and articles written in the West on Islam, which had already become much more expansive and diverse in its currents in the 1980s and 1990s after such major events as the Iranian Revolution of 1979, the Lebanese Civil War, the rise of Islamic movements among Palestinians, and Islamic resistance to the invasion of Afghanistan by the Soviet Union, turned into a torrent after the tragedy of September 11, 2001. Suddenly nearly everyone in the West and especially America was interested in learning more about Islam, and sales of the Quran rose dramatically. But unfortunately many tried to satisfy this rise of interest, which marked a unique opportunity to learn more about Islam in an authentic manner, through works which were based more on ignorance, misinformation, and in some cases disinformation, than on the truth. Those non-Muslims who tried to benefit from the situation for their particular political and religious agendas, sought to inundate the media as well as the journals and even shelves of books in major bookstores with images, ideas, and analyses that for the most part did little to create mutual understanding, there being fortunately some notable exceptions. As for the Islamic community in America, which found itself at the center of the storm created by the terrible events of that day, it was also not able to take full advantage of this unique opportunity to explain Islam on the basis of a full understanding of the Islamic intellectual and spiritual tradition, nor was it familiar with the nature of the audience it was now called upon to address. Again there were a few notable exceptions, and some laudable efforts were made towards that end, but by and large the Islamic community did not rise fully to the challenge which history presented to it, or at least it has not done so until now.

That opportunity has not, however, disappeared, and the thirst for greater understanding of Islam, along with the need to satisfy that thirst, continues. We can attest to this fact by the wide reception given to our own *The Heart of Islam*, written after the September 11th tragedy and published on the first anniversary of that event. The fact that the present book appears a couple of years later than the catastrophic event, which incited so much interest about Islam in America and the West in general, does not at all detract from its timeliness. In fact the present work is one of the most significant, timely, and fresh Muslim responses to that event, and marks an important step in bringing the deeper resources of the Islamic tradition to bear upon the task at hand, the task to present the authentic teachings of Islam to the West at this difficult moment of history as far as the relations between Islam and the West are concerned.

The authors of the essays contained in this volume are all members of a younger generation of Muslims who were either born or have lived for a long time in the West. They are all accomplished scholars, having studied in the best Western institutions of higher learning. They know Western thought and culture in depth, not only superficially. Furthermore, not only are they devout, practicing Muslims, but they are also deeply rooted in the Islamic intellectual tradition whose great intellectual power they bring to bear upon the solution to the problems at hand.

Until the middle of the twentieth century, scholarship on Islam in the West was for all practical purposes the monopoly of Western orientalists and missionaries, with the exception of a few Muslim scholars here and there who would write in French or English and even more rarely in other European languages. After the Second World War many more Muslim scholars began to write in European languages and some even lived in the West, while a number were of European origin. This group naturally increased in size as the number of Muslims living in Europe and America increased dramatically from the 1960s onward. But most of these scholars, especially those who had migrated from the Islamic world to the West, were either professionals such as physicians and engineers, who were pious and therefore wanted to write about Islam, or scholars of the Islamic sciences who had mastered a European language and began to write on Islamic subjects in that language. Members of the first category usually knew little of the intricacies of the traditional Islamic sciences while that of the second category knew a great deal about Islamic Law and the transmitted sciences, but usually little about the Islamic intellectual tradition, although there were some exceptions. Moreover, both groups, in contrast to European or American Muslims, were usually ignorant of the Western intellectual and religious tradition and the deeper roots of the problems with which they were seeking to deal and the more profound dimensions of the context in which Islam had to be presented to the Western intelligentsia.

The role of explaining the Islamic tradition to the West under the condition of knowing both worlds in depth was to be performed primarily by the traditionalist authors, chief among them René Guénon, Frithjof Schuon, Titus Burckhardt, and Martin Lings. This group consisted of individuals with the most profound knowledge of the Islamic tradition as well as of Christianity and Western philosophical schools. They spoke of Islam from within, in the language of the West, and they spoke with great authority and eloquence. Their significance in creating better understanding between Christianity and Islam, and in fact between all authentic religious traditions, can hardly be overemphasized. They created a whole body of writings which avoided the shortcomings of orientalist, missionary, and ordinary Muslim apologetic writings in the presentation of Islam to the West.

Moreover, these traditionalist authors provided a profound critique of the modern world which allowed those with intellectual discernment to understand in depth the nature of the forces which have brought chaos to humanity and now threaten human existence on earth itself. The influence of these authors began to be felt in the Islamic world itself and now grows from day to day in that world. In the West where official circles of learning sought to ignore them for a long time, they gradually began to exercise ever greater influence as the second half of the twentieth century came to a close.

The young scholars whose essays appear in this volume are well acquainted with the works of all the different categories of writers on Islam as well as with the texts of classical Muslim authorities. They know the works of Muslims writing in Western languages as well as in Islamic languages, belonging to schools as diverse as Sufism and puritanical rationalism and what is now called fundamentalism. They have also been fully trained in Western universities and so are familiar with the writings and ideas of Christian missionaries, classical orientalists and their successors, as well as the social scientists writing on the Islamic world. Moreover, they know deeply the works of the traditionalist authors and through them have gained not only the deepest insights into metaphysics as well as the nature of modernism, but also the means of presenting Islam to the Western world in such a way that it will be both authentic and comprehensible to their intended audience. Finally, they are fully aware of contemporary and current issues, and as young scholars, they work and breathe in a world in which the events of the day can hardly be neglected, especially those events which concern Islam, their religion, and its relation to the society in which they live.

The authors of this book are both Muslims and Westerners. They write as Western Muslims who are profoundly and authentically rooted in the Islamic tradition while being at the same time deeply respectful of Judaism and Christianity. They are also fully knowledgeable about Western thought and culture in their many facets. Furthermore, all these young scholars, as members of Western society, have experienced firsthand the reactions in their immediate ambience to the September 11th tragedy. They have heard the shrill voices against Islam itself and read the shallow criticisms made by so-called experts about this or that aspect of Islam. They have also read the more thoughtful and profound works on the causes of that event, on what transpires now in the Islamic world, on the nature of Islam, and on the future of Islam in the West.

The result of their meditations upon these experiences and readings is this groundbreaking volume, which presents a new and timely voice of several well-trained and serious engaged scholars writing about major issues that have come to the forefront as a result of the events of the past couple of years, but which of course have their roots in older historical realities. Anyone, whether he or she be a Muslim, a follower of another religion, or more generally anyone who is seriously interested in the relation between Islam and the West and Islam in the West, cannot but be attracted to this volume, which is the fruit of the thought of some of the best minds of the younger generation of Muslim scholars, who are at the same time part of Western society, bearing upon some of the most momentous issues of the day. These are issues which affect the lives of everyone, young and old, issues which everyone in the Islamic world and the West who has the necessary capability and vision must seek to address and solve for the sake of all of God's creatures wherever they might be, for as the Quran asserts, to God belong both the East and the West. As a person engaged for decades in the endeavor to create better understanding between Islam and the West, I must express my gratitude to the authors and especially the editor of this work, Joseph Lumbard, for making this valuable study and its publication possible.

And God knows best. *wa'Llāhu aʿlam.*

—Seyyed Hossein Nasr
Bethesda, Maryland
14th of Rajab, 1424
11th of September, 2003

Introduction

Like many in the West, the contributors to this book have been appalled and at times disheartened by the increasing tensions between Islam and the West. But unlike most such citizens, we are Muslims born in the West or immigrants to the West. We are thus faced with a predicament wherein the religion that has nurtured some of us for our entire lives, and some of us since the time we embraced Islam, has come to be identified for many of our neighbors and co-workers with the ideologies of a deviant if not heretical minority. Several Muslims have attempted to address such misinterpretations and misrepresentations in newspapers and magazines, on the radio and television. Some has been good, much has been mediocre, but most has been quite bad. It is painfully evident that many Muslims in the West, particularly the United States, have yet to fully navigate the complexities of living between two civilizations.

Despite the existence of many organizations, the Muslim communities of the Western world have not been able to bring the full intellectual resources of the Islamic tradition to bear upon contemporary issues. The increasing awareness of Islam in the West presents an opportunity for Muslims to share their traditions and their teachings with much of America and Europe, exploring ways in which the principles inherent in both civilizations can provide solutions to the dilemmas confronting all people in the modern world. But too often it has been left to non-Muslim scholars of Islam, such as John Esposito, Karen Armstrong, and Michael Sells, to represent the Islamic community to non-Muslims and defend it against myriad accusations. While many Muslims owe such scholars a debt of gratitude, we must also chasten ourselves for having been unprepared to carry the burden which was ours.

But the late twentieth and early twenty-first century has given rise to a new phase in the history of relations between Islam and the West.[1] The paradoxes of colonialism have produced a large crop of young Muslims who are of both the East and the West, Muslims who are as familiar with the writings of William Shakespeare, René Descartes and Mark Twain as with those of Jalāl al-Dīn Rūmī, Ibn Khaldūn and Naguib Mahfouz. At a time when the forces of technology and globalization are pushing us ever closer together, we must make use of all available means to ameliorate the tensions which arise from our mutual misunderstanding. This generation is uniquely qualified to help us all bridge the gap between Islam and the West, for they have spent much of their lives bridging it within themselves and their families.

The thousand-year history of writings on Islam in European languages, discussed by Ibrahim Kalin in his contribution to this volume, has never before seen a phase such as this. Distortion of Islamic history and Islamic teachings was an intricate component of the first European encounters with Islam. Being immersed in the sacred universe of Christianity, citizens of the Holy Roman Empire could not but see Islam as a heresy and its Prophet as the greatest of all charlatans—even as the anti-Christ. This faith-based rejection was, however, combined with a profound appreciation for the intellectual and cultural contributions of Islamic civilization. The great translation movements of Andalusia bear witness to a remarkable period of cross-fertilization which has forever bound Judaism, Christianity and Islam to a common intellectual heritage. In the Renaissance, however, hostilities towards Islam took a different direction. Islam was no longer the superior military and political force it had once been; there was thus no outward impetus to grant it respect. The roots of its contributions to European thought and culture could now be conveniently forgotten and seen as properly European. Islam therefore ceased to be viewed as a formidable political and theological adversary, and was now portrayed as the religion of primitive Arabs devoid of intellectual or cultural sophistication. This opened the door to new and different ways of conceptualizing the Orient. Enlightenment figures such as Voltaire employed Islamic images to undermine Christianity and in fact religion itself. In contrast, figures such as Goethe and Emerson displayed respect for Islam, though they had a somewhat unrealistic and romanticized view of the Orient.

With the dawning of the age of colonialism, European intellectuals gained greater access to things Islamic. But, acting as the intellectual complement to colonialism, they tended to employ these tools with all the hubris of those who see themselves as the saviors of less advanced peoples. This period of study gave rise to the academic treatment of Eastern traditions now known as Orientalism and led to some of the greatest distortions in the history of the interaction between Islam and the West.[2] The hostility of Christian polemic continued to determine the mode of analysis, but now its conclusions were conveyed through a presumed "scientific method" whose proponents rarely ventured to assess its premises. The guiding principle of the Orientalist enterprise was the unspoken presumption that Islam is not a divine revelation but a human creation, and an inferior one at that. Scholars such as Renan, Caetani, Hurgronge, Schacht, and Goldziher reported to their European peers that Islam was an arid Semitic religion of the desert whose adherents had "turned in a horizontal spiral around their techniques"[3] for over a thousand years. It was held by many that despite an early period of fertile intellectual activity, Muslims had failed to build upon this and had served as mere transmitters of the Greek tradition, returning it to its rightful European owners. While there were important and influential exceptions to this trend, for the most part the Orientalist enterprise served as the hand-maid of the colonialist enterprise, providing its ideological justification.

After World War I the West had essentially achieved a complete political triumph over the Islamic world. The Ottoman Empire had been divided into several politically unsustainable entities and the introduction of Western education, combined with a deep inferiority complex, had caused many Muslims to proclaim Western ideologies, sometimes openly rejecting the teachings of the Islamic tradition. Islam, however, continued to be practiced in forms which derive both from the Qur´ānic revelation and the unfolding and development of that sacred message through more than a thousand years of scholarship and devotion. Here the substance of the Islamic message continued to be manifest in the institutions and forms of society. This is what we refer to throughout this volume as "traditional Islam," which "... implies both horizontal continuity with the Origin and a vertical nexus which relates each movement of the life of the tradition in question to the meta-historical Transcendental Reality."[4] These forms of Islam based on a conscious attachment to established traditions which have the revelation as their central referent were represented by many eminent figures of the modern era, such as Maulanā Thanvī, ʿAbd al-Qādir al-Jazā´irī and Shaykh Aḥmad al-ʿAlawī, whose teachings have been examined in this volume. But the voices of such scholars were often unheard by those of the East and West who preferred to focus on the cacophony resulting from a deep existential crisis in the heartland of Islam. As a result, the majority of observers have only had access to the most conspicuous trends, those which clamor for attention: radical puritanical reformism, what we now call "fundamentalism," and intellectual capitulation in the form of almost every modern "ism." But these are modern phenomena which, as the first part of this volume demonstrates, represent a complete break with traditional Islamic teachings—not a conscious development from them or of them. Of all the possible "Islams" one could choose from, these are the least representative of its traditional teachings and classical heritage, for they have no scriptural, historical, or intellectual foundations. As such, they cannot provide sustainable solutions for Muslim people still rooted in their faith traditions.[5] Only the continuity of tradition in both its vertical and horizontal dimensions can provide a real foundation for genuine reformation.

Though Orientalist writings continued in this period and were joined by new approaches to the Islamic world in the field of the social sciences, the twentieth century also witnessed the rise of an entirely new approach to the Orient and the Islamic world, one which challenged the basic assumptions of the Orientalist enterprise. Writers such as René Guénon, Ananda

Coomaraswamy, Frithjof Schuon, and Titus Burckhardt began to examine the underlying principles of Eastern religions in a manner which did not assume the superiority of European culture or of modernity. These writers applied the principles of the teachings they espoused to the claims of rationalism, scientism and all of secular humanism in a manner that challenged the very foundations of modern Western civilization. Guénon's *The Reign of Quantity and the Signs of the Times* stands as a watershed event in European intellectual history, providing an acute philosophical assessment of the presuppositions of modernity and detailing the deleterious results of their applications. Coomaraswamy wrote of Hindu, Islamic, Christian, Greek, and Buddhist teachings in a manner that made clear to all the common principles underlying each tradition. Like Guénon he employed these principles to argue that, in relation to all traditional civilizations, modern civilization represents a monstrous deviation, for it is founded upon transient manifestations rather than eternal principles, upon sand rather than stone. Like Coomaraswamy, Burckhardt illustrated the manner in which traditional arts and crafts are a conscious manifestation of spiritual teachings. But his most significant contribution was to introduce Western audiences to the profound teachings of Islamic mystical theology represented by such figures as Ibn al-ʿArabī and ʿAbd al-Karīm al-Jīlī. Schuon expounded upon the quintessential spiritual message which lies at the heart of all religious traditions, and charted a course by which one can live in accord with tradition despite the vagaries and absurdities of the modern world. By examining the inner intellectual dimension of all religions, these authors exposed many of the traditional forms of intellectuality which had been obscured by the reductionist accounts of Western observers. In doing so they directly challenged the exclusivist claims of modern secularism and laid the groundwork for a revivification and re-articulation of the traditional teachings of all religions. Though conversant with the teachings of many religions, they were well aware that one can only *live* in one tradition. Thus Guénon, Schuon and Burckhardt each embraced Islam; they lived as Muslims, worshiped as Muslims and died as Muslims.

In the wake of these pioneers, the last few decades have seen the emergence of Muslim writers who are fully conversant with both European and Islamic intellectual traditions. Among these are authors such as Seyyed Hossein Nasr, Martin Lings, Charles Le Gai Eaton, and Jean-Louis Michon—all of whom have intellectual roots in both the East and West and consciously follow in the tradition of Schuon, Guénon and Burckhardt. In addition there are numerous other scholars, such as A. K. Brohi in Pakistan and Naquib al-Attas in Malaysia, who provide Islamic responses to the challenges of secular humanism with full awareness of both intellectual traditions. The writings of such authors have brought to Western audiences the intellectual traditions of Islam which have too long laid beyond the purview of Western academics who preferred to see the Islamic intellectual tradition as a thing of the past.

In revealing this most important dimension of Islam and applying its lessons to modern living, they have laid the foundation for the current generation of authors who are represented in this volume. Some are Muslim scholars who, like Seyyed Hossein Nasr, have been educated at the highest levels of the Western educational system while remaining firmly attached to their Islamic heritage. Others are young people of European origin who like Martin Lings have embraced Islam and spent many years living and studying in the Islamic world. Such scholars are deeply rooted in both traditions, such that the fruit of their trees is of both the East and the West. Having evaluated and built upon the many generations mentioned above, their appraisal of the current situation offers invaluable insights for a world where the children of these two civilizations are literally living on top of one another and their destinies are inevitably intertwined.

On the one hand, this generation of scholars functions as interpreters of the West for Muslims. On the other, they are ambassadors of Islam in the West, as well as interpreters of Islam for Western audiences. This book is thus addressed both to non-Muslims in the West and to Muslims the world over. It is hoped that both will benefit from greater exposure to the traditional teachings of Islam and the application of these teachings to the issues which now confront us all. Though scholars with this dual heritage have presented many essays and lectures in various forums, this collection represents the beginning of what we hope will be many collaborative efforts. The contributors are young Muslims from England, America, Pakistan, Iran, Turkey, and Egypt, representing a wide range of disciplines, from economics, sociology, and international relations to philosophy, comparative religion, and Islamic studies. In coordinating our efforts at every stage of this project, we strived to produce a volume which draws from several disciplines and perspectives while presenting a unified analysis. We have employed both traditional Islamic teachings and modern methodologies to provide in-depth analyses of Islam in the modern world. Such is the only means by which the aberrations now at large can be fully addressed, for the factors fomenting Islamic extremism arise from a meeting between East and West. Sustainable solutions must therefore draw from both civilizations.

The first part of the book, "Religious Foundations," is comprised of three essays which demonstrate that from a traditional Islamic perspective the acts of aggression which now dominate perceptions of Islam have no textual, historical, or intellectual legitimacy. David Dakake's "The Myth of a Militant Islam" counters the misunderstanding of Islam as an inherently violent faith by directly discussing Qur´ānic verses which have been misinterpreted by reporters, academics, and religious extremists of several traditions. The paper draws from the earliest and most authoritative Qur´ānic commentaries, the *ḥadīth* tradition (sayings of the Prophet Muḥammad), and early historical works to reveal the characteristics and, in particular, the limits that the first Muslims placed upon *jihād*. It concludes with a detailed analysis of distortions of Qur´ānic verses in the now infamous calls for "*jihād*" against the "Jews and Crusaders," showing the fundamentally anti-Islamic basis of such perspectives in light of the earliest sources.

Joseph Lumbard's "The Decline of Knowledge and the Rise of Ideology in the Modern Islamic World" examines the journey from the principles presented by David Dakake to the aberrations of today. This, he argues, results in part from an imbalance in the application of the Islamic sciences, which has allowed for the misinterpretations of both strident puritanical reformists and liberal secularists to persist and prevail. Lumbard maintains that the contributions of "the *iḥsānī* intellectual tradition," which combines the highest degree of intellectual and spiritual rigor, have been largely dismissed by both factions. Without the basic tools and fundamental insights of this tradition, Muslims have been unable to provide holistic solutions to the questions posed by the onset of modernism. Only when the legitimacy of the spiritual and intellectual traditions of Islam are recognized, and their teachings employed, will Muslims find sustainable solutions to the problems which now confront their societies.

To provide an historical illustration of the intellectual traditions discussed by Joseph Lumbard, Fuad Naeem's "A Traditional Islamic Response to the Rise of Modernism" examines the response of the famous Indian scholar Maulanā Ashraf ʿAlī Thanvī (d. 1942) to the rise of modernism in India. It details how Muslims of India, such as Sayyid Aḥmad Khān and Chirāgh ʿAlī, attempted to modernize and secularize Islam in response to the challenges posed by British colonization, and then presents Thanvī's poignant critique of distortions of Islam prevalent in the Indian subcontinent—a critique based upon the traditional teachings of the Islamic philosophical and spiritual traditions. Thanvī's approach stands in stark contrast to the ignorant reactionary approach of most fundamentalists, for it places thought before action and is based upon principles rather than slogans. Though his is a logical and philosophical critique of the highest order, Thanvī's aim is to address the root of all ignorance, the illness of the heart. From the perspective of traditional Islam, which Thanvī represents, it is only when the heart has been treated that political transformations can occur.

These three essays serve to familiarize the reader with the traditional teachings of Islam, which for over fourteen hundred years have established a norm that has enjoyed manifestations in many forms in both the Sunnī and Shīʿite worlds. Some have argued that radical militancy is endemic to

Islam and that Muslims must secularize in order to ameliorate these problems; but such an analysis belies a grave misunderstanding of Islam in all its many manifestations. In fact, were the teachings of Islam to be followed and a true Islamic revival to take place, militant extremists would no longer have an audience. Many analysts fail to realize that it is the very pressure to secularize which has produced the narrow interpretations characteristic of modern fundamentalism.[6] So long as Muslim peoples continue to feel a steady and suffocating pressure to secularize and Westernize, strident puritanical reductionism will continue to be seen by many as a viable, if not the only, alternative.

Whereas Part I clears the ground of common misconceptions, Part II, "Historical Dimensions," presents the historical background, and Part III, "Political Dimensions," applies the principles of traditional Islamic teachings to the exigencies of the moment in a contemporary language. The essays in these sections demonstrate that such teachings are essential for understanding the place of religious extremism and charting a path toward resolutions. Though written from within different academic disciplines, the authors provide complementary analyses based upon common principles. Important themes such as the conflict between tradition and modernity, the need for spiritual revival, and the decrepitude of fanaticism are woven throughout.

Drawing upon historical evidence and citing such figures as Ṣalāḥ al Dīn al-Ayyūbī (Saladin) and ʿAbd al-Qādir al-Jazāʾirī, Reza Shah-Kazemi's "Recollecting the Spirit of *Jihād*" provides examples of later generations of Muslims who acted in accord with the principles elucidated in Part I. It distinguishes between the stereotype of "jihadism" and the traditional Islamic understanding of *jihād*, demonstrating that Islamic and Western sources alike reveal a profound chivalry among Muslim warriors which derives from the precepts of the Qurʾān and the practice of the Prophet Muḥammad. As Shah-Kazemi writes: "The true warrior of Islam smites the neck of his own anger with the sword of forbearance; the false warrior strikes at the neck of his enemy with the sword of his own unbridled ego. For the first, the spirit of Islam determines *jihād*; for the second, bitter anger, masquerading as *jihād*, determines Islam. The contrast between the two could hardly be clearer."

Ibrahim Kalin's "Roots of Misconception: Euro-American Perceptions of Islam Before and After September 11" provides a historical framework for the analysis in Part III. He examines Western perceptions of Islam by addressing the religious, philosophical, and ideological factors that have shaped them, from medieval polemics to nineteenth-century romanticism. He then analyzes modern Euro-American perceptions of Islam, demonstrating how inherited ideologies have shaped presentations of Islam in forums as disparate as academia and Hollywood. Kalin concludes with a discussion of the confrontationist and accommodationist views of Islam in the U. S. While the former calls for an all-out confrontation and clash between the two civilizations, the latter views Islam as a sister civilization of the West and an intricate component of a tradition which is Judeo-Christian-Islamic, not only Judeo-Christian.

Waleed El-Ansary's "The Economics of Terrorism: How bin Laden is Changing the Rules of the Game" draws upon the observations in the previous essays to examine the strategic issues which must be accounted for in combating terrorism. El-Ansary applies modern game theory in an effort to understand the recent terrorist attacks against the United States, and analyzes the effectiveness of proposed strategies against terrorism. He argues that the inability of policy-makers to understand the world-views and self-images of many "terrorists" prevents them from envisioning effective counter-terrorism policies. The self-understanding of "terrorists" and "fundamentalists" must be seen in contrast to the self-understanding of traditional Muslims, which reveals terrorism and fundamentalism to be a deviation from the established norm. Unfortunately, the presuppositions of Orientalism, which most political analysts have inherited, prevent them from effectively evaluating the self-understanding of Muslims, thus leading to unnecessary antagonisms. This leads policy-makers into egregious strategic errors which have potentially disastrous consequences for us all.

Ejaz Akram's "The Muslim World and Globalization: Modernity and the Roots of Conflict" examines Muslim views of the West. It studies the political, economic, and social consequences of globalization in the contemporary Muslim world—particularly the Middle East—and argues that the inherently Euro-centric nature of globalization carries with it ideologies which are not conducive to the mores of local peoples. Drawing from the essays in Parts I and II, Akram illustrates why Muslims view many of the so-called "advantages" of globalization as disadvantages that challenge the principles by which they wish to live. He argues that tensions in many parts of the Islamic world can only be eased when Muslim peoples are able to choose ways of life and forms of government that rise organically from their own teachings and history. Until such time, we are condemned to patchwork reforms.

The essays in Parts II and III demonstrate that without a change of understanding in the light of common principles, all attempts to arrive at the political, intellectual, and economic solutions necessary to weed out terrorism will fail. The policy proposals that dominate the current political discourse are likely to backfire, for they are based on ideologies and do not account for realities. People of the Islamic world, people of the West, and people with roots in both worlds desire an end to all forms of conflict between the two civilizations. But to bring an end to the threats posed by radical extremists, we must recognize that they represent a deviation from a norm. When this norm is acknowledged and understood, people of both worlds will be better able to reach a common ground from which we can work together to address the negative consequences of fanaticism in all its forms. The legitimacy that the "religious authorities" of radical Muslim groups lend to their cause is, as the essays in Part I demonstrate, completely illegitimate from a traditional Islamic perspective. In order to formulate rulings they discard the principles and methodologies of Islamic scholarship, replacing them with conjecture and opinion. Select verses of scripture and sayings of the Prophet are then taken out of their context and used to justify positions which are unimaginable when such sayings are viewed in context.[7] Awareness of this, combined respect for the right of all civilizations to maintain alternative social values and economic systems, will enable us to eradicate the pseudo-religious legitimacy that is the cornerstone of terrorism. With diligent efforts the edifice of terrorism can then be brought down.

The influence of T. J. Winter of Cambridge University is evident in several essays among this collection. For the last decade he has been among those scholars who employ the insights of traditional Islamic intellectuality to answer the distortions of "fundamentalists" and illuminate the deleterious nature of the modern world. Like Seyyed Hossein Nasr and Martin Lings, T. J. Winter is a living exemplar of the "*iḥsānī* intellectual tradition" discussed in Joseph Lumbard's essay. He has been kind enough to let us reprint his essay "The Poverty of Fanaticism" as an epilogue to the volume. First written for Muslims after the attack on the World Trade Center in 1993, this essay also provides non-Muslims with insight into the dialogue which has been taking place among Muslims for many years. Like the first four essays in this collection, "The Poverty of Fanaticism" details the completely un-Islamic nature of modern fanaticism. But unlike these essays it provides important reflections from experiences within the Islamic community, showing that just as fanaticism has eaten away at the relations between the Islamic world and the West, so too has it eaten at the very core of the Muslim community. Considering that they were written some ten years ago, his words are eerily prescient of much that has since transpired. He concludes in a tone that expresses a sentiment shared by all the contributors to this volume:

> At this critical moment in our history, the *umma* (Islamic community) has only one realistic hope for survival, and that is to restore the "middle way," defined by that sophisticated classical consensus which was worked out over painful centuries of debate and scholarship. That consensus alone has the demonstrable ability to provide a basis for unity. But it can only be retrieved when we improve the state of our hearts, and fill them with the Islamic virtues of affection, respect, tolerance, and reconciliation. This inner reform, which is the

> traditional competence of Sufism, is a precondition for the restoration of unity and decency in the Islamic movement. The alternative is likely to be continued, and agonizing, failure.

It is our hope that these few essays will be a humble step toward introducing Muslims and non-Muslims alike to the traditional Islamic teachings that are necessary for bringing an end to the agonizing failure that has characterized relations between Islam and the West for too long. Our intention is not to lay blame, for nothing is to be gained from an endless cycle of recriminations. Our intention is only to identify the true nature of the illnesses which now afflict both the Islamic world and the West. In these flagitious times, when too much is determined by pelf and power, and when world leaders believe their juxtaposed ideological monologues constitute dialogue, there is an urgent need to move beyond subjective blame to objective analysis. Though some may blame the West for many of the illnesses in the Islamic world, the effects of colonization and globalization could never have been so far reaching had Muslims maintained their traditional teachings. Though others may blame Islam for the spread of wanton violence, such violence is a defining, if not *the* defining, feature of the twentieth century, and certainly did not originate in the Islamic world. In either case, neither Western civilization nor Islamic civilization can be exonerated. In answering the question "what went wrong?" it is incumbent upon us all to acknowledge that much has gone wrong the world over. To look at the other and ask this question is to answer the question itself; for what has gone wrong is that we of the West and we of the Islamic world have foisted the blame for our folly upon one another, rather than taking account of ourselves.

—Joseph E. B. Lumbard
Cairo, Egypt

Notes

1 On the face of it, the distinction between Islam and the West is improper, for Islam is a religion and the West is a geographical designation. Nonetheless, this has become an effective distinction for discussing some essential political and cultural issues. The West is no longer defined solely by its Christian heritage. It is now identified more closely with secular humanism and all the "isms" that have arisen therefrom. The term "the West" is thus used throughout these essays to identify a particular set of peoples that have a Judeo-Christian heritage, but who now live for the most part according to the principles of secular humanism. This can be contrasted to Islam, because Muslims the world over, though disagreeing on many things, identify themselves with a central core of beliefs and a common spiritual heritage which, despite many claims to the contrary, is not compatible with the ideologies of secularism.

2 For a study of the history of Orientalism see Edward Said, *Orientalism* (New York: Vintage Books, 1979). As Said observes in this much debated passage:

> The Orientalist surveys the Orient from above, with the aim of getting hold of the whole sprawling panorama before him—culture, religion, mind, history, society. To do this he must see every detail through the device of a set of reductive categories (the Semites, the Muslim mind, the Orient, and so forth). Since these categories are primarily schematic and efficient ones, and since it is more or less assumed that no Oriental can know himself the way an Orientalist can, any vision of the Orient ultimately comes to rely for its coherence and force on the person, institution, or discourse whose property it is.... [W]e have noted how in the history of ideas about the Near Orient in the West these ideas have maintained themselves regardless of any evidence disputing them. (Indeed, we can argue that these ideas produce evidence that proves their validity) (p. 239).

3 R. Brunschvig, "Perspectives," in G. E. von Grunebaum, ed., *Unity and Variety in Muslim Civilization* (Chicago: University of Chicago Press, 1955), p. 5.

4 Seyyed Hossein Nasr, *Traditional Islam in the Modern World* (London: Kegan Paul International, 1987), p. 13. For more on tradition in the traditionalist perspective see James S. Cutsinger, "An Open Letter on Tradition," *Modern Age* 36, no. 3 (1994).

5 The facile bifurcation of modern trends into "modern" and "fundamentalist" Islam is detrimental to our true understanding of Islam. Such an attitude is demonstrated in Daniel Pipes *Militant Islam Reaches America* (New York: W. W. Norton & Company, 2002). Pipes is correct in stating that there is a battle among Muslims for the soul of Islam; but rather than recognizing all of the nuances and the many groups involved in this struggle he argues: "A battle is now taking place for the soul of Islam. On one side stand the moderates, those Muslims eager to accept Western ways, confident to learn from outsiders, oriented towards democracy, and ready to integrate in the world. On the other stand the Islamists—fearful, seeking strong rule, hoping to push the outside world away" (p. 27). The notion that adopting Western ways is synonymous with integrating into "the world" is pure racism. Where is it that Muslims now live? As statistical analyses have demonstrated, most Muslims are eager for true democracy, but have little desire to adopt Western moral standards. Furthermore, the "Islamists" are quite eager to learn from the outside, as demonstrated by their use of rockets, guns and computers, and their manipulation of media outlets. In other essays, Pipes recognizes this paradox and

acknowledges the existence of a "traditional Islam," but he does not see it as a player in the battle for "the soul of Islam." This is far from the reality a Muslim experiences in the Islamic community, both within and outside of the Islamic world.

6 As Bruce Lawrence has observed in his influential study of Islamic fundamentalism, *Defenders of God: The Fundamentalist Revolt Against the Modern Age* (San Francisco: Harper & Row, 1989):

> Without modernity there are no fundamentalists, just as there are no modernists. The identity of fundamentalism, both as a psychological mindset and as a historical movement, is shaped by the modern world. Fundamentalists seem bifurcated between their cause and their outcome; they are at once the consequence of modernity and the antithesis of modernism.
>
> Either way, one cannot speak of premodern fundamentalists.... To speak about fundamentalism and to trace the lineage of any cadre of fundamentalists one must begin with the specific points of connectedness to, and interaction with, the process of the heralded global material transformation of our world that we call modernization, the result of which was modernity. (p. 6)

7 For a detailed analysis of this modern "pseudo-methodology" and the deleterious effects it has had within the Islamic world, particularly in the field of law, see Khalid Abou El Fadl, *Speaking in God's Name: Islamic Law, Authority and Women* (Cambridge: Oneworld Publications, 2001).

Part I

Religious Foundations

Chapter 1

The Myth of a Militant Islam

David Dakake

In the post-September 11th environment there is an urgent need for a clear enunciation of the views of traditional Islam in regard to *jihād*, so-called "holy war." The first matter which needs to be made clear is that *jihād* is not simply fighting or holy warfare. In Arabic, *jihād* literally means "effort," that is, to exert oneself in some way or another. Within the context of Islam, *jihād* has the meaning of exerting oneself for the sake of God, and this exertion can be in an infinite number of ways, from giving charity and feeding the poor, to concentrating intently in one's prayers, to controlling one's self and showing patience and forgiveness in the face of offenses, to gaining authentic knowledge, to physical fighting to stop oppression and injustice. Generally speaking, anything that requires something of us—that is, requires that we go beyond the confines of our individual ego and desires—or anything that we bear with or strive after for the sake of pleasing God can be spoken of as a "*jihād*" in Islam.[1] This understanding of *jihād* is such that when the "five pillars"[2] of the faith are taught, *jihād* is sometimes classified as a "sixth pillar" which pervades the other five, representing an attitude or intention that should be present in whatever one does for the sake of God.

This being said, there is no doubt that *jihād* has an important martial aspect. To understand this we should remember that within the Islamic tradition the term "*jihād*" has been understood to possess two poles: an outward pole and an inward pole. These two poles are illustrated in the words of the Prophet of Islam when he said to his companions, after they had returned from a military campaign in defense of the Medinan community: "We have returned from the lesser (*asghar*) *jihād* to the greater (*akbar*) *jihād*."[3] Here the lesser *jihād* refers to physical fighting, whereas having come back to the relative physical safety of their city of Medina, the Muslims faced yet a greater *jihād*—namely, the struggle against the passionate, carnal soul that constantly seeks its own self-satisfaction above all else, being forgetful of God. This famous saying of the Prophet emphasizes the hierarchy of the two types of *jihād*, as well as the essential "balance" that must be maintained between its outward and inward forms,[4] a balance often neglected in the approach of certain modern Islamic groups that seek to reform people and society from "without," forcing change in the outward behavior of men and women without first bringing about a sincere change in their hearts and minds. This is the lesson of the words of the Qur´ān when God says, "We never change the state of a people until they change themselves" (13:11).[5] This lesson, as we shall see when we examine the earliest military *jihād*, was not lost on the first Muslims.

In the present crisis, the pronouncements of many self-styled Middle East "experts" and Muslim "authorities" who have dealt with the subject of *jihād* have generally been of two kinds. There have been those who have sought, in a sense, to brush aside the whole issue and history of military *jihād* in Islam in favor of a purely spiritualized notion of "striving" in the way of God; and there have been those, both Muslim and non-Muslim, who have provided literal or surface readings of Qur´ānic verses related to *jihād* and "fighting" (*qitāl*) in an attempt to reduce all of Islam to military *jihād*.[6] The first view represents an apologetic attitude that attempts to satisfy Western notions of non-violence and political correctness but, in so doing, provides an "understanding" that lacks any real relationship to the thought of the majority of Muslim peoples throughout Islamic history. The second view, which would make Islam synonymous with "warfare," is the result either of sheer ignorance or of political agendas that are served by the perpetuation of animosity between peoples. This second position ignores entirely the commentary and analysis of the Islamic intellectual tradition that has served for over one thousand years as a key for Muslims to understand Qur´ānic pronouncements related to *jihād*. In this essay we will neither water down the analysis of *jihād* to suit those modernists who oppose any notions of legitimate religious struggle and conflict, nor disregard, as do the "fundamentalists," the intellectual and spiritual heritage of Islam which has defined for traditional Muslims the validity, but also the limitations, of the lesser *jihād*.

In carrying out this study we propose to examine those verses of the Qur´ān that deal with fighting, as well as those which define those who are to be fought against in *jihād*. We will also provide, along with this textual analysis of Qur´ānic doctrines of war, an historical analysis of the actual forms of the earliest *jihād* and the conduct of the *mujāhidūn*, the fighters in *jihād*, as exemplified by the Prophet of Islam and his successors, the "Rightly-guided Caliphs," given that their actions have served for Muslims as an indispensable example to clarify Qur´ānic pronouncements.[7] In this way, we hope to avoid both the etherialization of *jihād* by Muslim apologists, and the distortion of the tradition at the hands of the "fundamentalists." Lastly, we will examine "fundamentalist" interpretations of *jihād* and compare them with the traditional understanding of *jihād* in the early Qur´ānic commentaries and the actual history of Islam.

"Do Not Take Christians and Jews as *Awliyā´*"

Following the events of September 11th there is one verse of the Qur´ān which has often been quoted by radio announcers, talk-show hosts, and "fundamentalists" in both the East and the West. Before we deal with the actual issue of warfare or military *jihād*, it is necessary to say something about this verse which, if not understood correctly, can bias any further discussions. This verse appears in chapter 5, verse 51 of the Qur´ān:

> O, you who believe [in the message of Muḥammad], do not take Jews and Christians as *awliyā´*. They are *awliyā´* to one another, and the one among you who turns to them is of them. Truly, God does not guide wrongdoing folk.

The word *awliyā´* (sing. *walī*), which we left above in the original Arabic, has been commonly translated into English as "friends."[8] Given this translation, the verse appears to be a very clear statement opposing what we might term "normative" or "kindly relations" between Muslims and non-Muslims; but when we look at the traditional Qur´ānic commentaries of medieval times, which discuss the events surrounding the revelation of this verse, the modern translation becomes suspect. But before examining this issue in depth, it is necessary to clarify the importance of "verse context" in the Qur´ān. Here a comparison between the Biblical text and the Qur´ān is helpful.

Comparing the Bible and the Qur´ān, we can use certain images to illustrate some of the major stylistic differences between the two sacred scriptures. We could say, for example, that the Bible is like a "flowing stream"; when one reads the text there is a constant contextualization of the various verses, stories, chapters, and books. One begins reading with the story of Genesis, the creation of the world and the first man and woman, and then proceeds on through time, moving into the stories of the early patriarchs, then the later Hebrew judges and prophets, the coming of Christ, the post-Jesus community of the Apostles, and finally the end of the world in the Book of Revelation. As one reads the Bible there is a historical context established for each of the major stories and events which enables the reader to situate what is being said within time and space, and indeed priority. The orientation of events as related to the chapters and verses is made explicit through the historical "flow" of the stories and, in the case of the New Testament, the eventual culmination of the text and all history.

In contrast, if we were to use an image to illustrate the Qur´ānic revelation, it would be that of an individual standing upon a mountain at night as lightning flashes on him and in a valley below.[9] As this individual looks out upon the landscape shrouded in darkness, he would see sudden flashes, sudden illuminations of different portions of the mountain and the valley, but there would not appear to be any immediate relationship between these different illuminated regions, surrounded as they are by vast shadows. Of course, a relationship does exist between the different areas illuminated by the lightning, but that relationship is not explicit. It is hidden amid the darkness. This is something like the situation that is faced by the reader upon first examining the Qur´ān. One will often read sections of the text and wonder what is the relationship between the various pronouncements that one encounters, for the Qur´ān does not tell "stories" as the Western reader is accustomed to from the Biblical tradition. In fact, there is only one "full-length" story in the Qur´ānic text, in the chapter on the prophet Joseph. The rest of the Qur´ān is a series of verses grouped into chapters and sections, and often two verses right next to one another will actually refer to two completely different events in the life of the early Islamic community. It is for this reason that the Qur´ānic commentary tradition (*tafsīr*) deals so extensively with what is known in Arabic as *asbāb al-nuzūl*, or the occasions for God revealing particular Qur´ānic verses. Without reference to these "occasions" of revelation most of the verses of the Qur´ān would be susceptible to any and all forms of interpretation. This issue of the need for knowledge of the commentary tradition is, of course, further complicated—for those unable to read the original Arabic text—by translations, which often add yet another layer of difficulty for coming to terms with the meaning of the verses. When we examine verse 5:51, we encounter both these problems of context and translation.

The difficulties in understanding verse 5:51 begin with the translation of the Arabic word *awliyā´*, commonly rendered as "friends." In the context of this verse, the word *awliyā´* does not mean "friends" at all, as we use the term in English, and we know this from examining the occasion for its revelation. While it is true that *awliyā´* can mean "friends," it has additional meanings such as "guardians," "protectors," and even "legal guardians." When we consult the traditional commentaries on the Qur´ān, we are told that this verse was revealed at a particularly delicate moment in the life of the early Muslim community. To understand this verse it is thus necessary to explain the existential situation of the Muslims at this time in Arabia.

Before 5:51 was revealed, the Prophet of Islam and the Muslims had only recently migrated as a community from Makka to Medina, some 400 kilometers to the north. They had done so, according to Islamic histories, due to the persecution to which they were subjected at the hands of their fellow tribesmen and relatives in Makka. Most Makkans worshipped many idols as "gods" and feared the rising interest in the message of Muḥammad within the city, even though he was himself a son of Makka. The Makkans feared the growing presence of the Muslims amongst them because the Muslims claimed that there was only one true God, who had no physical image, and who required of men virtue, generosity, and fair and kind treatment of the weaker members of society. This simple message, in fact, threatened to overturn the order of Makkan society, based as it was upon the worship of multiple gods and the privilege of the strong and the wealthy. It also threatened to disrupt the economic benefits of this privilege, the annual pilgrimage season, when peoples from all over Arabia would come to worship their many idols/gods at the Kaᶜba—a cubical structure which the Qur´ān claims was originally built by Abraham and his son Ishmael as a temple to the one God, before the decadence of religion in Arabia.[10] The message of Islam threatened to replace the social and economic system of Makkan polytheism with the worship of the one God, Who—as in the stories of the Old Testament—would not allow that others be worshiped alongside Him. In this difficult environment the Prophet of Islam preached peacefully the message of monotheism and virtue, but he and his small band of followers were eventually driven from the city by torture, embargo, threats of assassination, and various other forms of humiliation and abuse. The Muslims then migrated to Medina where the Prophet had been invited to come and live in safety with his followers and where the main Arab tribes of the city had willingly accepted his message and authority.

According to one of the earliest and most famous Qur´ānic commentators, al-Ṭabarī (225-310 A.H. / 839-923 C.E.), it was not long after this migration to Medina that verse 5:51 was revealed. Specifically, al-Ṭabarī tells us that this verse came down around the time of the battle of Badr (2 A.H. / 623 C.E.) or perhaps after the battle of Uhud (3 A.H. / 625 C.E.).[11] In these early days the Muslim community constituted no more than a few hundred people and had already left the city of Makka; yet the Makkans continued to attempt to confront them militarily, and these two early battles, as well as others, were crucial events in the history of the early Islamic community. Militarily, the Makkans were a far more powerful force than the Muslims and they had allies throughout Arabia. Given the small numbers of the Muslims, the Prophet and his fledgling community faced the real possibility of utter annihilation should they lose any of these early conflicts. Al-Ṭabarī tells us that within this highly charged environment some members of the Muslim community wanted to make individual alliances with other non-Muslim tribes in the region. Within Medina there were Jewish tribes who constituted a powerful presence in the town and who were on good terms with the Makkans, and to the north of the city there were also Christian Arab tribes. Some Muslims saw the possibility of making alliances with one or more of these groups as a way of guaranteeing their own survival should the Makkan armies ultimately triumph. This was the stark reality of Arabia at that time; it was only through the protection of one's tribe or alliances with other tribes or clans that one's individual security was insured.

From the perspective of Islam, however, the Prophet realized that a young community, faced with great peril, could not allow such "dissension" in the ranks of the faithful as would be created by various individuals making bonds of loyalty with other groups not committed to the Islamic message. Indeed, from the Islamic point of view such actions, had they been allowed, would have been a kind of communal suicide that would have seriously undermined Muslim unity, broken the morale of the community (*umma*), and perhaps caused the many individuals making such alliances to lack fortitude in the face of danger.

Bearing these historical issues in mind, it becomes obvious that the translation of *awliyā´* as "friends" is incorrect. It should be rendered, in accord with another of its traditional Arabic meanings, as "protectors" or "guardians" in the strict military sense of these terms. The verse should be read as, "Do not take Christians and Jews as your protectors. They are protectors to one another ..." This is the true message of the verse, and the appropriateness of this understanding is supported by the fact that the Qur´ān does not oppose simple kindness between peoples, as is clear from verse 60:8, to which we shall now turn.

"To Deal Kindly and Justly"

Verse 60:8 says, "God does not forbid that you should deal kindly and justly with those who do not fight you for the sake of [your] religion or drive you out of your homes. Truly, God loves those who are just." Al-Ṭabarī tells us that this verse was revealed on the occasion of an incident involving the half-sister of one of the Prophet's wives.[12] According to him, Asmā´ bint Abī Bakr, who was a Muslim living in Medina, received some gifts from her mother, Qutaylah, who lived in Makka. Qutaylah had refused to convert to Islam and continued to practice the idolatrous ways of the Makkans. Asmā´ said, upon receiving the gifts, that she would not accept them, given that they came from one who had rejected the message of Islam and indeed one who had chosen to live among the arch-enemies of the Muslims; but then the above Qur´ānic verse was revealed to the Prophet, indicating that there was no need to be ungracious towards the one who gave these gifts, even though she had rejected the message of the Prophet and was living with the enemies of Islam.

Al-Ṭabarī goes even further in his analysis of the verse by criticizing those Muslims who say that 60:8 was later abrogated by another Qur´ānic verse which says, "Slay the idolaters wheresoever you find them" (9:5).[13]

Al-Ṭabarī says that the most proper interpretation of verse 60:8 is that God commanded kindness and justice to be shown "amongst all of the kinds of communities and creeds" (*min jamīʿ asnāf al-milāl wa'l-adyān*) and did not specify by His words some communities to the exclusion of others. Al-Ṭabarī says that here God speaks in general of any group that does not openly fight against the Muslims or drive them out of their homes, and that the opinion that this kindness was abrogated by later Qur'ānic statements makes no sense (*lā maʿnā li-qawl man qāla dhālik mansūkh*).[14] This understanding may seem to be in contradiction with our previous statement that the Makkans were indeed at war with the Muslims; however, Qutaylah, being a woman, could not technically be considered a "combatant" according to Islamic law. Indeed, this shows the essential distinction between combatants and non-combatants in the rules of Muslim warfare. This distinction, as we see from the example of Qutaylah, is to be upheld even in the context of engagement with an actively hostile enemy, as were the Makkans. Therefore, Islam does not oppose friendship and kindness between peoples who are not at war with one another and, even in the case of war, clear distinctions are to be made between "those who fight" and "those who do not fight." We shall examine this principle further in the next section.

"Slay Them Wheresoever You Find Them"

Another verse that is related to *jihād*, and also deals with the subject of those against whom *jihād* is to be waged, is 2:190-191. According to many accounts, this verse represents the first command given by God to the Muslims to carry out military *jihād*,[15] but this command had specific limitations placed upon it, as we shall see. The Qur'ānic text reads as follows:

> Fight in the way of God against those who fight you, but transgress not the limits. Truly, God does not love the transgressors [of limits].
>
> And slay them wheresoever you find them, and turn them out from where they have turned you out.

Al-Ṭabarī tells us that this verse is not to be read as a *carte blanche* to attack any and all non-Muslim peoples; rather, he says, the verse was revealed specifically in relation to fighting the idolaters of Makka, who are referred to in Arabic sources by the technical term *mushrikūn* or *mushrikīn* (sing. *mushrik*).[16] This term comes from a three-letter Arabic root "sh-r-k" which means "to associate" or "take a partner unto something," and the word *mushrikūn* literally means "those who take a partner unto God," that is to say, "polytheists" or "idolaters." It should be noted that from the point of view of Islamic law, this injunction to perform *jihād* against the polytheists does not pertain to either Jews or Christians. Neither Jews nor Christians are ever referred to within the Qur´ān by the terms *mushrik* or *mushrikūn*. They have, in fact, a very different status according to the Qur´ān, which often refers to the two groups together by the technical term *ahl al-kitāb* or "People of the Book," meaning people who have been given a scripture by God other than the Muslims. We shall discuss the status of Jews and Christians later, but what is important to recognize here is that this call to *jihād* was revealed in relation to a specific group of people, the idolaters of Makka, and within a specific context, a context of persecution and the driving of Muslims from their homes in Makka because of their religion. Indeed, this understanding is accepted not only by al-Ṭabarī but, he says, it is the view of most Qur´ān interpreters.[17]

In addition to this context for the first military *jihād*, there were also limits placed upon the early Muslims who carried out *jihād* against the *mushrikūn*. Verse 2:190 speaks of "fight[ing] in the way of God" but also of not transgressing the "limits." What are these limits? Al-Ṭabarī gives many accounts detailing the limits placed upon the *mujāhidūn*. He says, for instance, that the cousin of the Prophet of Islam, Ibn ᶜAbbās, commented upon verse 2:190 as follows: "Do not kill women, or children, or the old, or the one who greets you with peace, or [the one who] restrains his hand [from hurting you], and if you do this then you have transgressed."[18] Another tradition related by al-Ṭabarī comes from the Umayyad Caliph ᶜUmar ibn ᶜAbd al-ᶜAzīz or ᶜUmar II (99/717-101/720 C.E.), who explained the meaning of 2:191 as: "... do not fight he who does not fight you, that is to say women, children, and monks."[19]

These statements quoted by al-Ṭabarī are very much in keeping with other commands given specifically by the Prophet and the Rightly-guided Caliphs (Abū Bakr, ᶜUmar, ᶜUthmān and ᶜAlī) to the Muslim armies involved in *jihād*. These commands are noted in the various *ḥadīth* collections, i.e., records of the sayings of the Prophet and his companions, which along with the Qur´ān form the basis for determining the Islamic nature of any act. Some examples of these *ḥadīth* are:

> Nāfiᶜ reported that the Prophet of God (may peace be upon him) found women killed in some battles, and he condemned such an act and prohibited the killing of women and children.[20]

> When Abū Bakr al-Ṣiddīq [the trusted friend of the Prophet and first of the Rightly-guided Caliphs] sent an army to Syria, he went on foot with Yazīd ibn Abū Sufyān who was the commander of a quarter of the forces .... [Abū Bakr said to him:] "I instruct you in ten matters: Do not kill women, children, the old, or the infirm; do not cut down fruit-bearing trees; do not destroy any town; do not cut the gums of sheep or camels except for the purpose of eating; do not burn date-trees nor submerge them; do not steal from booty and do not be cowardly."[21]

> [The Umayyad Caliph] ʿUmar ibn ʿAbd al-ʿAzīz wrote to one of his administrators: We have learnt that whenever the Prophet of God (may peace be upon him) sent out a force, he used to command them, "Fight, taking the name of the Lord. You are fighting in the cause of the Lord with people who have disbelieved and rejected the Lord. Do not commit theft; do not break vows; do not cut ears and noses; do not kill women and children. Communicate this to your armies."[22]

> Once when Rabāḥ ibn Rabīʿah went forth with the Messenger of Allāh, he and [the] companions of the Prophet passed by a woman who had been slain. The Messenger halted and said: "She is not one who would have fought." Thereupon, he looked at the men and said to one of them: "Run after Khālid Ibn al-Walīd[23] [and tell him] that he must not slay children, serfs, or women."[24]

Such statements are common throughout the *ḥadith* collections and leave little doubt as to the limits set upon the military *jihād*, regardless of the enemy that is faced.

"Perform *Jihād* Against the *Kāfirūn*"

As we noted earlier, the Qur´ān does not speak of Jews or Christians as *mushrikūn* or polytheists. Therefore, none of the verses of the Qur´ān that pertain to fighting the *mushrikūn* pertain to them. However, it must be admitted that the Qur´ān does, within a limited context, speak of Jews and Christians as *kāfirūn*, a term often translated into English as "unbelievers," although its literal meaning is, "Those who cover over [the truth]" in some form or another. Unfortunately, the common translation of this term as "unbelievers" gives it nuances of meaning from Western cultural history that do not necessarily apply to the original Arabic, such as the fact that "unbelief" in English is synonymous with "atheism." In Arabic, however, *kufr* or "covering" does not necessarily refer to lack of faith but to a lack of correct thinking on one or more aspects of faith. In fact Muslims can also be *kāfirūn*. For instance, according to the traditional commentaries, verse 9:49, "There are some who say, 'Give me leave to stay behind and do not tempt me.' Surely they have fallen into temptation already and hell encompasses the unbelievers (*kāfirūn*)," refers to those Muslims who refused to respond to the Prophet's call to go on an expedition to Tabūk.[25]

The important question that could be asked, however, is: Does not the Qur´ān speak about fighting against the *kāfirūn*, such as in the verse "O Messenger, perform *jihād* against the unbelievers (*kāfirūn*) and the hypocrites (*munafiqūn*)" (9:73)? Does this verse not imply an essential militancy between Muslims on the one hand, and Jews and Christians on the other? In answering these questions we must refer to both Qur´ānic pronouncements and to the historical actions of the early Muslims in *jihād*.

We will deal with the issues of the Qur´ān first and then turn, in the next section, to what the Muslims actually did in *jihād*.

When we look at the comments of al-Ṭabarī regarding verse 9:73, as well as those of Ibn Kathīr (d. 774 A.H. / 1372 C.E.), perhaps the most famous of Sunnī Qur´ān commentators, both seem to condone the idea that this verse relates to violent or military *jihād*. Both make a distinction, however, between the two types of *jihād* mentioned in verse 9:73: *jihād* against the *kāfirūn*, and *jihād* against the *munafiqūn*. Each states that the *jihād* against the *munafiqūn* or hypocrites—i.e., those Muslims who knowingly disobey the commands of God—is "*bi´l-lisān*," meaning "with the tongue." That is to say, one should reprimand the Muslim hypocrites with critical speech, not with physical violence. Whereas, in regard to the *kāfirūn*, both commentators make reference to the idea that the *jihād* against them is "*bi´l-ṣayf*," or "by the sword."[26] This may seem to suggest that violent suppression of Jews and Christians is demanded, since we have already mentioned that both Jews and Christians—though never called *mushrikūn*—are sometimes referred to as *kāfirūn*. But before drawing this conclusion we must look more closely at how the Qur´ān defines the *kāfirūn*. Here it is useful to refer to a series of Qur´ānic verses referring to the "People of the Book," such as 98:1, 98:6, 5:78, and 2:105.

Verse 98:1 reads: "Those who disbelieved (*kafarū*) among (*min*) the People of the Book and the polytheists (*mushrikūn*) would not have left off erring until the clear truth came to them." This verse clearly indicates that "to disbelieve" is not a characteristic belonging to all Jews and Christians or People of the Book. Instead, it declares that disbelief is a characteristic of some "among" the People of the Book. This limiting of the declaration of unbelief is established by the Arabic preposition *min* within the quotation, which serves to distinguish a distinct species within a genus, namely, those unbelievers present within the larger believing Jewish and Christian communities. This delimitation is also to be seen in verse 98:6 which says, "Those who disbelieved (*kafarū*) among the People of the Book are in Hell-fire." Verses 5:78 and 2:105 are yet further examples of this qualifying and limiting of *kufr* or "unbelief" in regard to the People of the Book. They state, respectively:

> Those who disbelieved (*kafarū*) *among* the Tribe of Israel were cursed by the tongue of David and Jesus, son of Mary. [emphasis added]
>
> Neither those who disbelieved (*kafarū*) *among* the People of the Book, nor the polytheists (*mushrikūn*), love that anything good should be sent down to you from your Lord. [emphasis added]

We see in these verses that the Qur´ānic perspective, as regards the followers of faiths "other than Islam," is a subtle one, not simply a blanket condemnation of all non-Muslims. It is important to recall here the words of verses 113-115 of chapter 3 of the Qur´ān, which say:

> Not all of them are alike. Of the People of the Book are a group that stand (in prayer), rehearse the signs of God throughout the night and prostrate.
>
> They believe in God and the Last Day; they enjoin what is right and forbid what is wrong, and they hasten in (all) good works. These are among the righteous. Of the good that they do, nothing will be rejected of them, and God knows the God-fearing ones.

Keeping these Qur´ānic distinctions in mind, the injunction to fight the *kāfirūn* "by the sword" does not then apply to all Jews and Christians, but only to some "among" them. But this raises the question, who, among the Jews and Christians, are the Muslims to fight? To answer this question we must now turn to the historical facts of the *jihād* of the first Muslims.

The *Jihād* of the First Muslims

It is perhaps best to begin our discussion of historical *jihād* by recalling that the first *jihād* in Islam was not martial and had nothing to do with violence. The first *jihād* is referred to in the Qur´ān in verse 25:52, which states, "Do not obey the unbelievers (*kāfirūn*), but strive against them (*jāhidhum*) with it, a great striving." This somewhat enigmatic verse, traditionally understood to have been revealed at Makka, i.e., before any divine decree had been given as regards performance of military *jihād* (which came only later in the Medinan period), speaks of striving against the unbelievers by way of "it." Both al-Ṭabarī and Ibn Kathīr relate traditions from Ibn ʿAbbās and from Ibn Zayd ibn Ḥārith, the son of the Prophet's adopted son, telling us that this "it"—the means by which to carry out *jihād*—is the Qur´ān itself.[27] In other words, the earliest command to *jihād* was a kind of preaching of the Qur´ān to the Makkans, or perhaps a taking solace or refuge in the Divine Word from the persecutions that the Muslims were experiencing at that time in Makka. It was not military in nature. This brings up our first point regarding the historical form of military *jihād* and what may be its most misrepresented feature: the notion that the religion of Islam was spread through military force, that Jews, Christians, and other peoples of the Middle East, Asia, and Africa were forced to convert to Islam on pain of death.

"There is No Compulsion in Religion"

It has been a common view in the West, even to this day, to say that the religion of Islam spread through conquest. Although this Orientalist theory is now being shown to be a fallacy by modern scholarship,[28] it is important to mention that the peaceful spread of Islam throughout most of the Middle East,[29] Asia, and Africa was in fact due to principles flowing from the Qur´ānic revelation itself. Here and in the next section we will discuss some of these principles, beginning with the injunction found in verse 2: 256 which says, "There is no compulsion in religion." Our commentators tell us that this verse was revealed during one of three possible situations.

The first possible context for the revelation of 2:256 has to do with a practice that was fairly common among the women of Medina before Islam came to the city. Our commentators tell us that if a woman did not have any living sons, she would sometimes make a promise that if she gave birth to a child and the child lived, she would raise the child in the faith of one of the Jewish tribes of the city.[30] Apparently this practice was somewhat popular; we know this from the events following another of the early military engagements of Islamic history: the siege of the fortress of the Medinan Jewish tribe of Naḍīr (4 A.H. / 625 C.E.). The reason for the siege, according to Islamic sources, was that the Banū Naḍīr had broken an alliance that they had concluded with the Prophet[31] by secretly planning to assassinate him. As a result of this treason, the Muslims besieged the Banū Naḍīr for some ten days in their fortress just south of Medina. At the end of this siege the Banū Naḍīr accepted a punishment of exile from the region of Medina and the tribe left with their wealth packed on their camels, some heading north to the town of Khaybar, others going on further to Syria. Some of the Medinan Muslims protested the punishment of exile, saying to the Prophet: "Our sons and brothers are among them!"[32] Indeed, some of the children of the Medinans had been raised within the Jewish faith and were living with their adopted clan. In response to the dissatisfaction of the Medinan Muslims the words of the Qur´ān were revealed: "There is no compulsion in religion, for truth has been made clear from error," meaning essentially that these "sons and brothers" had made their choice to stay loyal to a treacherous group against the Prophet, as well as against their own Muslim relatives, and were party to a plan to murder God's messenger. In this way, the words of verse 2:256, although harsh from a certain point of view, also reveal an essential principle within the Muslim faith: no one can be compelled to accept a religion, be it Islam or any other faith. This particular narration of the context of 2:256 is highly significant for delineating the attitude of Muslims on this issue, occurring as it does during the *jihād* of the siege of the Banū Naḍīr and rejecting, within that context, any compulsion in religion.

Another variant on this same story speaks of the people of Medina desiring to compel those of their "sons and brothers" affiliated with another Jewish tribe in the city, the Banū Qurayẓah, into accepting Islam. This version (whose number of narrations in the sources is much fewer than that of the Banū Naḍīr narrations) makes no mention of there being any hostilities at that time between the Muslims and the Jews, but only recounts the desire of the Medinan Muslims to force their Jewish relatives into Islam. In these narrations the Prophet responds to their desire to compel their family members with the words of 2:256,[33] again affirming the absolute necessity of freedom in choosing one's faith.

This principle is also brought out in relation to a third possible context for the revelation of verse 2:256. This is said to be the conversion to Christianity of the sons of Abū´l-Ḥuṣayn, a companion of the Prophet. The story is told that the two sons of Abū´l-Ḥuṣayn were converted in Medina by Christian merchants visiting the city from Syria. They then returned to Syria with the merchants.[34] Upon hearing of what his sons had done, Abu´l-Ḥuṣayn went to the Prophet and asked for permission to pursue them and bring them back. The Prophet then recited to him, "There is no compulsion in religion ...." After Abū´l-Ḥuṣayn heard the words of the revelation, the narration concludes, "So he let them go their way" (*fa-khallī sabīlahumā*).[35]

Regardless of the version of the story that we examine, the message is always the same—to choose one's own religion is a free choice whether in time of peace or war. Ibn Kathīr's commentary upon 2:256 also reflects this fact when he says:

> God, the Exalted, said, "There is no compulsion in religion," that is to say, you do not compel anyone to enter the religion of Islam. Truly it is made clear [and] evident. It [Islam] is not in need such that one compel anyone to enter it. Rather, the one whom God guides to Islam and expands his breast and illuminates his vision, he enters into it by way of clear proof. It is of no use to enter the religion as one compelled by force.[36]

Although these words are hardly ambiguous, we should also note that there have been those in the Islamic tradition who have tried to say that this Qur´ānic verse was later abrogated, but this is not the opinion of either of our commentators. Both al-Ṭabarī and Ibn Kathīr note that 2:256 has never been abrogated by any other verse(s) of the Qur´ān and that although 2:256 descended in regard to a particular case (*khaṣṣ*), i.e., in regard to either the Jews of Medina or the Christians from Syria, nevertheless, its application is general (*ʿamm*).[37] This is to say, the verse applies to all People of the Book, who should be free from being compelled to accept Islam.[38]

"Had God Not Repelled Some Men by Means of Others ..."

A related issue which goes beyond the simple idea of not forcing anyone into Islam is the fact that one of the essential and expressed elements of the earliest military *jihād* was the protection of the rights of worship of the People of the Book, i.e., not simply avoiding using force to bring them into Islam, but actively using force to preserve and defend their houses of worship. This characteristic of the military *jihād* is mentioned in verses 22:39-40 and, as we shall see, it is confirmed by many historical examples.

We noted earlier that verses 2:190-191 are sometimes claimed to be the first verses revealed relating to military *jihād*. This claim is also made for verses 22:39-40.[39] It is, of course, impossible to determine on the basis of the narrations given in the sources which group of verses is truly the first to speak of military *jihād*, but the Islamic tradition in general has simply accepted ambiguity on this issue. Verses 22:39-40 say:

> Permission is given to those who are fought because they have been wronged. Surely, God is able to give them victory,
>
> Those who have been expelled from their homes unjustly only because they said: "Our Lord is God." And if it were not that God repelled some people by means of others, then monasteries, churches, synagogues, and mosques, wherein the Name of God is mentioned much would surely have been pulled down. Verily, God will help those who help Him. Truly, God is powerful and mighty.

Our commentators tell us that these verses were revealed just as the Prophet and his companions were leaving Makka and migrating to Medina.[40] Both al-Ṭabarī and Ibn Kathīr relay the words of Abū Bakr al-Ṣiddīq upon hearing the new revelation. He is reported to have said, "I knew [when I heard it] that it would be fighting (*qitāl*) [between the Muslims and the Makkans]."[41] It is also interesting to note that al-Ṭabarī relates traditions that state that the meaning of the phrase "if it were not that God repelled some people by means of others" is "if it were not for fighting and *jihād*" and "if it were not for fighting and *jihād* in the way of God."[42] Furthermore, Ibn Kathīr relates that many famous early figures of Islam "such as Ibn ʿAbbās, Mujāhid, ʿUrwah ibn al-Zubayr, Zayd ibn Aslam, Muqātil ibn Ḥayyān, Qatādah and others" also said that "this is the first verse revealed concerning *jihād*."[43] These commentaries are particularly important because all of them refer to the fact that *jihād* is to be understood, in its earliest sense, as a means by which "monasteries, churches, synagogues, and mosques" are to be preserved and protected.[44] The call to *jihād* then was not for the destruction of faiths other than Islam; rather, one of its essential aspects was the preservation of places of worship belonging to the monotheistic faiths and protecting them against those polytheists—in this case the idolaters of Makka—who might endanger them.

Some Applications of Qur´ānic Principles to the Military *Jihād*

When we turn to the many examples of the early military *jihād* found in the sources, we see that the Muslim armies were actually quite consistent in their application of the Qur´ānic doctrines mentioned in 22:39-40 and 2:256. Although the historical record does not speak definitively about the issue of whether or not these endeavors were strictly defensive—for as with all such undertakings, they involved both elements of true religious fervor and righteousness, as well as issues of the *Realpolitik* of the time—what can be said rather definitively is that the Muslim forces, in carrying out the early *jihād*, did act in accordance with the limits established by the Qur´ān and *ḥadīth*. We know this from the examination of the accounts presented in the various Islamic histories, such as al-Ṭabarī's universal history, *Ta´rīkh al-rusul wa´l-mulūk*, as well as other important historical works that specialize in the events of the early *jihād*, such as Balādhurī's (d. 279 A.H. / 892 C.E.) *Futūḥ al-buldān* or "Openings of the Nations." In these accounts, there is clear evidence of the importance Muslims attached to the idea of "no compulsion in religion," as well as to the preservation of the places of worship of the People of the Book. Balādhurī, for instance, recounts a text written by the Prophet to the Christian community of Najrān in southern Arabia guaranteeing them certain social and religious rights under Islamic rule. The text reads:

> Najrān and their followers are entitled to the protection of Allāh and to the security of Muḥammad the Prophet, the Messenger of Allāh, which security shall involve their persons, religion, lands, and possessions, including those of them who are absent as well as those who are present, their camels, messengers, and images [*amthila*, a reference to crosses and icons]. The state they previously held shall not be changed, nor shall any of their religious services or images be changed. No attempt shall be made to turn a bishop, a monk from his office as a monk, nor the sexton of a church from his office.[45]

Both al-Ṭabarī and Balādhurī make many references to similar treaties concluded between Muslim commanders during the early *jihād* effort and the various populations that fell under Islamic political control. Indeed, such examples are to be found on every major front of the Islamic conquests from Persia to Egypt and all areas in between.

Within the region of Syria, we have the example of the companion of the Prophet and commander of Muslim forces Abū ʿUbaydah ibn al-Jarrāḥ, who concluded an agreement with the Christian population of Aleppo granting them safety for "their lives, their possessions, city wall, churches, homes, and the fort." Abū ʿUbaydah is said to have concluded similar treaties at Antioch,[46] Maʿarrat Maṣrīn,[47] Ḥimṣ,[48] Qinnasrīn,[49] and Baʿlabakk.[50]

Balādhurī reports that after the surrender of Damascus, Khālid ibn al-Walīd wrote for the inhabitants of the city a document stating:

> In the Name of Allāh, the compassionate, the merciful. This is what Khālid would grant to the inhabitants of Damascus, if he enters therein: he promises to give them security for their lives, property, and churches. Their city shall not be demolished; neither shall any Moslem be quartered in their houses. Thereunto we give to them the pact of Allāh and the protection of his Prophet, the caliphs and the "Believers." So long as they pay the poll-tax,[51] nothing but good shall befall them.[52]

In addition to these accounts, al-Ṭabarī records the "Covenant of ʿUmar," a document apparently addressed to the people of the city of Jerusalem, which was conquered in the year 15 A.H. / 636 C.E. The document states:

> This is the assurance of safety (*aman*) which the servant of God ʿUmar, the Commander of the Faithful, has granted to the people of Jerusalem. He has given them an assurance of safety for themselves, for their property, their churches, their crosses, the sick and the healthy of the city, and for all the rituals that belong to their religion. Their churches will not be inhabited [by Muslims] and will not be destroyed. Neither they, nor the land on which they stand, nor their crosses, nor their property will be damaged. They will not be forcibly converted.... The people of Jerusalem must pay the poll tax like the people of [other] cities, and they must expel the Byzantines and the robbers....[53]

These conditions, respecting Christian practices and places of worship, were also given to other towns throughout Palestine, according to al-Ṭabarī.[54]

In regard to the Armenian front, we have references to treaties made with Jewish and Christian as well as Zoroastrian inhabitants of the region. It is noteworthy that both al-Ṭabarī and Ibn Kathīr in their Qur´ān commentaries mention Zoroastrians (*al-majūs*) within the classification of "People of the Book"[55]—Zoroastrianism being the other major faith, besides Judaism and Christianity, that was encountered by the Muslim armies as they spread out of Arabia and which, like Judaism and Christianity, possessed a sacred text. Balādhurī mentions the treaty concluded by the Companion of the Prophet, Ḥabīb ibn Maslamah al-Fihrī (d. 42 A.H. / 662 C.E.), with the people of the town of Dabīl which states:

> In the name of Allāh, the compassionate, the merciful. This is a treaty of Ḥabīb ibn Maslamah with the Christians, Magians [i.e., Zoroastrians], and Jews of Dabīl, including those present and absent. I have granted for you safety for your lives, possessions, churches, places of worship, and city wall. Thus ye are safe and we are bound to fulfill our covenant, so long as ye fulfill yours and pay the poll-tax....[56]

In addition to this, al-Ṭabarī mentions treaties that the Muslims made with the Armenians of al-Bāb and Muqan in the Caucasus mountains guaranteeing "their possessions, their persons, [and] their religion."[57]

When we turn to the region of Persia, Balādhurī mentions two agreements, one with the people of Rayy,[58] and the other with the people of Ādhārbayjān.[59] The texts of each of these agreements guarantees the safety of the lives of the inhabitants, as well as offering a promise not to "raze any of their fire temples," a reference to Zoroastrian *ātashkādas*. In al-Ṭabarī's history as well, treaties are recounted involving the town of Qūmis,[60] the peoples of Dihistān in the province of Jurjān,[61] and the people of Ādhārbayjān,[62] each treaty granting "safety … for their religion."

Finally, in Egypt we can point to the example of ʿAmr ibn al-ʿĀṣ, a companion of the Prophet and the commander of Muslim forces on the Egyptian front. He concluded a treaty with the Bishop of Alexandria on the orders of the Caliph ʿUmar, guaranteeing the safety of the city and agreeing to return certain Christian captives taken by the Muslims after an initial skirmish. According to al-Ṭabarī, ʿUmar's instructions to ʿAmr were as follows:

> … propose to the ruler of Alexandria that he give you the *jizya* in the understanding that those of their people who were taken prisoner and who are still in your care be offered the choice between Islam and the religion of their own people. Should any one of them opt for Islam, then he belongs to the Muslims, with the same privileges and obligations as they. And he who opts for the religion of his own people has to pay the same *jizya* as will be imposed on his co-religionists.[63]

ʿAmr also concluded an agreement with Abū Maryam, the Metropolitan of Miṣr. Al-Ṭabarī quotes ʿAmr's words in an apparent face to face meeting with the Metropolitan: "We call upon you to embrace Islam. He who is willing to do so will be like one of us. To him who refuses, we suggest that he pay the *jizya* and we will give him ample protection. Our Prophet … has determined that we keep you from harm…. If you accept our proposition, we will give you constant protection."[64] Al-Ṭabarī then quotes the actual text of the treaty agreed to between them as follows:

> In the name of God, the merciful, the compassionate.
>
> This is the text of the covenant that ʿAmr b. al-ʿĀṣ has granted the people of Miṣr concerning immunity for themselves, their religion, their possessions, churches, crucifixes, as well as their land and their waterways…. It is incumbent upon the people of Miṣr, if they agree on the terms of this covenant and when the rise of the Nile water comes to a halt to afford the *jizya*…. He who chooses [not to agree to these terms but] to depart will enjoy immunity, until he has reached his destination where he can be safe, or has moved out of the territory where our authority prevails.[65]

With these treaties in mind we can now return to a question which we raised earlier: Who, in the opinion of the early Muslims, were the People of the Book that had to be fought? In short, given this picture of the history, the answer to this question is that those who were to be fought among the People of the Book were only those who refused to submit to Islamic political authority, i.e., who refused to pay the poll-tax (*jizya*). The Muslims made no hair-splitting theological determinations regarding the issue of "true belief," as some might think is implied in certain Qur´ānic verses that we quoted earlier. All People of the Book were simply treated as "believers" within their respective religious communities, regardless of whether they followed, for instance, in the case of Christianity, a Monophysite, Arian, Jacobite, Nestorian, or Catholic rite. There was no litmus test of faith which the Muslims applied to determine true belief on the part of the people who came under their political control, other than the self-declarations of those people themselves to be Jews, Christians, or Zoroastrians, and their willingness to pay the *jizya*.[66] The earliest *mujāhidūn*, the Prophet, his companions, and their immediate successors, essentially placed all People of the Book under the general category of "faith." This fact played itself out not only in terms of treaties concluded between Muslims and non-Muslims, which as we have seen demonstrate no theological scrutiny of non-Muslim communities, but also in terms of the very composition of the "Muslim" forces involved in the *jihād*, to which we will now turn.

The Composition of the Forces of *Jihād*

In relation to the practice of the military *jihād* we can see that Islam's universal perspective on faith also had an important effect on the make-up of the "Muslim" armies. Here we can point to the fact that military *jihād* was not seen as the exclusive prerogative of Muslims. This is particularly true during the formative years of the Islamic conquests, i.e., from the first command to military *jihād* in Medina through the early Umayyad period. Again, this is made clear in various treaties that the Muslims concluded with both the Jewish and Christian populations of the Near East at this time. Perhaps the most famous of these treaties is the Constitution of Medina, which was composed during the lifetime of the Prophet himself and which speaks of the Jews and Muslims fighting together as one *umma* or community.

The Constitution of Medina

The Constitution of Medina, recorded in Ibn Isḥāq's (d. 151 A.H. / 768 C.E.) *Sīrāṭ Rasūl Allāh* (*The Biography of the Messenger of God*), the most important historical account of the life of the Prophet, indicates that *jihād* was for any community willing to fight alongside the Muslims (with the exceptions of polytheists). Ibn Isḥāq prefaces his account of the Constitution by saying:

> The Messenger of God (God bless and preserve him) wrote a writing between the Emigrants and the *Anṣār*,[67] in which he made a treaty and covenant with the Jews, confirmed their religion and possessions, and gave them certain rights and duties.[68]

The text of the treaty then follows:

> In the name of God, the Merciful, the Compassionate!
> This is a writing of Muḥammad the prophet between the believers and Muslims of Quraysh and Yathrib[69] and those who follow them and are attached to them *and who crusade (jāhada) along with them.* They are a single community distinct from other people.... Whosoever of the Jews follows us has the (same) help and support..., so long as they are not wronged [by him] and he does not help [others] against them.[70] [emphasis added]

Here we see that the participation in "military *jihād*," translated above as "crusade," is open to those "attached" to the Prophet and the Muslims, and that together they constitute a "single community" (*umma wāḥida*) in the face of all others. It is interesting to note that the claim that animosity has always existed between Muslims and Jews does not accord with this very early document dealing with military cooperation and mutual protection between the two communities.[71] Indeed the treaty seems not only to form a basis for an important military alliance between the Muslim and Jewish communities, but it also anticipates orderly and peaceful interactions on a general social level. Thus the Constitution goes on to say:

> The Jews bear expenses along with the believers so long as they continue at war. The Jews of Banū ʿAwf are a community (*umma*) along with the believers. To the Jews their religion (*dīn*) and to the Muslims their religion. [This applies] both to their clients and to themselves, with the exception of anyone who has done wrong or acted treacherously; he brings evil only on himself and on his household. For the Jews of Banū´n-Najjār the like of what is for the Jews of the Banū ʿAwf. For the Jews of Banū´l-Ḥarīth the like.... For the Jews of Banū Saʿīdah the like.... For the Jews of Banū Jusham the like.... For the Jews of Banū´l-Aws the like.... For the Jews of Banū Thaʿlabah the like of what is for the Jews of Banū ʿAwf....[72]

Another portion of the document speaks even more directly to the social attitudes that should form the basis of interactions between the two communities:

> Between them [Muslims and Jews] there is help (*naṣr*) against whoever wars against the people of this document. Between them is sincere friendship (*naṣ´ḥ wa-naṣīḥa*) and honorable dealing, not treachery. A man is not guilty

of treachery through [the act of] his confederate. There is help for the person wronged.[73]

What this document shows is that early in the life of the Islamic community, there was the anticipation of normal and "friendly" relations between the Jews and Muslims and indeed, help between them in terms of war. These ideas are also supported by the authenticity generally accorded to the Constitution by modern scholarship. In terms of this authenticity, both the language and the content of the document suggest that it is an early piece of work, i.e., pre-Umayyad.[74] This is due to the fact that later falsifiers, writing during the time of the Umayyads or the ʿAbbāsids, would not likely have included non-Muslims as members of the *umma* (a term later reserved for the Muslim community exclusively), nor retained the other articles of the document (from which we did not quote) that speak against the Quraysh,[75] nor made such prevalent and constant use of the term *mu´minūn* (believers) rather than *muslimūn* to refer to the followers of the Prophet and his message.[76] Both Julius Wellhausen and Leone Caetani placed the writing of the document sometime before the battle of Badr. Hubert Grimme argued for a date just after Badr, and W. Montgomery Watt, a date following siege of the Banū Qurayẓah (5 A.H. / 627 C.E.).[77] In any case, it is clear that we are dealing here with a document whose early date of composition is claimed both from within and from without the tradition, suggesting a high degree of reliability that it does indeed express early Islamic attitudes toward the openness of the institution of military *jihād.*

Christians in Jihād

Another important point regarding the armies of *jihād* is that traditional Islamic histories give accounts of Christians taking part in some of the early battles alongside the Muslim armies. This is discussed by Fred Donner in his book *The Early Islamic Conquests.* He notes that, according to Muslim historical sources, in the very early period of *jihād,* Christian Arabs from tribes such as the Banū Ṭayyi´ of Najd, the Banū al-Namir ibn Qāsiṭ of the upper Euphrates river valley, and the Banū Lakhm participated in the *jihād* with the Muslim armies.[78] Other allusions to this kind of activity can be found in al-Ṭabarī's *Ta´rīkh* where he notes, for instance, a treaty signed during the reign of the caliph ʿUmar by Surāqah ibn ʿAmr in 22 A.H. / 642 C.E. Surāqah was a commander of Muslim forces in Armenia, which was predominantly Christian. The treaty discusses the poll-tax which the Christian population is to pay to the Islamic government, unless they are willing to supply soldiers to the *jihād* effort, in which case the poll-tax would be cancelled.[79] In addition to this account, Balādhurī notes many other agreements in the *Futūḥ al-buldān* concluded by Muslim commanders with the

Christian populations of various regions. Such is the case of the Jarājimah, a Christian people from the town of Jurjūmah.[80] This town had been under the control of the patrician and governor of Antioch but surrendered to the Muslim armies, commanded by Ḥabīb ibn Maslamah al-Fihrī, when they attacked the town. Balādhurī recounts the terms of the peace between Ḥabīb and the Jarājimah as follows:

> Terms were made providing that al-Jarājimah would act as helpers to the Moslems, and as spies and frontier garrison in Mount al-Lukam. On the other hand it was stipulated that they pay no tax, and that they keep for themselves the booty they take from the enemy in case they fight with the Moslems.[81]

Here *jihād* is an endeavor open to the Christian Jarājimah. Another treaty concluded with them during the reign of the Umayyad Caliph al-Walīd ibn ʿAbd al-Malik (86-96 A.H. /705-715 C.E.), states:

> Al-Jarājimah may settle wherever they wish in Syria... ; neither they nor any of their children or women should be compelled to leave Christianity; they may put on Moslem dress; and no poll-tax may be assessed on them, their children, or women. On the other hand, they should take part in the Moslem campaigns and be allowed to keep for themselves the booty from those whom they kill... ; and the same amount taken from the possessions of the Moslems should be taken [as tax] from their articles of trade and the possessions of the wealthy among them.[82]

These agreements, along with the many others that we have noted in the previous sections, in addition to revealing something of the martial applications of Islam's universal perspective on faith, also demonstrate that historically *jihād* was directed against those who stood in opposition to the political authority of the Islamic state. It was not directed against a people simply because they professed a faith other than Islam. The point of the *jihād* was not to establish a world populated only by Muslims; it was to create a social order in which the freedom to practice the worship of God was guaranteed, for Muslims as well as for the People of the Book. Although military *jihād* had as its goal the establishment of this Islamic authority, there were also certain essential and religiously unavoidable limitations placed upon the means to achieving this goal. These limitations were defined by the injunctions of the Qur'ān and the *ḥadīth* and manifested, as well as clarified, by the conduct of the earliest *mujāhidūn*, the Prophet, and his companions. These teachings and examples have served as an indispensable guide to Muslims throughout their 1400-year history, not only in terms of *jihād* but in relation to all matters of faith. When we look at the attempts of certain contemporary figures to revive the military *jihād*, their words and actions must always be judged by way of the limits and examples mentioned in the early tradition. This is the only way to determine the essential "Islamicity" of their claims and to know if their actions constitute some form of reprehensible (*makrūh*) or forbidden (*ḥarām*) innovation (*bidʿa*) upon the tradition.[83] Muslims have always been cautioned to exercise the utmost care when introducing new interpretations or practices, as a famous *ḥadīth* of the Prophet states: "Beware of newly invented matters, for every invented matter is an innovation, every innovation is a going astray, and every going astray is in Hell-fire."[84]

Some Contemporary Fundamentalist Interpretations of *Jihād*

To begin our analysis it is perhaps best to start with the form of the *jihād* envisaged by the modern fundamentalists; that is to say, is the form of this *jihād* consistent with the established principles of the Islamic faith or not? It has been claimed that the *jihād* which Muslims must now wage involves "killing Americans and their allies—civilian and military" (*qatl al-amrikān wa ḥulfāyhim madiniyyūn wa ʿaskariyyūn*). Any such declaration would immediately place the endeavor outside the bounds of true *jihād* whose limits, as we noted earlier, would clearly exclude, for instance, attacks upon women and children. In fact, the categories of "civilian" and "military" often used by these extremists are somewhat alien to the Islamic tradition which always speaks on this issue of warfare in terms of "those who fight against the Muslims" and "those who do not," the tradition being unanimous in defining "those who do not" as women and children, with other categories often times included such as monks and the elderly. Therefore, the declarations making "lawful" the indiscriminate killing of civilians unequivocally transgress the limits of warfare defined in the traditional sources. Indeed, some claim that now is the time for a new *fiqh* or jurisprudence in Islam that would leave behind such traditional constraints.[85] Some have even attempted to cast their arguments in the guise of religion by calling their declarations of *jihād* "*fatwās*"[86] and by quoting liberally from the Qur´ān. Of course, the determination of the "Islamicity" of any *fatwā* must be in relation to its content, and yet if we analyze the Qur´ānic verses chosen by extremists to justify their own exegesis reveals that, far from being representatives of traditional Islam and the "pious forefathers" (*salaf*) of the Muslim community, their perspective is actually what we might call the "other side of the coin" of modernism, due to its near total disregard for the established contexts of the verses they quote.[87]

One verse often mentioned in this regard is verse 9:5: "But when the forbidden months are past, then fight and slay the polytheists [*mushrikūn*] wherever you find them, seize them, beleaguer them, and lie in wait for them in every stratagem [of war]." It is interesting that this verse should be cited in the context of calls for Muslims to fight Jews and Christians, particularly since this verse has nothing to do with the issue of the People of the Book. As we mentioned earlier, the Qur´ān does not refer to Jews and Christians as *mushrikūn* but reserves this term for the idolatrous Arabs of Muḥammad's time. In the case of verse 9:5, however, we are not dealing with a reference to the idolaters of Makka specifically because, according to tradition, the ninth chapter of the Qur´ān was revealed after the conquest of Makka by the Muslims, that is to say, at a time when there were no longer any polytheists in the city as a result of conversion to Islam. The *mushrikūn* referred to in verse 9:5 are therefore the Arab polytheists/idolaters who remained in other parts of Arabia not yet under Muslim control. This being the case, the use of 9:5 would represent a misappropriation of this verse to an end other than the one intended from its established traditional context of fighting the "pagan" Arabs.

Other verses which have become popular proof texts for the jihadist position are 9:36 and 2:193. The verses are, respectively: "And fight the polytheists [*mushrikūn*] together as they fight you together," and "Fight them [i.e., the *mushrikūn*] until there is no more oppression and religion is for God." These verses have been cited as direct support for killing civilians, yet both these verses, as with verse 9:5, refer directly to fighting the *mushrikūn*, not Jews or Christians and certainly not civilians. Neither al-Ṭabarī nor Ibn Kathīr have much to say regarding 9:36, except to emphasize that the Muslims should act together or in unison during warfare against the polytheists. The injunction to "fight the polytheists together as they fight you together," which has sometimes been taken to mean that Muslims should respond in kind to the attacks of an enemy, cannot be understood as an invitation to transgress the established Islamic rules of warfare. It is telling in this regard that al-Ṭabarī and Ibn Kathīr only refer in their comments on 9:36 to the verse's meaning in relation to the "unity" of the *umma*, and do not mention issues of responding in kind to offenses, which would seem to be a subject worthy of at least some comment, if indeed that was the verse's intended meaning.

In terms of verse 2:193, Ibn Kathīr sees it as part of a series of related verses beginning with 2:190. Like al-Ṭabarī, he mentions that these verses refer to the first military *jihād* against the *mushrikūn* of Makka, and he also emphasizes the fact that these verses are in no way an invitation to kill non-combatants, even those who live among the communities of the enemies of Islam. Like al-Ṭabarī, Ibn Kathīr in his comments quotes many narrations about the "transgressing of limits" in warfare, such as the words of the famous Qur´ān commentator and theologian Ḥasan al-Baṣrī (d. 728 C.E.), who said that the acts which transgress the limits of war are:

> ... mutilation (*muthla*), [imposing] thirst (*ghulūl*), the killing of women (*nisā´*), children (*ṣibyān*), and the old (*shuyūkh*)—the ones who have no judgment for

themselves (*lā ra´y lahum*), and no fighters are among them, [the killing of] monks and hermits (*aṣḥāb al-ṣawāmiʿ*), the burning of trees, and the killing animals for other than the welfare [of eating]."[88]

In addition to this, Ibn Kathīr mentions various sayings of the Prophet with meanings similar to the words of Ḥasan al-Baṣrī, such as:

When he [the Prophet] dispatched his armies, he said, "Go in the name of God! Fight in the way of God [against] the ones who disbelieve in God! Do not act brutally![89] Do not exceed the proper bounds! Do not mutilate! Do not kill children or hermits!"[90]

As if such statements were not enough, from the Islamic point of view, to reject the indiscriminate violence endorsed by many fundamentalists, Ibn Kathīr also relays another *ḥadīth* in which the Prophet tells the story of a community of people who were weak and poor and were being fought by a stronger group who showed animosity and harshness towards them. The Prophet says that the weaker group was eventually given help by God to overcome their enemies, but in their success, these weak ones became oppressors of those who had first tried to oppress them. He concludes with the words, "And God was displeased with them till the Day of Resurrection." The meaning of this prophetic story says Ibn Kathīr, is: "When they [the weak] possessed power over the strong, then they committed outrageous/unlawful/brutal acts (*aʿtadū*) against them ... and God was displeased with them by reason of this brutality (*iʿtidā´*)." Thus, Ibn Kathīr points out an important principle of warfare in Islam: acts of brutality committed against Muslims are not an excuse for Muslims to respond in kind. This idea, so clear in the traditional sources, stands in direct contrast to the positions of the fundamentalists, which through their use of Qur´ānic citations seeks to hide what ultimately can only be described as disobedience to these teachings of the Prophet.

Another Qur´ānic verse often quoted is 4:75: "And why should you not fight in the way of God and those who are weak—men, women, and children, whose cry has been: 'Our Lord, rescue us from this town, whose people are oppressors, and raise for us, from you, one who will help.'" This verse has been mentioned as justification for open warfare against the West and to inspire Muslims to fight America and her allies who threaten the Muslim lands in particular. According to our commentators, however, the reason for the revelation of 4:75 was the fact that even after the Prophet had made his migration to Medina, there were still some Muslims who remained in Makka although they could not practice their religion, and some Makkans who wished to be Muslims but would not convert out of fear of their fellow tribesmen.[91] In both cases these difficulties were due to the weakness of these people vis-à-vis the polytheistic members of their own clans who sought to oppress them with threats and even torture. Therefore, verse 4:75 was revealed to call the Muslims of Medina to a two-fold *jihād*: (1) to free their brethren who were left behind in Makka from religious oppression, and (2) to give those Makkans who desired to convert the ability to do so without fear of reprisals from the enemies of Islam. This clearly established context is very different from the manner in which the verse is understood by extremists, for the least that can be said is that in the West, unlike many places in the "Islamic" world itself, Muslims are basically free to worship as they see fit, nor is there any attempt to stop men or women from converting to Islam. Clearly then, the use of 4:75 as a proof text for *jihād* against the West and America is at best disingenuous considering the traditional understanding of the circumstances surrounding its revelation.

In addition to these verses, some cite verse 3:139 and make an indirect reference to verse 4:89 in their call for each Muslim to kill Americans and plunder their wealth "in any place he finds them." Verse 3:139, which says, "Do not lose heart, and do not be sad. For you will gain mastery if you are believers," like so many misplaced quotations, actually occurs in the context of the fight against the Makkan polytheists at the battle of Uhud, while 4:89 refers to the *munafiqūn* or "hypocrites" among the early Islamic community. The *munafiqūn*, as mentioned earlier, were those Muslims who disobeyed God's commands knowingly. Many of them converted to Islam only out of a sense of the advantage that could be gained from not openly opposing the Prophet while his power was waxing. Secretly they hoped for and worked toward victory for the polytheists. It is in regard to these traitors within the Muslim community that the verse speaks with such harshness, not in reference to those outside of the *umma*.

One last verse that is popular in modern jihadist literature is verse 9:38:

> O you who believe, what is the matter with you that when you are asked to go forth in the way of God, you cling heavily to the Earth. Do you prefer the life of this world to the Hereafter? ... Unless you go forth, He will punish you with a grievous torment and put others in your place.

According to our commentators, this verse relates to the military expedition (*ghazwa*) led by the Prophet to Tabūk, a region in what is today northwestern Saudi Arabia. During this expedition the Muslims went out in search of Byzantine military in the region. It is said that the Muslims stayed, maneuvering in the field some ten days, but did not encounter any Byzantine forces. As regards the use of this verse, it has been quoted with the hope of encouraging Muslims today to "go forth" against America and her allies, as the early *mujāhidūn* did against another world power, the Byzantines. The expedition to Tabūk, however, did not constitute some kind of special case in which the Islamic limits of warfare were neglected. Although the Muslims potentially would be facing a foe far more capable and powerful than any they had yet encountered, namely, the standing army of the Byzantine Empire which had only recently conquered much of Persia, this did not constitute an excuse for transgression. Despite the danger, at no time in the expedition did the Prophet ever give orders to his army to "transgress" or discard the limits set upon *jihād*. Therefore, any such use of this verse within the context of encouraging such transgression is inconsistent with the historical reality of the *ghazwa* to Tabūk. In fact, the expedition was an occasion for establishing treaties of protection very similar to those we have mentioned in previous sections of this essay, those concluded with the people of Ayla and the Christians of Dūma.[92]

In the case of each of these verses we have cited, extremists have tried to apply them in ways which entail clear innovations from their generally accepted meanings. Such "exegesis" not only goes against basic aspects of the science of Qur´ānic commentary, it also introduces innovation into the very practice of Islam itself, by making *jihād* into a path of unbounded bloodshed. In this manner, the "fundamentalists" violate the fundamental principles of warfare in Islam and betray the example of the Prophet, as well as that of the first Muslims engaged in *jihād*, and as Reza Shah-Kazemi shows in a following essay, many generations into the modern era. In fact their teachings are a not-so-subtle perversion of the very Islam they claim to want to preserve. So systematic is their disregard of the facts of early Islamic history and the circumstances surrounding the revelations of the Qur´ān that one is left wondering what of Islam, other than a name, would they claim to save?

Conclusion

We have attempted to show in this paper that, properly understood, the traditional doctrine of *jihād* leaves no room for militant acts like those perpetrated against the United States on September 11th. Those who carried out these crimes in the name of God and the Prophet, in fact, followed neither God nor the Prophet, but followed their own imaginings about "religion" without any serious understanding of the traditional sources of the Islamic faith. No textual justifications for their acts can be found in the Qur´ān, nor can one cite examples of such brutality and slaughter of innocents from the life of the Prophet or the military *jihād* of the early decades of Islam. The notion of a militant Islam cannot be supported by any educated reading of the source materials, be they the Qur´ān and its commentaries, the *ḥadīth* tradition, or the early Islamic historical works. On the contrary, what is clear when looking at these texts is the remarkable degree of acceptance and, indeed, respect that was shown to non-Muslims, Jews and Christians in particular, at a time—the early medieval period—when tolerance and acceptance of religious differences were hardly well known attitudes. Even in cases of warfare, the Muslim armies acted with remarkable dignity and principle, irrespective of the weakness or strength of their opposition. In short, the early Islamic community was characterized not by militancy, but primarily by moderation and restraint.

These traits were not in spite of the religion of Islam but because of it. This can be seen in the Qur´ān in Chapter 2, verse 143, where God says to the Muslims, "We have made you a middle people," that is, a people who avoid extremes, and in another famous verse which says, "… and He [God] has set the Balance [of all things]. Do not transgress the Balance!" (55: 7-8). Traditional Muslims saw all of life in terms of balance, from simple daily activities to fighting and *jihād*. Each activity had its limits and rules because God had set the balance for all things. It has primarily been certain modernized Muslims, whose influences are not the traditional teachings of the faith, but the attitudes and excesses of modernity (only cloaked with turbans and beards), who have transgressed all limits and disregarded the Balance that is true Islam.

Notes

[1] As regards women, for example, there are *ḥadīth* that declare that the "*jihād* of women" is making the pilgrimage (*ḥājj*) to Makka. See Bukhārī, *Ṣaḥīḥ al-Bukhārī* (Medina: Dār al-Fikr, n.d.), vol. 4, pp. 36, 83-84 (*Kitāb al-jihād, ḥadīth* n. 43, 127, 128). There are also *ḥadīth* concerning the various types of death that qualify one as a martyr (*shahīd*), i.e., as having died like a fighter in *jihād*. One such type of death is said to be the death of a woman in childbirth. Other traditions in *Ṣaḥīḥ al-Bukhārī* imply that women can fulfill the duty of *jihād* by attending to the wounded on the battlefield (see *Ṣaḥīḥ*, vol. 4, pp. 86-87, *ḥadīth* n. 131-134). See also Muslim, *Ṣaḥīḥ Muslim* (printed with commentaries) (Beirut: Dār al-Kutub al-ʿIlmiyya, 1978), vol. 5, pp. 153, 157.

[2] These are: 1) testifying that there is only one true God and that Muḥammad is His messenger, 2) praying five times a day, 3) paying a charity-tax every year, 4) fasting during the month of Ramaḍān, and 5) making a pilgrimage to Makka once in one's life, if one has the means and the health to do so.

[3] See ʿAljunī, *Kashf al-khafā´* (Beirut: Dār Iḥyā´ al-Turāth al-ʿArabī, 1968), *ḥadīth* n. 1362.

[4] It should be noted that "outward *jihād*" is by no means only military in nature. The arena of outward *jihād* is the level of human action. It is not concerned with inner attitudes of the soul, such as sincerity and love (which constitute the realm of the inner *jihād*) but with proper outward action alone, as defined by the religious law (*sharīʿa*).

[5] The word translated here as "themselves," *anfusihim* in Arabic, may be more literally translated as "their souls." This demonstrates an essential Qur´ānic perspective: the inner struggle (i.e., "until they change *their souls*") takes precedence over the outer struggle (i.e., the particular state in which a people exist at the moment) and furthermore, that no amount of purely outward actions can overcome hypocrisy of soul.

[6] There are a few important exceptions to this categorization. Among them are the articles of Khaled Abou El Fadl, "The Place of Tolerance in Islam," in the book by the same title, eds. J. Cohen and I. Lague (Beacon Press, 2002), "The Rules of Killing at War: An Inquiry into the Classical Sources," *Muslim World* 89, no. 2 (April 1999), and Sherman Jackson, "Jihad and the Modern World," *The Journal of Islamic Law and Culture* (Spring/Summer 2002).

[7] For examples of how these traditional teachings were followed in later generations see Reza Shah-Kazemi's "Recollecting the Spirit of *Jihād*" in this volume.

[8] Although it is incorrect in this context, the six major translations of the Qur´ān available in English, those of A. J. Arberry, Marmaduke Pickthall, N. J. Dawood, Yusuf Ali, Ahmad Ali, and El-Hilali/Khan, all translate the word *awliyā´* as "friends."

[9] We owe this image to Dr. Seyyed Hossein Nasr.

[10] Qur´ān 2:125-129.

[11] Al-Ṭabarī, *Jāmiʿ al-bayān ʿan ta´wīl āy al-qur´ān* (Beirut: Dār al-Fikr, 1995), vol. 4, pp. 372-373.

[12] *Ibid.*, vol. 14, pp. 83-84.

[13] We will look more closely at verse 9:5 when we examine the *fatwā* of the World Islamic Front later in this essay.

[14] Al-Ṭabarī, vol. 14, p. 84.

15 *Ibid.*, vol. 2, p. 258. It should be noted that there is another group of verses, 22:39-40 which is also considered to have been the first verses to speak about the military *jihād.* We shall have occasion to speak about this later in the essay.

16 *Ibid.*, vol. 2, p. 258.

17 *Ibid.*, vol. 2, p. 258.

18 *Ibid.*, vol. 2, p. 259.

19 In addition, al-Ṭabarī reports a second narration of these words of ʿUmar ibn ʿAbd al-ʿAzīz with only slight changes in phrasing, *Ibid.*, vol. 2, p. 259.

20 See Mālik ibn Anas, *Muwaṭṭa´*, trans. M. Rahimuddin (New Delhi: Tāj, 1985), p. 200 (*Kitāb al-jihād, ḥadīth* n. 957). See also Bukhārī, *Ṣaḥīḥ*, vol. 4, pp. 159-160 (*Kitāb al-jihād, ḥadīth* n. 257-258), Abū Dāwūd, *Sunan Abī Dāwūd* (Beirut, Dār al-Kutub al-ʿIlmiyya, 1996), vol. 2, p. 258 (*Kitāb al-jihād, ḥadīth* n. 2668), and Muslim, *Ṣaḥīḥ*, vol. 5, p. 56 (*Kitāb al-jihād*).

21 Mālik, *Muwaṭṭa´*, p. 200 (*Kitāb al-jihād, ḥadīth* n. 958). Other similar instructions are also given to the Muslim armies prohibiting the killing of children and the mutilating of bodies, see Muslim, *Ṣaḥīḥ*, vol. 5, pp. 46-50 (*Kitāb al-jihād*).

22 Mālik, *Muwaṭṭa´*, p. 201 (*Kitāb al-jihād, ḥadīth* n. 959). A similar version of this *ḥadīth* in the *Sunan* of Abū Dāwūd mentions not killing the elderly, in addition to the categories of women and children, see Abū Dāwud, *Sunan*, vol. 2, p. 243 (*Kitāb al-jihād, ḥadīth* n. 2614).

23 Khālid ibn al-Walīd (d. 22 A.H. / 642 C.E.) was a companion of the Prophet and one of the famous early commanders of Muslim forces.

24 Quoted from *Bidāyat al-mujtahid wa nihāyat al-muqtaṣid* of Ibn Rushd, translated by Rudolph Peters in *Jihād in Mediaeval and Modern Islam* (Leiden: E. J. Brill, 1977), p. 17. For a similar version of this *ḥadīth* see Abū Dāwūd, *Sunan*, vol. 2, p. 258 (*Kitāb al-jihād, ḥadīth* n. 2669).

25 See *Ṣirāṭ Rasūl Allāh* of Ibn Isḥāq, trans. by A. Guillaume in *The Life of Muḥammad* (Oxford: Oxford University Press, 1978), pp. 602-603.

26 Al-Ṭabarī, *Jāmiʿ al-bayān*, vol. 6, pp. 233-234; and Ibn Kathīr, *Tafsīr al-Qur´ān al-aʿẓīm* (Riyādh: Dār al-Salām, 1998), vol. 2, pp. 488-489.

27 Al-Ṭabarī, *Jāmiʿ al-bayān*, vol. 11, p. 30; Ibn Kathīr, *Tafsīr*, vol. 3, p. 429.

28 See for example R. Bulliet, *The Patricians of Nishapur* (Cambridge: Harvard University Press, 1972) and *Islam: The View from the Edge* (New York: Columbia University Press, 1994) where he speaks about the case of the conversion of the Persian plateau. Bulliet has carried out demographic studies showing that for three centuries following the Muslim's political conquest of the region the land of Iran remained a majority Zoroastrian population, in direct contradiction to any notions of forced conversion.

29 It was only the polytheistic Arab tribes in the Arabian Peninsula who were compelled to enter Islam. Those Arab tribes who were already People of the Book were not forced to accept the religion. Numerous examples of this can be found in the histories, particularly in regard to the Christian Arabs. See the accounts of the Arabs of Najrān (al-Ṭabarī, *Ta´rīkh al-rusul wa´l-mulūk*, ed. M. J. de Goeje [Leiden: E. J. Brill, 1964], vol. 1, pp. 1987-1988 and p. 2162), the Banū Namir, Banū Iyād, and Banū Taghlib (al-Ṭabarī, *Ta´rīkh*, I, p. 2482 and pp. 2509-2510), the Banū Ghassān (Balādhurī's *Futūḥ al-buldān,* trans., P. Hitti as *The Origins of the Islamic* State [New York: AMS Press], vol. 1, p. 209),

the Banū Ṣāliḥ ibn Ḥulwān (Balādhurī, *Origins*, vol. 1, p. 223), the Banū Ṭayyi´ and the Arabs of the settlement of Ḥaḍir Ḥalab (Balādhurī, *Origins*, vol. 1, p. 224), and the Arabs of Baᶜlabakk (Balādhurī, *Origins*, vol. 1, p. 198).

30 Al-Ṭabarī, *Jāmiᶜ al-bayān*, vol. 3, p. 21; Ibn Kathīr, *Tafsīr*, vol. 1, p. 417.

31 We shall speak of this alliance known as the Constitution of Medina later in this essay.

32 Al-Ṭabarī, *Jāmiᶜ al-bayān*, vol. 3, p. 22. See also Wāḥidī, *Asbāb al-nuzūl* (Beirut: ᶜĀlam al-Kutub, 1970), p. 58 and Abū Dāwūd, *Sunan*, vol. 2, pp. 262-263 (*Kitāb al-jihād, ḥadīth* n. 2682).

33 See al-Ṭabarī, *Jāmiᶜ al-bayān*, vol. 3, p. 23.

34 Al-Ṭabarī, *Jāmiᶜ al-bayān*, vol. 3, p. 220; Ibn Kathīr, *Tafsīr*, vol. 1, p. 417; Wāḥidī, *Asbāb al-nuzūl*, pp. 58-59.

35 It should also be noted that in the case of one version of this story (see al-Ṭabarī, *Jāmiᶜ al-bayān*, vol. 3, p. 22 and Wāḥidī, *Asbāb al-nuzūl*, pp. 58-59), the Prophet, after pronouncing the Qur´ānic verse, then says, "God banish them! They are the first ones to disbelieve" (*abᶜadahumā Allāh, hum awwal man kafara*). This statement requires some explanation and needs to be understood in the context of the time. It can be said from the Islamic point of view that the actions of Abū´l-Ḥuṣayn's sons represent a grave error, because they were rejecting a prophet within his own lifetime, a prophet whom they knew personally. The actions of Abū´l-Ḥuṣayn's sons represent a denial of the immediate presence of the truth, and this is very different than, for instance, someone choosing not to accept the message of Islam today; one who never had the chance to actually see the Prophet, who was the living embodiment of submission to God. Like the words of Christ, "He who has seen me has seen the truth," the Prophet said, "He who has seen me has seen his Lord," thereby placing great responsibility on the shoulders of those who were privileged to encounter him. The strident words of the Prophet about the sons of Abū´l-Ḥuṣayn need to be understood in this context.

36 Ibn Kathīr, *Tafsīr*, vol. 1, p. 416.

37 Al-Ṭabarī, *Jāmiᶜ al-bayān*, vol. 3, p. 25; Ibn Kathīr, *Tafsīr*, vol. 1, p. 417.

38 Moreover this injunction is reflected elsewhere in the Qur´ān, such as in the verse, "For each we have given a law and a way, and had God willed He could have made you one people, but that He might put you to the test in what He has given you [He has made you as you are]. So vie with one another in good works. To God will you all be brought back, and He will inform you about that wherein you differed" (5:48). The universality and indeed acceptance of other "ways" and "laws" evident in this verse is to be seen even more directly in verse 2:62: "Those who say 'We are Jews' and 'We are Christians' and 'We are Sabians,' all who believe in God and the Last Day and do good works, they have their reward with their Lord and neither shall they fear nor grieve." The word "Sabians" may be a reference to the remnants of a group of followers of St. John the Baptist, but in any case the message of this verse is very far from the fallacious notion that Islam denies the truth of other faiths. Indeed, the Qur´ān demands that Jews and Christians judge according to what God has given them in the Torah and the Gospel. This is evident in the Qur´ānic statement, "Truly, We revealed the Torah. In it is a guidance and light. By it the prophets who submitted [to God] judged the Jews ... with what they were entrusted of the Book of God, and they were witnesses to it. Therefore, fear not men, but fear Me. Sell not My signs for little gain. Whoever does not judge by that which God has revealed, those are the unbelievers. We ordained therein [within

the Torah]: a life for a life, an eye for an eye, nose for a nose, an ear for an ear, a tooth for a tooth, and wounds for retaliation. But if any one remits it then it is a penance for him, and whosoever does not judge by that which God has revealed, they are wrong-doers" (5:44-45). In relation to the followers of the Gospel, the Qur´ān says, "We sent him [Jesus] the Gospel. Therein is a guidance and a light.... Let the People of the Gospel judge by that which God has revealed therein. Whosoever does not judge by that which God has revealed, those are the corrupt" (5: 46-47). Therefore, not only are the People of the Torah and of the Gospel not to be compelled to accept Islam, but they must, according to the Qur´ān, be free to make their own decisions based upon what their scriptures reveal to them. Moreover, for them not to do so is displeasing to God.

39 Al-Ṭabarī, *Jāmiʿ al-bayān*, vol. 10, p. 227-228; Ibn Kathīr, *Tafsīr*, vol. 3, p. 303.

40 Al-Ṭabarī, *Jāmiʿ al-bayān*, vol. 10, p. 226; Ibn Kathīr, *Tafsīr*, vol. 3, p. 302.

41 Al-Ṭabarī, *Jāmiʿ al-bayān*, vol. 10, p. 227; Ibn Kathīr, *Tafsīr*, vol. 3, p. 303.

42 Al-Ṭabarī, *Jāmiʿ al-bayān*, vol. 10, p. 229.

43 Ibn Kathīr, *Tafsīr*, vol. 3, p. 303.

44 Maḥmūd Shaltūt (d. 1963), the former Shaykh al-Azhar, arguably the most important exoteric authority in the Islamic world, commented upon these verses in his book *al-Qur´ān wa´l-qitāl* (*The Qur'an and Fighting*, trans. Peters [in *Jihād*, p. 43]) as follows: "These verses are, as we have said, the first verses of fighting. They are clear and do not contain even the slightest evidence of religious compulsion. On the contrary, they confirm that the practice that the people ward off each other is one of God's principles in creation, inevitable for the preservation of order and for the continuation of righteousness and civilization. Were it not for this principle, the earth would have been ruined and all different places of worship would have been destroyed. This would have happened if powerful tyrants would have held sway over religions, free to abuse them without restraint and to force people to conversion, without anyone to interfere. These verses are not only concerned with Muslims, but have clearly a general impact ...."

45 Balādhurī, *Origins*, vol. 1, p. 100.

46 *Ibid.*, vol. 1, p. 227.

47 *Ibid.*, vol. 1, p. 229.

48 *Ibid.*, vol. 1, p. 187.

49 *Ibid.*, vol. 1, p. 223.

50 *Ibid.*, vol. 1, pp. 198-199.

51 The poll-tax or *jizya* was required to be paid by the People of the Book to the Islamic state according to verse 9:29 of the Qur´ān and certain ḥadīth. This tax, unlike feudal taxation in Europe, did not constitute an economic hardship for non-Muslims living under Muslim rule. The tax was seen as the legitimate right of the Islamic state, given that all peoples—Muslim and non-Muslim—benefited from the military protection of the state, the freedom of the roads, and trade, etc. Although the *jizya* was paid by non-Muslims, Muslims were also taxed through the *zakāt*, a required religious tax not levied on other communities.

52 Balādhurī, *Origins*, vol. 1, p. 187.

53 Al-Ṭabarī, *The History of al-Ṭabarī, v. XII: The Battle of al-Qādisiyya and the Conquest of Syria and Palestine*, trans. Y. Friedmann (Albany: SUNY Press, 1985), p. 191. The use

of the word "Byzantines" here should not be conflated with "Christians." "Byzantines" refers to those people who were the administrators of Byzantine authority in the lands that were now conquered by the Muslims. The very fact that the word "Byzantines" is used, and not "Christians" is significant. This shows that it was not "Christianity" but rather the political and military opposition of Byzantium that was at issue. It was because of this opposition that the Byzantines needed to be expelled. Byzantine administrators and officials, like the "robbers" also mentioned in the quotation, were a possible source of social unrest and political chaos. Just as there cannot be two kings ruling a single kingdom, the Muslims needed to remove any vestiges of Byzantine political authority in the lands they now controlled. This did not mean the removal of the vestiges of "Christianity" from those lands, for the quotation itself also mentions preserving the rights of Christians to practice their faith and maintain their churches, crosses, etc., under the new Islamic government.

54 *Ibid.*, pp. 191-192. Al-Ṭabarī indicates that similar letters were written to "all the provinces" around Jerusalem as well as to the "people of Lydda and all the people of Palestine."

55 Al-Ṭabarī, *Jāmiʿ al-bayān*, vol. 3, pp. 24-25; Ibn Kathīr, *Tafsīr*, vol. 2, pp. 457-458. This position has been generally agreed upon by most of the early scholars of Islamic law; see for instance the comments of Ibn Rushd in his *Bidāyat al-mujtahid*, in Peters, *Jihād*, p. 24.

56 Balādhurī, *Origins*, vol. 1, p. 314.

57 Al-Ṭabarī, *The History of al-Ṭabarī, v. XIV: The Conquest of Iran*, trans. G. Rex Smith (Albany: SUNY Press, 1994), pp. 36-38.

58 Balādhurī, *Origins*, vol. 2, p. 4

59 *Ibid.*, p. 20.

60 Al-Ṭabarī, *The History of al-Ṭabarī, v. XIV: The Conquest of Iran*, p. 28.

61 *Ibid.*, p. 29.

62 *Ibid.*, p. 33.

63 Al-Ṭabarī, *The History of al-Ṭabarī, v. XIII: The Conquest of Iraq, Southwestern Persia, and Egypt*, trans. G. H. A. Juynboll (Albany: SUNY Press, 1985), pp. 164-165.

64 *Ibid.*, pp. 167-168.

65 *Ibid.*, pp. 170-171.

66 The issue as to whether the Muslims may accept the *jizya* from the *mushrikūn* or polytheists, thereby granting them protected (*dhimmī*) status under the Islamic state, like the status of the People of the Book, has been debated by scholars of Islamic law. For various opinions on this issue see Ibn Rushd, *Bidāyat al-mujtahid*, in Peters, *Jihād*, pp. 24-25.

67 These terms may need some explanation. The people of the city of Makka were almost all members of an Arabic tribe known as Quraysh, and the Prophet and the vast majority of his early followers in Makka were also members of this tribe. When the Prophet left Makka for the city of Medina, an event known as the *hijra* or migration, those members of his community who journeyed with him were given the title of *muhājirūn* or "Emigrants." As for the term *anṣār*, it refers to those people of Medina who accepted the Islamic message and invited the Prophet and the Emigrants to the city, giving them refuge from their situation of persecution in Makka. For this reason these

residents of Medina were given the title of *anṣār* or "Helpers," due to the fact that they gave safe haven to the Prophet and the Emigrants.

68 W. M. Watt, *Muḥammad at Medina* (Oxford: Clarendon Press, 1956), p. 221.

69 The term "Yathrib" actually refers to the city of Medina. Before the time of Islam, Medina was called "Yathrib." The name "Medina" came to be used later as a result of the fact that the city was eventually renamed "Madīnat al-Nabī" (The City of the Prophet). Today the city is simply referred to by the first part of this title, Medina, or "The City."

70 Watt, *Muḥammad*, p. 221.

71 It may be asked if this pact of mutual protection does not contradict the point made earlier concerning verse 5:51. We stated that 5:51 essentially tells the Muslims not to take Jews (or Christians) as their "protectors" in a military sense, and yet the Constitution seems to be doing just that by stating that between Muslims and Jews is "help against whoever wars against the people of this document." Is this not then taking Jews as "protectors"? In answer to this question it needs to be said that the specific context of 5:51 is that of individual Muslims taking alliances with those outside the *umma* in order to save their own individual lives and thereby endangering the unity and internal strength of the Muslims. It does not refer to a context in which the Muslims, as an *umma*, agree to a treaty for the benefit and safety of the *umma* as a whole. This issue points out the necessity of clearly understanding the *asbāb al-nuzūl* of Qur´ānic passages. Without such understanding a mistake could be made such that all agreements of help or assistance between Muslims and non-Muslims would be seen as compromising Islam; but this is simply not the context of 5:51. Indeed if it were, it would compromise practically the entire early history of the *jihād* effort which is filled with agreements of protection and assistance, as we see with the Constitution and as we shall see in other parts of this essay.

72 Watt, *Muḥammad*, p. 222.

73 *Ibid.*, p. 224.

74 The Umayyad Dynasty ruled the Islamic world immediately following the end of the "Rightly-guided caliphate" (40 A.H. / 661 C.E.) until they were overthrown by the ʿAbbāsids in 132 A.H. / 750 C.E., who established their own dynasty, which ruled over all Muslim lands (in a nominal way from the 4th c. A.H. / 10th c. C.E. onward) until the Mongol conquest of their capital at Baghdad in the 7th c. A.H. / 13th c. C.E., at which time the last ʿAbbāsid caliph was killed.

75 Such comments criticizing the tribe of Quraysh would have been construed by the Umayyads (see note 67) as a critique of their legitimacy, given that the Umayyad's drew their legitimacy from their status as descendents of one of the prominent clans of Quraysh. The importance that they placed upon this Qurayshi lineage was as a result of the fact that, within the tribe of Quraysh, they were not descendents of the immediate clan of the Prophet, i.e. the clan of Hāshim, but of another clan within Quraysh, the clan of ʿAbd Shams. Thus, it was not through their immediate clan but through their more distant Qurayshi heritage that they could claim a relation to the Prophetic substance of Muḥammad.

76 Although the Qur´ān discusses both *mu´minūn* and *muslimūn* in referring to those who followed the message of Muḥammad, most early theological and sectarian documents refer to members of the Islamic community as *mu´minūn* or "believers," rather than *muslimūn* specifically. For example, the early sectarian writings of the Khārijites and Murjiʿites always discussed issues of membership in the Islamic

community in terms of "believers" and non-believers, not in terms of Muslims and non-Muslims.

77 Watt, *Muḥammad*, pp. 225 - 227.

78 Fred M. Donner, *The Early Islamic Conquests* (Princeton: Princeton University Press, 1981), p. 200.

79 Al-Ṭabarī, *The History of al-Ṭabarī, v. XIV*, p. 36. The text of the treaty is:

> In the name of God, the Compassionate, the Merciful. This is the safe-conduct Surāqah b. ʿAmr, governor of the Commander of the Faithful, ʿUmar b. al-Khaṭṭāb, has granted to Shahrbarāz, the inhabitants of Armenia, and the Armenians [in al-Bāb]. [He grants] them safe-conduct for their persons, their possessions, and their religion lest they be harmed and so that nothing be taken from them. [The following is imposed] upon the people of Armenia and al-Abwāb, those coming from distant parts and those who are local and those around them who have joined them: that they should participate in any military expedition, and carry out any task, actual or potential, that the governor considers to be for the good, providing that those who agree to this are exempt from tribute but [perform] military service. Military service shall be instead of their paying tribute. But those of them who are not needed for military service and who remain inactive have similar tribute obligations to the people of Azerbaijan [in general] .... If they perform military service, they are exempt from [all] this.

80 Jurjūmah was located in the border region between modern-day Syria and Turkey.

81 Balādhurī, *Origins*, vol. 1, p. 246.

82 *Ibid.*, p. 249.

83 For a full explanation of the traditional Islamic teachings on innovation (*bidʿa*) see T. J. Winter's "The Poverty of Fanaticism" in this volume.

84 al-Nawawī, *An-Nawawī's Forty Ḥadīth*, trans. by E. Ibrahim and D. Johnson Davies (Malaysia: Polygraphic Press Sdn. Bhd., 1982), p. 94 (*ḥadīth* 28). This *ḥadīth* is also to be found in the *Sunan* of Abū Dāwūd and the *Jāmiʿ* of Tirmidhī. Other *ḥadīth* related by al-Nawawī concerning the issue of innovation are: "He who establishes (*aḥdatha*) something in this matter of ours that is not from it, it is rejected (*radd*)!" and "The one who acts [in a way that is] not in agreement with our matter, it is rejected!" (see p. 40).

85 We should not have the impression that modern fundamentalists represent the first time that the traditional Islamic limits of warfare have been disregarded. The Khārijite movement, whose roots go back to a religio-political dispute in the first Islamic century, represent one of the most famous examples of just such transgression. The Khārijites were perfectly willing to attack "civilians," although their dispute was essentially with other members of the Muslim community rather than with non-Muslims. They declared a sentence of "excommunication" (*barā'a*) upon anyone who did not accept their perspective on Islam. According to the Khārijites, such excommunicated people—men, women, and children—were afforded no protection under the laws of religion for their lives or property. Therefore, the Khārijites considered it perfectly legal to kill such persons. It is important to mention that throughout the early history of Islam the Khārijite position was condemned and even physically opposed by every major Muslim group, Sunnī and Shīʿite.

86 The choice of this word is a calculated political maneuver to co-opt the authority

of the 1400-year Islamic legal tradition. Within the science of Islamic jurisprudence (*fiqh*), a *fatwā* refers to a religious opinion issued by a scholar of law (*sharī ͑a*). Most fundamentalists have had no formal training in the study of Islamic law.

87 For an examination of the relationship between modernism and fundamentalism, see Joseph E. B. Lumbard's "The Decline of Knowledge and the Rise of Ideology in the Modern Islamic World," in this volume.

88 Ibn Kathīr, *Tafsīr*, vol. 1, p. 308.

89 The command here in Arabic, *lā ta ͑tadū*, means "not to act brutally," but it can also mean "not to commit excess, outrage, unlawful action, or violate women."

90 Ibn Kathīr, *Tafsīr*, vol. 1, pp. 308-309.

91 Al-Ṭabarī, *Jāmi ͑ al-bayān*, vol. 4, p. 220; Ibn Kathīr, *Tafsīr*, vol. 1, p. 698.

92 See Guillaume, *The Life of Muḥammad*, pp 607-608.

Chapter 2

The Decline of Knowledge and the Rise of Ideology in the Modern Islamic World

Joseph E. B. Lumbard

Throughout the twentieth century, Muslim scholars called for a revival of the Islamic intellectual tradition in order to address the moral and spiritual malaise which has too long afflicted Muslim peoples the world over. Both Sunnīs and Shīʿites, from the heartland of medieval Islamic civilization such as Syria, Egypt, and Iran, to its later lands such as Malaysia and West Africa, to its most recent penetrations into Europe and America, have long decried the intellectual decrepitude of modern Islamic civilization. To many scholars of Islam, both Muslim and non-Muslim, the rise of violence, punctuated by the events of September 11, 2001, are the latest symptoms of an underlying illness, a cancer which has been eating at the collective moral and intellectual body of the international Islamic community. In retrospect, such events were not a surprise but a painful indication of how deep this crisis has become. Unfortunately, the solutions sought by the American-led coalition involve significant risks, and to the minds of many condone senseless violence and wanton killing as a just response to senseless violence and wanton killing.[1] Critics of the policy maintain that such a response rarely does more than beget the same violence from whence it was begotten. If this is correct, removing one or two more heads from the hydra of religious extremism will only succeed in breeding more of the same. In any case, what is needed is to strike a fatal blow to the heart of this beast, a beast whose name is ignorance.

From an Islamic perspective, it could be said that ignorance is our only true foe and that knowledge is our only true need, for when applied and lived, knowledge provides all that is necessary to overcome our spiritual, moral, emotional, and even physical decrepitude. Viewed in this light, the myriad social, economic, and political problems which have given rise to extremist reactions are in part the symptoms of an underlying intellectual crisis. The role of European and American influence in contributing to this is discussed in Ibrahim Kalin's and Ejaz Akram's contributions to this volume. In this essay we will discuss the role of modern ideological trends within Islam itself. But as these are relatively recent developments, which for the most part represent deviations from the traditional Islamic sciences, we must delve into Islamic intellectual history in order to fully address these issues. Historical contextualization of movements in the Islamic world is important for non-Muslims because an inability to appreciate the subtleties and complexities of the Islamic intellectual tradition leads to egregious misunderstandings, which can in turn lead to devastating political miscalculations, as is demonstrated by Walid El-Ansary in his essay "The Economics of Terrorism." It is also of central importance for Muslims because much of the thought now produced in the Islamic world is not in fact Islamic. Western ideologies are presented by both dogmatic literalists and modern "liberal" secularists with a thin veneer of Islamic terms and sayings, while the voice of traditional Islamic thought is often muted and ignored. But through the work of scholars such as S. H. Nasr and Hamza Yusuf Hanson in America, A. K. Brohi and Suheyl Umar in Pakistan, ʿAbd al-Halīm Maḥmūd in Egypt, Naquib al-Attas in Malaysia, and Martin Lings, Ḥassan Gai Eaton, and T. J. Winter in England, it can continue to be heard.

Many of the most influential modern Muslim thinkers, such as Sayyid Aḥmad Khān (d. 1898), Muḥammad ʿAbduh (d. 1905), Jamāl al-Dīn Afghānī (d. 1897) and Rashīd Riḍā (d. 1935),[2] were so awed by the technological achievements of Western civilization that they freely surrendered the ground of intellectuality to the secular humanistic and scientistic (as opposed to scientific)[3] world-view that gave rise to them. While, as Fuad Naeem has demonstrated,[4] the secularism and modernism of Sayyid Aḥmad Khān and his followers in India is immediately evident, that of ʿAbduh and Afghānī has been more insidious. They tried to be modernist without being secularist, not realizing that the former opened the door to the latter. In adopting foreign theories and analytical models without fully evaluating them, both modernist and puritanical reformist (to avoid the amoeba-word "fundamentalist") Muslims have abandoned the guidance of their own intellectual heritage. But in order to be effectively assimilated into the Islamic world, such modes of thought must first be evaluated. Then what is found to be of value can be incorporated organically through a genuine intellectual and civilizational discourse, as happened in the encounter between Islam and Greek thought in the ninth and tenth centuries. When, however, one intellectual tradition is abandoned outright, there is no basis for the evaluation of another intellectual tradition and none of the fertile ground that is necessary for effective assimilation. Recovering the Islamic intellectual tradition is thus an essential, if not the essential, step to ameliorating the malaise which Muslims and non-Muslims alike have long bemoaned and decried. When this has occurred, Muslim peoples will be better prepared to engage Western civilization without surrendering to it altogether or opposing it outwardly while capitulating inwardly.

Indications of Islam's intellectual decline can be found in all the traditional Islamic sciences. On the one hand, jurisprudence (*fiqh*) has been abused by extremists so as to excuse and even promote suicide killings. On the other, it has been abandoned by modernists because they believe it is rooted in a medieval code of life which is not applicable in the "new world order." Puritanical reformists have distorted theology so as to deny the immanence and closeness of God, affirming only the transcendence and remoteness of the Divine. Modernists, such as Sayyid Aḥmad Khān and Chirāgh ʿAlī of India, have rejected every facet of theology and philosophy which does not accord with an Enlightenment and positivist notion of reason. Doctrinal literalists have decontextualized the teachings of the Prophet Muḥammad so as to deny women rights that were granted to them from the beginning of Islam, whereas many modernists have rejected the authenticity of the sayings of the Prophet, and even the Qur'ān. Both have almost completely abandoned the principles of Islamic thought. Puritanical reformists do so because they favor an opaque literalism which denies the efficacy of our speculative, intuitive, and imaginal faculties. Modernists do so because they have capitulated to the mental habits of their conquerors, conditioned as they are by relativism, scientism, and secular humanism. Each side continues to advance its position, but there is no dialogue; for in the absence of the traditional Islamic modes of interpretation, there is no basis for a common discourse among Muslims.[5]

All of the dimensions of this intellectual decline cannot be covered in one essay, or even one book. Here we will focus on one dimension of the Islamic intellectual heritage whose true nature has been abandoned, rejected, and forgotten for much of the modern period. In this essay it is referred to as the "*iḥsānī* intellectual tradition." *Iḥsān* is an Arabic word which comes from the root *ḥasana*, meaning to be beautiful, good, fine, or lovely. The word *iḥsān* is the noun form of the verb *aḥsana*, which means to make beautiful, good, fine, or lovely. *Iḥsān* thus means making beautiful or good, or doing what is beautiful or good. The *iḥsānī* intellectual tradition begins with the teachings of the Qur'ān and the Prophet Muḥammad, who told his companions that "God has ordained *iḥsān* for everything."[6] In perhaps his most famous teaching on the subject he said: "*Iḥsān* is to worship God as if you see Him, and if you do not see Him, He nonetheless sees you."[7] The central manifestation of the practice of *iḥsān* took form in what is traditionally known as Sufism (Islamic mysticism), where the emphasis is on making one's heart and soul beautiful so that beauty will arise naturally from within. But the *iḥsānī* tradition has taken on many forms, under many names, throughout Islamic history. Wherever there has been a vibrant Islamic civilization, be it Sunnī or Shīʿī, the *iḥsānī* intellectual tradition has been present in one form or another. Though it is not absent from the modern world, its political, social, and intellectual influence has decreased dramatically.

Like the philosophy of Plotinus, Meister Eckhart or Shankaracharya, the *iḥsānī* intellectual tradition comprises a science of Ultimate Reality in which metaphysics, cosmology, epistemology, psychology, and ethics are elaborated in terms of the attachment of all things to their one true origin, which is also their ultimate end. From this perspective, philosophy is not simply ratiocinative deduction and speculation; rather, it is the science of the Real. But to truly see the Real without the obfuscations of passional predilections and mental constructs, one must first perfect the organ of thought and perception—i.e., the intellect, which according to most traditional Islamic thinkers, resides in the heart. As Mullā Ṣadrā, a preeminent representative of this tradition, writes: "Know that philosophy is the perfection of the human soul to the extent of human possibility through perception of the realities of existent things as they are in themselves and judgment of their existence verified through demonstrations, not derived from opinion and tradition."[8] From the perspective of the *iḥsānī* intellectual tradition, perception and understanding are not merely a way of knowing, they are moreover a way of being, and any form of perception or understanding which is not informed by the awareness of God's omnipotence and omnipresence is not in keeping with the ultimate purpose of being human. Not all the solutions to the malaise of Islamdom lie within this dimension of the Islamic tradition. Nonetheless, its absence from contemporary discourse is among the most severe of the symptoms indicating the illness of the whole. But before we examine some teachings of the *iḥsānī* intellectual tradition, we must first look to the Islamic view of the human being; for all of the Islamic sciences, from philosophy to jurisprudence, are designed to address the one shortcoming of man from whence all other shortcomings stem—ignorance.

From one perspective, the message of Islam is one of knowledge having come to cure ignorance, truth having come to abolish error. The conception of the human being expounded in the Qur´ān and the sayings of the Prophet Muḥammad is not of a fallen being in need of redemption, but of a forgetful being in need of remembrance, an ignorant being in need of knowledge and thus of instruction. Where a Christian may see the ills of the human condition as a result of original sin, a Muslim will see these same ills as the result of ignorance or forgetfulness. In Islamic anthropology, the human is believed to have been created according to a norm (*fiṭra*) in which he knows that there is no god but God, that God is the only source of truth and reality, that God is the Origin of all things, that all things continually exist through God, and that all things will return to God. This is the vision of *tawḥīd*, which literally means "making one" and can best be expressed as "asserting the unity of God." Throughout the centuries this vision of *tawḥīd* is the one thing which has been agreed upon by all Muslim scholars, of whatever sect or creed. Arguments have never centered on the veracity of *tawḥīd* itself, but upon the best means of recognizing and averring it.

As humankind has exhibited a tendency to be heedless of *tawḥīd*, and to forget and ignore its implications, the Qur´ān states that God has sent messengers to remind them of this essential truth. It is in this spirit that the Qur´ān tells us, "Verily this is a reminder" (73:19, 76:29). This reminder is the truth of *tawḥīd*, a truth expressed in the first testimony of the faith, "There is no god but God" (*lā ilāha illā Llāh*). It is to remind humankind of this truth that every prophet has been sent. In the Qur´ān, God specifically addresses Moses: "I am God! There is no god but I. So worship Me ...." (20:14). The seventh chapter of the Qur´ān tells us that the Prophets Noah, Hūd, Ṣāliḥ and Shuʿayb all said to their people in different lands and in different ages, "O my people! Worship God! You have no other god but Him" (7:59, 7:65, 7: 73, 7:85). In another passage we are told, "Ask those of Our messengers We sent before thee: Have We appointed gods to be worshiped apart from the Merciful?" (43:45). But the answer to this has already been given: "And We never sent a messenger before thee except that We revealed to him, saying, 'There is no god but I, so serve Me'" (21:25). It is a fundamental principle of the Qur´ān that every human collectivity has been sent a prophet: "And We have sent to every people a messenger, that they may worship God" (16: 36). Every human collectivity has thus been sent a reminder of *tawḥīd*, of God's oneness and its consequences. From this perspective, the purpose of revelation is not to bring a new truth, but to reaffirm the one truth, the only truth that is, the only truth that has ever been.

From another perspective, the central message of the Qur´ān is expressed in this verse: "Truth has come and falsehood has vanished. Falsehood is ever bound to vanish!" (18:81). In this spirit the text reads, "And we have made the book descend as a clarification for all things" (16:89). The emphasis of Islam is to experience this clarification and thus to know. As is revealed, "We have made it descend as an Arabic Qur´ān, that you may know" (12:2). Such verses do not refer to a knowledge experienced through transmission from one generation to the next; rather, they call humankind to an immediate knowledge of things *as they are in themselves* (*kamā hiya*). To possess such knowledge is the human norm, the *fiṭra*. The function of the Islamic intellectual tradition is therefore not only to transmit and preserve textual authorities which clarify *tawḥīd* from one generation to the next, but moreover to cultivate the intellect through which one is able to aver this basic truth through one's own experience and consciousness. Through the intellect all things are known as signs of God. As the Qur´ān says: "We shall show them our signs on the horizons and in themselves until it becomes clear to them that it is the truth" (41:53). The specific trait which distinguishes man from all else in creation is his ability to read all of God's signs. The human intellect is in a sense the ultimate decoder, which when refined and polished can witness the face of the Divine in all of Its many modes in all of creation; for as the Qur´ān says: "Wheresoever you turn there is the face of God" (2:115). To see all things as signs of God and be called to the remembrance of God in all modes of knowing is thus the human norm. Islam understands such knowledge to be the goal of all religions. This is not knowledge of facts and information, but knowledge of things as they are in themselves, a knowledge in which everything is given its proper place because everything is seen in relation to God, and the relations between things are understood on the basis of their relationship to God. From this point of view, to know things outside of God is not to truly know them, for nothing can exist outside of its relationship to God; no existent exists outside of its dependence upon Absolute Existence. It is for this reason that the Prophet Muḥammad would often pray: "Oh God show me things as they are in themselves. Show me truth as truth and give me the strength to follow it. Show me falsehood as falsehood and give me the strength to avoid it."[9]

The Early Intellectual Tradition

Based upon the centrality of knowledge in the Islamic understanding of man, the quest for knowledge is a religious duty. As the Qur´ān reads, "He who has been given wisdom has been given a great good" (2:269). For generations Muslims have sought to comply with the command of the Prophet Muḥammad: "Seeking knowledge is an obligation for every Muslim."[10] Such knowledge does not have as its end the utilitarian goals which we associate with modern scientific and rational pursuits; rather, it has as its end the remembrance of God. As the great scientific tradition of Islam attests, knowledge pertaining to worldly endeavors is not outside the scope of Islam. It is in fact incumbent upon every Muslim to seek such knowledge when the exigencies of life demand it. But the first obligation for every Muslim is to learn the principles of both the practices and beliefs of the religion. All subsequent knowledge should then be understood in light of the principles of the religion. What does not support that does not support one's final end—salvation. The pursuit of such knowledge is therefore believed to be deleterious. As such the Prophet would often pray, "I seek refuge in God from knowledge which has no benefit."[11] He further said, "The world is accursed, accursed is what is in it, save the remembrance of God and what supports it, and the teacher and the student."[12] The injunction to seek knowledge must thus be understood as an injunction to seek knowledge which inculcates remembrance, for all else is accursed. It is for this reason that Islamic scientists never discovered many of the technological applications of modern science, applications which allow us to perform fundamental tasks more rapidly, but do not necessarily increase the quality of life and may distract us from what is most important. By and large the fundamental concern of Muslim scientists was not control of the material realm for worldly pursuits. Rather, they wished to understand the signs of God's creation so as to better understand the Divine.

Throughout Islamic history, Muslims have traveled extensively in the quest for knowledge. To understand the nature of this knowledge we need, therefore, to investigate some aspects of the historical development of the Islamic sciences and the Islamic pedagogical tradition. The first centuries of Islam (ca. 700 to 900 C.E.) were a time of small diverse communities of scholars often seen to be part of a larger movement known as the *Ahl al-ḥadīth*, meaning those devoted to the study, preservation, and application of the teachings of the Prophet Muḥammad.[13] The scholars now known as the *Ahl al-ḥadīth* exhibited many tendencies and would often focus their efforts on divergent, though complementary, aspects of the tradition bequeathed by the Prophet Muḥammad. Although they agreed on several basic tenets, they would often have contentious disagreements over others. What identifies them with a single educational and intellectual movement is their common belief that the Qur´ān and the *sunna*, or wont, of the Prophet Muḥammad were the primary, if not the only, appropriate sources of religious knowledge.[14] Not only was the content of their teachings based upon words transmitted from the Prophet, so too was their mode of teaching modeled upon that of the Prophet and his community. Thus the *Ahl al-ḥadīth* movement was not based so much upon a single method or doctrine as it was an expression of the widely held belief that the guarantee of authenticity, and therefore of orthodoxy, was not only the verbal and written transmission of the sayings of the Prophet Muḥammad, but the conveyance of the authority contained therein through adherence to his *sunna* in the very manner of transmission.[15] Not only was the content of the Islamic message preserved in the sayings of the Prophet, so too was the manner of instruction preserved in detail. The widespread *ḥadīth* movement thus worked to preserve the *sunna* of the Prophet in the actions, minds, and hearts of the Islamic community. It is important to understand the contours of this movement because modern Islamic revivalist movements also claim close adherence to the *sunna* of the Prophet Muḥammad. The nature of their dedication is, however, quite different. There were those among the *Ahl al-ḥadīth* who took recourse to a literalist interpretation of scripture while suspending the speculative and intuitive capabilities, and stressing the saving nature of faith alone. But this was never the whole of the Islamic tradition. It was always balanced by other modes of interpretation. To understand the true nature of the early community, and how much it differs from the current situation, we would thus do well to examine some of the subtleties of this movement.

Because they based themselves upon the Prophetic model, a central component of the *Ahl al-ḥadīth* movement was the training of the soul (*tarbiyat al-nafs*) and the purification of the heart. Emphasis on the purification of the heart follows directly from the teachings of the Prophet Muḥammad, such as: "There is in man a clump of flesh. If it is pure, the whole body is pure. If it is polluted the whole body is polluted. It is the heart";[16] and "God does not look at your bodies, nor at your forms. He looks at your hearts."[17] As the Qur´ān tells us, the day of judgment is "a day when neither wealth nor sons shall profit, except for one who comes to God with a sound heart" (26:88-89). While the health of the heart has always been a concern for traditional Islamic scholars of every discipline, as for all serious Muslims, the individuals most dedicated to the purification of the heart are those historically identified as Sufis, usually defined as the mystics of Islam. But as the impetus for inner purification stems directly from the Prophet, most Sufis of the early Islamic community were in some way aligned with the *Ahl al-ḥadīth* movement. Sufis sat with non-Sufis in circles where both jurisprudence and *ḥadīth* were taught, and there is no evidence that they were isolated from the social and intellectual influence of the populist movement of the *Ahl al-ḥadīth*. What distinguishes Sufis from other representatives of this movement is not that they sought inner purification, for this is a concern of all Muslims. They were, however, singularly devoted to purification and believed that it cultivated an unadulterated mode of perception.

Many Sufis not officially recognized as *ḥadīth* scholars also had some knowledge of both *fiqh* (jurisprudence) and *ḥadīth*. The biographical dictionaries of the Sufis, in which are recorded the companions and sayings of many famous Sufis, also serve as repositories of *ḥadīth* known to have been transmitted by famous Sufi figures. Having observed this trend, Marshall Hodgson, one of the foremost scholars of Islamic history, argues that Sufism was closely associated with the *Ahl al-ḥadīth* movement. As he observes: "In some cases it is hard to draw a line between what was Sufi mystical self-examination and what was Ḥadīthī moralism."[18] Nonetheless, there has been a tendency among Western scholars and modern Muslims to see Sufism as an esoteric, mystical movement disengaged from the rest of the Islamic community, rather than an integral part of it,[19] even though the primary historical sources do not support this view.

The tendency to separate Sufism from other forms of Islamic scholarship and practice arises from a theoretical dichotomy which juxtaposes free esoteric spirituality with restrictive exoteric conformism. Events such as the hanging of the famous Sufi Manṣūr al-Ḥallāj in 922 C.E. and the execution of the jurist and Sufi teacher ʿAyn al-Quḍāt Hamadānī in 1132 C.E. are viewed in isolation, as evidence of an irreconcilable antagonism between a stultified nomo-centric interpretation of the religion and an inspired personal experience of the Divine. But as Omid Safi has observed, this understanding derives from conceptualizing Islamic civilization through post-Enlightenment theories of religion.[20] When subject to scrutiny, such simplistic bifurcations often tell us more about the theoreticians who pose them than about their subject matter.

The idea of mysticism as a special category of non-rational or supra-rational spiritual consciousness received one of its first articulations in the nineteenth century in William James' *The Varieties of Religious Experience*, wherein mysticism is portrayed as an emotional, trans-rational experience akin to drug-induced hallucinations. Spiritual methods were interpreted by James as the methodical cultivation of ecstatic moments of cosmic consciousness, and the entire enterprise was seen to be private and individualistic.[21] But Sufis have long decried those who would only seek ecstatic experiences. The goal has been simply to remember God constantly and to see things as they are in themselves. Any experiences, visions, or ecstatic states were seen as accidental, and novices were even warned not to be deluded by visions and delights, for in relation to the ultimate quest, they are as smoke to fire. As the famous Sufi Shaykh Abū Ḥafṣ ʿUmar al-Suhrawardī (d. 1234) explains in his Sufi manual *Gifts of the Gnostic Sciences* (*ʿAwārif al-maʿārif*), to seek wondrous experiences through spiritual exercises is "... pretension itself and sheer folly." Though such rigors may lead to supernatural experiences that help one to better understand divine mysteries, people are only to engage in such practices "for the soundness of religion, inspecting the states of the soul and sincerity of action towards God."[22]

Following upon the trend begun by James, mysticism was described by the tremendously influential Evelyn Underhill as a movement "whose aims are wholly transcendent and spiritual. It is in no way concerned with adding to, exploring, re-arranging or improving anything in the visible universe."[23] Such notions prompted some critics to chastise mysticism for "... its tendency to flee the responsibilities of history and engage in premature adventures into eternity."[24] But the idea that being ever-mindful of the transcendental and the spiritual would necessarily turn one away from the affairs of this world is rarely found in Sufism. Sufis speak of turning away from the world with the meaning of cutting the internal entanglements that come through greed, lust, and pride. It is not that the Sufi is not in the world, but that the world is not in him or her. As Abū ʾl-Qāsim al-Qushayrī (d. 1072), author of one of the most important handbooks of early Sufism, writes: "The sign of the sincere Sufi is that he feels poor when he has wealth, is humble when he has power, and is hidden when he has fame."[25] Any licit act, even war, is open to the saint, so long as he acts from the inner peace to which he has attained and remains in that peace. As Ibn ʿAṭā'illāh al-Iskandarī (d. 1309), a Shaykh of the Shādhiliyya Sufi order who was also an accomplished jurisprudent, writes in the second line of his famous book of Sufi aphorisms, *al-Ḥikam*, "Your desire to disengage, even though God has put you in the world to earn a living, is hidden passion. And your desire to earn a living in the world, even though God has disengaged you, is a fall from supreme aspiration."[26] From this perspective, Sufism, like the religion of Islam of which it is a fundamental expression, is a middle way in which everything is to be given its proper due. The world is not to be shunned outright, but it is not to be sought in itself. Though representatives of the Sufi tradition sought inner purification, stillness, and unmediated knowledge of the Divine, many—such as Najm al-Dīn Kubrā (d. 1221), who perished in battle against the Mongols, Amīr ʿAbd al-Qādir al-Jazā'irī (d. 1883), whose struggle against the French occupation of Algeria has been examined in Reza Shah-Kazemi's "Recollecting the Spirit of *Jihād*," and ʿUthmān Dan Fodio (d. 1817), who transformed the religious life of Hausaland—sought to have the affairs of this world arranged in accord with transcendent principles, seeing this as one of the meanings of being God's vicegerent on earth (*khalīfat Allāh fi'l-arḍ*).

Sufism has almost never been a matter of personal religious expression which stood in contradistinction to communal institutional religion. Rather, those who we now identify as Sufis were a group that sought to live both their personal and communal lives in constant awareness of the Divine. They sought to find their true center and act from that center. As the famous Muslim historian Ibn Khaldūn (d. 1406) writes:

> Sufism belongs to the sciences of the religious law that originated in Islam. It is based on the assumption that the practice of its adherents had always been considered by the important early Muslims, the men around Muḥammad and the men of the second generation, as well as those who came after them, as the path of truth and right guidance. The Sufi approach is based upon constant application to divine worship, complete devotion to God, aversion to the false splendor of the world, abstinence from the pleasure, property, and position to which the great mass aspire, and retirement from the world into solitude for divine worship. These things were general among the men around Muḥammad and the early Muslims.[27]

Thus the place of Sufism, as understood by both its champions and its traditional analysts, is very different from the notions advanced in most modes of modern discourse, be they Islamic or non-Islamic.

In their contributions to this volume, Waleed El-Ansary and Ibrahim Kalin have observed how religious polemicists, orientalists, and political scientists among others have long interpreted and represented Islam through simplistic cultural essentialisms which are usually more problematic than useful. This, too, is the case with Sufism. For years scholars and laymen, both Western and Muslim, have been guilty of assuming that the divisions and juxtapositions which modern man employs to analyze the world are reflections of age-old dichotomies. On the one hand, it is assumed that Islam is a rigid, desert religion of the sword whose most native expression is found in rigid reformist movements (what many like to call "Islamic fundamentalism"). On the other hand, Sufism is seen as a free, even supra-Islamic, expression of individual spirituality. In the early nineteenth century, many scholars looked for its origins in Hinduism and some in Christianity. Perhaps the best example of the tendency to view Sufism as an extra-Islamic phenomenon is found in one of the earliest treatises of orientalist studies of Sufism, an essay by Lt. James William Graham entitled "A Treatise on Sufism, or Mahomedan Mysticism":

> With regard to the religion (if it can be so termed in the general acceptation of that word) or rather doctrine and tenets of Sufis, it is requisite to observe, first, that any person, or a person of any religion or sect, may be a Sufi: the mystery lies in this: — a total disengagement of the mind from all temporal concerns and worldly pursuits; an entire throwing off not only of every superstition, doubt, or the like, but of the practical mode of worship, ceremonies, &c. laid down in every religion, which the Mahomedans term *Sheryat*, being the law or canonical law; and entertaining solely mental abstraction, and contemplation of the soul and Deity, their affinity, and the correlative situation in which they stand: in fine, it is that spiritual intercourse of the soul with its Maker, that disregards and disclaims all ordinances and outward forms....[28]

Developments in recent scholarship have provided many corrections to these errors, but such notions persist. An example of this is found in Julian Baldick's *Mystical Islam*, where he writes that Islam developed more slowly than is usually believed, "... and that in the slow process of development Christian materials were used to build the mystical side of the religion, the side which was to become Sufism."[29] But a close examination of the original sources reveals that the proponents of Sufism drew upon the same materials as other scholars and were an integral component of the scholarly community as a whole. The *Ahl al-ḥadīth* movement, the jurisprudents and the Sufis comprised intertwining circles whose methods, interests, and members overlapped. Whereas the jurisprudents, the Qur´anic exegetes and the *Ahl al-ḥadīth* transmitted knowledge in a way which could properly be called teaching (*taʿlīm*), the Sufis put more emphasis on inner training (*tarbiya*) for the sake of purification (*tazkiya*). But *taʿlīm* and *tarbiya* are by no means mutually exclusive. They are in fact complimentary parts of a greater whole. By observing how closely connected the Sufis were with the *Ahl al-ḥadīth*, we can see that *tarbiya* and *tazkiya* were not just individual spiritual practices, but an important aspect of early Islamic pedagogy and thus intellectuality.

A study of the biographies of early Sufis demonstrates that the sayings of the Prophet Muḥammad were an intricate component of their discourse and thus of their self-understanding. Well-established Sufis also reached a high degree of competency in other fields. A noted *ḥadīth* scholar and one of the foremost authorities of early Sufism, Abū ʿAbd al-Raḥmān al-Sulamī (d. 1021) compiled the biographies and teachings of over one hundred Sufis from the early Islamic period in a book entitled *Generations of the Sufis* (*Ṭabaqāt al-ṣūfiyya*). Among those he recorded as companions of the Sufis and of the *Ahl al-ḥadīth* are men such as Abu´l- ʿAbbās al-Sayyārī (d. 953-4), a Sufi Shaykh, a jurist, and a noted *ḥadīth* scholar. According to Sulamī, all the *Ahl al-ḥadīth* were Sayyārī's companions.[30] Ruwaym b. Aḥmad al-Baghdādī (d. 915) was among the most revered Sufi Shaykhs of Baghdad. He is recorded by Sulamī as a practicing jurist, a noted reciter of Qur´ān, and a scholar of Qur´ānic exegesis (*tafsīr*).[31] The most famous of the early Sufis, al-Junayd al-Baghdādī (d. 910), known as the Shaykh of Shaykhs, was also a practicing jurist who studied with many scholars known to be directly aligned with the *Ahl al-ḥadīth*. Foremost among his teachers were Abū Thawr (d. 855), the pre-eminent jurist of his day in Baghdad, and Ibn Surayj (d. 918), heralded by many as the leading scholar of *uṣūl al-fiqh* (the principles of jurisprudence) in his day. It is said of Junayd, "His words were connected to the texts (i.e., the Qur´ān and the *ḥadīth*)."[32]

In addition to these points of convergence, there were also points of divergence. But the importance of *ḥadīth* and the *sunna* was never disputed. Many Sufis entered the path of Sufism because they found that the sciences of jurisprudence and *ḥadīth* did not offer sufficient knowledge of God. But in such cases one does not always find condemnations of the jurists and the *Ahl al-ḥadīth* themselves; rather, a belief that their sciences are limited in scope and function when not complemented by the inner training which cultivates those very actions that the jurist can only regulate. The goal of the Sufi community was not to toss aside the transmitted knowledge of the jurists and the *Ahl al-ḥadīth*, but to recognize its proper place in the scope of all knowledge. As another famous Sufi, Abū Bakr al-Wāsiṭī (d. 942), said in a commentary on the *ḥadīth*, "Question the scholars, befriend the wise, and sit with the great ones":[33] "Question the scholars with regard to what is lawful and unlawful. Befriend the wise who wayfare by means of it (i. e., wisdom) on the path of truthfulness, clarity [and sincerity]. Sit with the great ones who speak of God, allude to His lordship, and see by the light of His nearness."[34] Although he is calling others to seek more than the knowledge obtained from scholars, even the injunction to go beyond the transmitted wisdom of the Islamic tradition in order to "see by the light of God" is believed to have a foundation in transmitted knowledge.

Given these observations, the Sufis of the early Islamic period should be viewed as one of the many groups among the broad based *Ahl al-ḥadīth* movement. Not only were many trained in the sciences with which this movement is commonly associated, more importantly, they shared with them in the common understanding that the Qur´ān and *sunna* of the Prophet are the criteria of all knowledge. As the famous Sufi Abū Yazīd al-Bisṭāmī (d. 849 or 875) is reported to have said: "The *sunna* is abandoning this world, and religious obligation (*al-farīḍa*) is companionship with the Master (i. e., the Prophet), because the whole of the *sunna* points to abandoning this world, and all of the Book points to companionship with the Master. So who has learned the *sunna* and the obligation has become complete."[35] Indeed, the path of Sufism is defined by the foremost Qur´ān commentator of the early Sufis, Sahl al-Tustarī (d. 896), in a manner that emphasizes the centrality of the *sunna*: "Our principles (*uṣūl*) are seven: holding fast to the Book, emulating the Messenger of God through the *sunna*, eating what is permissible, desisting from doing harm, avoiding misdeeds, repentance, and fulfilling the rights [of God and all things]."[36] Moreover, those who inclined to the Sufi way often saw the Qur´ān and the *sunna* as the instruments by which to measure the validity of their insights and inspirations, the validity of what is seen "through the light of God." Abū Sulaymān al-Dārānī (d. 830) said, "Whenever one of the subtle teachings of the Tribe (i.e., the Sufis) descends into my heart for a few days, I do not yield to it unless it is with two just witnesses, the Book and the *sunna*."[37] Abū Ḥafṣ al-Naysāburī goes further, making the Qur´ān and the *sunna* the criteria not only for the validity of one's knowledge, insights, and inspirations, but for the purity of one's state at every moment: "Whoever does not weigh his actions and states in every moment by the Book and the *sunna* and is not attentive to his incoming thoughts (*khawāṭir*), he will not be counted in the book of men (*dīwān al-rijāl*) (i.e., he will not be counted among the Sufis)."[38] The most influential of the early Sufis, al-Junayd al-Baghdādī, said, "All paths (*ṭuruq*) are blocked to mankind, save he who imitates the Messenger, follows his *sunna*, and adheres to his path. Then the path of all good things is opened to him."[39] His students report, "We heard Junayd say more than once, 'We teach what is determined by the Book and the *sunna*.' Whoever does not memorize the Qur´ān, record *ḥadīth* or study jurisprudence does not emulate him."[40]

While all the subtleties of the early Sufi movement and its interconnections with the *Ahl al-ḥadīth* movement cannot be examined here, this short survey should be enough to indicate the extensive personal, methodological, and theological affiliations between the two movements. The fundamental methodological distinction is that the Sufis believed that "the wisdom which derives from the impressions upon the heart of one of God's friends" should accompany the Qur´ān and *sunna* as legitimate sources of religious knowledge.[41] Their substantiation for this was derived from the *sunna* itself. As another compiler of Sufi teachings, Abū Naṣr al-Sarrāj (d. 988) writes in his *Kitāb al-Luma*ʿ (*The Book of Illumination*), one of the most important handbooks of early Sufism:

> The source of that is the tradition regarding faith when Gabriel asked the Prophet about the three roots: about *islām* (surrender), *īmān* (faith) and *iḥsān* (doing beautiful), the outer, the inner, and the reality. *Islām* is the outer, *īmān* is the inner and the outer, and *iḥsān* is the reality of the outer and the inner. That is the saying of the Prophet, "*Iḥsān* is to worship God as if you see Him, and if you do not see Him, He nonetheless sees you." And Gabriel corroborated that for him.[42]

Sufis such as Sarrāj and Junayd saw themselves as the transmitters of the living prophetic *sunna* pertaining to the cultivation of praiseworthy states (*aḥwāl*) and noble character traits (*akhlāq*), and believed that jurisprudence and knowledge of *ḥadīth* in and of themselves were limited to the transmitted *sunna*, which pertains more to actions and beliefs. This is not to say that they had contempt for scholars who limited their concerns to these domains. Many of the Sufis saw themselves as part of the larger community of scholars all of whom were "the inheritors of the Prophets."[43] The Sufis saw their way as a science among the Islamic sciences which is superior because it cultivates not only external obedience to the teachings of the Qur´ān and the *sunna*, but also the character traits and states of soul from which such actions arise. As Sarrāj writes:

> The Sufis also have a special place among the people of knowledge regarding the observance of verses from the book of God, and reports from the Messenger of God. What a verse has annulled and the decree of something which a report has abolished calls to the noble character traits (*makārim al-akhlāq*). It encourages the excellence of states and the exquisiteness of deeds (*a*ʿ*māl*), and imparts high stations in the religion and sublime way-stations particular to a group among the believers. A group of the companions [of the Prophet Muḥammad] and the generation after them adhered to that. That is modes of comportment from the Messenger of God and character traits from his character traits, since he said: "God taught me comportment and made beautiful my comportment."[44] And God said: "Verily you are (fashioned) upon a great character" (68:4). That is found in the records of the scholars and the jurisprudents, but they do not have a comprehension and understanding of that like their comprehension in the other sciences. Other than the Sufis, none of the possessors of knowledge who are abiding in justice have a share in that, other than consenting to it and believing that it is true.[45]

Like any group, the Sufis were sometimes loved and sometimes hated, at times supported and at times persecuted; but they were part and parcel of the early intellectual tradition, and thus an important component of the overall pedagogical effort to establish a society based upon the Qur´ān and the teachings of the Prophet Muḥammad, a society based upon submission, faith, and "doing beautiful"—*islām, īmān*, and *iḥsān*. The efforts of figures such as Seyyed Aḥmad Khān, Muḥammad ʿAbduh, the Wahhābīs, and some factions among the Muslim Brotherhood to curtail their influence, if not abolish them altogether, is thus an indication of how far Muslims have strayed from their own traditions.

The *Iḥsānī* Tradition

As is evident from Sarrāj, the Sufis saw themselves as that group among the scholars who were especially devoted to the science of doing beautiful or doing good (*iḥsān*). To understand the central thrust of the Sufi movement, we must therefore examine the Qur´ānic roots of *iḥsān*. The verb "to make beautiful" (*aḥsana*) and its derivatives occur over fifty times in the text and it is often found in the *ḥadīth*. According to these sources, the first to make beautiful is God Himself, "Who made beautiful everything which He created" (32:6). It is God who "formed you, made your forms beautiful, and provided you with pleasant things" (40:64). "He created the heavens and the earth through truth, formed you and made your forms beautiful, and to Him is the homecoming" (64:3). God is thus the first to make beautiful (*muḥsin*), and to do beautiful is to imitate the Creator as best a human can. This is fundamentally important for understanding the place of *iḥsān*, for while *islām* and *īmān* are important Qur´ānic concepts, neither pertains to, nor can pertain directly to God. God cannot submit, He can only be submitted to, and God does not believe or have faith, He knows. *Iḥsān* is thus the dimension of the religion wherein one draws closest to God by being as God-like as one can be: "Do what is beautiful as God has done what is beautiful to you" (28:77). In this vein, the Prophet Muḥammad would pray, "Oh God, You have made beautiful my creation (*khalq*), make beautiful my character (*khuluq*)."[46] From this perspective, doing beautiful is not only a way of performing specific actions, it is a way of being. Only when God has beautified one's character is the human servant then able to do beautiful, for only the like comes from the like. This in turn leads to the continued beautification of one's self. As the Qur´ān says: "Is not the recompense of doing beautiful, other than doing beautiful?" (55:60). So just as God has beautified man's form, so too He may then beautify his character, and when the character is beautified, the servant performs acts of beauty by which he participates in the inner beautification of his soul and moves towards his

Lord: "Those who do what is beautiful will receive the most beautiful and more" (10:26). Indeed, God "will recompense those who do what is beautiful with the most beautiful" (53.31). And what is most beautiful is God Himself: "God is beautiful and He loves beauty,"[47] "and to Him belong the most beautiful Names" (18:110, 20:8, 59:24).

The Prophet Muḥammad said to his companions: "God has ordained doing beautiful for everything. So when you kill, make the killing beautiful, and when you sacrifice, make the sacrificing beautiful. You should sharpen your blade so that the sacrificial animal is relieved."[48] While the first part of this *ḥadīth* is a re-affirmation of the general principle expounded in the Qur´ān, the second demonstrates that even acts which seem ugly can and must be done with beauty. Doing things with beauty is thus obligatory in all licit acts. As a Muslim, one should therefore do all things as if one sees God, for as observed above, "*Iḥsān* is to worship God as if you see Him, and if you do not see Him, He nonetheless sees you."[49] It is thus to do all things as an act of worship, for as God says, "I did not create jinn and man, except to worship Me" (51:56).

This, however, requires an initial understanding of beauty. On the intellectual level, the Sufis saw themselves as those who developed the science by which the beauty which has been ordained for everything is discerned and properly observed. This, however, was not a science which could be cultivated through transmission, like the sciences of *ḥadīth* and of law, but through discipline and inner purification; in order to do what is beautiful one must train oneself to be beautiful. As Abu ´l-Ḥasan an-Nūrī (d. 908), one of the most famous of the early Sufis said, "Sufism is neither regulations nor sciences, rather it is character traits."[50] This emphasis on inner cultivation is such that some Sufis identified the entire enterprise of Sufism with the adoption of noble character traits in accordance with the teachings of the Prophet Muḥammad: "I was only sent to complete the beautiful character traits";[51] and "Among the best of you is the most beautiful in character traits."[52] Without this active inner purification, Sufism would be but another science among the transmitted sciences. Thus, without Sufism or some form of the *iḥsānī* tradition, Islam is liable to become an ideology devoid of spiritual efficacy, and its central teaching—*lā ilāha illā Llāh*—is reduced to a slogan.

The Place of Sufism in the Middle Period

The preceding discussion has demonstrated that in the early period Sufis did not see themselves as a group completely separate from the *ʿulamā´* and the *fuqahā´*, and were not aloof from the corresponding intellectual disciplines. Nonetheless, they saw their science, the science of character traits (*akhlāq*) and of doing beautiful (*iḥsān*), as the means by which the fullness and depth of the other sciences was to be realized. In the fifth and sixth Islamic centuries both Sufism and the more standard intellectual disciplines came to be identified with particular institutional manifestations. *Fiqh* (jurisprudence) and *kalām* (theology) came to be taught in the *madrasa* (college), while many Sufis began to congregate in *khānqāhs* or *ribāṭs*, where they could study and dedicate themselves to private and collective spiritual practices. Both institutes were funded by a variety of sources, from well-wishing individual patrons to power-brokering Sultans and viziers. Unfortunately, the facile bifurcation between jurisprudence and Sufism employed by many scholars has caused the relationship between these institutions to be misunderstood and thus misrepresented. In analyzing tenth century Iranian politics, one scholar describes an antagonism between Sufis and jurisprudents which he calls:

> ... a reflection of two fundamentally opposed interpretations of the Koranic revelation and the Muḥammadan legacy. The positive nomocentricity of Islamic law found the language of Islamic mysticism as quintessentially flawed in nature and disposition. The feeling was mutual. The Sufis, too, rejected the rigid and perfunctory nomocentricity of the jurists as quintessentially misguided and a stultification of the Koranic message and the Prophetic traditions.[53]

As in the early period, there are too many convergences between the Sufis, the jurists, and their supporters to provide any evidence that such a dichotomy existed. The most influential political figure of this time period, the Saljuq vizier Niẓām al-Mulk (1063-1092), was renowned for his support of both Sufis and *ʿulamāʾ*. He established both *madrasas* and Sufi *khānqāhs*, as did relatively unknown individuals such as Abū Saʿd al-Astarābādī (d. 1048-9)[54] and Abū Saʿd al-Kharkūshī (d. 1013 or 1016).[55] Abū ʿAlī al-Daqqāq (d. 1015), renowned as a Sufi master, is also said to have founded a *madrasa* in the city of Nasā.[56] He and his more famous son-in-law, Abu ʾl-Qāsim al-Qushayrī (d. 1072), author of one of the most influential handbooks of Sufism, are said to have taught in a *madrasa* which later became known as the Qushayriyya *madrasa*.[57] Shaykh Abū ʿAlī al-Fārmadī (d. 1084), known as the Shaykh of Shaykhs in the city of Nishapur, is said to have professed a love for his Shaykh which soon inspired him to move from the *madrasa* to the *khānqāh*.[58] Al-Fārmadī was in turn a teacher of both Abū Ḥāmid al-Ghazālī (d. 1111) and Aḥmad al-Ghazālī (d. 1126), two brothers who are known to have traveled freely between *madrasa* and *khānqāh* and were revered for having reached the highest levels in *fiqh*, *kalām*, and Sufism. The more famous and influential of the two, Abū Ḥāmid, rose to the highest level of the *madrasa* system and was appointed chair of Shāfiʿī law at the Niẓāmiyya *madrasa* in Baghdad, the most influential educational institution of its day. After leaving his teaching position for over ten years he returned to his homeland of Khurāsān, where he spent his last days providing instruction in a "*khānqāh* for the Sufis, and in a *madrasa* for the sake of those who seek knowledge."[59]

Though only a handful of figures have been mentioned, the free movement of such intellectuals between the *khānqāh* and the *madrasa* demonstrates that in medieval Islamdom there was no hard line between the Sufis and the *ʿulamāʾ*, nor between the *madrasa* and the *khānqāh*. The lines which have been drawn by secularist and revivalist Muslim interpreters, as well as orientalists, are more a result of the modern mind, which imposes Enlightenment and Protestant Christian notions of mysticism upon the medieval Islamic world: a world in which most intellectuals, though they frequently criticized one another's predilections (as in any healthy intellectual environment), participated in the same discourse. Their particular interests and resulting identities often differed, but still overlapped. Failure to admit this basic historical reality has led generations of Muslims to discard an integral part of their faith and has blocked many more from understanding and experiencing the fullness of their tradition. When this occurs, the religion is reduced to an ideology, and when it is reduced to an ideology it no longer functions to purify hearts, but rather to justify individual aspirations and political ambitions.

Abū Ḥāmid al-Ghazālī

Though the aforementioned Abū Ḥāmid al-Ghazālī was the most accomplished scholar in both jurisprudence and theology of his day, in his later years he became a chief proponent of the *iḥsānī* intellectual tradition. His later writings argue for the primacy of Sufi knowledge received through inner purification and the actualization of one's inherent noble character traits, a knowledge which he and others referred to as "knowledge by presence" (*al-ʿilm al-ḥuḍūrī* or *al-ʿilm al-ladunī*). His belief in the primacy of "knowledge by presence" did not take hold among all Muslim scholars and many disputed his claims. But his *Revival of the Religious Sciences* became the most popular book in the history of Islam and his writings exercised an influence in all fields of scholarship throughout the Islamic world, from his native Iran to India, Morocco, Indonesia, and even Muslim China. His view of knowledge and the relation between the Islamic sciences is therefore one which has been widely contemplated and which did much to shape medieval Islamic civilization. Even if a scholar was vehemently opposed to the primacy of Sufi knowledge, or knowledge by presence, he would have been influenced by this notion because he had to account for it as an important player in the intellectual dialogue of his day. To understand the manner in which the *iḥsānī* intellectual tradition continued in the middle period, and to see more clearly what some of the central concerns of most Muslim intellectuals until the modern period were, we would thus do well to examine the contours of Ghazālī's thought.

Ghazālī left a vast corpus of writings which dramatically changed the direction of philosophy, theology, jurisprudence, and Sufism. But due to his attack on the philosophers in *Tahāfut al-falāsifa* (*The Incoherence of the Philosophers*), several Western scholars and modernist Muslims have held him responsible for the intellectual decline of Islamic civilization. He is often seen as the implacable adversary of philosophy and the fundamental cause for the demise of philosophy, and thus intellectuality, in the Islamic world. This is a lamentable misunderstanding, for although Ghazālī's intention in the *Tahāfut* was clearly to deconstruct, in many other works it was to reconstruct. In works such as *The Niche of Lights* and even Ghazālī's magnum opus, *The Revival of the Religious Sciences*, one finds a recurrent implementation of philosophical terminology and philosophical modes of discourse.

As T. J. Winter, one of the leading authorities on the teachings of Ghazālī, has demonstrated, Ghazālī's presentation of the soul and its virtues in the twenty-second book of *The Revival*, "On Breaking the Two Desires" is borrowed directly from the *Tahdhīb al-akhlāq* (*The Refinement of Character Traits*) of the Neoplatonic Islamic philosopher Abū ʿAlī ibn Miskawayh (d. 1030), a follower of the Islamic peripatetic tradition, whose primary representatives are al-Fārābī (d. 950) and Ibn Sīnā (d. 1037).[60] Like Ibn Miskawayh, Ghazālī begins with the three faculties of the soul: the rational, the irascible, and the appetitive, and the four Platonic virtues, or "principles of virtue": Wisdom (*al-ḥikma*), Courage (*al-shujāʿa*), Temperance (*al-ʿiffa*) and Justice (*al-ʿadl*) from which derive all secondary virtues. As with Ibn Miskawayh and others before him, Ghazālī believes that the human objective is to maintain the four cardinal virtues in perfect equilibrium (*iʿtidāl*). But he differs from Ibn Miskawayh in two fundamental ways. First, he argues that the good deeds which result from equilibrium are not only recognized by the intellect, but also confirmed by the revealed law (*sharīʿa*). Secondly, he believes that the Prophet Muḥammad is the only person to have attained complete equilibrium. Stylistically, Ghazālī differs in that he precedes the discussion with selections from Qur'ān, *ḥadīth*, and the sayings of Sufis, such as the aforementioned Abū Bakr al-Wāsiṭī and Sahl al-Tustarī. Thus, although this is clearly a Neoplatonic discussion of virtue, Ghazālī introduces it in a manner which thoroughly Islamicizes it, and then employs it to support fundamental assertions of the Islamic faith.

A far more complex issue is Ghazālī's use of emanationist vocabulary and concepts in the *Niche of Lights*, where he presents the relationship between God and the many levels of creation as a hierarchy of lights by which subsequent degrees of creation become manifest:

> The low lights flow forth from one another just as light flows forth from a lamp. The lamp is the holy prophetic spirit. The holy prophetic spirits are kindled from the high spirits just as a lamp is kindled from a light. Some of the high things kindle each other, and their hierarchy is a hierarchy of stations. Then all of them climb to the Light of lights, their Origin, their First Source. This is God alone, who has no partner.[61]

Ghazālī's presentation is distinguished from that of earlier Islamic philosophers in that at every turn he is careful to couch his discussion in language which preserves the integrity of Divine oneness and omnipotence, precisely what he accuses the philosophers of failing to do. As he writes, "The only true light is His light. Everything is His light—or, rather, He is everything. Or, rather, nothing possesses selfhood other than He, except in a metaphorical sense. Therefore, there is no light except His light."[62] In other words, for Ghazālī, God as light is the true light of everything and nothing has any light in and of itself; it is God's light within it that allows it to be. It is God's light within it that is its very being. This is something which can be found in Ibn Sīnā's discussion of existence insofar as all that is other than God is not truly existent in itself, but is a possible existent (*mumkin al-wujūd*) deriving its existence from absolute existence (*al-wājib al-wujūd*). But for Ghazālī this does not suffice to preserve the complete integrity of God's oneness and singularity. His view of existence is much closer to the Sufi understanding of the oneness of existence (*waḥdat al-wujūd*) than to that of the early Islamic peripatetics, which, although it opens towards the oneness of existence, does not express it outright.

Following upon the well-known saying of the Sufi master Maʿrūf al-Karkhī (d. 815), "There is nothing in existence except God," Ghazālī sees all of creation as having two faces: a face towards itself and a face towards its Lord. Viewed in terms of the face of itself it is non-existent; but viewed in terms of the face of God, it exists:

> "Everything is perishing save His face" (28:88), not that each thing is perishing at one time or at other times, but it is perishing from beginninglessness to endlessness. It can only be so conceived since, when the essence of anything other than He is considered in respect of its own essence, it is sheer non-existence. But when it is viewed in respect of the "face" to which existence flows forth from the First, the Real, then it is seen as existing not in itself but through the face turned to its Giver of Existence. Hence the only existence is the Face of God.[63]

Here the tools of philosophy are used to unpack the meaning within one of the terse sayings of early Sufism in order to give a particular Sufi doctrine a more dialectical architecture.

These two examples clearly indicate that Ghazālī found value in the intellectual contributions of philosophy. The potential benefit of philosophy is alluded to in his autobiographical treatise, *The Deliverer from Error*, where he argues that one must not reject philosophy out of hand, but must develop a strong mind in order to discern what is of value within it:

> Those with weak minds know truth by men, not men by truth. The intelligent person follows the saying of ʿAlī, "Do not know truth through men. Know truth and then you will know its people." So the intelligent person knows truth then looks at the claim itself. If it is truth he accepts it....[64]

For Ghazālī this means that one "must be zealous to extract the truth from the claims of those who are misguided, knowing that the gold mine is dust and gravel."[65] He thus advises his readers to sift truth from falsehood. He likens this process to that of a money changer who does not reject everything a counterfeiter brings to him, but instead uses his knowledge of true currency and false currency to sort the good from the bad and make use of the good. This is in fact what Ghazālī does with philosophy. He rejects the arguments and conclusions of philosophy which he finds are non-Islamic, but then incorporates many aspects of philosophy into an Islamic, that is a Qur´ānic, world view.

In the philosophy of the early Islamic peripatetics, Ghazālī found powerful tools, which if not tempered by the light of revelation, could lead to a syllogistically imprisoned vision of the truth; that is to say, a vision of the truth which is confined to the mind such that it does not open the heart. Like the money changer, he extracted the good aspects of peripatetic philosophy and incorporated them into an intellectual economy which was fully Islamic. Rather than being a Muslim who is a philosopher, as in the case of Ibn Sīnā, al-Farābī, and Ibn Miskawayh, Ghazālī can be seen as perhaps the first to be a fully Islamic philosopher.[66] Rather than converting Muslims to philosophy, he formed a crucial step in the conversion of philosophy to Islam, a trend which was to unfold in the school of Ibn al-ʿArabī (d. 1240) and the philosophy of Suhrawardī (d. 1191), and which came to full fruition in the seventeenth century through the writings of the Iranian philosopher Mullā Ṣadrā (d. 1640).

To understand what is meant by an "Islamic philosopher," we must look deeper into Ghazālī's epistemology. In a short treatise composed for a disciple, Ghazālī begins by criticizing one who seeks knowledge out of "... preoccupation for the grace of the soul and the paths of the world. For he thinks that knowledge in itself will be his deliverance, that his salvation lies within it and that he has no need for work, and this is the belief of philosophy."[67] Instead he enjoins a combination of knowledge and action in which action is always based upon sound knowledge. As the Prophet Muḥammad has said in a *ḥadīth* often cited by Ghazālī: "He who acts according to what he knows, God teaches him what he did not know."[68] Developing upon this teaching, Ghazālī writes, "Knowledge without action is madness, action without knowledge is non-existent."[69] This does not, however, refer to the mere outer actions of the body. It refers to inner actions whereby one disciplines oneself by "severing the passions of the lower soul and killing its caprice with the sword of spiritual exercises ..."[70] For Ghazālī, this knowledge is indeed the most important form of knowledge:

> If you study and examine knowledge, your knowledge must rectify your heart and purify your soul, as if you know your life span will not last more than a week. It is necessary that you not busy that time with the knowledge of jurisprudence, character traits, the principles [of religion and jurisprudence], theology and the like because you know that these sciences will not benefit you. Rather, you should occupy yourself with observing the heart and recognizing the qualities of the soul and the accidents resulting from its attachment to the world. You should purify your soul of blameworthy character traits and occupy yourself with the love of God and servitude to Him, and with being characterized by beautiful characteristics. Not a day or night passes, but the death of the servant may come.[71]

Through this one opens the eye of the heart whereby one may reach the knowledge of unveiling which Ghazālī describes as "the very end of knowledge" from which all other forms of knowledge derive.[72]

According to his own account, the understanding of the proper relation between the Islamic sciences, which Ghazālī developed in his later writings, is based entirely upon the clarity of understanding he obtained by devoting himself to the discipline of Sufism, which for him:

> ... is composed of both knowledge and action. The outcome of their action is cutting off the obstacles of the soul, refraining from blameworthy character traits and their depraved attributes, so that the heart may arrive from it to freeing the heart from what is other than God and to adorning it with the remembrance of God.[73]

When this has been achieved, one can attain to immediate witnessing, which Ghazālī believed to be the only true path to certainty, all else being merely confirmation through the imitation of what others have said. But like Sarrāj and other Sufi scholars before him, he believed that most Islamic scholars were not on this path: "This knowledge is not obtained through the types of knowledge with which most people are occupied. Thus, that knowledge does not increase them except in boldness to disobey God."[74] As such, he saw a radical need for a revivification of the Islamic sciences, one based on the preeminence of that knowledge received through inner purification and constant remembrance of God—knowledge by presence.

In both *The Revival of the Religious Sciences* and a smaller treatise entitled *The Treatise on Knowledge by Presence*, Ghazālī outlines a hierarchy of knowledge in which all modes of knowledge are subordinate to knowledge by presence.[75] He is indefatigable in promoting his belief that the fundamental objective of all learning is to wipe away ignorance and return to the state of purity which is the human norm—the *fiṭra*: "Learning is not but the return of the soul to its substance and bringing what is within it into actuality, seeking the completion of its essence and the attainment of its joy."[76] For Ghazālī the goal of knowledge is not advancement in the practical affairs of the world, but a wisdom deriving from a living intelligence that is able to see things as they are in themselves, and is able to realize the applications of that wisdom on all planes and in all affairs. Following the Sufi tradition before him, Ghazālī believed that when this is achieved, one realizes that one was a "knower" (*ʿārif*) before, but that attachment to the body and its concomitant desires clouded one from the knowledge for which man is created. As this is a knowledge which corresponds to the human norm, it is not a knowledge obtained through learning, though learning can help to actualize it. Rather, this is a way of knowing which requires no intermediary: "Knowledge by presence is that which has no intermediary between the soul and the Creator for its acquisition. It is like the light from a lamp of the unseen [realm] falling upon a pure, empty, and subtle heart."[77] "Those who arrive at the level of knowledge by presence have no need for much obtaining and toil in instruction. They study little and know much...."[78] This is thus a knowledge obtained through inspiration (*ilhām*); it is to the saints (*awliyāʾ*) what revelation (*waḥy*) is to the prophets.

The seat of this knowledge, according to Ghazālī and many who came before him and followed after him, is the heart or intellect, which is the spirit that God blew into the form of man, a spirit alluded to in the Qurʾānic verse, "And I blew into him from My spirit" (15:29, 38:72). It is through this eternal seat of consciousness that the full awareness of *tawḥīd* is realized. From this point of view, things can only be understood in relation to the Creator, who is the Origin and the End and who sustains all things at every moment. Every branch of knowledge must therefore have this understanding as its end, otherwise it is oriented towards a knowledge which is not grounded in the fullness of *tawḥīd*, and thus a knowledge which does not assist the human being in achieving the perfection and felicity of the human norm. In other words, all true sciences were seen by Ghazālī as applications of *tawḥīd*. All knowledge sought in this way is sought with *iḥsān* because it is sought in order to know God and to attain human perfection. It ennobles the human condition by helping one to understand, emulate, and participate in the *iḥsān* of God and His creation. All aspects of a person's education, from the study of language, grammar, and mathematics, to the study of jurisprudence, ethics, and metaphysics, should thus be integrated into this overarching vision. For if one knows a thing without knowing its relation to God, one does not really know the thing, but rather has compound ignorance (*al-jahl al-murakkab*) because he thinks he knows what he does not know. Is this not the case of so many today?

Ibn al-ᶜArabī

There were many other proponents of this view, some with very different emphases than that of Ghazālī and Sarrāj, and Junayd before them, but nonetheless with the same central concern that all knowledge and learning be oriented towards a vibrant actualization of *tawḥīd*, lest it become a dead letter. Though the transmission of the religious texts which affirm *tawḥīd* was emphasized, this was joined to the inculcation of active and free remembrance of God. For true faith cannot be taught; it must arise from within. Foremost among the later scholars to write of the knowledge by presence, or knowledge by tasting (*dhawq*) as it is also known, is the great Shaykh of Murcia, Muḥyi ´d-Dīn Ibn al-ᶜArabī (d. 1240). The writings of Ibn al-ᶜArabī and his disciples came to be the most influential expression of the *iḥsānī* intellectual tradition until and into the modern period. To know the form in which this tradition continued we must therefore look to him.

Ibn al-ᶜArabī did not often refer to himself and those of his ilk as Sufis, he preferred the term verifiers (*muḥaqiqqūn*): "I mean by 'our companions' those who possess hearts, witnessings, and unveilings, not the worshipers or ascetics, and not all Sufis, save those among them who are the people of truths and verification (*taḥqīq*)."[79] Nonetheless, in many ways he was the intellectual and spiritual descendant of the early Sufi movement. His writings often unpack the meanings contained within the terse and allusive sayings of earlier luminaries of the Sufi tradition, such as the aforementioned Junayd al-Baghdādī, Bayāzīd al-Bisṭāmī, and Sahl al-Tustarī, all of whom he considered to be verifiers. Thus many of the teachings attributed to him are in fact teachings which had been within the Islamic community from the beginning, but were now expressed in a new mode. Like his predecessors, he saw Sufism as the perfection of character traits:

> The people of the path of God say Sufism is character, so whoever surpasses you in character surpasses you in Sufism.... Among the conditions of being designated a Sufi is that one be wise, possessing wisdom. If he is not, then he has no share of this heart, for it is entirely wisdom and it is entirely character traits. It necessitates complete gnosis, a superior intellect, and strong control over one's soul, so that selfish desires do not rule over it.[80]

Thus for Ibn al-ᶜArabī wisdom, knowledge, or gnosis is intrinsically bound to virtue and character, i.e., to doing beautiful.

The school which developed from Ibn al-ᶜArabī's mode of expressing these teachings came to be known as the school of *ᶜirfān* or *maᶜrifa*, which can best be translated as the school of gnosis.[81] The word *ʿirfān* derives from the verb *ʿarafa* which means to know, but also means to recognize. *ʿIrfān* thus refers to the recognition and realization of that knowledge which is the birthright of man, the knowledge of things as they are in themselves. From this perspective, to attain to gnosis is to realize the fullness of God and His creation, which is to return to the human norm. According to Ibn al-ʿArabī, gnosis is distinct from what is learned through transmission and reflection:

> All knowledge which can only be attained through practice, godfearingness, and wayfaring is gnosis because it derives from a verified unveiling (*kashf muḥaqqaq*) in which there is no obfuscation. In contrast, knowledge obtained through reflective consideration is never free from obfuscation and bewilderment, nor from rejecting that which leads to it.[82]

While Ghazālī argued for the primacy of knowledge by presence, Ibn al-ʿArabī wrote directly from the perception derived through knowledge by presence. Like Ghazālī, he saw it as the defining characteristic of being human. According to Ibn al-ʿArabī, only when a human fully experiences knowledge by presence can he truly be called human. To experience such knowledge is to see the truth (*ḥaqq*) of all things, and one who sees these truths is the verifier. Gnosis could thus be seen as the science of verification: "Verification is the gnosis (*maʿrifa*) of truth which is demanded by the essence of each thing. The verifier fulfills that through knowledge."[83] One who has attained to verification witnesses the *ḥaqq* or truth of everything. But *ḥaqq* is a deceptively simple word, for in addition to truth it can also mean true, reality, real, right, or due. It is one of the names of God who is *al-Ḥaqq* or the True, the Real. To verify the truths, rights, or realities of all things is thus to see the self-disclosure of the ultimate Truth within all. As William Chittick, one of the foremost scholars of Ibn al-ʿArabī, writes:

> The goal of *taḥqīq* is to see the face of God wherever you turn, in every creature and in oneself, and then to act according to the *ḥaqq* [truth] of God's face. If we understand anything in the universe without taking the Divine face into account, then we have lost the thing's *ḥaqq*. By losing sight of the thing's *ḥaqq*, we have lost sight of God, and by losing sight of God, we have lost sight of *tawḥīd*.[84]

To verify the truth is a command deriving from the Qurʾānic revelation itself: "Do not dress truth in falsehood and hide the truth, though you know" (2:42). According to the Qurʾān, both the revelation and creation are truth and are brought through truth. The Qurʾān states, "And what We have revealed to you from the book is the truth" (35:31). Several verses affirm that the Qurʾān has descended through truth: "That is because God brought down the book through truth" (2:176); and "We brought down upon you the book through truth, that you may judge between the people in accordance with what God has shown you" (4:105). As regards creation, the text declares, "He is the one who created the heavens and the earth through truth" (6:73). Indeed, humans are challenged to recognize this fundamental reality: "Do you not see that God created the heavens and the earth through truth?" (14:19). Several verses of the Qur´ān respond to this question; one reads: "He did not create the heavens and the earth and what is between them except through truth" (30:8). It is in fact through Himself that God has created and revealed, for He Himself is the Truth: "That is your God, the Lord, the Truth" (10:33); and "That is because God is the Truth" (22:62). All that concerns us as humans is thus to be understood by knowing the ultimate Truth directly, and the other truths, which are in fact an unfolding of this one Truth, through creation and revelation. To know things outside of the truth is to be guided by caprice (*hawā´*) and conjecture (*ẓann*), regarding which the Qur´ān cautions: "Do not follow their caprices over what has come to you from the truth" (5:48); and "Verily conjecture is of no avail against the truth" (10:37). The view of verifying the truth or *taḥqīq* advanced by Ibn al-ᶜArabī and his followers thus derives from a thoroughly Qur´ānic understanding of the universe. God is the Truth, truth is from God (18:29), and truth belongs to God (18:44). God reveals through truth, creates through truth, and guides through truth to truth. To see the truth of things is thus the only way to truly see things. It is in fact to see God, for He is the Truth which has made all things descend through truth, i.e. through Himself.

Man is unique in that he is the only being that is able to see all things as they are, the only being able to recognize all of these truths. The Qur´ān teaches that Adam was taught the names of all things (2:31-33). According to Ibn al-ᶜArabī, these names are the traces of God's own self-disclosure of Himself through Himself. As Chittick explains:

> The traces of God's names and attributes are externalized as the specific and unique characteristics of each thing. Every creature in the universe knows God in a specific differentiated and determined way, defined by the attributes that thing displays, or by the word that it embodies. Each thing displays the signs of God and gives news of Him through occupying its own specific niche in the never repeated speech that is the universe.[85]

The one being who is able to hear this never-ending speech, and thus witness all the traces of God's names and attributes, is man. He cannot know things outside of God because things do not exist outside of God. So his knowledge of all things is in fact his knowledge of God. But it is also knowledge through God, which according to Ibn al-ᶜArabī is the only true knowledge there is:

When one wants to recognize (*ʿarafa*) things, he cannot recognize them through what his faculties give him. He should endeavor in many acts of obedience until the True (*al-ḥaqq*) is his hearing, his seeing, and all his faculties. Then he will know all affairs through God and will recognize God through God.... When you know God through God and all things through God, no ignorance, obfuscation, doubt, or uncertainty will come upon you.[86]

As such, all knowledge is in fact *tawḥīd*, attesting to unity. If one does not see something as displaying the Truth, he cannot really know that thing, for he is being heedless of God, the Origin and End of that thing. If he thinks he knows it, he actually has compound ignorance, because he thinks he knows what he does not know. To know is thus to remember God, for it is to see God in all things: "Wheresoever you turn there is the face of God" (2:115). According to Ibn al-ʿArabī, to not see this face is ignorance, and this is the greatest of sins from which all other sins derive:

The greatest sin is what kills hearts. They do not die except through the absence of the knowledge of God. This is what is named ignorance. For the heart is the house that God has chosen for Himself in this human configuration. But such a person has usurped the house, coming between it and the owner. He is the one who most wrongs himself because he has deprived himself of the good that would have come to him from the owner of the house had he left the house to Him. This is the deprivation of ignorance.[87]

Ibn al-ʿArabī went on to become the most influential intellectual figure of the next six or seven centuries. A glance at the intellectual landscape of Islam after Ibn al-ʿArabī shows that he had a profound influence on Islamic intellectual discourse in all lands until the middle of the nineteenth century. As Alexander Knysh has demonstrated in his study of the Shaykh's historical influence: "... from the 7th/13th C.E. onward practically every Muslim thinker of note took it upon himself to define his position vis-à-vis the controversial Sufi master."[88] And as Itzchak Weismann has demonstrated, all the responses to modernism in late Ottoman Damascus necessarily had to respond in some way to the thought of this great master. Among such movements, that of ʿAbd al-Qādir al-Jazāʾirī saw in the teachings of Ibn al-ʿArabī the tools for a re-establishment of an intellectual elite able to respond in full to the intellectual and institutional pressures of their times.[89]

As with Ghazālī, Ibn al-ʿArabī and his followers, whether one agreed with them or not, were a force with which any serious intellectual had to reckon. Thus, through the influence of Ghazālī, Ibn al-ʿArabī and the many who followed them, the *iḥsānī* intellectual tradition, which developed as a conscious elaboration of the teachings of the early Sufi tradition, was a central component of Islamic intellectual *and* political discourse until the middle of the nineteenth century. The belief that there is a transcendent source of knowledge which can be obtained without the intermediary of instruction and which is necessary in order to fully understand the knowledge contained in the transmitted sciences thus had an important presence throughout the Islamic world from the time of the earliest scholarly circles of the *Ahl al-ḥadīth* until the dawn of the modern period. It has never died out; but in their efforts to keep pace with the modern world, both rigid puritanical and secular liberal reformists have attempted to deny that it was an inherently Islamic phenomenon. In doing so, they have denied their own heritage.

The Modern Period

In the modern period, the intellectual landscape of Islam has undergone dramatic changes due to seismic shifts resulting from the challenges of foreign military, economic, and cultural domination. Though not immediately apparent, the foremost of these challenges are those posed by Western thought and its concomitant methodologies, for it is through our ideologies that our institutions are formed. Yet despite its transformations, the Islamic world remains profoundly Islamic in so far as the culture, social mores, and worldview of the people inhabiting it have been molded by the teachings of Islam. Nonetheless, the most vocal trends of the modern period are in danger of removing even this from the Islamic world, for they do not represent Islamic responses to the challenges of the West, responses based upon *islām*, *īmān*, and *iḥsān*. The solutions to the difficulties of the Muslim world lie not in the complete capitulation or drastic rejectionism which characterize secularist and radicalist movements respectively, but in the interaction with other civilizations on the basis of traditional Islamic teachings. Such a solution is being sought by intellectuals in many parts of the Islamic world. But the loudest voices still belong to those who have in large part rejected or misunderstood their intellectual heritage. For the non-specialist, who has little familiarity with the intellectual tradition of Islam, its voice is easily drowned out by the cries of radicals and the Western bias towards "liberal intellectuals" such as Mohamed Arkoun and Abdul-Karim Soroush. So long as such figures are held up by the West as the leaders of a coming intellectual revolution—the "Martin Luthers of Islam" as is so often said—more Muslim youth will be radicalized by these obvious efforts toward continued intellectual colonization.

The intellectual imbalance and stultification in the modern Islamic world derives not from the failure to modernize and secularize as critics such as Bernard Lewis, Daniel Pipes, and Salman Rushdie would have it, but from a widespread rejection of the Islamic intellectual tradition, usually in the name of progress. There are important exceptions, such as Shaykh ʿAbd al-Ḥalīm Maḥmūd (d. 1974) of al-Azhar University in Cairo and the late ᶜAllamah Ṭabāṭabā'ī (d. 1981) in Iran, whose *Uṣūl-i falsafa* (*The Principles of Philosophy*) provides a thorough critique of dialectical materialism from the standpoint of Mullā Ṣadrā's philosophy. Another exception is Maulanā Ashraf ᶜAlī Thanvī (d. 1943) in the Indian subcontinent, whose response to modernism has been examined in depth by Fuad Naeem. In addition, the last fifty years has witnessed a resurgence of traditional Islamic teachings in many parts of the Islamic world. But by and large the teachings of Sufism and their subsequent unfolding have been rejected by the most visible and politically active trends of the modern period—be they liberal secularists or religious dogmatists. Unlike earlier opponents of the *iḥsānī* intellectual tradition, most modern critics have not seriously studied the works of its representatives. Sufism continues to be practiced on a popular level, but many of the central teachings of such figures as Junayd, Sarrāj, Ghazālī, Ibn al-ᶜArabī and their intellectual descendants are discounted out of hand by their opponents, or presented in a trite and hackneyed manner by many of their supposed proponents. There are notable exceptions, but for most of the liberal and doctrinal reform movements in the Islamic world,

> Sufism became the scapegoat through which Islam's "backwardness" could be explained. In this view Sufism is the religion of the common people and embodies superstition and un-Islamic elements adopted from local cultures; in order for Islam to retain its birthright, which includes modern science and technology, Sufism must be eradicated.[90]

This rejection of Sufi teachings and their later intellectual elaborations is among the most significant losses endured by the Islamic world. It is indeed an essential part of what makes much of the current Islamic world "modern." For in order to be lived in its fullness, every aspect of the Islamic tradition must be present. As C. S. Lewis has observed: once you have rejected a part of a religious tradition, you have *ipso facto* rejected the entire tradition. Not every individual will be fully inclined to each aspect of a particular religious tradition, but every aspect must be present for people of different predilections to work together in weaving a social fabric that allows for the expression and actualization of the full tradition. Law and creed, which could be said to correspond to *islām* and *īmān* respectively, are an integral component of any Islamic society, but without the vivifying presence of a full-fledged *iḥsānī* tradition, they become opaque and are soon bereft of that light by which God guides. It is for this reason that Sarrāj referred to *iḥsān* as the reality (*ḥaqīqa*) of the religion. The rejection of intellectual Sufism as a major component of the modern intellectual discourse has thus contributed to a catastrophic myopia. Not only have many Muslim thinkers demonstrated a shallow understanding of non-Islamic elements, they have also distorted the religion itself. In attempting to reconstruct and reinterpret the Islamic tradition in light of the perceived achievements of the times, modernist thinkers of the past, such as Sayyid Aḥmad Khān, Muḥammad ʿAbduh and Jamāl al-Dīn Afghānī abandoned the rigorous intellectual discernment of traditional Islamic intellectuality—the first outright, the others with more subtlety. They lost sight of their intellectual traditions and unwittingly surrendered the ground of intelligence to a secular humanist tradition, whose ideologies they tried to foist upon others by reading them into their own traditions or simply by adding the adjective "Islamic." Their legacy has been carried through the twentieth century and into the twenty-first by thinkers such as Mamadiou Dia of Senegal, Farid Esack of South Africa, Mohamed Arkoun of Algeria, Abdul-Karim Soroush of Iran, Jawdat Saʿīd of Syria, and Fatima Merinissi of Morocco to name a few. Though such thinkers may call upon the Qur´ān and *ḥadīth* as proof texts for their assertions, they are rooted in mental habits that developed in a secular universe that rejects the centrality of revelation, if not its very veracity.

Though each has different players with different shades of emphasis, both stringent reformism and liberal modernism constitute artificial limitations of traditional Islamic knowledge inspired by the influence of secular ideologies. This has led to the inversion of Islamic thought and the destruction of Islamic civilization. As Seyyed Hossein Nasr writes, "In trying to render back to Islam its power on the stage of history, many of these movements have disfigured the nature of Islam itself."[91]

Stringent reformists, such as the Wahhābīs of Saudi Arabia, the *Jamāʿat-i Islāmī* (Society of Islam) in Pakistan, and the more militant elements among the Muslim Brotherhood in Egypt and Syria, propose strict adherence to the Qur´ān and the *sunna*, but in doing so arrogantly discard thirteen centuries of Islamic intellectual history, claiming that there is no need for help from the great thinkers of the past in order to understand and interpret the texts which they themselves preserved and transmitted. They then seek refuge in religious fervor, while closing the door to analysis and deliberation regarding the problems which confront the Islamic world. This approach stirs deep passions in the hearts of people who yearn to live a pious Islamic life, but denies many of the forms of guidance by which such passions were traditionally channeled towards the Divine. In the absence of such guidance a narrow ideological interpretation of the faith comes to predominate. Those who fail to adopt this interpretation are then seen as unbelievers, or at best as misguided.

Modernism originates from the secularizing and humanistic tendencies which began with the Renaissance and resulted in a scientistic and reductionist understanding of reality. But as this mode of thought did not rise organically from within the Islamic intellectual tradition, its expressions in the Islamic world have consisted largely of warmed-over Western ideologies under a thin veneer of Islamic terminology. Liberalizing modernists join with doctrinaire reformists in eschewing the great interpreters of the past, but go further, at times arguing for the abandonment of the Qur´ān and *sunna*. Reformists join with modernists in thinking that one can adopt the outward trappings of modern science without evaluating the *weltanschauung* from which it arose. The reformists err in thinking that man can function on the transmitted sciences alone and has no need for developing the critical interpretive skills cultivated through the Islamic intellectual sciences. The modernists err in thinking that one can discard much of the transmitted traditions, such as *ḥadīth* and jurisprudence, or that these must now be interpreted through Western methodologies. Both take recourse to theories and methodologies which are decidedly un-Islamic, if not anti-religious. Rather than calling upon the guidance of scholars of the past, most of the figures who have dominated modern Islamic discourse have joined with many Western thinkers in an ill-conceived movement towards an undefined goal known as progress.

Liberal modernist Muslim thinkers and radical reformist activists are two sides of the same coin. Whereas medieval thinkers like Ghazālī were able to analyze and utilize intellectual tools from outside influences, radical reformists reject them outwardly while submitting inwardly, and modernists attempt to patch them onto the fabric of Islam, some claiming that they have been a part of that fabric all along. Both movements represent a subversion of traditional values and teachings from within the Islamic tradition. In an effort to transform Islamic civilization, each has in fact hastened the onset of the very illnesses they sought to ameliorate. Rather than contemplating and evaluating Western civilization through the Islamic intellectual tradition, modernists have embraced many tenets of Western thought out of a deep sense of inferiority—a sense which results from mistaking the power of Western nations for the truth of Western ideologies. Finding these movements within their midst, the reformists have retreated to fanatical adherence and pietistic sentimentalism. The modernists fail to offer solutions because they begin with intellectual capitulation. The reformists fail because they only provide intermediate solutions which are fideistic and voluntaristic at best. But such a response cannot provide lasting solutions to the challenges posed by the West, because these are at root intellectual challenges which demand an intellectual response.

The diatribes of fanatical rejectionism must be transformed into a logical and objective critique, and the sycophancy of liberalist capitulation must be supplanted by analysis and comprehension. This is what Ghazālī advised when saying that one must become like the moneychanger, who through the power of discernment is able to discern truth from falsehood and thus snatch truth from the words of all, be they of one's own tradition or from another. But in order for this to be achieved, an intellectual universe which is fully Islamic must first be re-established, that is to say an intellectual universe based upon *tawḥīd.* Through the sciences which developed in the *iḥsānī* intellectual tradition, an objective critique of the modern world which is based upon the verities contained in the Islamic revelation can be developed. Nothing that is objectively true can be rejected through the methodologies of this tradition, for it is in the nature of Islam that it accepts all that bears witness to the Divine—every truth cannot but bear witness to the one Truth. But such sciences must be implemented on all levels, for man is not only a mental being, but a spiritual, emotional, psychological, and physical being as well. In short, the preservation of the transmitted sciences which has continued to the present day must be combined with a rediscovery of the intellectual sciences and a revitalization of the training of the soul and the methods of cultivating inner discernment. This is the way to which Abū Naṣr al-Sarrāj alluded in the introduction to his *Book of Illumination*; it is to combine *islām, īmān,* and *iḥsān* in a single composite intellectual approach wherein one seeks to know things as they are in themselves. As William Chittick argues:

> The only way to think in Islamic terms is to join thought with the transcendent truths from which Islam draws sustenance. This needs to be done not only by having recourse to the guidelines set down in the Koran and the Hadith, but also by taking guidance from the great Muslim intellectuals of the past, those who employed the Koran and the Hadith to clarify the proper role of thought in human affairs.[92]

The choice of great thinkers from whom one seeks guidance is not limited to a narrow definition of "orthodoxy," but extends to all those Islamic thinkers, Sunnī and Shīʿī, who have tried to lend clarity to the understanding of reality enjoined by the Qur´ān and *ḥadīth.* Those intellectuals who have been chosen for this essay are but a few luminaries from an extensive tradition, one which continues into our own day and is now showing signs of new life. In order for the malaise of the Islamic world to be fully addressed and the radical reform movements to be brought back into the fold of the Islamic tradition, the *iḥsānī* intellectual tradition needs to be accorded its proper place in a way of life that is fully and truly Islamic. In applying the principles of Islam to the modern world, while avoiding the passionate rhetorical battles which rage around them, the representatives of this tradition exemplify this saying of Abū Saʿīd b. Abī ´l-Khayr: "A [true] man is one who sits and rises among others, sleeps and eats, and interacts with others in the bazaar, buying and selling, who mixes with people, yet for one moment is not forgetful of God in his heart."[93] But such a path is not achieved by focusing upon reform of the world, of Islam, or of one's nation. It is first and foremost a reform of one's self. As Seyyed Hossein Nasr has written in his seminal analysis of modern Islam, *Islam and the Plight of Modern Man*:

> … the real reform of the world begins with the reform of oneself. He who conquers himself conquers the world, and he in whom a renewal of the principles of Islam in their full amplitude has taken place has already taken the most fundamental step toward the "renaissance" of Islam itself, for only he who has become resurrected in the Truth can resurrect and revive the world about him, whatever the extent of that "world" might be according to the Will of Heaven.[94]

This fully reformed state of being is that of the *fiṭra*, the human norm. To live in this state is to surrender the house of the heart to its true owner. When this is done, the crispations of the heart are stilled such that one can see the truth of all things, for one sees things as they are in themselves, as discrete manifestations of God's names and qualities. But what has been forgotten and must again be remembered—not only by Muslims but by people the world over—is that to see truth and to know truth one must, as Vaclav Havel has said, "live in truth." To live in truth is the way of Islam. From an Islamic perspective, it is the way of all religions; it is the way of man.

Notes

[1] As journalist Robert Fisk observes: "I'm beginning to suspect that 11 September is turning into a curse far greater than the original bloodbath of that day, that America's absorption with that terrible event is in danger of distorting our morality. Is the anarchy of Afghanistan and the continuing slaughter in the Middle East really to be the memorial for the thousands who died on 11 September?" ("America's Morality Distorted by 11 September," *The Independent*, March 7, 2002).

[2] For the a brief introduction to the views of Jamāl al-Dīn Afghānī, Muḥammad ʿAbduh and Rashīd Riḍā see Albert Hourani, *Arabic Thought in the Liberal Age, 1789-1939* (London: Oxford University Press, 1962), chs. 5-8; and Malcolm Kerr, *Islamic Reform: The Political and Legal Theories of Muḥammad ʿAbduh and Rashīd Riḍā* (Berkeley, 1966).

[3] We have in mind here the distinction made by Wolfgang Smith: "There is a sharp yet oft-overlooked distinction between scientific knowledge and scientistic belief. And the difference is simple: authentic knowledge of a scientific kind refers necessarily to things that are observable in some specific sense, and affirms a verifiable truth; scientistic belief, on the other hand, is distinguished precisely by the absence of these positivistic attributes." Wolfgang Smith, *Cosmos and Transcendence* (Peru, Illinois: Sherwood Sugden & Co., 1984), p. 9. Smith goes on to demonstrate that most of the theories which the common educated person takes at face value as scientific propositions are in fact scientistic beliefs arising from the bias of secular humanism.

[4] See his contribution to this volume, "A Traditional Islamic Response to the Rise of Modernism."

[5] It is not the purpose of this essay to chronicle all the subtleties of various modern trends, but rather to allude to general errors which most of these trends exhibit. For a more nuanced examination see W. C. Smith, *Islam in Modern History* (Princeton: Princeton University Press, 1977); J. O. Voll, *Continuity and Change in the Modern Islamic World* (Syracuse: Syracuse University Press, 1994); J. Esposito, *Voices of Resurgent Islam* (New York: Oxford University Press, 1983); and S. H. Nasr, *Traditional Islam in the Modern World* (London: Kegan Paul International, 1989).

[6] Muslim, *Kitāb aṣ-ṣayd*, 57.

[7] This is part of a famous *ḥadīth*, known as the *ḥadīth* of Gabriel:

> ʿUmar ibn al-Khaṭṭāb said: One day when we were with the Messenger of God, a man with very white clothing and jet black hair came up to us. No mark of travel was visible on him, and none of us recognized him. Sitting down before the Prophet, leaning his knees against his, and placing his hands on his thighs, he said, "Tell me Muḥammad about submission (*islām*)." He replied, "Submission means that you should bear witness that there is no god but God and that Muḥammad is the Messenger of God, that you should perform the ritual prayer, pay the alms tax, fast during Ramaḍān, and make the pilgrimage to the House if you are able to go there." The man said, "You have spoken the truth." We were surprised at his questioning him and then declaring that he had spoken the truth. He said, "Now tell me about faith (*īmān*)." He replied, "Faith means that you have faith in God, His angels, His books, His messengers, and the last day, and that you have faith in the measuring out, both its good and its evil." Remarking that he had spoken the truth, he then said, "Now tell me about doing

what is beautiful (*iḥsān*)." He replied, "Doing beautiful means that you should worship God as if you see Him, for if you do not see Him, He nonetheless sees you." Then the man said, "Tell me about the Hour." The Prophet replied, "About that he who is questioned knows no more than the questioner." The man said, "Then tell me about its marks." He said, "The slave girl will give birth to her mistress, and you will see the barefoot, the naked, the destitute, and the shepherds vying with each other in building." Then the man went away. After I had waited for a long time, the Prophet said to me, "Do you know who the questioner was ʿUmar?" I replied, "God and His Messenger know best." He said, "He was Gabriel. He came to teach you your religion" (Muslim, *Kitāb al-īmān*, 1; Bukhārī, *Kitāb al-īmān*, 37).

8 Ṣadr al-Dīn Shīrāzī, *al-Ḥikma al-mutaʿāliyya fī l-asfār al-arbaʿa al-ʿaqliyya* (Tehran, 1387/1958), vol. 1, p. 20.

9 This is an oft-cited saying of the Prophet Muḥammad which is not, however, found in any of the canonical collections.

10 Ibn Māja, *Muqaddima*, 17.

11 Muslim, *Kitāb al-Dhikr*, 73; Tirmidhī, *Kitāb al-Daʿawāt*, 68.

12 Tirmidhī, *Kitāb al-Zuhd*, 14; Ibn Māja, *Kitāb al-Zuhd*, 3; Abū Dāwūd, *Muqaddima*, 32.

13 A *ḥadīth* is a saying, action, or description of the Prophet Muḥammad which has been transmitted by his companions and by the generations of Muslims which followed. The word *ḥadīth* is also used to apply to the entire collection of such sayings. Over time an intricate science developed for determining the authenticity of sayings attributed to Muḥammad. In the third and fourth centuries, the most authentic *ḥadīth* were assembled in collections which have been recognized as authoritative since that time. After the Qur´ān, the *ḥadīth* are the most important source of knowledge for the Islamic sciences. But as the body of preserved *ḥadīth* is far more substantial in quantity than the text of the Qur´ān, more of the specific injunctions and teachings of Islam are to be found in the *ḥadīth* than in the Qur´ān.

14 Lauri Silvers-Alario, "The Teaching Relationship in Early Sufism: A Reassessment of Fritz Meir's Definition of the shaykh al-tarbiya and shaykh al-taʿlīm" (forthcoming), p. 10. I am indebted to many of Professor Silvers-Alario's observations in elucidating the place of Sufism in the early period.

15 Muḥammad Qasim Zaman, *Religion and Politics under the Early ʿAbbāsids* (Leiden: E. J. Brill, 1997), pp. 212-213.

16 Bukhārī, *Kitāb al-īmān*, 39.

17 Aḥmad b. Ḥanbal, 2: 285, 2: 539; Muslim, *Kitāb al-birr*, 33; Ibn Māja, *Kitāb az-zuhd*, 9.

18 Marshall G. Hodgson, *The Venture of Islam* (Chicago: University of Chicago Press, 1990), vol. I, p. 393.

19 As will be demonstrated in the following pages, the arguments of scholars such as Montgomery Watt that the *Ahl al-ḥadīth* were at odds with Sufis are no longer tenable. See Montgomery Watt, *The Formative Period of Islamic Thought* (Oxford: Oneworld Press, 1998), p. 264. For an example of a modern Muslim who also takes this approach see Fazlur Rahman, *Islam*, 2nd ed. (Chicago: The University of Chicago Press, 1979), pp. 128-132.

[20] Omid Safi, "Bargaining with Baraka: Persian Sufism, Mysticism, and Pre-Modern Politics," *Muslim World* 3-4 (2001): 259-287.

[21] William James, *The Varieties of Religious Experience* (New York: Macmillan Publishing Co., 1961), pp. 312-14.

[22] Shihāb al-Dīn Abū Hafṣ ʿUmar as-Suhrawardī, *ʿAwārif al-maʿārif* (Cairo: Maktabat al-Qāhira, 1393/1973), p. 196.

[23] Evelyn Underhill, *Mysticism: A Study in the Nature and Development of Man's Spiritual Consciousness* (London: Methuen, 1911; reprint, New York: Image Books, 1990), p. 81.

[24] Reinhold Niebuhr, from his introduction to William James' *The Varieties of Religious Experience*, p. 7.

[25] Abu ʾl-Qāsim ʿAbd al-Karīm al-Qushayrī, *ar-Risāla al-Qushayriyya*, ed. ʿAbd al-Ḥalīm Maḥmūd and Maḥmūd b. ash-Sharīf (Cairo: Dār al-Kutub al-Ḥadītha, 1972-4), p. 557.

[26] Ibn ʿAṭāʾillāh al-Iskandarī, *Sufi Aphorisms (Kitāb al-Ḥikam)*, trans. Victor Danner (Leiden: E. J. Brill, 1984), p. 23. (Translation slightly modified).

[27] Ibn Khaldūn, *The Muqaddimah: An Introduction to History*, trans. Franz Rosenthal, ed. N. J. Dawood, Bollingen Series (Princeton: Princeton University Press, 1969), p. 358.

[28] Lt. James William Graham, "A Treatise on Sufism, or Mahomedan Mysticism," *Transactions of the Literary Society of Bombay* 1 (1819): 90-91.

[29] Julian Baldick, *Mystical Islam* (London: I. B. Tauris & Co., 1989), p. 9.

[30] Abū ʿAbd ar-Raḥmān al-Sulamī, *Ṭabaqāt aṣ-Ṣūfiyya*, ed. Nūr al-Dīn Sharība (Cairo: Maṭbaʿat al-Madanī, 1987), p. 440.

[31] *Ibid.*, p. 180; Abū Bakr Aḥmad b. ʿAlī al-Kātib al-Baghdādī, *Taʾrīkh Baghdād* (Beirut: Dār al-Kutub al-ʿArabī, 1966), vol. VII, p. 430-432.

[32] Abū Nuʿaym al-Isfahānī, *Hilyat al-awliyāʾ*, ed. Muṣṭafā ʿAbd al-Qādir ʿAṭā (Beirut: Dār al-Kutub al-ʿIlmiyya, 1997), vol. 10, p. 274.

[33] This *ḥadīth* is not found in any of the canonical collections.

[34] Abū Naṣr al-Sarrāj, *Kitāb al-Lumaʿ*, ed. ʿAbd al-Ḥalīm Maḥmūd and Taha ʿAbd az-Zāqī Surūr (Cairo: Dār al-Kutub al-Ḥadīthiyya, 1970), p. 164.

[35] Sulamī, p. 74.

[36] *Ibid.*, p. 210. The concept of fulfilling the rights of all things is central to Sufism. It is a fundamental tenet of *tawḥīd*. It is to understand the truth (*ḥaqq*) of each thing as a sign of God, the existence of which originates only from God, belongs only to God, and returns only to God. As such its reality (*ḥaqīqa*) can only be understood through an understanding of God and His attributes, and it is only through such understanding that we can act properly in those matters for which there is not an immediate and evident ruling in the *sharīʿa*. This will be expanded upon in the section on Ibn al-ʿArabī.

[37] Sulamī, p. 78.

[38] al-Isfahānī, vol. X, p. 244.

[39] al-Isfahānī, vol. X, p. 276.

[40] al-Isfahānī, vol. X, p. 274.

41 Sarrāj, *Kitāb al-Luma*ᶜ, p. 22.

42 *Ibid.*, p. 22. Here Sarrāj is referring to the *ḥadīth* of Gabriel, one of the best known *ḥadīth* of the Islamic tradition. This *ḥadīth* has been used for generations as a key for understanding the different dimensions of the Islamic intellectual tradition. See note 7 (Muslim, *Kitāb al-īmān*, 1; Bukhārī, *Kitāb al-īmān*, 37).

43 This is an allusion to a *ḥadīth*, "The scholars (*ᶜulamāʾ*) are the inheritors of the Prophets" (Bukhārī, *Kitāb al-ᶜilm*, 10; Abū Dāwūd, *Kitāb al-ᶜilm*, 1; Ibn Māja, *Muqaddima*, 17; Dārimī, *Muqaddima*, 32; Aḥmad b. Ḥanbal, 5:196).

44 This saying is cited as a *ḥadīth*, but I have not been able to find it in any of the canonical collections.

45 Sarrāj, *Kitāb al-Luma*ᶜ, p. 31.

46 Aḥmad b. Ḥanbal, 1:403.

47 Muslim, *Kitāb al-īmān*, 147; Ibn Māja, *Kitāb al-duᶜā*ʾ; Aḥmad b. Ḥanbal, 4:133.

48 See note 6.

49 See note 7.

50 Sulamī, p. 167.

51 Aḥmad b. Ḥanbal, 2:381.

52 Bukhārī, *Kitāb al-adab*, 38; Abū Dāwūd, *Kitāb as-sunna*, 14; Tirmidhī, *Kitāb ar-riḍā*ᶜ, 11; *Kitāb al-īmān*, 6; Ibn Māja, *Kitāb az-zuhd*, 31; Dārimī, *Kitāb ar-riqāq*, 74.

53 Hamid Dabashi, "Historical Conditions of Persian Sufism during the Seljuk Period" in *Classical Persian Sufism: from its Origins to Rumi*, ed. Leonard Lewisohn (London: Khaniqahi Nimatullahi Publications, 1993), p. 150.

54 Tāj al-Dīn Abū Nasr ᶜAbd al-Wahhāb b. ᶜAlī as-Subkī, *aṭ-Ṭabaqāt al-Shāfiᶜiyya al-kubrā* (Cairo: ᶜIsā ʾl-Bābī al-Ḥalabī, 1964-76), vol. 4, pp. 293-4.

55 *Ibid.*, vol. 3, p. 369.

56 Nūr al-Dīn ᶜAbd ar-Raḥmān Jāmī, *Nafaḥāt al-uns min ḥaḍarāt al-quds*, ed. Maḥmūd ᶜĀbidī (Tehran: Intishārāt-i Iṭṭilaᶜāṭ, 1380 HS), p. 295.

57 Richard Bulliet, *The Patricians of Nishapur* (Cambridge: Harvard University Press, 1972), p. 151.

58 Muḥammad Ibn Munawwar Mayhanī, *Asrār-i tawḥīd fī maqāmāt Shaykh Abī Ṣaᶜīd*, ed. Muḥammad Riḍā Shafīᶜī Kadkanī (Tehran: Muʾassisiy-eh Intishārāt-i Āgāh, 1376 HS), vol. 1, p. 119; Jāmī, *Nafaḥāt al-uns*, pp. 373-4.

59 Jāmī, p. 376.

60 For these observations we are indebted to T. J. Winter, who has examined the influence of Ibn Miskawayh upon the *Kitāb Riyāḍat an-nafs* of the *Iḥyāʾ* in the introduction to his translation of the latter. See Abū Ḥāmid al-Ghazālī, *On Disciplining the Soul (Kitāb Riyāḍat al-nafs) and On Breaking the Two Desires (Kitāb Kasr al-shahwatayn): Books XXII and XXIII of The Revival of the Religious Sciences*, trans. T. J. Winter (Cambridge: Islamic Texts Society, 1995), pp. xlv-lviii.

61 Abū Ḥāmid al-Ghazālī, *The Niche of Lights*, trans. David Buckman (Provo, Utah: Brigham Young University Press, 1998), p. 20.

62 *Ibid.*, p. 20 (translation slightly modified).

[63] *Ibid.*, p. 16.

[64] Abū Ḥāmid al-Ghazālī, *Majmūʿa Rasāʾil al-Imām al-Ghazalı*, n. e. (Beirut: Dār al-Fikr, 1416/1996), p. 546.

[65] *Ibid.*, p. 546.

[66] This is not to say that the early Muslim peripatetics were not Muslims and that the nature of their philosophical inquiry was not shaped by the teachings of Islam. They marked the first stage of Islamic philosophy in which questions that arose from the Islamic context and questions bequeathed by the Greek tradition were analyzed through a methodology learned from Greek philosophy. Nonetheless, it is Islamic philosophy in that *tawḥīd* is at the root of philosophical inquiry, revelation is considered as a reality, and God is understood to be the Origin and End of all things. For elaboration on this point see S. H. Nasr, "The Meaning and Concept of Philosophy in Islam" in *History of Islamic Philosophy*, ed. Seyyed Hossein Nasr and Oliver Leaman (New York: Routledge, 1996), pp. 21-26 and "The Qurʾān and *Ḥadīth* as Source and Inspiration of Islamic Philosophy," *ibid.*, pp. 27-39.

[67] Ghazālī, *Majmūʿah*, p. 257.

[68] *Ibid.*, p. 262. This *ḥadīth* is not found in any of the canonical collections.

[69] *Ibid.*, p. 258.

[70] *Ibid.*, p. 260.

[71] *Ibid.*, p. 266.

[72] *Ibid.*, p. 230.

[73] *Ibid.*, p. 552.

[74] *Ibid.*, p. 564.

[75] For a comprehensive treatment of Ghazālī's classification of the Islamic sciences see Osman Bakar, *Classification of Knowledge in Islam* (Lahore: Suhail Academy, 2000), chs. 8 & 9.

[76] Abū Ḥāmid al-Ghazālī, *Majmūʿa*, p. 234.

[77] *Ibid.*, p. 232.

[78] *Ibid.*, p. 233.

[79] Ibn al-ʿArabī, *al-Futuḥāṭ al-Makkiyya*, n. e. (Cairo: 1911; reprint Beirut: Dār Ṣādir, n.d.), vol. 1, p. 261.

[80] *al-Futuḥāṭ al-Makkiyya*, vol. 2, p. 266.

[81] The use of the word "gnosis" does not here imply any historical link to the Christian Gnostic movement. It is used with the original meaning of the word, "a special knowledge of spiritual mysteries" (OED vol. 1, p. 1163), p. 248.

[82] *al-Futuḥāṭ al-Makkiyya*, vol. 2, pp. 297-8.

[83] *Ibid.*, vol. 2, p. 267.

[84] William Chittick, "Time, Space, and the Objectivity of Ethical Norms: The Teachings of Ibn al-ʿArabī," *Islamic Studies* 39, no. 4 (2000): 585.

[85] William Chittick, "The Cosmology of Dhikr" lecture delivered at "Paths to the Heart:

Sufism and the Christian East" conference, University of South Carolina, October 2001. See *Paths to the Heart: Sufism and the Christian East*, ed. James Cutsinger (Bloomington, IN: World Wisdom, 2002), pp. 48-63.

86 *al-Futuḥāt al-Makkiyya*, vol. 2, p. 298.

87 *Ibid.*, vol. III, p. 179.

88 Alexander D. Knysh, *Ibn ʿArabī in the Later Islamic Tradition: The Making of a Polemical Image in Medieval Islam* (Albany: SUNY Press, 1999), p. 1.

89 Itzchak Weismann, *Taste of Modernity: Sufism, Salafiyya, and Arabism in Late Ottoman Damascus* (Leiden: E. J. Brill, 2001).

90 William Chittick, "Sufism: Sufi Thought and Practice," in *Oxford Encyclopedia of the Modern Islamic World*, p. 107.

91 Seyyed Hossein Nasr, *Traditional Islam in the Modern World* (London: Kegan Paul International, 1987), p. 305.

92 William Chittick, "The Rehabilitation of Islamic Thought," p. 1.

93 Muḥammad Ibn Munawwar, *Asrār-i tawḥīd*, vol. 1, p. 199.

94 Seyyed Hossein Nasr, *Islam and the Plight of Modern Man* (Chicago: Kazi Publications, 2001), p. 195.

CHAPTER 3

A TRADITIONAL ISLAMIC RESPONSE TO THE RISE OF MODERNISM

FUAD S. NAEEM

In the face of the conflicts and uncertainties that prevail today in both the West and the East, it has become ever more important to identify the roots of the problems now confronting the world, not only their external and accidental manifestations. Attempting to correct accidents without addressing their core causes is akin to treating symptoms without treating the internal disease that produces them. Recent events have brought to the forefront long-held views in the West of a confrontation and opposition of world-views between Islam and the West. Mainstream analyses in the West, whether in academia or the media, have posited a clash between forward-looking Western civilization and a backward and stagnant Islam, represented by the exploits of so-called "fundamentalist" Muslims. Such analyses stop at only the most superficial aspect of the problem and do not penetrate to the roots of either modern Western civilization or Islam, nor of the various political and social reformist and revivalist movements labeled "fundamentalist." Other essays in this volume offer a critical assessment of prevalent analytical trends and their methodologies; here we will examine alternatives presented by the Islamic intellectual tradition.[1]

A very different understanding of the reality of the conflict between the West and Islam emerges when one examines the philosophical principles and presuppositions that lie behind each civilization and that determine the more contingent and external aspects of that civilization. From one perspective, the underlying reality of Islam, as of any religion, is tradition, while that of modern Western civilization—as opposed to its medieval Christian heritage—is modernism and secularism.

Tradition, states the prominent Muslim intellectual Seyyed Hossein Nasr,

> implies both the sacred as revealed to man through revelation and the unfolding and development of that sacred message in the history of the particular humanity for which it was destined in a manner that implies both horizontal continuity with the Origin and a vertical nexus which relates each movement of the life of the tradition in question to the meta-historical Transcendental Reality.[2]

From this perspective, traditional Islam refers to both the Qur´ānic Revelation and the Prophetic *Sunna*[3] in themselves, as well as the subsequent life and activity of the Islamic community, whether it be in law, philosophy, art, mysticism, politics, or social life, which can be seen as a historical commentary upon, and continuity of, the original Revelation. As for modernism, it refers to a world-view, with a whole body of ideas and their resultant institutions, that emerged in Europe as a result of the Renaissance in the fifteenth and sixteenth centuries and the Enlightenment in the eighteenth and nineteenth centuries, and which revolted against religion in all the various areas of life and replaced it with humanism, rationalism, and secularism. As a result of these ideas, the Western world transformed itself from the deeply Christian civilization of the Middle Ages to the largely secular humanistic civilization it has become in modern times.[4]

Modernism in the Islamic world emerged from the direct influence of these foundational ideas of the modern West, often wed to the political and military power of colonialism. Fundamentalism, or literalist reformism,[5] although it serves as an umbrella term comprising many different movements with different beliefs and aims, generally implies a rejection of traditional Islamic scholarship and especially its intellectual and spiritual traditions; it calls for a return to the Qur´ān and the *ḥadīth* (the sayings of the Prophet Muḥammad), interpreting these primary sources of Islam in a purely literalist and exclusivist manner, often in opposition to the traditional understanding and interpretation of these sacred texts.[6] The groups denoted by the term often have a puritanical emphasis and an agenda for Islamic revival on a social and political level but with little interest in the spiritual and intellectual aspects of Islam. Neither fundamentalism nor modernism is integral to Islamic civilization; both are reactions to the modern secular Western world, which has dominated the Islamic world for the last two centuries, first politically and militarily through colonialism, and later ideologically and culturally.[7] They are also both united in their opposition to traditional Islam. Seyyed Hossein Nasr has, therefore, spoken of the two as "opposite sides of the same coin."[8]

The neglect in the West of the voice of traditional Islam prevents us from seeing the whole tapestry of Islamic civilization. It has led to reducing Islam to a misleading dichotomy of "fundamentalist" and modernistic currents, which are followed by only a relatively small number of Muslims. With this background, it is often proposed by intellectuals such as Salman Rushdie, Bernard Lewis, and Daniel Pipes that Islam must modernize if it does not want to succumb to the forces of fundamentalism. What is completely disregarded is that Muslims cannot embrace modernism, as they cannot embrace puritanical literalism, and still remain true to their faith. Islam's traditional understanding of itself as a message of salvation that affirms the primacy of God, and seeks to awaken men and women to their true spiritual nature and make possible the actualization of their God-given possibilities, stands in stark contrast to an anthropocentric, rationalistic, and materialistic framework which relegates the sacred to the private sphere—the very framework that determines much of modern Western civilization. The modern world lacks a sense of transcendence and limits reality to its most outward and material aspect, while Islam is a religion based on the Transcendence of God; a religion which, like all religions, asks men and women to transcend their lower selves. The issue of Islam's incompatibility with modernism is ignored by both Westerners and modernized Muslims who have become estranged from their own spiritual and intellectual heritage.

This study provides an example of the manner in which traditional Muslims have responded to the same challenges from modern thought that resulted in the emergence of the modernist and fundamentalist movements in the Islamic world. This response, by the great Indian religious scholar, Sufi, and philosopher Maulanā Ashraf ʿAlī Thanvī (1863-1943), is neither a capitulation to modern Western civilization in the manner of liberal Muslim modernists, nor a blindly puritanical and political rejection of modernity without any understanding of its nature or arguments. Rather, it is an intellectual response in defense of the principles of traditional Islam, indeed of religion itself, which uses logic and philosophy to answer, on their own grounds, the claims of modernism.

Maulanā Thanvī was at once a religious, intellectual, and spiritual figure. He is therefore an exemplar of what Joseph E. B. Lumbard has called the "*iḥsānī* intellectual tradition," which combines intellectuality with spirituality, theoretical doctrine with spiritual practice.[9] Thanvī's analysis and refutation of the principles of modernism is not a merely theoretical exercise, but is meant to remove the obstacles to intellectual and spiritual understanding and growth for the pious and practicing Muslim. This is a goal Thanvī states explicitly as the *raison d' être* of his whole written corpus. Indeed, it is the *raison d'être* of the whole Islamic intellectual tradition.

This study is divided into two parts, the first concerning the rise of modernism in Muslim India; the circumstances that surrounded this rise; and the ideas of the modernists themselves. This will also enable us to understand the larger phenomenon of modernism in the Islamic world; for the different modernist movements in different parts of the Islamic world are remarkably similar in basic outlook. This is largely due to their being influenced by similar notions and ideologies that have originally been borrowed from the West. With this background in mind, one can properly approach the second and more important part of this study, the response of Maulanā Ashraf ʿAlī Thanvī to the modernism that was spreading in the Indian Subcontinent, especially among the Western-educated classes. Maulanā Thanvī's response to modern ideas, especially scientism and rationalism, is the response of a traditional *ʿālim* (religious scholar, pl. *ʿulamāʾ*), well versed in the Islamic intellectual tradition, using this tradition to refute what he believed to be false doctrines. The approach of Thanvī is quite rare in the annals of Muslim thought in modern times, for the traditional *ʿulamāʾ* generally did not respond to modern ideas and ways upon their arrival in the Muslim world in the nineteenth and early twentieth centuries—except on a juridical (*fiqhī*) level, and more rarely on a theological (*kalāmī*) level. This was largely due to the fact the *ʿulamāʾ* were among the last in Islamic society to be directly exposed to modern ideas. Also, since few in the Islamic world other than the *ʿulamāʾ*, including those of the exoteric and the esoteric religious sciences like Sufism,[10] were intellectually qualified to answer the claims of modernism, the responses that were made were usually facile and inadequate. It is something quite remarkable then that a traditional scholar and Sufi of the caliber of Maulanā Thanvī undertook to write a critique of modernism on a purely intellectual level, and governed by the principles of *ḥikma* (Islamic philosophy), or more properly, theosophy, understood in its original sense.[11] Although Maulanā Thanvī was replying to particular ideas promulgated by the modernists of India, his treatise was intended as a general refutation of the very principles behind modernism in its various forms as they manifested themselves in the Islamic world as a whole. Therefore, it furnishes criteria of truth, from the Islamic point of view, that can be applied to modernist ideas in general in the Islamic world.

To understand the depth and breadth of Thanvī's critique of modernism, scientism, and rationalism, we will examine his book *al-Intibāhāt al-mufīda ʿan al-ishtibāhāt al-jadīda* (*The Beneficial Intimations Regarding the Newly-Arisen Doubts*) topic by topic, beginning with first principles and proceeding to various Islamic doctrines that have been misinterpreted or rejected by modernists. But before proceeding to Maulanā Thanvī's critique, we will began with an exposition of the rise of modernism in India and the circumstances that led to this emergence, briefly examining the ideas of figures like Sayyid Aḥmad Khān (1817-1898) and those whom he influenced.

The Rise of Modernism in Muslim India

The Indian Muslims encountered Europeans for the first time when Vasco da Gama sailed around the Cape of Good Hope, ironically with the help of Muslim navigators, and reached India in 1497. The age of exploration had begun and with it the continual encroachment of European powers into foreign lands. By the first decade of the seventeenth century, the British East India Company was already established and had jurisdiction over its own citizens in India. The Company gradually expanded, and in the aftermath of the collapse of the Mughal Empire at the death of the last great Mughal emperor Aurangzeb in 1707, it was able to expand its power rapidly. In 1757, it acquired large portions of Indian territory and its jurisdiction covered a number of Indian provinces. By 1790, Governor-General Cornwallis had enough power of jurisdiction to abolish Islamic law and replace it with the newly created Anglo-Muḥammadan law. Under Wellesley (1798-1805), British imperialism became a vital force in the political life of the Subcontinent and by 1803, the British had entered the capital of the Mughal Empire itself, Delhi. Thereafter, the Mughal emperor was to become only a puppet of the British so long as the Mughal Empire survived.

These developments on the political front clearly demonstrate that the Muslims had ceased to be the rulers of India and had been replaced by the British, who now ruled over them. It was in light of this situation that the son of the great religious scholar, theologian, and Sufi Shāh Walī Allāh (1703-1762), Shāh ʿAbd al-Azīz (1746-1824), the greatest religious authority of his day, issued his famous *fatwā* (religious verdict), stating that India had still been *dār al-islām* (the abode of Islam), under the rule of the Marathas, the chief Hindu adversaries of the Muslims in the turbulent period after Aurangzeb's death, but that under the British, it had become *dār al-ḥarb* (the abode of conflict). In this pronouncement can be seen a keen presentiment of the notion that the British were not common enemies like the Marathas, but represented something far more ruinous for the Muslims. Shāh ʿAbd al-Azīz understood that the Hindu and Sikh enemies might kill and plunder the Muslims but left Islam alone, while the British aimed to destroy Islam itself, which they demonstrated by replacing the injunctions of the *sharīʿa* (Islamic law) with British law. Here then was the first awareness among Indian Muslims of the struggle between tradition and modernity, although it was primarily on a political level.

Shāh ʿAbd al-Azīz's concerns were not unfounded, for the British next discouraged the use of Persian, the *lingua franca* of Muslim India and the language in which the majority of Muslim religious literature was composed, thus undermining the whole heritage of Islam in India. By 1835, Persian had been abolished as the language of public instruction and replaced by English. This transition marked another important stage in what was to become the struggle between tradition and modernity in Muslim India. Consequently, it was in this period that the religious scholars (*ʿulamāʾ*), seeing the forced decline of Persian, began to cultivate Urdu as a language for the preservation of religion. This process was begun by two of Shāh Walī Allāh's other sons, Shāh Rafīʿ al-Dīn (1750-1818) and Shāh ʿAbd al-Qādir (1754-1813), both of whom translated the Qurʾān into Urdu, the former in a literal rendering and the latter in a more idiomatic fashion.

In the course of the nineteenth century and the early twentieth century, the *ʿulamāʾ* cultivated Urdu and translated much of the corpus of Islamic doctrine and practice as it existed in the Indian Subcontinent into it, enabling the preservation and continuity of traditional Islam. Maulanā Ashraf ʿAlī Thanvī, with over a thousand books attributed to him in every field from metaphysics and philosophy to Sufism and jurisprudence, written largely in Urdu, had no small part to play in this task, but his efforts were carried out largely in the early twentieth century.

The aims of British domination were primarily political and economic. Therefore, despite the enforcement of Anglo-Muḥammadan law and the English language upon the Muslim populace, the threat to the Islamic tradition at a truly intellectual, and not merely political, level was not to come directly from them. It came at the hands of a number of Muslim thinkers themselves influenced by the British and their notions of progress and civilization, rationalism and naturalism. Herein began the true battle between the Islamic tradition in India and the modernity spawned by the Renaissance, the Scientific Revolution, the French Revolution, and other modern developments in Europe, which was inherited by the nineteenth-century Britain that ruled over India. Historically, this struggle began in the aftermath of the Uprising of 1857, largely led by Muslims, in which they were thoroughly defeated and subsequently treated very harshly by the British, bearing the brunt of British hostility and suppression. This defeat and oppression shook the Islamic community of India and left them in a state of crisis. Being subdued and ruled by the enemy, the Muslims had three options: join the enemy, continue to oppose him, or carry on as before. The traditional *ʿulamāʾ* and the Sufis were to adopt this third option and concentrated on preserving and transmitting traditional Islamic teachings. The second option, due to the strength of the enemy, was not seriously adopted until the beginning of the Independence Movement in the second quarter of the twentieth century, and was then adopted generally by groups of a reformist stance, although many among the *ʿulamāʾ* also partook in it. As for opposition on an intellectual level, this was always present on the part of the traditional Islamic authorities.

The first position, that of adopting the ways of the British, was the one taken by the proponents of Westernization and modernism, who were to find their voice in Sayyid Aḥmad Khān, the most important modernist of Muslim India. The primary forerunner of Sayyid Aḥmad Khān was Karamat ʿAlī Jawnpurī (d. 1873), the first important ideological modernist produced by Muslim India. Jawnpurī, in his early years, was associated with the *mujāhidūn* movement of Sayyid Aḥmad Barelvī, but later turned to modern ideas. Jawnpurī's significance lies in his celebration of modern science, an attitude that was passed down to generations of Indian Muslim modernists and which still remains a curious aspect of modernism among Muslims of the Subcontinent. Scientism has had a greater attraction for Indian modernists than perhaps for any other modernist movement in the Islamic world. This is undoubtedly due largely to the influence of nineteenth-century British philosophy, with its empiricism, and the scientism of philosophers such as Spencer (who is still studied in the Subcontinent after being almost completely forgotten in the West). Karamat ʿAlī's views, developed well before the uprising, though published in 1865, assert a wholehearted embracing of modern science. He was the first to propagate the well-known modernist position still prevalent today among the majority of Muslim modernists—that modern science is really Islamic science that was passed down to the Europeans by the Arabs and it is, therefore, the duty of the Muslims to reclaim it. He is also the author of another popular notion, namely that all the claims of modern science are to be found in the Qur´ān, an assertion often made by both modernists and "fundamentalists" alike to this day. Regarding this point, Karamat ʿAlī states:

> The whole Koran is full of passages containing information on physical and mathematical sciences. If we would but spend a little reflection over it we should find wondrous meanings in every word it contains. The Koran has most satisfactorily confuted all the systems of ancient philosophy; it plucked from the root the physical sciences as prevalent among the ancients. What a strange coincidence exists between the Koran and the philosophy of modern Europe.[12]

Sir Sayyid Aḥmad Khān (1817-1898) was among the most important modernists in the entire Islamic world. His influence on the intellectual life of the Indian Subcontinent has been far-reaching and substantial. Although his own doctrinal views concerning Islam were harshly condemned by the *ʿulamā´* and sharply criticized even by his supporters, his influence was to reach many different sectors of the Muslim populace and intelligentsia. This occurred mainly in two ways: firstly, through his educational theories and their implementation at the college at Aligarh, the main foundation from which modernism was spread among Muslims in India, and secondly, through his followers and those who were influenced by his ideas. Several of his followers, or those influenced by his ideas, such as the nationalistic poet Altāf Ḥusayn Hālī (1837-1914), the historian and apologist Sayyid Amīr ʿAlī (1849-1928), the inventor of the Urdu novel Naẓīr Aḥmad (1831-1912), and the religious scholar ʿAllamah Shiblī Numānī (d. 1914), were able to cloak Sir Sayyid's ideas in terms and forms which were far less repugnant to both Muslim orthodoxy and the ordinary Muslim believer. Sir Sayyid's equation of Islam and nineteenth-century British thought, with its naturalism, rationalism, scientism, and empiricism, is the best-known formulation of the modernist position in Muslim India. Among his primary doctrines was the identity between nineteenth-century British naturalism and empiricism and Islam, reason as the ultimate judge of truth, and a vast reinterpretation of Islam based upon it. For the representatives of traditional Islam, the consequences of these and other ideas that will be mentioned below were enormous, for they threatened the entire intellectual and practical structure upon which the Islamic tradition was founded. It was primarily in response to the ideas such as those of Sayyid Aḥmad Khān and the school of thought he inaugurated that Maulanā Thanvī undertook the task of composing a critique of this modernism by means of the traditional Islamic intellectual sciences.

Sayyid Aḥmad Khān, who had been pro-British during the 1857 Uprising, is a perfect example of one who responded to the aftermath of the Uprising by asserting that it was in the best interests of the Muslims of India to assimilate Western culture. To this end, he believed that Muslims needed to receive modern Western education and for this purpose founded his famous college at Aligarh in 1874. His movement was to become known as the Aligarh Movement. In the teachings in this university and in his books, he presented a modernized and secularized version of Islam that he felt would be in conformity with modern science and progress. His interpretation of Islam was based upon reason as understood in modern Western philosophy, and which he judged to be the ultimate criterion of truth, following the rationalism that had prevailed in the West since Descartes. In addition he held that Islam was in complete conformity with nature, following the schools of naturalism popular in Victorian Britain. The consequence of this was the negation of all supernatural and miraculous elements of the Islamic tradition.

These ideas of progress, rationalism, scientism, and other Enlightenment and post-Enlightenment notions have been among the staple beliefs of modernists, not only in India, but all over the Muslim world. Sayyid Aḥmad Khān wanted to demonstrate to the British that Islam was respectable by modern Western standards, a task numerous modernists were to attempt after him, especially Amīr ʿAlī, and that Islam was not incompatible with Victorian ideals and values. This notion has often been repeated by modernists who present modern Western values as Islamic values that the Islamic world has forgotten.[13]

Sayyid Aḥmad Khān was severely condemned by the *ʿulamāʾ*, and *fatāwā* (religious verdicts) were passed declaring him a *kāfir* (infidel). The *ʿulamāʾ* were incensed both by the heterodoxy of his religious ideas and by his being a layman, not trained in the religious sciences, who had arrogated to himself the right to discuss subtle theological and judicial matters. Among his main theological works is his *Taḥrīr fī usūl al-tafsīr* (*The Principles of Exegesis*), which is a rationalistic interpretation of the Qurʾān consisting of fifteen points in which he demonstrates that the Qurʾān, if interpreted according to his methodology, is in complete conformity with science and reason, for "between the Word of God and the work of God there can be no contradiction."[14] The eminent *ʿālim* and founder of the school at Deoband, Muḥammad Qāsim Nanautvī (1833-1877) wrote a point by point refutation of this tract in his *Taṣfiyat al-ʿaqāʾid* (*Clarification of Religious Tenets*),[15] a work in the orthodox theological tradition (*kalām*) and one of the first and only major intellectual responses from the traditional *ʿulamāʾ* against modernist ideas at that time. This tract can be seen as a precursor to the work of Maulanā Thanvī, who also studied at Deoband, but Maulanā Thanvī's response to the tenets of modernism is of a more philosophical and intellectual nature than the generally theological response of Maulanā Nanautvī. Many other *ʿulamāʾ* also criticized Sayyid Aḥmad Khān's views, as did a wide range of individuals and organizations across Muslim India, from the anti-modernist satirist Akbar Allāhabādī, to Sir Sayyid's fellow modernist Muḥsin al-Mulk, to various journals and newspapers. It is also interesting that even orthodox Christian Indian writers refuted Sayyid Aḥmad's rationalism and naturalism, perhaps driven by the fact that he interprets the Bible, on which he wrote a tract, in accordance with his modernistic views.

To give a concrete idea of the kind of rationalism and naturalism Sayyid Aḥmad Khān was expounding, and how it challenged traditional Islamic ideas, it is necessary to turn to his specific views. He believed *waḥy* (traditionally understood as prophetic revelation) to be ultimately the same as reason, and also natural law. It is the most developed form of reason and can also be called prophetic intuition. He believed that it is this that is called Gabriel by Islamic theological texts, not a supernatural archangel. For him prophethood is a natural faculty, not a gift of God, and therefore revelation is a natural phenomenon, like the fruit of other faculties, and not a message brought by an angel from Heaven. Sayyid Aḥmad's naturalism is based upon the ideas of nineteenth-century scientists who viewed nature "as a closed system of the universe which obeys certain laws of mechanics and physics and which is invariably characterized by a uniformity of behavior in which there cannot be any exception."[16] Sayyid Aḥmad Khān grafted upon this anti-theistic and mechanistic view a theistic and teleological view that was completely opposed to it. This is why he had to remove all supernatural elements from Islam in order to lessen this divide.

This anti-supernaturalism, followed by many in his movement, went to absurd lengths to interpret and rationalize the Qurʾān and Islamic doctrines in accordance with the mechanistic view of nature. He believed that Qurʾānic eschatology, angelology, demonology, and cosmology could not be contrary to scientific reality and must be interpreted in its terms. Thus, angels are really only the properties of created things like hardness in stone, fluidity in water, and cognition of external reality in man. A secondary meaning of "angel" in the Qur´ān is divine moral support. Likewise, Satan refers to the dark passions of man; the *jinn* are projections of evil, disease, and other calamities, or in certain instances refer to wild men living in the forests and deserts. From this perspective, the portrayal in the Qur´ān, as in the Bible, of natural disasters as Divine punishment is rooted in popular superstition and has been borrowed in scripture to make an ethical point.

Since prophets are sent to promulgate the divine law of nature, and miracles go completely against this law, they must all be rejected. Those miracles mentioned in scripture are to be regarded as symbolic, metaphorical, or legendary. The laws of nature are immutable and they are pledges of God to His creation that cannot be broken. Therefore, to believe in a miracle is to believe in the suspension or reversal of these laws and thus to repudiate faith in the Divine pledges and accuse God of falsehood. By his deistic view of the universe, Sayyid Aḥmad Khān viewed God only through *tanzīh* (transcendence or remoteness),[17] and turned Him into a mere *prima causa*. This, in turn, resulted in opinions on his part that are astonishing to any traditional Muslim, like the notion that private prayer could not be heard.

Another important facet of Sayyid Aḥmad's thought is his acceptance of Darwinism, which was to have a wide influence among modernist Muslims for generations to come. He was perhaps the first modernist in the Islamic world to attempt to reconcile the Darwinian theory of evolution with Islamic tenets of Creation and the Fall of Adam. He interpreted the Qur´ānic statement that "semen" or "seed" is the nucleus of life as a metaphorical illustration of the primeval movement of life emerging from inert matter. The literal reference in the Qur´ān and the Bible to the creation of the universe is the use by God of popular belief for the sake of argument. Scripture must speak to the common people in terms they can understand. Sayyid Aḥmad also interpreted the Fall of Adam as being metaphorical, Adam here denoting human nature. To rationalize these novel opinions and positions, Sayyid Aḥmad Khān asserted—contrary to the traditional Islamic view which allowed only the learned (*ʿulamā´*) to interpret the Qur´ān on the basis of traditional norms—that any Muslim could interpret the Qur´ān according to his own view, whether the interpretation be literal, analytical, or symbolic. Such viewpoints as the ones mentioned above, which were to be repeated in various forms by his followers, show the danger his modernism posed to traditional Islam and how, in the eyes of traditional Muslim authorities, it was ready to cast aside eternal and established truths for the fashionable theories of the day.

In addition to his novel views concerning Islamic doctrine, Khān also critiqued Islamic law and practice as traditionally understood. If the doctrinal views of Sayyid Aḥmad Khān demonstrate his naturalism, these views demonstrate his rationalism. For example, hẹ stated that all *ḥadīth* (sayings of the Prophet Muḥammad), repugnant to reason (which for him often amounted to Victorian custom) should be discarded. Similarly, he tried to reinterpret Islamic law in terms of European norms, such as rationalizations of polygamy and *jihād*, allowing of interest, and eating meat not ritually slaughtered, among other things. He also rejected the traditional views on authenticity of the great canonical collections of *ḥadīth* as well as the traditional schools of Islamic law. In this question, he and his disciple Chirāgh ʿAlī (d. 1895), who went to extremes in the rejection of the *ḥadīth* and Islamic law, foreshadowed the opinions of Orientalists like Joseph Schacht and Ignaz Goldziher, both of whom claimed that the *ḥadīth* were fabrications by later generations of Muslims and were not the authentic words of the Prophet Muḥammad. In this domain, Sayyid Aḥmad started a popular trend among modernists, and later, by the fundamentalists, of doubting and rejecting aspects of Islamic law, the methodology of jurisprudence (*fiqh*) and its principles, such as *ijmāʿ* (consensus), and *qiyās* (analogy), and the sources of the law, particularly the *ḥadīth.*

The Aligarh modernists, as well as others who bore the influence of Sayyid Aḥmad Khān, were to elaborate certain aspects of his thought. Sometimes they took it further away from traditional Islam, such as in the radical skepticism of Chirāgh ʿAlī, and at other times they brought it closer to traditional teachings, such as in the case of the religious scholar Shiblī Numānī. Here will be mentioned just a few brief notes about his most important followers, for the substance of modernism in India is to be found in Sayyid Aḥmad Khān himself.

Chirāgh ʿAlī was a radical proponent of modernism and his espousal of modern Western civilization was even more extreme than Sir Sayyid's. He attempted to interpret Islamic law completely in terms of Western ideas of humanism and rationalism. He stated that since man is born free, the basis of law should be humanistic. Religion and the social system are distinct, he stated, in accordance with European ideals, and he criticized Islamic law for blending the religious and what Western thought called the secular, a dichotomy rarely looked upon with favor in traditional Islamic discourse.[18] He added that the Prophet never combined church and state, another conception borrowed from European sources. Islamic law, he said, is based on surviving pagan rites and inauthentic *ḥadīth*, which comprised, according to him, the entire corpus, and therefore, it should be adapted in accordance with the demands of the times. He thus demanded radical changes in Islamic law, especially in all those aspects not conforming to Western standards, such as polygamy, divorce, and *jihād.* He rejected all sources of law except the Qur'ān itself. He stated that Islam was not hostile to progress if one rid it of theology, and that there was nothing in Islam which was opposed to modern civilization. Under Chirāgh ʿAlī's interpretation, Islam is turned into a second-rate bourgeoisie Protestantism marked by excessive rationalism. This can be seen, for example, in his assertion that Islam is easy; one can perform religious obligations without sacrificing worldly prosperity and one can adopt whatever one finds to be good in another civilization, without any interference from one's religion.

It was in the field of literature that Sayyid Aḥmad Khān's ideas were to be diluted enough to find a wide circulation. This was done at the hands of two eminent literary men, Altāf Ḥusayn Hālī, whose fame as a great Urdu poet became widespread, and Deputy Naẓīr Aḥmad Dehlavī, the father of the Urdu novel. Hālī's poems, instead of using traditional themes, speak of modern topics such as justice and fatherland and often have a very sentimental quality that appeals to the masses. He was a devoted disciple of Sayyid Aḥmad Khān and drew largely on his teachings, which he subtly conveyed in his poems. Naẓīr Aḥmad inaugurated the Urdu novel, which he modeled after Victorian moralistic novels and which was filled with the liberal ideas of Sayyid Aḥmad. Yet he was more conservative than Sir Sayyid and supported certain elements of tradition. Through him, the diluted ideas of Sir Sayyid were disseminated to a large public. A major part of this audience consisted of women, for Naẓīr Aḥmad often wrote on women's issues. Maulanā Thanvī, in his treatise against modernism, does not address the ideas of men of literature, since his purpose is a philosophical and theological critique. But in his popular book for women, *Bihishtī Zevar* (*Celestial Ornaments*),[19] he condemns the novel harshly as a useless form of entertainment that is ruinous to religion. He specifically condemns four novels of Naẓīr Aḥmad that support modern feminist and liberal views. Thanvī also wrote a critique of Naẓīr Aḥmad's translation of the Holy Qur´ān, named *Iṣlāḥ tarjama Dehlavī* (*Correction of the Translation of Dehlavī*).

Mention should also be briefly made of Syed Amīr ʿAlī, among the most famous of the Indian modernists, and strongly influenced by both Karamat ʿAlī Jawnpurī and Sayyid Aḥmad Khān. Amīr ʿAlī's emphasis was not on doctrine, but on the social and political aspects of Islam. He attempted to glorify Islamic history on the basis of the prevalent Western notions of progress and civilizationism. To this end, he wrote his famed book of apologetics *The Spirit of Islam* in English, a work that portrayed Islam as fully consistent with modern beliefs and ideologies. In this work, he emphasized those aspects of Islam that could be rationalized and brought in conformity with nineteenth-century liberalism and humanism, such as political freedom, social justice and equality, and fair distribution of wealth, among others. Even religious practices are explained by him in a rationalistic manner. Amīr ʿAlī was to have a far-reaching influence not only on Muslims themselves but even on the Western understanding of Islam, due to the popularity of his book in the Western world. *The Spirit of Islam* stands to this day as perhaps the definitive work of Muslim apologia before the onslaught of Western values and ideas.

Muḥammad Iqbāl (1873-1938), one of the most important intellectual figures in the modern Muslim world, cannot be truly counted as a member of the school of Sayyid Aḥmad Khān, despite his avowed modernism, especially in his early days. Iqbāl undoubtedly was influenced by Sir Sayyid in various domains, but his intellectual development was independent and shows a different strand of modernistic influence associated with figures such as Friedrich Nietzsche and Henri Bergson. He stands as a complex figure to be studied on his own, and since much of his work was of a more philosophical nature, his modernistic ideas did not wield as great an influence on the mainstream religious discourse of Muslim India as Sayyid Aḥmad Khān's. His influence, though, was to grow with time and came to be a significant force in the intellectual life of Muslim India and Pakistan in the second half of the twentieth century.

Finally, mention needs to be made of ʿAllamah Shiblī Numānī, whose importance for the critique of modernism by Maulanā Thanvī is only second to Sir Sayyid. Shiblī was not a fervent modernist like individuals associated with the Aligarh movement. His position was much closer to traditional orthodoxy and he often defended tradition. It is exactly this trait that in some ways made him more dangerous to the traditional point of view than many ardent modernists. Through the influence of the ideas of Sayyid Aḥmad Khān, he was able to introduce modernist ideas into the very bosom of tradition. He served as head of the *Nadwat al-ʿulamāʾ*, an important Islamic institution in modern India, which, by combining traditional and modern education, tried to steer a course between the schools of Aligarh, the hotbed of modernism, and Deoband, the defender of traditional orthodoxy. His position was very close in many ways to that of the al-Manār group in Egypt, with whom he maintained links first through Muḥammad ʿAbduh (1849-1905) and then Rashīd Riḍā (1865-1935). His interpretation of Islam is that of general orthodoxy, but colored with rationalism and supporting various ideas of modernism. For example, he criticized the traditional schools for continuing to teach Greco-Islamic science, and supported the teaching of modern science, but made no critical assessment of it. That he is very much influenced by Sir Sayyid and modern scientism is shown by his interpretation of Rūmī's famous verse "I died as a mineral and became a plant, I died as a plant and rose to animal state ...."[20] as referring not to the spiritual transformation of man as traditionally understood, but to evolutionism in a Darwinian sense. Similarly, his rationalism is apparent in his well-known biography of the Prophet, where he rejects most miraculous elements in the life of the Prophet and states that they are not a proof of prophethood, the criteria of prophethood being only purity of character and soundness of teaching—a claim that Maulanā Thanvī specifically challenges. An element of historicism influenced by Orientalists, some of whom he knew personally and whose methods he admired, is also present in his biographies and other works.

The Response to Modernism

As mentioned earlier, Western scholarship has produced extensive literature on modernism in the Islamic world and their opponents in fundamentalist and reformist groups, but has not sufficiently studied the vast majority of both common Muslims and Muslim intellectuals and scholars, who remained traditional and produced works in continuity with traditional Islamic scholarly and intellectual ideas and methods. In the case of Muslim India, this has led to study upon study of figures such as Sayyid Aḥmad Khān and Muḥammad Iqbāl, who were anomalies in their milieu, while traditional Islam and its representatives have been largely ignored. For example, the inner revivals within the Sufi orders of India in late nineteenth and early twentieth centuries, such as the Chishtiyya and Qādiriyya, major traditional figures such as the Sufi poet Khwāja Ghulām Farīd (d. 1903), or the activities of traditional schools such as those of Farangī Mahall, Khayrabād, and Bareilly, and to a large extent even Deoband, have been largely ignored by Western Islamicists,[21] and remain areas where much work needs to be done.

All traditional schools, as well as the *Ahl-i-ḥadīth*, perhaps the most important fundamentalist group in India at this time, were completely opposed to modernism and the errors that it promulgated, especially among the educated classes. But some were more vocal and responsive than others. By the beginning of the twentieth century, the followers of traditional Islam were roughly divided into three groups: those associated with Aḥmad Rezā Shāh (1856-1921) and the school of Bareilly, those associated with the school of Deoband, and the rest of the traditional population, including those associated with older schools like those of Farangī Mahall and Khayrabād. Out of these, the last remained the most unaffected by modernism and were therefore the least responsive, continuing to teach Islam according to the traditional methods and choosing to focus on the internal dimensions of the religion. This was largely the attitude of almost all traditionalists, some of whom, however, took a more active stance towards the new ideas affecting the understanding of Islam both in the intelligentsia and the populace around them. The school of Bareilly founded by Aḥmad

Rezā Shāh, a charismatic *ʿālim* and *shaykh* of the Qādiriyya Sufi order, adherents of which are known as Barelvīs, fought to preserve Sufism as it was traditionally and popularly practiced in India, from attacks by both modernists and reformers as well as from other Sufi schools like the Deobandīs, who sought to replace popular Sufism with a more sober, law-bound, and intellectual Sufism. The response of the school of Bareilly to modernism was one of hostility and rejection both from a theological and, especially, a juristic standpoint. An account of their complete response still needs much further scholarly work.

The school of Deoband is the best known of the aforementioned schools, and has become one of the major institutions of learning in the Sunnī world. The school of Deoband is often characterized as reformist, which usually implies puritanical ideas and a break from tradition, but this characterization is not accurate. The Deobandīs no doubt have certain characteristics that they share with reformist groups, such as opposition to various popular practices of Sufism and an emphasis on the revival of Islam, but in all essential matters of doctrine and practice, they remain completely orthodox and traditional.[22] The school of Deoband should not be viewed as an autonomous reformist movement, but as a result of the inner revival of the Chishtiyya-Sabiriyya Sufi order in the latter half of the nineteenth century. This is demonstrated by the fact that the school of Deoband was set up in response to a suggestion by the great Chishti-Sabirī master Ḥājjī Imdād Allāh (1817-1899), who, though he had migrated to Makka permanently after the failed Uprising of 1857 in which he took part, was the spiritual master of the founders of the seminary at Deoband, Muḥammad Qāsim Nanautvī, and Rashīd Aḥmad Gangohī (1829-1905). He was also the master of Maulanā Ashraf ʿAlī Thanvī. Deoband's opposition to certain popular Sufi practices needs to be seen not as puritanical reform, but rather as an attempt to focus on essential Sufism, as was the case with other Sufi revivals in the Islamic world, like those of the Darqawiyya and Sanūsiyya in North Africa. Deoband should be seen as a school dedicated to the preservation and revival of traditional Islam. Though it often stayed aloof and focused on cultivating the inward faith of Muslims like other traditional schools, Deoband did, when the occasion demanded, respond to notions that were erroneous in its point of view and that had gained currency. This is seen both in documents such as Nanautvī's aforementioned response to Sayyid Aḥmad Khān, and in the participation of certain Deobandī *ʿulamāʾ* in religious debates against missionary Christians and Arya Samaj Hindu revivalists, who aimed to convert Muslims back to Hinduism. In addition, this attitude is to be found in numerous *fatāwā* that were given by Deobandī scholars against both modern ideas and practices. It is most importantly found in the main thrust of Deobandī teaching, which was to preserve and revive traditional Islam first in the hearts of the believers and then in society at large in the face of modernism and puritanical movements. It was Maulanā Thanvī who was able to provide Deoband's and, much more importantly, Muslim India's greatest response to the tenets of modernism.

Maulanā Ashraf ʿAlī Thanvī

Maulanā Ashraf ʿAlī b. ʿAbd al-Ḥaqq al-Farūqī Thanvī was born in 1863 at Thānā Bhāwan and received his education at his hometown and in the seminary at Deoband. At Deoband, he wrote to the Chishtī-Sabirī master Ḥajjī Imdād Allāh in Makka and was accepted as his disciple, formal initiation being performed when Maulanā Thanvī made the pilgrimage to Makka a few years later. At the tender age of twenty, he graduated from Deoband and moved to Kanpur, where he was to teach for the next twenty years and where he first achieved fame due to his lucid discourses on various Islamic subjects being printed in the form of pamphlets. In 1898, he moved back permanently to Thānā Bhāwan, which was also the hometown of Ḥājjī Imdād Allāh, and took residence at his *khānqāh*. There, and at the school of Islamic learning he established at Thānā Bhāwan, he imparted religious and spiritual knowledge until his death in 1943. He was the most eminent religious figure of his time, a prolific author, and believed to be the greatest Sufi saint of modern India. He led a very active life, teaching, preaching, writing, lecturing, and making occasional journeys.

There are over one thousand works attributed to him in Urdu, Persian, and Arabic, mostly in the fields of *tafsīr* (Qur´ānic exegesis), *ḥadīth* (Prophetic traditions), *manṭiq* (logic), *kalām* (dialectical theology), *ḥikma* (traditional philosophy and theosophy), *ʿaqā´id* (doctrine), and *taṣawwuf* (Sufism), the esoteric and mystical tradition of Islam. His most famous works are his twelve-volume commentary on the Qur´ān, *Bayān al-Qur´ān*, and his handbook for women, *Bihishtī Zevar* (*Celestial Ornaments*), which is found in almost every Muslim household in the Subcontinent. He also wrote a multi-volume commentary on the *Mathnawī*, the masterwork of Jalāl al-Dīn Rūmī (1207-1273), following his spiritual master Hajjī Imdād Allāh who would give discourses on the *Mathnawī* at the *Ḥarām Sharīf*, the Blessed Sanctuary at Makka. In addition, Maulanā Thanvī wrote a Sufi commentary on the poems of the greatest Persian Sufi poet Ḥāfiẓ (1320-1389). Maulanā Thanvī is also well known for being a great defender of the doctrines of Ibn ʿArabī (1165-1240), perhaps the greatest writer on esoteric subjects in Islam, to whom he devoted several works, including a multi-volume commentary on the celebrated *Fuṣūṣ al-Ḥikam* (*Bezels of Wisdom*) that also attempts to vindicate the monumental but controversial work from the point of view of the Law. Maulanā Thanvī wrote many tracts giving a lucid presentation of traditional Islamic doctrines and beliefs, several of which have received multiple printings.[23] That Maulanā Thanvī was a great opponent of modernism will become clear through his treatise *al-Intibāhāt al-mufīda ʿan al-ishtibāhāt al-jadīda* (*The Beneficial Intimations Regarding the Newly-Arisen Doubts*), his principal tract against modernism, which will be investigated below. His other works against modernism and modern philosophy include *Taʿālīm al-dīn maʿ takmīl al-yaqīn* (*Teachings of Religion for the Perfection of Certitude*), *Iṣlāḥ al-khiyāl* (*Rectification of Thought*), and *al-Qaṣad al-mashīd lil-ʿaṣr al-jadīd* (*Lofty Intentions for the New Era*). He also translated the tract of Ḥusayn al-Jasr Tarabulisī, the *Risāla Ḥāmidiyya*, against the assumptions and methodology of modern science, from Arabic to Urdu, under the title *Islam awr Science* (*Islam and Science*). He addressed the issue of modernism in many of his other works on beliefs, religious practices, ethics, and Sufism, and pointed out how modern ideas were detrimental to the traditional Islamic understanding of the topics he discussed. Among such works can be counted, by way of example, his celebrated *Ḥayāt al-muslimīn* (*The Life of the Believers*), a tract on the meaning and importance of Islamic beliefs and practices. His work *al-Maṣāliḥ al-ʿaqliyya* (*Intellectual Counsels*) is an elucidation of the rationality of specific Islamic beliefs and practices in light of the criticism and misinterpretation they received at the hands of the modernists. This is a work in the tradition of the great philosopher, Sufi, and religious scholar Shāh Walī Allāh (1703-1762) and his monumental *Ḥujjat Allāh al-balīgha* (*The Conclusive Proof from God*), a work that seeks to explain Islamic beliefs and practices in a philosophical and rational manner.

Much of his enormous corpus is devoted to Sufism and the journey on the spiritual path. Being a great Sufi master, he was an exceptional Sufi psychologist. (A glimpse of his remarkable thought on this subject is given in Muḥammad Ajmal's article, "Sufi Science of the Soul.")[24] Maulanā Thanvī's voluminous Sufi writings, as well as biographies written by those who knew him, bear witness to his reputation as one of the greatest Sufi masters of Muslim India in modern times.[25] Unfortunately, very little exists on or by Maulanā Thanvī in Western languages, an exception being the translation of his aforementioned tract against modernism, translated proficiently by Muhammad Hasan Askari, the renowned Pakistani traditionalist, and Karrar Husain, under the title *Answer to Modernism*. A partial translation of his *Bihishtī Zevar* by Barbara Metcalf also exists. A number of other works of Maulanā Thanvī have also been translated in India, Pakistan, and South Africa, but the translations are generally not of a scholarly nature.

Maulanā Ashraf ʿAlī Thanvī is known in the Indian Subcontinent as *Ḥakīm al-Ummat*, a title that signifies that he was both a wise man and physician of the Muslim *umma* (the community of believers), a title well-suited for a man who so successfully combined a lucid intellect with deep spirituality and a gift for spiritual healing. All of Maulanā Thanvī's corpus of books, whatever may be the subject they discuss, can be seen as an attempt to clear away doubts and errors and thereby lead the reader towards a more religious and spiritual existence. In the treatise *Intibāhāt*, the Maulanā responds to and defeats the prevalent errors of modernism in the wake of the Western domination of India, and thereby removes the barriers for the Muslim, especially those with a Western education, that prevent him or her from penetrating into the truth of his or her own tradition. Maulanā Thanvī writes with a lucid and clear logicality and a penetrating intellect, as well as deep and powerful spirituality. It is this combination that makes him such an insightful and forceful critic of the modern world.

Maulanā Thanvī's Answer to Modernism

> In the case of our modernists, besides the paucity of knowledge, the pursuit of one's desires is the thickest veil which conceals the truth from their eyes.[26]
>
> —Maulanā Ashraf ʿAlī Thanvī Chishti

Maulanā Ashraf ʿAlī Thanvī's *al-Intibāhāt al-mufīda ʿan al-ishtibāhāt al-jadīda* is a refutation of the very principles of modernism, especially in its facets of rationalism and scientism, which were so popular among modernists in India. He accomplishes this daunting task by using the eternal principles that have been preserved in the Islamic tradition through the science of *ḥikma* (divine philosophy or theosophy) to undermine the very foundations of modern ideas and theories. What is particularly striking about the treatise is the impeccable logic and crystalline lucidity, and its ability to meet and overcome modernism on its own grounds. The treatise is divided into roughly twenty chapters, each being a lecture given to university students at Aligarh University on a particular topic concerned with the Islamic tradition. In the early discourses, Thanvī lays down very clearly the traditional philosophical principles that he would use to clear away modern errors and reassert the truth of Islamic teachings. One by one, he takes the diverse topics of the Islamic tradition that the modernists have expounded erroneously and refutes their propositions, reasserting the traditional Islamic position.

The introduction begins by stating that certain people—these being specifically Sayyid Aḥmad Khān and Shiblī Numānī, although the Maulanā never mentions any names—have asserted the need for an *ʿilm al-kalām al-jadīd*, a new dialectical theology.[27] If this means revising the principles of the old *ʿilm al-kalām*, then this demand is questionable, for these principles are sufficient and comprehensive; but if the demand means elaborating these principles in view of new situations that have arisen, then it is valid. He states:

> What is new in this case is that certain doubts have newly arisen. In fact, it would demonstrate the comprehensiveness of the "old" *ʿilm-al kalām* all the more conclusively, and show that, no matter what the doubts are and in what age they arise, the same "old" principles are more than sufficient to meet them adequately.[28]

He adds that what those making these demands really desire is that:

> ... the injunctions of the *sharīʿa* with regard to the doctrinal beliefs as well as to the religious practices, enjoying universal conformity, resting on explicit statements in the Holy Qur´ān and the *ḥadīth*, preserved and handed down from generation to generation, should be so modified in the light of new scientific researches as to bring them in conformity with the latter, even though the validity of these researches is neither confirmed by observation nor proved conclusively by rational argument. This object is patently absurd. All the propositions which are popularly known as "new researches" have not attained the degree of certainty; actually, most of them are merely hypothetical and conjectural.[29]

These doubts are not all new, adds Maulanā Thanvī, for they have been mentioned even by the ancient philosophers and the *mutakallimūn* (theologians). Some doubts include those that have been forgotten and are now being repeated afresh, while others are being presented in a new form. Yet others are truly new, for they are founded upon assumptions that result from the "new researches." For Thanvī, only in combating these newly-arisen doubts and employing a mode of expression suited to the contemporary mentality is speaking of a new *ʿilm al-kalām* legitimate—and there is undoubtedly need for such an *ʿilm al-kalām*:

> If Allāh helps someone compile from the writings of the atheists and critics of Islam all those objections and doubts that are based on the confrontation between Islam on the one hand, and science or the new principles introduced by western civilization on the other, and then to write a detailed refutation, such a work[30] would genuinely deserve the name of a "new" *ʿilm-al kalām*.[31]

Henceforth, Maulanā Thanvī embarks on such a task. His first priority is to elucidate what *ḥikma* is, for therein lies the foundation of all Islamic metaphysics and philosophy:

> What the Greek and Muslim philosophers call *ḥikma* (wisdom), or philosophy, is a general term which does not exclude any science or branch of knowledge, and the *sharīʿa* is also included in it.... Philosophy is the knowledge of real entities as they are, the object of such knowledge being that the self acquires thereby some kind of excellence. Thus, every science deals with the characteristics of a certain form of reality.[32]

Following this quintessential definition, Thanvī elucidates the branches of this *ḥikma*, which, according to a traditional primary classification, are two: knowledge which pertains to that whose scope is under our will and power, or practical philosophy (*al-ḥikmat al-ʿamaliyya*), and knowledge that pertains to that which is beyond us, or theoretical philosophy (*al-ḥikmat al-naẓariyya*). Practical philosophy can be further divided into ethics (*tahdhīb al-akhlāq*), domestic economy (*tadbīr al-manzil*), and politics (*siyāsat al-mudun*), and theoretical philosophy can be divided into metaphysics (*ilāhiyyāt*), mathematics (*riyāḍiyyāt*), and physics (*ʿilm al-ṭabīʿa*).

The purpose of the *sharīʿa*, he asserts, is to fulfill one's obligations to God and to creatures. Therefore, mathematics and physics are not treated by the *sharīʿa*. This leaves us with four branches of *ḥikma* that concern the *sharīʿa*. Of these, metaphysics is the only theoretical branch, and a sub-division of it is the "science of doctrines and beliefs" (*ʿilm al-ʿaqāʾid*). It is this with which the Maulanā says we are concerned in these discourses, for doubts are related to belief, and the purpose here is to discuss "only those things about which people with a Western education have sometimes come to feel a doubt."[33]

First Principles

The first chapter of the *Intibāhāt* is called precisely that which it expounds, namely, "First Principles." The purpose of this chapter is to clearly explicate the principles of Islamic philosophy that are necessary to refute erroneous concepts. Maulanā Thanvī begins the chapter with the heading: "One's inability to understand something is no argument for its being false,"[34] which recalls the famous dictum of Islamic philosophy, *ʿadam al-wijdān lā yadullu ʿalā ʿadam al-wujūd*, "the non-existence of knowledge of something is not proof of its non-existence."[35] Thanvī elaborates this principle by explaining that the inability to understand that a certain thing exists is wholly different from certain knowledge that it does not exist. The former signifies that, due to lack of observation, the mind cannot comprehend the causes and modes of the existence of a thing, but can produce no evidence, whether rational or based on report, to establish its non-existence. On the other hand, certain knowledge that a thing does not exist signifies that the mind can produce a sound argument, whether rational or based on report, to establish its non-existence. He gives the illustration of a man who has never seen a railway train, and hears of this carriage that runs without a beast. He would be unable to understand such a phenomenon, but he would not have any sound argument to deny its truth. According to his habitual observation, carriages were always pulled by beasts and he had not seen anything contrary to this phenomenon. Yet he could not have a valid argument to state that the railway does not exist. Similarly, one who denies the Islamic belief that on the Day of Judgment man will have to walk along a bridge called *ṣirāṭ* that will be finer than a hair, has the same status as the man who denied the railway train, for he has not experienced anything like it.

The next principle of philosophy asserted by Maulanā Thanvī is: "If a thing is rationally possible, and its existence is attested by sound report, then it is necessary to accept its existence. On the other hand, if its non-existence is attested by sound report, then it is equally necessary to accept its non-existence."[36] In lieu of this, he invokes the famous Islamic philosophical principle that goes back to the renowned peripatetic Islamic philosopher Ibn Sīnā (Avicenna) (979-1037) who states that being is of three kinds: necessary (*wājib*), impossible (*mumtanī*), and contingent or possible (*mumkin*). Firstly, there are facts that are necessary rationally, such as "one is the half of two." Secondly, there are facts whose non-existence is necessary by reason, such as "one is equal to two." Thirdly, there are facts whose existence is neither affirmed nor denied by necessity of reason, their existence or non-existence being equally possible. Such for example is the case of the statement that "the area of such a town is greater than that of the other town." In such a case, reason must either make a direct examination or accept the findings of those who have made such an examination. Until it does one of these two, reason cannot regard the statement as true or false. Such a fact is termed "possible." If one can find an argument based on sound report that such a thing is true, then it is necessary to believe in it, and if one finds similarly that it is false, then one must accept its non-existence. Similarly, Maulanā Thanvī says: "It is rationally possible for the Heavens to exist as the Muslims in general believe them to do. That is to say, reason does not possess any argument either to confirm or to deny this fact, but admits both probabilities."[37] So, to establish the truth of the matter, reason must depend on sound report, which is provided by the Holy Qur´ān and *ḥadīth* that such a thing does exist. Thus reason must, of necessity, affirm their existence.

It is important to note here that Maulanā Thanvī does not limit his epistemology to reason and sound report but takes into account other modes of knowing such as *kashf*, or spiritual unveiling, and *ilhām*, or intuition. In this treatise, he uses only those modes of knowing that would be most familiar to his audience, which consisted largely of modernized Muslims who were educated with the background of British rationalism and empiricism. He therefore employs a dialectical mode of argumentation and does not focus upon mystical and higher modes of knowing. There are several places in the treatise where he does allude to such knowledge, as in his discussion of eschatology and the inner meanings of religious rites. In many of his other works, Maulanā Thanvī discusses at length higher modes of knowing such as intuition and unveiling. He states in one of his writings and even alludes in the *Intibāhāt* to the notion that one believes in the truths of religion based on intuition. He also states in one of the last chapters of the *Intibāhāt* that a sage can have immediate knowledge of Divine matters.

The third principle that Maulanā Thanvī declares is another classical Islamic philosophical principle and is effective in undermining the very foundations of both rationalism and empiricism:

> What is rationally impossible is something totally different from what is merely improbable. The impossible is opposed to reason itself, while the improbable is opposed merely to habit. The predicates of reason and those of habit are quite distinct, and it is erroneous to identify them with each other. What is impossible can never exist, but what is merely improbable may exist. It is the impossible alone which can be described as irrational, while the improbable is only something which reason cannot understand by itself.[38]

As the Maulanā has demonstrated, the impossible is that by which the non-existence of a thing is necessary by reason, while the improbability of a thing might make it astonishing (like a train running without a beast), but it is not permissible to deny that which is only improbable but not rationally impossible. In addition, what is astonishing is the force of habit whereby "all those things which are not supposed to be astonishing are all in reality very astonishing,"[39] but we have grown used to them through repeated observation. Such is the case of a male seed entering the womb and becoming a human. This is far more astonishing than a railway train, but we do not consider it astonishing due to repeated observation. Similarly, a person who is used to listening to a gramophone speak does not find it astonishing, yet might find the Islamic belief that hands and feet speak on the Day of Judgment to be so astonishing that he considers it impossible—which would be a clear error in logic. If one encountered a thing that seemed improbable, but there existed a sound report testifying to its truth, then it would be necessary to believe in it. Such is the case of Islamic beliefs like the passage over the bridge of *ṣirāṭ* after death, which is based on the report of a truthful reporter, the Holy Prophet. Therefore, it would be a rational error to deny it and try to interpret it away.

The fourth philosophical principle that Maulanā Thanvī enunciates is a direct attack upon the claims of modern science and the resultant scientism and empiricism so in vogue among proponents of modernism: "If a thing exists, it is not necessary that it must also be sensible and visible."[40] Thanvī states that there are three ways of ascertaining the truth of a fact: one, through personal observation; two, through sound report from a truthful reporter; three, through rational argument. Among these three categories, existence is common to all, but only one of them involves sense perception. Thus, if we state that a certain fact exists, it is not necessary that it be perceptible by the senses nor is it necessary that a fact not perceptible by the senses must be non-existent. By way of illustration, he demonstrates that the Holy Qur´ān states that there are seven Heavens above us, and just because we cannot see them does not mean that they do not exist.

The fifth philosophical principle used by Maulanā Thanvī is the following: "It is not possible to prove a purely reported fact by a purely rational argument. So it is not also permissible to demand such an argument."[41] This is especially directed at the demands of the modernists who, considering the scientific method as the ultimate criterion of truth, want a rational proof for every religious tenet. Maulanā Thanvī states that, as mentioned, one of the ways of ascertaining a fact is through sound report. Now, a fact accepted through sound report is not arguable through a purely rational argument. To illustrate this, he gives the example of someone telling us that a battle was fought between the kings Darius and Alexander the Great. Thanvī proceeds:

> Now if another person were to demand a rational argument in order to establish this fact, even the greatest philosopher would not be able to present any other argument except this—the existence of two such kings and [that] a war between them is not impossible, but possible enough; and trustworthy historians have reported that this possibility did actually come into existence, and since it is rationally necessary to affirm a fact as real when we learn from a truthful reporter that what was possible did really come into existence, we must necessarily accept the report about the two kings as an actual fact.[42]

Similar is the case of the coming of the Day of Judgment, the resurrection of the dead, and the beginning of a new life. Since these are all sound reports, if a man asserts them, no one can justifiably demand a rational argument from him. For to silence his opponents, all he would have to do is to say that there is no argument to prove these facts impossible, even though they may not understand them—these two things not being identical; they are, however, rationally possible, and based on sound report, which means that they must be accepted.

The sixth principle of Islamic philosophy that Maulanā Thanvī utilizes follows in the line of the last one: "There is some difference between a precedent and an argument. It may be justifiable to demand an argument from the man who makes an assertion, but it is not valid to demand a precedent from him."[43] He illustrates this principle with an example: he asks us to suppose there is a man who asserts that King George V had his coronation at Delhi. Now, if another man comes and states that he will believe it only if he is given a precedent and that otherwise he would consider it unreal, it would only be sufficient for the first man to state that there is no precedent, for this has not happened before, yet there are sound witnesses to the event and the newspapers have reported it. Similarly, says Maulanā Thanvī: "If man asserts that human hands and feet will speak on the Day of Judgment, no one can have the right to demand a precedent from him, nor can any one justifiably refute him merely on the ground that he has failed to cite a precedent."[44] It is, of course, necessary for him to put forward an argument to support his contention, and that would only be the argument based on sound report mentioned earlier.

Maulanā Thanvī's last philosophical principle in this first foundational chapter on first principles is fourfold. There are only four rationally possible situations in which there can be a contradiction between a rational argument and an argument based on report. These are as follows: One, that both the arguments are final and conclusive; such a situation is impossible, for two truths cannot contradict each other. Two, both are approximative; in this case, although they can be reconciled through some non-literal interpretation, the regular rule of language is the literal and so the report would be taken as literal and this would invalidate the rational argument. Three, the report is final and the rational argument approximative; in this case, the report would certainly prevail. Four, the rational argument is final and the report approximative, either in its connotation or its authenticity; here the rational argument would be given precedence and the report treated in a non-literal way. After this, the Maulanā asserts: "Thus, the last situation is the only one in which Reason (*dirāya*) is to be given precedence over Tradition (*riwāya*). And it is not justifiable to adopt this procedure in all possible situations."[45] This completes Maulanā Thanvī's major principles of Islamic philosophy with which he answers the basic propositions of modernism as it manifested itself in Muslim India. These principles contain all that is needed to address the specific errors of the modernists.

Applications of the Principles

After the elucidation of the principles, which in essence contain a response to any of the modernists' main positions, Maulanā Ashraf ʿAlī Thanvī approaches various aspects of Islamic doctrine and belief that have been rejected or misinterpreted by the modernists of India due to the effect of Westernization and the resulting skepticism, scientism, and rationalism. These points are treated in a series of discourses, each of which encompasses a certain area of Islamic doctrine and belief challenged by the modernists. The topics Maulanā Thanvī addresses—each the subject of a chapter—are: the temporality of matter; the omnipotence of God; prophethood; four separate chapters on the four sources of the *sharīʿa* (according to the Ḥanafī school of law that Maulanā Thanvī followed): the Qur'ān, the *ḥadīth*, *ijmāʿ* or consensus, and *qiyās* or analogy; the angels, *jinn*, and Satan; the events after death; certain features of the physical universe; the question of destiny; the pillars of Islam and modes of worship; mutual transactions and politics; social customs; moral attitudes; and rational argumentation. As can be seen, these cover the whole spectrum of traditional Islam, from fundamental doctrines to social practices. In this study, certain salient aspects of Maulanā Thanvī's thought concerning these subjects and his criticism of the modernists will be brought out.

The first of these intimations pertains to the temporality of matter. Maulanā Thanvī writes: "By putting their faith in Western science and following its lead blindly, many Muslims have fallen into two grave errors with regard to the doctrine of the Unity of God which is the very basis of Islam. In committing these errors, such blind followers of science are being fully faithful neither to science nor to Islam."[46] The first of these errors is the belief that matter is eternal, which denies the doctrine of *tawḥīd* (Divine Unity)—for then matter is eternal alongside Allāh. The Maulanā says that the Greeks were also guilty of this error:

> ... but they, at least, had some kind of argument, however flimsy and dependent upon a sophistical use of words.... On the other hand, modern scientists and their followers do not possess an argument which could pretend to even that much degree of validity.[47]

Their judgment is no more than a presumption, Maulanā Thanvī claims. By making this distinction between the Greeks and modern scientists, Thanvī demonstrates that he was among the few Muslim *ʿālims* who understood that modern science, as opposed to pre-modern or traditional science, posed a serious threat to the Islamic tradition because of the philosophical assumptions upon which it is based. As to the modern objection that it is inconceivable that existence could come out of non-existence, and that matter must thus be eternal, he asserts that the inability to understand something is no proof of its falsity. He then utilizes the Aristotelian distinctions to argue that there can be no matter without form, for modern science asserts that in the beginning primeval matter was devoid of substantial form (*al-ṣūrat al-jismiyya*). This is so because matter is purely potential and it is form that gives it actuality. He then offers another argument based upon classical Islamic philosophy to refute Greek science as well. Belief in the eternity of matter turns Islamic metaphysics on its head. This is so because if matter is the cause of its own existence, then it is necessary being. It would thus have no need of any other being, even if it be necessary, like God. Maulanā Thanvī then refutes, in detail, many different theories in which matter and some of its constituents, like the atom, are held to be eternal. He also refers readers to his own major philosophical work, *Dirāyat al-ʿiṣma*, as well as to Mullā Ṣadrā's (1571-1640) celebrated *Sharḥ hidāyat al-ḥikma*

(*Commentary upon the Book of Guidance* of Athīr al-Dīn Abharī),[48] for a further analysis of some of the main arguments he makes in this chapter.

Maulanā Thanvī asserted that there are two errors that threaten the Unity of God, the first being the eternity of matter. The second, discussed in the second intimation, pertains to the omnipotence of God. Here, the Maulanā attacks the idea—championed by Sayyid Aḥmad Khān and his followers—that nothing can ever happen contrary to the law of nature. By doing this, they negate God's attribute of omnipotence. He states that the modernists employ two arguments, one rational and one traditional. The rational argument is based on the premise that since habitually things happen in nature in a certain way they must always happen in that way and so miracles cannot happen. This is, of course, as Maulanā Thanvī has demonstrated, taking the improbable for the impossible. The Maulanā expands upon this and shows its falsity through the rules of logic, and then proceeds to criticize the indiscriminate use of Qur´ānic verses and other traditional materials to prove naturalistic theories, such as the Qur´ānic verse, "And you will not find any change in the way of God" (35:43), interpreted to mean that the laws of nature, being the ways of God, cannot be changed. Maulanā Thanvī proceeds further to repudiate particular positions, especially the one held by Sayyid Aḥmad Khān that God would be breaking His promise if He allowed miracles to happen, because "the habitual way of Allāh" is taken to be a promise and interpreted as the law of nature.

Maulanā Thanvī's critique of the prevalent errors regarding prophethood forms one of the richest chapters in his treatise. Here he outlines a series of errors found among the modernists concerning the nature and scope of prophethood. He first criticizes the notion that *waḥy* (Divine Revelation) is a natural phenomenon, as argued by proponents of naturalism. He then points out a few errors concerning the nature of miracles. He asserts that the followers of modern science do not accept miracles as they are but make far-fetched rationalizations in which miracles are made to look like habitual facts. If this cannot be done, they make other kinds of rationalizations, for example Moses' stick turning into a snake is explained as mesmerism or hypnotism. The answer to such claims is to assert once again that the impossible and the improbable are not the same. Another error regarding miracles, one explicitly stated by Shiblī Numānī, whose name Maulanā Thanvī does not mention, is "that miracles are not adjudged to be a proof of prophethood, but the excellence of a prophet's teaching and the excellence of his moral conduct are supposed to be the only valid arguments for establishing his prophethood."[49] Those that claim this, continues the Maulanā, say that if supernatural events are taken as proofs of prophethood, then mesmerism and conjuring tricks too will be proofs of prophethood. But this is a very flimsy argument, for mesmerism and tricks are not, in fact, supernatural events and can be traced back to hidden causes that experts of such arts can easily detect; the imposter can therefore be exposed, and could even be challenged in the art of such tricks. Excellence of teaching and moral conduct are also proofs of prophethood, but Divine Wisdom has its own way of disposing things. He illustrates this by explaining the nature of the audience of the prophets:

> The audience of the prophets (peace be upon them) was composed of two kinds of people. On the one hand were the elite—people who had intelligence enough to recognize the highest excellence of teaching and moral conduct (which is itself a miracle). On the other hand were the dull-witted ordinary people who, being unable to recognize the highest degree of excellence, could not derive the correct conclusion from the testimony of teaching and moral conduct, and were thus liable to the fatal error of accepting every just and good man as a prophet. So Divine Wisdom ordained a special mode of argument which should be proper to their level of understanding, and which should provide a compulsive recognition of the validity of the claim to prophethood, without requiring any exertion of the will or of the mind on their part.[50]

Another error concerning prophethood, contends Thanvī, is that prophets are said to be concerned only with affairs of the other world, while in affairs of this world one is supposed to be absolutely independent of prophetic injunctions. Such a position is maintained as we have seen by those like Chirāgh ʿAlī who attempt to equate Islam with secularized Christianity. Maulanā Thanvī states that since worldly rulers, through law and governance, interfere with our personal lives, why should not the real Ruler have this right? He then argues against those who maintain that the injunctions of the *sharīʿa* should be modified according to the requirements of the age, and who argue that in the conditions prevailing in the modern world it is difficult to follow the *sharīʿa*, and that it should thus be modified. "The real source of the difficulties is our present way of life and not the injunctions of the *sharīʿa*,"[51] replies the Maulanā. In any case, he says that the *sharīʿa* is not difficult to follow, rather "it is only the fear of some personal loss that conjures up a suspicion that the *sharīʿa* is very restrictive and difficult to be practiced."[52]

The next error that Maulanā Thanvī points out concerns the injunctions of the *sharīʿa*:

> Some people invent certain *raisons d'être* for these injunctions on the basis of their personal opinion, and insist on making the validity of the injunctions depend solely on the presence or absence of these very *raisons d'être*. In consequence of this, they start misinterpreting, distorting, and even annulling the injunctions laid down by the Holy Qur´ān and the *ḥadīth*. Thus, we have heard of some people who somehow convinced themselves that the *raison*

> *d'être* of the ritual ablutions (*wuḍū'*) was no more than cleanliness, and finding themselves clean enough, did not think it necessary to perform the ablutions at all before offering prayers.[53]

Such, he continues, is also the case of the ritual prayer, and of other rites such as fasting, almsgiving (*zakāt*), and the pilgrimage to Makka, as well as prohibitions such as interest, all of which are treated in this same facile manner. In a later passage on the pillars of Islam, he writes:

> The *raison d'être* for ritual prayer is supposed to be moral discipline; that for ritual ablution, mere cleanliness; that for fasting, control over animal energy; that for ritual almsgiving (*zakāt*), helping those who do not possess the means of "progress"; that for the pilgrimage of Mecca (*ḥājj*), collective gathering for the furtherance of trade, commerce, culture, and for encouraging "progress"; that for the recitation of the Holy Qur'ān, mere information and acquaintance with the contents of the book; that for devotional prayer, only satisfaction of the soul; that for openly declaring the word of Allāh, mere peace and freedom.[54]

Not only is this patent heresy, argues Thanvī, but it is completely unsupported by rational argument. This is so because different individuals could, according to their whims, posit different *raisons d'être* and there would be no rational criterion to prefer one opinion over another. A corollary of this attitude, continues Maulanā Thanvī, is that some people trying to defend Islam against its detractors try to offer similar rationalizations and *raisons d'être*. He warns:

> Now, there is a great danger in adopting such a procedure. The *raisons d'être* thus suggested are purely conjectural. If any of them is found to be questionable, the related injunction itself thereby becomes dubious and defective. Thus, it amounts to providing the detractors of Islam with a permanent opportunity for disputing and negating the Islamic injunctions.[55]

Another grave error concerning prophethood, asserts Maulanā Thanvī is that some modernists believe that salvation is possible for even those who deny prophethood, for the prophets themselves came to attest to the Unity of God, and as long as a man does that, there is no harm in denying the prophets. Thanvī argues that one who denies prophethood denies God, for it is the prophets who have brought His Word, which itself attests to their truth. To support this argument, he cites an example: "And a precedent from the worldly life is this. If a man were to acknowledge George V as his king, but were to keep defying the Viceroy of India, would his behavior be considered meritorious, or even pardonable by the king?"[56]

In the intimation concerning the Holy Qur'ān, Thanvī identifies two grave errors among modernists. One is to consider it the sole repository of the injunctions of the *sharīʿa*. This was the position of Chirāgh ʿAlī and many reformist groups to come, who rejected all other sources of law. This,

Maulanā Thanvī states, is used to justify all sorts of un-Islamic practices by stating they are not forbidden explicitly in the Qur´ān. The second error is the one that relates specifically to modernists and apologists and this is the "attempt ... to bring the verses of the Holy Qur´ān into conformity with the theories of modern science through fanciful interpretations, and also to prove that the Holy Qur´ān propounds and confirms these very theories."[57] Maulanā Thanvī's thought on this subject is especially enlightening and insightful:

> One too often finds in newspapers and journals nowadays that as soon as people come across a scientific discovery made in the West, they try as best as they can to discover an indication of this theory in some verse of the Holy Qur´ān, and a proof of one's own intelligence. What is worse, even some religious scholars have been found guilty of this error. What is basically wrong with this approach is that it is to be a mark of the highest perfection for the Holy Qur´ān to contain scientific theories.[58]

This misconception, continues the Maulanā, is due to the fact that no attention has been paid to the essential nature of the Holy Qur´ān. He writes:

> The Holy Qur´an, in fact, is not a book of physical science, nor of history, nor of geography. It is a book which deals with the cure of souls, just as books on medicine deal with the cure of bodies. It would not be a defect or deficiency in a book of medicine, if it does not discuss the problems of shoe-making or cloth-weaving.[59]

If it did so unnecessarily, it would indeed be a defect. In addition, when one is arguing for a certain proposition, the premises must be already acceptable to the audience or need to be made acceptable through proper argument. Otherwise, an argument of any validity could not be made. So if the theories of modern science are what the verses of the Qur´ān are meant to indicate, this means that the Qur´ān was arguing with its earliest audience, the desert Arabs, with premises that were neither universally acceptable nor had yet been established through proof and were therefore unintelligible to the Arabs and worthless as the basis of argument. Another great defect of this approach, asserts Maulanā Thanvī, is that scientific theories are sometimes proved to be wrong. If these theories come to be accepted by the Muslims as being affirmed by the Qur´ān and are then proven wrong, it would cast doubt on the Qur´ān itself. The final great defect with this approach, cited by Maulanā Thanvī, is as follows:

> The fourth defect in this approach is that it totally goes against our self-respect, for if we make the interpretation of the Qur´ān dependent upon scientific discoveries, would not the European scholars point out that although the Qur´ān was revealed such a long time ago, yet no Muslim, not even the Holy

> Prophet himself (peace be upon him), has ever understood it, and that the Muslims should be grateful to the West for having made it possible for them to understand and interpret the Qur´ān correctly? Were they to do so, what reply would we have?[60]

Thanvī's comments and arguments concerning the widespread doubts that had fallen around the science of *ḥadīth* are equally insightful. It is claimed, he states, that the *ḥadīth* are not authentic because they were not written down in the time of the Prophet and it is unnatural for men to have exact memories. Also, each man understands things in his own way, so that when these *ḥadīth* were passed down, they were no longer reliable. Maulanā Thanvī retorts: "In fact, this error results from disregarding the lives of the early *muḥaddithūn*[61] and the *fuqahā´*.[62] Some people have simply imagined them to be like themselves in the matter of a weak memory, a want of zeal, and a lack of piety."[63] Maulanā Thanvī then proceeds to give a masterly discourse filled with actual examples of the great memory, zeal, and scrupulousness of the early *muḥaddithūn*. The Maulanā adds that one reason memory is so weak in the present age is that, due to literacy, men cannot remember anything unless it is written down, and have lost that faculty of memory which so-called "illiterate" people still possess. Also, certain human faculties are especially developed in accordance with the needs of an age, and in those days in Arabia the memory was especially developed, just as in the West today mental dexterity is especially developed so as to pursue scientific discoveries and inventions. The Maulanā then proceeds—using the criteria he has established earlier—to take to task the notion that a *ḥadīth* contrary to reason cannot be accepted.

As for the denial of the reality of the angels, the *jinn*, and Satan, Maulanā Thanvī asserts that what cannot be perceived is not necessarily unreal. The same applies to the events in the grave, events of the Day of Judgment and Heaven and Hell. Regarding the latter articles of Islamic belief, he adds that things which are improbable are not impossible, and that not all things need have a precedent in order to be true. Concerning the events of the grave, Maulanā Thanvī hints at certain metaphysical notions like the soul passing to the *ʿālam al-arwāḥ* (the world of spirits), but since his argument is logical and dialectical in this treatise, he does not pursue this line of thought. He also relates other doctrines of a metaphysical and mystical nature very briefly, such as the subtle or imaginal body (*al-jism al-mithālī*). Overall, in discussing these matters, he opens the way to a treatment of them which goes beyond just reason and sense perception, and which is rooted in the elaborate eschatological doctrines of later Islamic theosophical philosophy, although in this treatise he does not treat these subjects in detail.[64]

One of the most interesting discourses in Maulanā Thanvī's treatise addresses those claims of modern science that contradict Islamic doctrine.

This is one of the rare occasions in modern Islamic history when a traditional *ʿālim* has directly addressed the claims of modern science in an intellectual, and not merely juridical, manner. In this intimation, he begins by reasserting that the purpose of the *sharīʿa* is not to discuss the physical universe, but that there are certain statements made about the natural world in the Qur´ān and *ḥadīth*, and what opposes these—such as certain claims of modern science—needs to be rejected. Then Maulanā Thanvī challenges Darwin's theory of evolution. He affirms that this theory goes directly against the Qur´ān and *ḥadīth,* which state that man is born of human seed. Darwin himself, Maulanā Thanvī states, has confessed that this theory is purely due to his own speculations, and it is clear from their own statements that Muslim modernists believe in this theory only in imitation of Darwin. He adds that even this imitation of theirs is imperfect, both in respect of its motivating cause and its particular detail. Darwin, he continues, affirmed this ridiculous hypothesis because he was a materialist and an unbeliever, and not having had faith, had to invent the cult of evolution in order to explain the origin of all things. But those who believe in the existence of the Creator, says Maulanā Thanvī, that is, people of all religions, and especially Muslims, have no need for a cult of evolution, for profession in a Creator who created man in his present form is sufficient for them. Modernist Muslims do not have the same cause for this belief as Darwin did, that is, unbelief. And they cannot have the same particular detail, for Darwin said that a species of beast evolved by stages into man, the implication being a large number of individuals from a beastly species turned into a human species all at one time. Islam asserts that Adam was one individual. Maulanā Thanvī adds: "In our days certain insolent, unscrupulous, and impudent people have had the temerity to suggest that Adam is the name of the ape which first turned into man. May Allāh protect us from such things!"[65]

Maulanā Thanvī then proceeds to discuss a number of physical phenomena in which theories of modern science have been understood to contradict some element of the Islamic tradition. For example, the manner of production of rain, thunder, and lightning that is mentioned in the *ḥadīth* is different than modern science has observed. Here he applies the principle of logic that there cannot be contradiction between two partial propositions, which he demonstrates both versions to be. He similarly addresses questions such as the cause of plague being sins or *jinn* as tradition asserts, or germs as science asserts, and again shows that there is no real contradiction. He also addresses astronomical issues, like the plurality of worlds and the plurality of heavens. In such cases, he reasserts the principle that the lack of observation of something is not proof of its non-existence. Also, the motion of the sun and the moon is discussed and affirmed, as well as the rising of the sun from the West at the end of time. He also states that if Gog and Magog have not been discovered in the North, it does not mean they do not exist.[66]

There are many other discourses and points and arguments against modernism in this treatise that cannot be mentioned, much less discussed in detail, due to the scope of this study. Let us draw the study to a close by quoting from two important passages from the end chapters of the *Intibāhāt*, which demonstrate clearly that Maulanā Thanvī is not only an impeccable logician and philosopher, but also a master spiritual psychologist. Maulanā Thanvī states the real root of the tendencies of the modernists in the following terms: "The real root of all error is the love of worldly life and the flattery of worldly people. To tell the truth, our modernists only seek to flatter a certain set of worldly people [namely, the westernized rulers of society], by distorting Islamic principles in the light of their postulates ..."[67]

Maulanā Thanvī thus identifies the errors of the modernists with an error in their intention and their will, in which the intelligence does not play any real role, for all their thinking is being done in accordance with worldly desire. His intimation regarding moral attitudes is one of the most insightful of all despite its brevity. Here, Maulanā Thanvī relates how the true meaning of virtue and vice has become increasingly confused in modern times:

> A special error that is usually committed in this matter is that certain virtues have been falsely mixed up with certain vices, and vice versa, and a proper demarcation has not been made between the two categories. Consequently certain moral attitudes which are reprehensible in their essential nature, have been given fine names, and thus considered to be commendable, while others have been dealt with in the opposite manner. Let us cite a few instances of the first kind. What is nowadays regarded as "progress" is in its essential nature the greed for money and social position; what is called "honor" is in fact pride; the quality known as "love for one's nation" is basically the spirit of tribalism which blinds one to the distinction between right and wrong; what is called "statesmanship" is in fact deceit and cunning; what is known as "keeping up with the march of time" is in reality mere hypocrisy; and so on and so forth. Now, as for the instances of the second kind, that is, of those moral attitudes which are commendable but are nowadays (vices), being included among the reprehensible ones: contentment, which is supposed to be the lack of initiative; acceptance of and resignation to the will of God, which is condemned as idleness; jealous regard for religion and firmness of faith, which is called dogmatism and fanaticism; indifference to one's physical appearance, which is described as debasing; courtesy, which is supposed to be meanness and pettiness of mind; fear of God and piety, which is considered to be mere whimsicality; keeping oneself away from unnecessarily mixing with people, which is called misanthropy; and so on and so forth.[68]

It is fitting that this quotation comes from the last pages of the *Intibāhāt al-mufida*, for it demonstrates that though this treatise is of an impeccably philosophical and logical nature, its central concern is the spiritual life, for it was written by a spiritual master with a profound understanding of spiritual psychology. As such, the treatise exemplifies the spiritual attitude of traditional Islam and its emphasis on wisdom (*ḥikma*), which contains within itself both intellectual as well as existential knowledge, which is none other than virtue (*iḥsān*).

Conclusion

In this treatise, Maulanā Thanvī illustrates powerfully and insightfully how, through recourse to the Islamic intellectual tradition, contemporary Muslims can tread a way which avoids both the intellectual capitulation of the modernists, and the blind rejectionism of the puritanical reformists vis-à-vis the challenges the modern Western world poses for Islam. In this, Thanvī follows the way of his great forbearers like al-Ghazālī (1058-1111), Ibn ʿArabī, and Shāh Walī Allāh of Delhi, who demonstrated synthetically that the ways of the intellect and the ways of revelation are harmonious and not contradictory. One of the Names of God in Islam is *al-Ḥaqq*, the Truth. In light of this, the Islamic intellectual and spiritual tradition has always emphasized the primacy of truth, wherever it may be found, for all divergent truths are unified in and testify ultimately to the one Truth, God. This is why Islam does not need to be reformed or modernized; it already contains within itself the principles necessary for renewal from within. These principles provide the discernment to both integrate truth wherever it is found and to reject falsehood decisively.

For Thanvī and for the tradition he inherited and passed on, the essence of Islam is wisdom and spirituality and only he who has rectified himself inwardly, which means protecting the mind from error and protecting the heart from vice, can rectify the external world. This is a far cry indeed from the ideas and concerns of the generality of modernists and fundamentalists in the Islamic world of today, who employ the opposite approach of trying to reform the outward before reforming the inward. Thus, they focus their energies almost exclusively on the social and political dimensions of Islam. This preoccupies them with the issue of worldly power and the fact that the Islamic world at the present time does not wield such power becomes for them a definite sign of its weakness. The modernists mistake the power of the modern West with the truth of its ideas and thereby seek to modernize Islam in order to make it more powerful. The fundamentalists attempt to empower Islam through the increase of its political power, an enterprise that can and has resulted in violent means. The approach of traditional Islam, which is the approach of Maulanā Thanvī, challenges both methodologies by demonstrating that the enduring power of Islam lies not in its political strength but its truth, and the intellectual and moral soundness and strength that only truth can provide.

The issues Thanvī raises can be elaborated further and can be of great use, not only to Muslims, but to all who seek to reverse the deleterious effects of modernism and secularism. Maulanā Thanvī demonstrates the reality of our world and our human existence, issues that the varying and ever-changing ideologies of the modern world can never sufficiently address, in that they begin with man, who is contingent, and not with the Divine, who is absolute. At a time when the Western world is itself asking questions about its modernist heritage of secularism, rationalism, humanism, and the like,[69] and the thirst for genuine spirituality is growing rapidly in the West,[70] the Islamic intellectual and spiritual tradition can provide decisive and far-reaching answers. Neither puritanical movements which limit truth to a narrow literalist vision, nor liberal modernism, which relativizes it, can achieve this task. It is, therefore, important that the Western world recognize and engage the voice of traditional Islam, which is still the voice of the majority of Muslims, amongst both the masses and the religious authorities. If a civilizational dialogue is to be conducted, it must start here, for this is where the intellectual and spiritual tradition of Islam resides and where the true face of Islam, as it has been practiced for the last fourteen hundred years, is found. Furthermore, it is pertinent for Muslims themselves to reclaim their intellectual and spiritual heritage from the modernist and the puritanical movements that threaten it. If Islam is to flourish as a religion, it can only do so through its spiritual and intellectual traditions, which alone stand the test of time and the ebbs and flows of worldly fortunes. The neglect of this venerable tradition can only result in loss for the Islamic world and for all of mankind.

Notes

1 See the essays of Ibrahim Kalin, Waleed El-Ansary, and Ejaz Akram in this volume.

2 Seyyed Hossein Nasr, *Traditional Islam in the Modern World* (London: Kegan Paul International, 1987), p. 13.

3 The *Sunna* refers to the Way of the Prophet, which comprises both his words and his deeds, and which has been taken as the perfect model for the life of the Muslims since the beginning of Islam.

4 See Tage Lindblom, *The Tares and the Good Grain: the Kingdom of Man at the Hour of Reckoning* (Macon, GA: Mercer University Press, 1983), and Martin Lings, *Ancient Beliefs and Modern Superstitions* (New York: Routledge, 1980), as analyses and critiques of the modern, secular, humanistic, and scientistic worldview. For an Islamic critique, see Seyyed Hossein Nasr, "Reflections on Islam and Modern Thought," in *Traditional Islam in the Modern World*, pp. 97-114.

5 On the phenomenon of fundamentalism, see Bruce Lawrence, *Defenders of God: The Fundamentalist Revolt Against the Modern Age* (San Francisco: Harper & Row, 1989).

6 For an examination of this divide between modern and traditional interpretations of the Qur´ān and the *ḥadīth*, see David Dakake's "The Myth of a Militant Islam," in this volume.

7 For a masterly analysis of the different responses of Islam to the Western world, see Seyyed Hossein Nasr, *Traditional Islam in the Modern World*. See also his *Islam and the Plight of Modern Man* (London, 1975; revised and enlarged edition, Chicago: Kazi Publications, 2001). An excellent summary of these different responses is given in the last chapter of Victor Danner, *The Islamic Tradition: An Introduction* (Amity, NY: Amity House, 1988). A thorough study of Islamic movements in the last two centuries is found in John O. Voll, *Islam: Continuity and Change in the Modern World* (Syracuse: Syracuse University Press, 1994). For a discussion of modernism in the Islamic world, H. A. R. Gibb's, *Modern Trends in Islam* (Chicago: University of Chicago Press, 1950) is still useful. See also John Esposito et al., *Contemporary Islamic Revival: A Critical Survey and Bibliography* (New York, 1991).

8 Remark at the "Paths to the Heart: Sufism and the Christian East" conference, University of South Carolina, October 2001.

9 See his article "The Decline of Knowledge and the Rise of Ideology in the Modern Islamic World," in this volume.

10 It is important to note that in the period with which we are concerned, Sufism had been, to a large extent, reconciled with the jurisprudence and theology that the *ʿulamā´* generally represented, this being especially true of the Indian subcontinent since Shāh Walī Allāh (d. 1762). Therefore, the designations of *ʿālim* and *Sufi* often coincided in the same person, a prime example being Maulanā Thanvī himself.

11 For an exposition of the meaning of *ḥikma*, or theosophy, see Seyyed Hossein Nasr, *Ṣadr al-Dīn Shīrāzī and his Transcendent Theosophy* (Tehran, 1997), ch. 5.

12 Quoted in Aziz Aḥmad, *Islamic Modernism in India and Pakistan 1857-1964* (Oxford: Oxford University Press, 1967), pp. 22-23.

13 This is seen, for example, in the influential Egyptian modernist Muḥammad ʿAbduh's assertion to the effect that he found real Islam in Paris!

14 Quoted in *Muslim Self-Statement in India and Pakistan 1857-1968*, eds. Aziz Aḥmad and G. E. Von Grunebaum (Wiesbaden: Otto Harrassowitz, 1970), p. 4.

15 For a complete translation of this treatise by Nanautvi, as well as the tract mentioned above by Sayyid Aḥmad Khān, see *Ibid.*, pp. 25-42, 60-76.

16 Quoted in Aziz Aḥmad, *op. cit.*, p. 44.

17 Traditional Islamic metaphysics and theology views God's relation to man in terms of both *tanzīh*, Transcendence or otherness, and *tashbīh*, Immanence or similitude. See William Chittick, *The Sufi Path of Knowledge: Ibn ʿArabi's Metaphysics of Imagination* (Albany: SUNY Press, 1989).

18 See Naquib al-Attas, *Islam and Secularism* (Lahore: Suhail Academy, 1997) and Seyyed Hossein Nasr, "Religion and Secularism, their Meaning and Manifestation in Islamic History," in his *Islamic Life and Thought* (Albany: SUNY Press, 1981), pp. 7-15.

19 See Barbara Metcalf's translation, *Perfecting Women: Maulanā Ashraf ʿAlī Thanawī's Bihishti Zewar: a Partial Translation with Commentary* (Berkeley: University of California Press, 1990).

20 Seyyed Hossein Nasr, *The Need for a Sacred Science* (Albany: SUNY Press, 1993), p. 17-18.

21 An important exception is the work of Barbara Metcalf, especially in her work *Islamic Revival in British India: Deoband, 1860-1900* (Princeton: Princeton University Press, 1982), where she also addresses the ideas of other important traditional schools.

22 In the last twenty years, a gradual politicization of many Deobandī schools in Pakistan has taken place, which has resulted in a form of Deobandism which is akin to a militant Wahhābism and is quite removed from the traditional Sufi piety of the founders of Deoband. On this, see Ahmad Rashid, *Taliban: Militant Islam, Oil, and Fundamentalism in Central Asia* (New Haven: Yale University Press, 2000).

23 See Seyyed Vali Reza Nasr, *Mawdudi and the Making of the Islamic Revivalism* (Oxford: Oxford University Press, 1995), p. 159.

24 *Islamic Spirituality: Foundations*, ed. S. H. Nasr (New York: Crossroad Publications, 1991), pp. 294-307.

25 His best-known biography is by his disciple Khwāja ʿAzīz al-Ḥasan Majdhūb, *Ashraf al-Sawāniḥ* (Multan, 1416 AH) in four volumes.

26 Maulanā Ashraf ʿAlī Thanvī, *Answer to Modernism*, trans. Muhammad Hasan Askari and Karrar Husain (Karachi: Maktaba Darululoom, 1976; reprint, Delhi, 1981).

27 It should be noted that in the later centuries in the Sunnī world *kalām* came to have a more comprehensive meaning and scope than did the purely dialectical theology of an al-Ashʿarī, and came to possess elements taken from *falsafa* (philosophy), *ḥikma* (theosophy), and *taṣawwuf* (Sufism). This is especially true of the Indian Subcontinent, where mainstream theology after Shāh Walī Allāh came to include even the ideas of Mullā Ṣadrā (1571-1640) and especially Ibn al- ʿArabī.

28 Thanvī, *Answer to Modernism*, p. 1.

29 *Ibid.*, p. 2.

30 Maulanā Thanvī adds that the model of such a book has already been published by Ḥusain al-Jasr al-Tarabulisī under the title *Al-Risāla al-ḥāmidiyya*.

31 Thanvī, *Answer to Modernism*, p. 5.

32 *Ibid.*, p. 9.

33 *Ibid.*, p. 12.

34 *Ibid.*, p. 14.

35 S. H. Nasr, *Traditional Islam in the Modern World*, p. 15.

36 Thanvī, *Answer to Modernism*, p. 17.

37 *Ibid.*, p. 18.

38 *Ibid.*, p. 20.

39 *Ibid.*, p. 21.

40 *Ibid.*, p. 23.

41 *Ibid.*, p. 25.

42 *Ibid.*, p. 25.

43 *Ibid.*, p. 26.

44 *Ibid.*, p. 27.

45 *Ibid.*, p. 29.

46 *Ibid.*, p. 35.

47 *Ibid.*, p. 35.

48 Also known by the title *Sharḥ al-hidāyat al-athīriyya*, this is Mullā Ṣadrā's best-known work in the Indian Subcontinent and is on the syllabi of the major *madrasas* to this day, including Deoband.

49 Thanvī, *Answer to Modernism*, p. 50.

50 *Ibid.*, p. 51.

51 *Ibid.*, p. 54.

52 *Ibid.*, p. 54.

53 *Ibid.*, p. 55.

54 *Ibid.*, p. 106.

55 *Ibid.*, p. 56.

56 *Ibid.*, p. 58.

57 *Ibid.*, p. 59.

58 *Ibid.*, p. 63.

59 *Ibid.*, p. 63.

60 *Ibid.*, p. 67.

61 Scholars of *ḥadīth* (sayings of the Prophet Muḥammad).

62 Scholars of *fiqh* (jurisprudence).

63 Thanvī, *Answer to Modernism*, pp. 68-9.

64 For Maulanā Thanvī's elaborate treatment of esoteric and metaphysical subjects, see

his *Al-Takashshuf ʿan muhimmat al-taṣawwuf* (Deoband, 1972).

65 Thanvī, *Answer to Modernism*, p. 96.

66 The rising of the sun from the West and the breaking of the barrier of Gog and Magog from the North are two Islamic eschatological beliefs that are considered as signs of the end of times, according to certain Qur´ānic verses and prophetic traditions.

67 Thanvī, *Answer to Modernism*, p. 113.

68 *Ibid.*, p. 117-18.

69 This can be seen in the contrasting phenomena of the resurgence of religion in the West and the rise of postmodernist philosophy that critiques the whole modernist enterprise.

70 As is evidenced, for example, by the tremendous popularity of Eastern spirituality and New Age subjects.

Part II

Historical Dimensions

Chapter 4

Recollecting the Spirit of *Jihād* [1]

Reza Shah-Kazemi

> When we think how few men of real religion there are, how small the number of defenders and champions of the truth—when one sees ignorant persons imagining that the principle of Islam is hardness, severity, extravagance, and barbarity—it is time to repeat these words: "Patience is beautiful, and God is the source of all succor" (*Ṣabr jamīl, wa'Llāhu'l-musta'ān*) (Qur'ān, 12:18).
>
> —Emir ʿAbd al-Qādir al-Jazā'irī[2]

If these words were true in 1860, when the Emir wrote them, they are sadly even truer today. In the aftermath of the earth-shaking events of September 11, many in the West and in the Muslim world are rightly appalled by the fact that the mass-murder perpetrated on that day is being hailed by some Muslims as an act of *jihād*. Only the most deluded souls could regard the suicide attacks as having been launched by "*mujāhidīn*," striking a blow in the name of Islam against legitimate targets in the heartland of the enemy. Despite its evident falsity, the image of Islam conveyed by this disfiguration of Islamic principles is not easily dislodged from the popular imagination in the West. There is an unhealthy and dangerous convergence of perception between, on the one hand, those—albeit a tiny minority—in the Muslim world who see the attacks as part of a necessary anti-Western *jihād*; and on the other, those in the West—unfortunately, not such a tiny minority—who likewise see the attacks as the logical expression of an inherently militant religious tradition, one that is irrevocably opposed to the West.

Although of the utmost importance in principle, it appears to matter little in practice that Muslim scholars have pointed out that the terror attacks are totally devoid of any legitimacy in terms of Islamic law and morality. The relevant legal principles—that *jihād* can only be proclaimed by the most authoritative scholar of jurisprudence in the land in question; that there were no grounds for waging a *jihād* in the given situation; that, even within a legitimate *jihād*, the use of fire as a weapon is prohibited; that the inviolability of non-combatants is always to be strictly observed; that suicide is prohibited in Islam—these principles, and others, have been properly stressed by the appropriate experts of Islamic law (*sharīʿa*); and they have been duly amplified by leaders and statesmen in the Muslim world and the West. Nonetheless, here in the West, the abiding image of "Islamic *jihād*" seems to be determined not so much by legal niceties as by images and stereotypes; in particular, in the immediate aftermath of the attacks, the potent juxtaposition of two scenes: the apocalyptic carnage at "Ground Zero"—where the Twin Towers used to stand; and mobs of enraged Muslims bellowing anti-Western slogans to the refrain of "*Allāhu Akbar.*"

In such a situation, where the traditional spirit of Islam, and of the meaning, role and significance of *jihād* within it, is being distorted beyond recognition, it behooves all those who stand opposed both to media stereotypes of "jihadism" and to those misguided fanatics who provide the material for the stereotypes, to denounce in the strongest possible terms all forms of terrorism that masquerade as *jihād*. Many, though, will understandably be asking the question: if this is a false *jihād*, what is true *jihād*? They should be given an answer.[3]

Islamic Principles and Muslim Practices

In a previous essay of this volume, David Dakake has established the traditional Islamic principles which reveal the totally un-Islamic nature of this ideology of "jihadism." We will complement this critique with images, actions, deeds, personalities, and episodes that exemplify the principles in question, thereby putting flesh and blood on the bare bones of theory. For the salience of intellectual argument, especially in the domain being considered here, is immeasurably deepened through corroboration by historically recorded cases where the spirit of authentic *jihād* is vividly enacted; and the pretensions of the self-styled warriors of Islam can be more acutely perceived in the light cast by true *mujāhidīn*.

There is a rich treasure of chivalry from which to draw for this purpose in Muslim history. What follows is a series of scenes drawn from this tradition which might serve as illustrations of key Qur´ānic and prophetic values which pertain to principled warfare. For it is one thing to quote Qur´anic verses; quite another to see them embodied in action.

As regards the very idea of principled warfare, it is no exaggeration to say that, throughout the Middle Ages, the very name "Saladin" was a byword for chivalry, and this remains to some extent true even to this day. The contemporary chronicles—by Muslims and Christians alike—that describe his campaigns and his consistent fidelity to the most noble principles of dignified warfare speak volumes. Again and again, often in the face of treachery by his adversaries, Saladin responded with magnanimity and justice. Suffice it to draw attention to his forbearance, mercy, and generosity at the moment of his greatest triumph: the reconquest of Jerusalem on Friday

2nd October, 1187, a memorable day indeed, being 27th of Rajab—the anniversary of the Prophet's *Laylat al-Mi'rāj*, his ascent through the heavens from Jerusalem itself. After detailing many acts of kindness and charity, the Christian chronicler Ernoul writes:

> Then I shall tell you of the great courtesy which Saladin showed to the wives and daughters of knights, who had fled to Jerusalem when their lords were killed or made prisoners in battle. When these ladies were ransomed and had come forth from Jerusalem, they assembled and went before Saladin crying mercy. When Saladin saw them he asked who they were and what they sought. And it was told him that they were the dames and damsels of knights who had been taken or killed in battle. Then he asked what they wished, and they answered for God's sake have pity on them; for the husbands of some were in prison, and of others were dead, and they had lost their lands, and in the name of God let him counsel and help them. When Saladin saw them weeping he had great compassion for them, and wept himself for pity. And he bade the ladies whose husbands were alive to tell him where they were captives, and as soon as he could go to the prisons he would set them free. And all were released wherever they were found. After that he commanded that to the dames and damsels whose lords were dead there should be handsomely distributed from his own treasure, to some more and others less, according to their estate. And he gave them so much that they gave praise to God and published abroad the kindness and honor which Saladin had done to them.[4]

Saladin's magnanimity at this defining moment of history will always be contrasted with the barbaric sacking of the city and indiscriminate murder of its inhabitants by the Christian Crusaders in 1099. His lesson of mercy has been well expressed in the words of his biographer, Stanley Lane-Poole:

> One recalls the savage conquest by the first Crusaders in 1099, when Godfrey and Tancred rode through streets choked with the dead and the dying, when defenseless Moslems were tortured, burnt, and shot down in cold blood on the towers and roof of the Temple, when the blood of wanton massacre defiled the honor of Christendom and stained the scene where once the gospel of love and mercy had been preached. "Blessed are the merciful, for they shall obtain mercy" was a forgotten beatitude when the Christians made shambles of the Holy City. Fortunate were the merciless, for they obtained mercy at the hands of the Moslem Sultan .... If the taking of Jerusalem were the only fact known about Saladin, it were enough to prove him the most chivalrous and great-hearted conqueror of his own, and perhaps of any, age.[5]

Saladin, though exceptional, was but expressing essentially Islamic principles of conduct, as laid down by the Qur'ān and the Prophet. These principles of conduct were exemplified in another telling incident which occurred some fifty years before Saladin's victory; a mass conversion of Christians to Islam took place, as a direct result of the exercise, by unknown "Saracens," of the cardinal Muslim virtue of compassion. A Christian monk, Odo of Deuil, has bequeathed to history a valuable record of the event; being openly antagonistic to the Islamic faith, his account is all the more reliable. After being defeated by the Turks in Phyrgia in 543/1147, the remnants of Louis VII's army, together with a few thousand pilgrims, reached the port of Attalia. The sick, the wounded and the pilgrims had to be left behind by Louis, who gave his Greek allies 500 marks to take care of these people until reinforcements arrived. The Greeks stole away with the money, abandoning the pilgrims and the wounded to the ravages of starvation and disease, and fully expecting those who survived to be finished off by the Turks. However, when the Turks arrived and saw the plight of the defenseless pilgrims, they took pity on them, fed and watered them, and tended to their needs. This act of compassion resulted in the wholesale conversion of the pilgrims to Islam. Odo comments:

> Avoiding their co-religionists who had been so cruel to them, they went in safety among the infidels who had compassion upon them .... Oh kindness more cruel than all treachery! They gave them bread but robbed them of their faith, though it is certain that, contented with the services they [the Muslims] performed, they compelled no one among them to renounce his religion.[6]

The last point is crucial in respect of two key Islamic principles: that no one is ever to be forced into converting to Islam; and that virtue must be exercised with no expectation of reward. On the one hand, "There is no compulsion in religion" (2:256); and on the other, the righteous are those who "feed, for love of Him, the needy, the orphan, the captive, [saying] we feed you only for the sake of God; we desire neither reward nor thanks from you" (76:8-9).

The "Ontological Imperative" of Mercy

Mercy, compassion, and forbearance are certainly key aspects of the authentic spirit of *jihād*; it is not simply a question of fierceness in war, it is much more about knowing when fighting is unavoidable, how the fight is to be conducted, and to exercise, whenever possible, the virtues of mercy and gentleness. The following verses are relevant in this regard: "Warfare is ordained for you, though it is hateful unto you" (2:216); "Muḥammad is the messenger of God; and those with him are fierce against the disbelievers, and merciful amongst themselves" (48:29); "And fight in the way of God those who fight you, but do not commit aggression. God loveth not the aggressors" (2:190). The Prophet is told in the Qur´ān: "It was by the mercy of God that thou wast lenient to them; if thou hadst been stern and fierce of heart they would have dispersed from around thee" (3:159).

Repeatedly in the Qur´ān one is brought back to the overriding imperative of manifesting mercy and compassion wherever possible. This is a principle that relates not so much to legalism as to the deepest nature of things; for, in the Islamic perspective, compassion is the very essence of the Real. A famous saying of the Prophet tells us that, written on the very Throne of God are the words, "My mercy takes precedence over My Wrath." Mercy and compassion (*raḥma*) express the fundamental nature of God. Therefore nothing can escape from divine mercy: "*My compassion encompasses all things*" (7:156; emphasis added). The name of God, *al-Raḥmān*, is coterminous with Allāh: "Call upon Allāh or call upon al-Raḥmān" (17: 10). The divine creative force is, again and again in the Qur´ān, identified with *al-Raḥmān*; and the principle of revelation itself, likewise, is identified with this same divine quality. The chapter of the Qur´ān named *al-Raḥmān* (55) begins thus: "Al-Raḥmān, taught the Qur´ān, created man."

This "ontological imperative" of mercy must always be borne in mind when considering any issue connected with warfare in Islam. The examples of merciful magnanimity given above are not only to be seen as instances of individual virtue, but also and above all, as natural fruits of this "ontological imperative"; and no one manifested this imperative so fully as did the Prophet himself. Indeed, Saladin's magnanimity at Jerusalem can be seen as an echo of the Prophet's conduct at his conquest of Mecca. As the huge Muslim army approached Mecca in triumphal procession, a Muslim leader, Saᶜd ibn Ubada, to whom the Prophet had given his standard, called out to Abu Sufyān, leader of the Quraysh of Mecca, who knew that there was no chance of resisting this army:

> "O Abū Sufyān, this is the day of slaughter! The day when the inviolable shall be violated! The day of God's abasement of Quraysh" .... "O Messenger of God," cried Abū Sufyān when he came within earshot, "hast thou commanded the slaying of thy people?—and he repeated to him what Saᶜd had said. "I adjure thee by God," he added, "on behalf of thy people, for thou art of all men the greatest in filial piety, the most merciful, the most beneficent." "This is the day of mercy," said the Prophet, "the day on which God hath exalted Quraysh."[7]

The Quraysh, having full reason to be fearful, given the intensity of their persecution of the early Muslims, and their continuing hostility and warfare against them after the enforced migration of the Muslims to Medina, were granted a general amnesty; many erstwhile enemies were thereby converted into stalwart Muslims. This noble conduct is embodied in the following verse from the Qur´ān: "The good deed and the evil deed are not alike. Repel the evil deed with one which is better, then lo! He, between whom and thee there was enmity [will become] as though he were a bosom friend" (41:34).

The principle of "no compulsion in religion" was referred to above. It is to be noted that, contrary to the still prevalent misconception that Islam was spread by the sword, the military campaigns and conquests of the Muslim armies were on the whole carried out in such an exemplary manner that the conquered peoples became attracted by the religion which so impressively disciplined its armies, and whose adherents so scrupulously respected the principle of freedom of worship. Paradoxically, the very freedom and respect given by the Muslim conquerors to believers of different faith-communities intensified the process of conversion to Islam. Arnold's classic work, *The Preaching of Islam*, remains one of the best refutations of the idea that Islam was spread by forcible conversion. His comprehensive account of the spread of Islam in all the major regions of what is now the Muslim world demonstrates beyond doubt that the growth and spread of the religion was of an essentially peaceful nature, the two most important factors in accounting for conversion to Islam being Sufism and trade. The mystic and the merchant were the most successful "missionaries" of Islam.

One telling document cited in his work sheds light on the nature of the mass conversion of one group, the Christians of the Persian province of Khurāsān; and may be taken as indicative of the conditions under which Christians, and non-Muslims in general, converted to Islam. This is the letter of the Nestorian Patriarch, Isho-yabh III to Simeon, Metropolitan of Rev-Ardashir, Primate of Persia:

> Alas, alas! Out of so many thousands who bore the name of Christians, not even one single victim was consecrated unto God by the shedding of his blood for the true faith. (The Arabs) attack not the Christian faith, but on the contrary, they favor our religion, do honor to our priests and the saints of our Lord and confer benefits on churches and monasteries. Why then have your people of Merv abandoned their faith for the sake of these Arabs?[8]

This honoring of Christian priests, saints, churches, and monasteries flows directly from the practice of the Prophet—witness, among other things, the treaty he concluded with the monks of St. Catherine's monastery in Sinai;[9] and it is likewise rooted in clear verses relating to the inviolability of all places "wherein the name of God is oft-invoked." Indeed, in the verse giving permission to the Muslims to begin to fight back in self-defense against the Meccans, the need to protect all such places of worship, and not just mosques, is tied to the reason for the necessity of warfare:

> Permission [to fight] is given to those who are being fought, for they have been wronged, and surely God is able to give them victory; those who have been expelled from their homes unjustly, only because they said: Our Lord is God. Had God not driven back some by means of others, monasteries, churches,

synagogues and mosques—wherein the name of God is oft-invoked—would assuredly have been destroyed (22:39-40).

Islam and "The People of the Book": Tolerance or Terrorism?

The long and well-authenticated tradition of tolerance in Islam springs directly from the spirit of this and many other verses of similar import. We observe one of the most striking historical expressions of this tradition of tolerance—striking in the contrast it provides with the intolerance that so frequently characterized the Christian tradition—in the fate of Spanish Jewry under Islamic rule. Before looking at this particular case, we should note that, in general terms, active, systematic persecution of Jews is virtually unknown under Muslim rule. It is important to stress this fact in the strongest possible terms in the present context, and to debunk the pernicious lie that is circulating in our times, the lie that there is in Islam an inherent, deep-rooted, theologically sanctioned hostility to Judaism. One must not regard the present anger on the part of most Muslims against the actions of those who support Israeli policies as some atavistic resurgence of a putative anti-Semitism ingrained in the Islamic view of the world. Today, it is the extremists on both sides—that is the "jihadists" and the Zionists—who share an interest in promoting this myth of an intrinsically and eternally anti-Jewish Islam; it is of the utmost importance to show the falsity of this notion.

One should also add here that it is not just the "moderates" on both sides who come together for the sake of peace and justice in opposing this false characterization of Muslim-Jewish relations; it is also the lovers of traditional, orthodox Judaism that come together with those from other religions, to denounce, for the sake of veracity, that deviation from Judaism which many Jews believe Zionism represents. Thus we find such groups as the Neturei Karta—traditional Jews opposed to Zionism on irrefutable theological grounds—joining hands with Muslim human rights groups to defend the legitimate rights of the Palestinians against the injustices perpetrated against them in the Holy Land.[10] One must take care to distinguish, therefore, not only between Judaism and Zionism, but also between legitimate opposition to particular policies of the state of Israel—policies that reflect and embody Zionist aspirations in different degrees—and illegitimate "*jihād*" against Jews or Westerners simply on account of the fact that they are Jews or Westerners. The first expresses a legitimate grievance; the second makes of this grievance the pretext for terrorism.

As regards the refutation of the myth that Muslim-Jewish relations have traditionally been antagonistic and oppressive, a cursory perusal of the historical record suffices. Even so fierce a critic of Islam as Bernard Lewis cannot but confirm the facts of history as regards the true character of Muslim-Jewish relations until recent times. In his book, *The Jews of Islam*, he writes that even though there was a certain level of discrimination against Jews and Christians under Muslim rule,

> Persecution, that is to say, violent and active repression, was rare and atypical. Jews and Christians under Muslim rule were not normally called upon to suffer martyrdom for their faith. They were not often obliged to make the choice, which confronted Muslims and Jews in reconquered Spain, between exile, apostasy and death. They were not subject to any major territorial or occupational restrictions, such as were the common lot of Jews in premodern Europe.[11]

He then adds the important point that this pattern of tolerance continued to characterize the nature of Muslim rule vis-à-vis Jews and Christians until modern times, with very minor exceptions.

It is not out of place to note here that the phenomenon of anti-Semitism has absolutely nothing to do with Islam. It was, as Professor Schleifer notes, "Church Triumphant"—that is the Byzantine Church which triumphed over the Roman Empire, and founded its new capital in Constantinople in the fourth century—it was this Church that was to "unleash upon the world the phenomenon of anti-Semitism. For if we are to differentiate between the vicissitudes which any minority community may endure, and a 'principled' and systematic hostility, then one can boldly state, with the consensus of modern historians, that anti-Semitism originated as a Christian phenomenon."[12]

The story of anti-Semitism in Europe—the violent episodes of what today would be labeled "ethnic cleansing"—is too well-known to need repeating here. But it should be borne in mind that at the same time as the Christian West was indulging in periodic anti-Jewish pogroms, the Jews were experiencing what some Jewish historians themselves have termed a kind of "golden age" under Muslim rule. As Erwin Rosenthal writes, "The Talmudic age apart, there is perhaps no more formative and positive time in our long and checkered history than that under the empire of Islam."[13]

One particularly rich episode in this golden period was experienced by the Jews of Muslim Spain. As has been abundantly attested by historical records, the Jews enjoyed not just freedom from oppression, but also an extraordinary revival of cultural, religious, theological, and mystical creativity. As Titus Burckhardt writes, "The greatest beneficiaries of Islamic rule were the Jews, for in Spain (*sephārād* in Hebrew) they enjoyed their finest intellectual flowering since their dispersal from Palestine to foreign lands."[14] Such great Jewish luminaries as Maimonides and Ibn Gabirol wrote their philosophical works in Arabic, and were fully "at home" in Muslim Spain.[15] With the expulsion, murder, or forced conversion of all Muslims and Jews following the *reconquista* of Spain—brought to completion with the fall of

Granada in 1492—it was to the Ottomans that the exiled Jews turned for refuge and protection. They were welcomed in Muslim lands throughout North Africa, joining the settled and prosperous Jewish communities already there, while also establishing new Jewish communities.

It was at this time also that Jews were suffering intense persecution in central Europe; they likewise looked to the Muslim Ottomans for refuge. Many Jews fleeing from persecution in central Europe would have received letters like the following, from Rabbi Isaac Tzarfati, who reached the Ottomans just before they captured Constantinople in 1453. This was his reply to those Jews of central Europe who were calling out for help:

> Listen, my brethren, to the counsel I will give you. I too was born in Germany and studied Torah with the German rabbis. I was driven out of my native country and came to the Turkish land, which is blessed by God and filled with all good things. Here I found rest and happiness.... Here in the land of the Turks we have nothing to complain of. We are not oppressed with heavy taxes, and our commerce is free and unhindered.... every one of us lives in peace and freedom. Here the Jew is not compelled to wear a yellow hat as a badge of shame, as is the case in Germany, where even wealth and great fortune are a curse for the Jew because he therewith arouses jealousy among the Christians.... Arise, my brethren, gird up your loins, collect your forces, and come to us. Here you will be free of your enemies, here you will find rest....[16]

Given the fact that so much of today's jihadist propaganda is directed against the Jews, it is important to stress that this tolerance of the Jews under Muslim rule is one expression of an underlying theological harmony between the two religions—a harmony that is conspicuously absent when one compares Christian and Jewish theology. Islam was never considered the messianic fulfillment of Judaism, as was Christianity; it was put forward as a restoration of that primordial Abrahamic faith of which both Judaism and Christianity were alike expressions. Islam calls adherents of both faiths back to that pristine monotheism; far from rejecting their prophets, the Qur´ān asserts that all the prophets came with one and the same message, and that therefore there should be no distinction made between any of the prophets:

> Say: We believe in God and that which is revealed unto us, and that which is revealed unto Abraham and Ishmael and Isaac and Jacob and the tribes, and that which was given unto Moses and Jesus and the prophets from their Lord. We make no distinction between any of them, and unto Him we have submitted (3:84).

The consequences of this acceptance of the pre-Qur´ānic scriptures—albeit conditioned by the need to beware of certain "distortions" (*taḥrīf*), distortions which, however, the Qur´ān does not specify—these consequences were far-reaching as regards theological relations between Muslims and Jews. As the Jewish scholar Mark Cohen notes:

> Rabbinic exegesis of the Bible—so repugnant to Christian theologians—bothered Muslim clerics only insofar as it distorted pristine Abrahamic monotheism. Thus the Islamic polemic against the rabbis was much less virulent and had far less serious repercussions. The Talmud was burned in Paris, not in Cairo or Baghdad.[17]

Therefore, the refusal of the Jews to follow the *sharīʿa* was not a challenge to Islamic belief; this in contrast to the Jewish rejection of Christ as messiah, which not only challenged a cardinal tenet of Christian dogma, but also deeply insulted Christian faith and sensibility. Whereas in Christendom, the Jews were reviled as the killers of Jesus, in Islam, the Jews were "protected," as *dhimmīs*,[18] by the very Law that they refused to follow for themselves. To quote Cohen again:

> More secure than their brethren in the Christian West, the Jews of Islam took a correspondingly more conciliatory view of their masters. In Europe, the Jews nurtured a pronounced hatred for the Christians, whom they considered to be idolaters, subject to the anti-pagan discriminatory provisions of the ancient Mishnah.... The Jews of Islam had a markedly different attitude towards the religion of their masters. Staunch Muslim opposition to polytheism convinced Jewish thinkers like Maimonides of Islam's unimpeachable monotheism. This essentially "tolerant" view of Islam echoed Islam's own respect for the Jewish "people of the Book"....[19]

In presenting this argument, one is not trying to argue for the supremacy of Islam over Christianity, nor simply to apportion blame for the phenomenon of anti-Semitism, nor to argue that there is an inherent and insuperable antagonism between Christianity and Judaism. Rather, the aim in making these points is to try and demonstrate the irony as well as the falsity of the claim that Islam is inherently anti-Jewish. Both theology and history point in the opposite direction: that there is a profound affinity between the two faiths, both in theory and in practice. If there are theological problems that need to be resolved, and a history of intolerance to exorcise, the onus falls much more on Christianity than Islam. For Jews found sanctuary and dignity in Islam, not persecution; fleeing to the Muslim world from the not infrequent campaigns of Christian persecution, they were met with tolerance and respect. It is this that must be stressed in any discussion of the historical and theological background to contemporary Jewish-Muslim relations, given the grave challenges to these relations posed by the propaganda of the extremists on both sides, that is, the jihadists and the islamophobes.

The tolerance extended by Islam to the "People of the Book" (and, indeed, all believers, including Hindus, Buddhists, and Zoroastrians) should be seen, again, as arising not only out of a sense of virtue or justice or expediency on the part of the majority of the rulers and dynasties throughout Muslim history—and thus as some kind of interesting historical prefiguration of modern, secular tolerance; rather, the fact that this phenomenon of Muslim tolerance is so clearly defined must be seen as organically connected to the spirit of the Qur´ānic revelation, a spirit grasped in depth by traditional Muslims, and deliberately ignored or subverted by modern extremists of both the religious and secular varieties. This spirit is well expressed in the following verses:

> Truly those who believe, and the Jews, and the Christians, and the Sabeans—whoever believeth in God and the Last Day and performeth virtuous deeds—surely their reward is with their Lord, and no fear shall come upon them, neither shall they grieve (2:62).

> Of the People of the Scripture there is a staunch community who recite the revelations of God in the watches of the night, falling prostrate. They believe in God and the Last Day, and enjoin right conduct and forbid indecency, and vie with one another in good works. These are of the righteous. And whatever good they do, they will not be denied it; and God knows the pious (3:113-114).

Not an Eye for an Eye: The Emir ʿAbd al-Qādir

The life-blood of terrorism is hatred; and this hatred is often in turn the disfigured expression of grievance—a grievance that may be legitimate even when the manner of addressing it is not.[20] In the present day, few doubt that the ongoing injustices in Palestine, Iraq, Chechnya and other parts of the Muslim world give rise to legitimate grievances; but there is nothing in Islam that justifies the killing or injuring of civilians, nor of perpetrating any excess as a result of hatred, even if that hatred is based on legitimate grievances. The pursuit of justice must be conducted in accordance with justice; the means should not undermine the end: "O ye who believe, be upright for God, witnesses in justice; and let not hatred of a people cause you to be unjust. Be just—that is closer to piety" (5:8).

Going back to the recent past, the principle here established is perfectly exemplified in the conduct of the Emir ʿAbd al-Qādir, leader of the Algerian Muslims in their heroic resistance to French colonial aggression between 1830 and 1847. The French were guilty of the most barbaric crimes in their "*mission civilisatrice*"; the Emir responded not with bitter vengefulness and enraged fury but with dispassionate propriety and principled warfare. At a time when the French were indiscriminately massacring entire tribes, when they were offering their soldiers a ten-franc reward for every pair of Arab ears, and when severed Arab heads were regarded as trophies of war, the Emir manifested his magnanimity, his unflinching adherence to Islamic principle, and his refusal to stoop to the level of his "civilized" adversaries, by issuing the following edict:

> Every Arab who has in his possession a Frenchman is bound to treat him well and to conduct him to either the Khalifa or the Emir himself, as soon as possible. In cases where the prisoner complains of ill treatment, the Arab will have no right to any reward.[21]

When asked what the reward was for a live French soldier, the Emir replied: "eight douros." When asked what the reward was for a severed French head, the reply was: "twenty-five blows of the baton on the soles of the feet." Many in his ranks, including within the council of *khalīfas*, were keen to respond in kind to the French atrocities, to "fight fire with fire"; but the Emir could not be swayed from what he knew was right, and resisted all calls for revenge. Indeed, he set the highest of standards himself in regard to the need to transcend the human desire for revenge. A captured and wounded French soldier who had himself thrice inflicted wounds on the Emir in previous battles was accorded medical treatment and taken care of in exemplary fashion.[22] Such stories and incidents abound in the astonishing story of the Emir's war of national self-defense. One understands why General Bugeaud, Governor-General of Algeria, referred to the Emir not only as "a man of genius whom history should place alongside Jugurtha," but also as "a kind of prophet, the hope of all fervent Muslims."[23] When he was finally defeated and brought to France, before being exiled to Damascus, the Emir received hundreds of French admirers who had heard of his bravery and his nobility; the visitors by whom he was most deeply touched, though, were French officers who came to thank him for the treatment they received at his hands when they were his prisoners in Algeria.[24]

Also highly relevant to our theme is the Emir's famous defense of the Christians in Damascus in 1860. Now defeated and in exile, the Emir spent his time praying and teaching. When civil war broke out between the Druzes and the Christians in Lebanon, the Emir heard that there were signs of an impending attack on the Christians of Damascus. He wrote letters to all the Druze shaykhs, requesting them not to "make offensive movements against a place with the inhabitants of which you have never before been at enmity." Here we have an expression of the cardinal principle of warfare in Islam: never to initiate hostilities: "And fight in the way of God those who fight you, but do not commit aggression. God loveth not the aggressors" (2:190).

The Emir's letters proved to no avail. When the Druzes were approaching the Christian quarters of the city, the Emir confronted them, urging them to observe the rules of religion and of human justice.

> "What," they shouted, "you, the great slayer of Christians, are you come out to prevent us from slaying them in our turn? Away!"
> "If I slew the Christians," he shouted in reply, "it was ever in accordance with our law—the Christians who had declared war against me, and were arrayed in arms against our faith."[25]

This had no effect upon the mob. In the end, the Emir and his small band of followers sought out the terrified Christians, giving them refuge, first in his own home, and then, as the numbers grew, in the citadel. It is estimated that no less than fifteen thousand Christians were saved by the Emir in this action; and it is important to note that in this number were included all the ambassadors and consuls of the European powers. As Churchill prosaically puts it:

> All the representatives of the Christian powers then residing in Damascus, without one single exception, had owed their lives to him. Strange and unparalleled destiny! An Arab had thrown his guardian aegis over the outraged majesty of Europe. A descendant of the Prophet had sheltered and protected the Spouse of Christ.[26]

The French Consul, representative of the state that was still very much in the process of colonizing the Emir's homeland, owed his life to the Emir. For this true warrior of Islam, there was no bitterness, resentment or revenge, only the duty to protect the innocent, and all the "People of the Book" who lived peacefully within the lands of Islam. It is difficult to conceive of a greater contrast between the Emir's conduct and the present self-styled *mujāhidīn*, who indiscriminately portray the West as the enemy *tout court*, and perpetrate correspondingly illegitimate acts against Westerners. The Emir's action exemplifies well the Qur´ānic verse: "God forbiddeth you not from dealing kindly and justly with those who fought not against you on account of your religion, nor drove you out of your homes. Truly God loveth those who are just" (60:8).

It is interesting to note that another great warrior of Islam, Imām Shāmil of Dagestan, hero of the wars against Russian imperialism,[27] wrote a letter to the Emir, when he heard of his defense of the Christians. He praised the Emir for his noble act, thanking God that there were still Muslims who behaved according to the spiritual ideals of Islam, the ideals of what Joseph E. B. Lumbard has called "the *iḥsānī* intellectual tradition" in this volume:[28]

> I was astonished at the blindness of the functionaries who have plunged into such excesses, forgetful of the words of the Prophet, peace be upon him, "Whoever shall be unjust towards a tributary,[29] who shall do him wrong, who shall lay on him any charge beyond his means, and finally who shall deprive him of anything without his own consent, it is I who will be his accuser in the day of judgment."[30]

The Greater *Jihād*

While the Emir fought French colonialism militarily, in the following century another great Sufi master in Algeria, Shaykh Aḥmad al-ʿAlawī, chose to resist with a peaceful strategy, but one which pertained no less to *jihād*, in the principial sense of the term. One has to remember that the literal meaning of the word *jihād* is "effort" or struggle, and that the "greater" *jihād* was defined by the Prophet as the *jihād al-nafs*, the war against the soul. The priority thus accorded to inward, spiritual effort over all outward endeavors must never be lost sight of in any discussion of *jihād*. Physical fighting is the lesser *jihād* and only has meaning in the context of that unremitting combat against inner vices, the devil within, that has been called the greater *jihād*. This spiritual and moral struggle is what truly articulates the "spirit of *jihād*"; everything else flows by way of consequence from this inner refusal to allow the lower elements of the soul from dominating the will, the intelligence, and the personality of the individual.

One contemporary Sufi master vividly contrasts the kind of inner warfare that characterizes the true "warriors of the spirit" from the mass of ordinary believers. He does so in connection with the Qur´ānic distinction, within the category of those who are saved in the Hereafter, between the "companions of the right" (*aṣḥāb al-yamīn*) and "the foremost" (*al-sābiqūn*) (56:8-10):

> Every Muslim is at war with the devil. As regards *those of the right*, however, this warfare is desultory and intermittent, with many armistices and many compromises. Moreover the devil is aware that as fallen men they are already to a certain extent within his grasp, and having by definition no faith in the Divine Mercy, he cannot foresee that they will escape from his clutches in the life to come. But as regards *the foremost*, he feels them actually throwing off his domination in the present, and they even carry the war into his territory. The result is a terrible retaliation ... [31]

The individual's moral and spiritual effort in this inner struggle is a necessary but not sufficient condition for victory; only by means of heaven-sent weapons can the war be won: sacred rites, meditations, incantations, invocations—all of which are summed up in the term "remembrance of God" (*dhikr Allāh*). No action can be compared with this remembrance, which the Qur´ān refers to as "greater" or "greatest" (*akbar*): "Recite that which hath been revealed to thee of the Scripture and observe the prayer. Truly prayer preserveth from lewdness and iniquity; but the remembrance of God is greater" (29:45). In many sayings of the Prophet, this remembrance is given primacy over all other practices; the following saying is particularly relevant in the present context. The Prophet asked his companions: "Shall I not tell you about the best and purest of your works for your Lord, and the most exalted of them in degree, and the work which is better for you than silver and gold, and better for you than encountering your enemy, with you striking their necks and them striking your necks?" Upon being asked what this thing is, he replied: "The constant remembrance of God."[32]

In this light, the strategy of the Shaykh al-ʿAlawī can be better appreciated. It was to put first things first, concentrating on the "one thing needful" and leaving the rest in God's hands. It might be seen, extrinsically, as an application, on the plane of society, of the following esoteric principle, enunciated by one of his spiritual forbears, Mulay ʿAlī al-Jamal: "The true way to hurt the enemy is to be occupied with the love of the Friend; on the other hand, if you engage in war with the enemy, he will have obtained what he wanted from you, and at the same time you will have lost the opportunity of loving the Friend."[33]

The Shaykh al-ʿAlawī concentrated on this love of the Friend, and on all those values connected to this imperative of remembrance; doing so to the exclusion of other, more overt forms of resistance, military and political, against the French. The Shaykh's spiritual radiance extended not just to a few disciples but, through his many *muqaddams*, to hundreds of thousands of Muslims whose piety was deepened in ways that are immeasurable.[34] The Shaykh was not directly concerned with political means of liberating his land from the yoke of French rule, for this was but a secondary aspect of the situation, inasmuch as the underlying aim of the French "*mission civilisatrice*" in Algeria was to forge the Algerian personality in the image of French culture.[35] In the measure that one perceives that the real danger of colonialism was cultural and psychological rather than just territorial and political, the spiritual indomitability of the Shaykh and his many followers assumes the dimensions of a signal victory. The French could make no inroads into a mentality that remained inextricably rooted in the spiritual tradition of Islam.

Lest this approach be regarded as a prescription for unconditional quietism, one should note that the great warrior, the Emir himself, would have had no difficulty whatsoever in asserting its validity: for even while outwardly engaging with the enemy on the battlefield, he was never for a moment distracted from his remembrance of the "Friend." The advice of Mulay ʿAlī not to "engage in war with the enemy" concerns above all the inner dimension: not to fight the demon that is within oneself on its own terms, using one's own limited resources, but to defeat it by means of the remembrance of God. Although capable of being expressed on the social plane in terms of overt disavowal of military or political activity, it is also perfectly compatible with an activist stance, such as that adopted by the Emir. There is no contradiction here, only a shift of emphasis, the underlying principle remaining the same. It is only when outward efforts eclipse, marginalize or deny the inner struggle that this underlying principle is absent.

The Emir fought without bitterness and rage; and this explains the absence of any resentment towards the French when he was defeated by them, submitting to the manifest will of God with the same contemplative resignation with which he went into battle in the first place. One finds expressed here a supreme example of the contemplative warrior, engaging the enemy without attachment, that is, acting without being bound in any way by the fruits of action. One may suspect us of romanticizing somewhat, and of overstating the Emir's capacity to deal with the exigencies of a brutal war whilst simultaneously plumbing the depths of contemplative experience; it is therefore useful to present the following account, written by a Frenchman, Léon Roche, who entered the inner circle of the Emir's entourage by pretending to have converted to Islam. During the siege of Ayn Madi in 1838, Roche was traumatized by the fighting and killing, and sought out the Emir; entering his tent, he pleaded with the Emir to help him.

> He calmed me and had me drink an infusion of *schiehh* (a kind of absinthe common in the desert). He supported my head, which I could no longer hold up, on one of his knees. He was squatting in the Arab fashion. I was stretched out at his side. He placed his hands on my head, from which he had removed the *haik* and the *chechias*, and under this gentle touch I soon fell asleep. I awoke well into the night. I opened my eyes and felt revived. The smoky wick of an Arab lamp barely lit the vast tent of the emir. He was standing three steps away from me. He thought I was asleep. His two arms were raised to the height of his head, fully displaying his milky white *bernous* and *haik* which fell in superb folds. His beautiful blue eyes, lined with black lashes, were raised. His lips, slightly open, seemed to be still reciting a prayer but nevertheless were motionless. He had come to an ecstatic state. His aspirations towards heaven were such that he seemed no longer to touch the earth. I had on occasion been granted the honor of sleeping in Abd al-Kader's tent and I had seen him in prayer and been struck by his mystical transports, but on this night he represented for me the most striking image of faith. Thus must the great saints of Christianity have prayed.[36]

From this account one sees that the following "official" description of the Emir, given as the conclusion to a pamphlet defining army regulations in 1839, was not simply pious propaganda:

> Il Hadj Abdel Kader cares not for this world, and withdraws from it as much as his avocations permit.... He rises in the middle of the night to recommend his own soul and the souls of his followers to God. His chief pleasure is in praying to God with fasting, that his sins may be forgiven.... When he administers justice, he hears complaints with the greatest patience.... When he preaches, his words bring tears to all eyes, and melt the hardest hearts.[37]

This remarkable combination of roles—warrior and saint, preacher and judge—recalls perhaps the greatest model of all Muslim *mujāhidīn*, ʿAlī ibn Abī Ṭālib, son-in-law and cousin of the Prophet, the fourth Caliph of Islam and first Shīʿī Imām, unrivalled hero of all the early battles of Islam. His importance in the Islamic firmament can be gauged from the following sayings of the Prophet: "I am the city of knowledge and ʿAlī is its gate." He also said, in a *ḥadīth* bearing the highest degree of authenticity (*mutawātir*): "For whoever has me as his master (*mawlā*), ʿAlī is his master." And the Prophet referred to ʿAlī as having the same rank in relation to him as Aaron had in relation to Moses, except that ʿAlī was not a prophet. This paragon of spiritual wisdom and impeccable virtue stands forth as the most compelling holy warrior in the Islamic tradition. As Frithjof Schuon puts it, "ʿAlī appears above all as the 'Solar Hero,' he is the 'Lion' of God; he personifies the combination of physical heroism on the field of battle with a sanctity wholly detached from the things of the world; he is the personification of the wisdom, both impassive and combative, which the Bhagavad-Gita teaches."[38]

One of the great lessons of principled warfare, of "fighting in the path of God," imparted by ʿAlī was immortalized by Rūmī in his poetic rendering of the famous incident in which ʿAlī sheathed his sword instead of finishing off his defeated enemy, who had spat at him in a last gesture of defiance. Although the immediate spiritual significance of the action is clearly ʿAlī's refusal to kill on the basis of personal anger—the warrior must be detached from self, and fight wholly for God—it is also given a deeper metaphysical meaning by Rūmī. In his *Mathnawī*, Rūmī turns the incident into a sublime commentary on the Qur´ānic verse, "Ye slew them not, but God slew them. And thou (Muḥammad) didst not throw when thou threwest, but God threw" (8:17). The last part of the verse refers to the throwing by the Prophet of a handful of dust in the direction of the enemy before a battle. But the verse as a whole alludes to the reality that the true, ontological agent of all actions is God Himself; man's actions are good only if he is conscious of this, and insofar as he is effaced in this consciousness. Rūmī puts the following words into the mouth of ʿAlī, who replies to the question of the baffled, defeated warrior on the ground: why did you not kill me?

> He said, "I am wielding the sword for God's sake, I am the servant of God, I am not under the command of the body.
>
> I am the Lion of God, I am not the lion of my passion: my deed bears witness to my religion.
>
> In war I am (manifesting the truth of) *thou didst not throw when thou threwest*: I am (but) as the sword, and the wielder is the (Divine) Sun.

> I have removed the baggage of self out of the way, I have deemed (what is) other than God to be non-existence.
>
> I am a shadow, the Sun is my lord; I am the chamberlain, I am not the curtain (which prevents approach) to Him.
>
> I am filled with the pearls of union, like a (jeweled) sword: in battle I make (men) living, not slain.[39]
>
> Blood does not cover the sheen of my sword: how should the wind sweep away my clouds?
>
> I am not a straw, I am a mountain of forbearance and patience and justice: how should the fierce wind carry off the mountain?"[40]

The true warrior of Islam smites the neck of his own anger with the sword of forbearance;[41] the false warrior strikes at the neck of his enemy with the sword of his own unbridled ego. For the first, the spirit of Islam determines *jihād*; for the second, bitter anger, masquerading as *jihād*, determines Islam. The contrast between the two could hardly be clearer.

The episodes recounted here as illustrations of authentic *jihād* should be seen not as representing some unattainably sublime ideal, but as expressive of the sacred norm in the Islamic tradition of warfare; this norm may not always have been applied in practice—one can always find deviations and transgressions—but it was continuously upheld in principle and more often than not gave rise to the kind of chivalry, heroism, and nobility of which we have offered a few of the more striking and famous examples here.

This sacred norm stood out clearly for all to see, buttressed by the values and institutions of traditional Muslim society. For those who look hard enough it can still be discerned through the clouds of passion and ideology. The Emir bewailed the paucity of "champions of truth" in his time; in our own time, we are confronted with an even more grotesque spectacle: the champions of authentic *jihād* being blown to pieces by suicide-bombers claiming to be martyrs for the faith. One of the truly great *mujāhidīn* in the war against the Soviet invaders in Afghanistan, Ahmed Shah Massoud, fell victim to a treacherous attack by two fellow-Muslims, in what was evidently the first stage of the operation that destroyed the World Trade Center. It was a strategic imperative for the planners of the operation to rid the land of its most charismatic leader; a hero who could credibly be used by the West as a figure-head for the revenge attack on Afghanistan that was provoked, anticipated, and hoped for, by the terrorists. The reason why Massoud was so popular was precisely his fidelity to the values of noble warfare in Islam; and it was this very fidelity to that tradition that made him a dangerous enemy of the terrorists—more dangerous, it may be said, than that more abstract enemy, "the West." To present the indiscriminate murder of Western civilians as "*jihād*," the values of true *jihād* needed to be dead and buried.

The murder of Massoud was thus doubly symbolic: he embodied the traditional spirit of *jihād* that needed to be destroyed by those who wished to assume its ruptured mantle; and it was only through suicide—subverting one's own soul—that this destruction, or rather, this apparent destruction, could be perpetrated. The destruction is only apparent in that, on the one hand: "They destroy [but] themselves, they who would ready a pit of fire fiercely burning [for all who have attained to faith]" (85:4-5). [42] And on the other hand: "Say not of those who are slain in the path of God: They are dead. Nay, they are alive, though ye perceive not" (2:154).

Finally, let it be noted that, while it is indeed true that the martyr is promised Paradise, the real martyr (*shahīd*) is one whose death truly bears "witness" (*shahāda*) to the Truth of God. It is consciousness of the Truth that must animate and articulate the spirit of one who "fights in the path of God"; fighting for any cause other than the Truth cannot be called a "*jihād*," just as the one who dies fighting in such a cause cannot be called a "martyr." Only he is a martyr who can say with utter sincerity: "Truly my prayer and my sacrifice, my living and my dying are for God, Lord of all creation" (6: 162).

Notes

1 This is an expanded version of an article first published in the journal *Sacred Web*, no. 8 (2001).

2 This statement was made in a letter written by the Emir in 1860. Quoted in Charles Henry Churchill, *The Life of Abdel Kader* (London: Chapman and Hall, 1867), p. 323.

3 One of the best answers to this question is contained in the series of essays on *jihād* by Abdullah Schleifer. He mounts an excellent critique of the political reduction of *jihād*, using as his basis "traditional Islamic consciousness," and including, as a case-study of *jihād* conducted according to this consciousness, the little known *mujāhid* in the struggle against the colonization of Palestine in the 1920s and 1930s, ʿIzz al-Dīn al-Qassām. This case-study forms part 1 of the series, which was published in the journal *Islamic Quarterly* 23, no. 2 (1979); part 2, "Jihad and Traditional Islamic Consciousness" is in vol. 27, no. 4 (1983); part 3, is in vol. 28, no. 1 (1984); part 4, in vol. 28, no. 2 (1984); and part 5, in vol. 28, no. 3 (1984).

4 Quoted in Stanley Lane-Poole, *Saladin and the Fall of the Kingdom of Jerusalem* (Beirut: Khayats Oriental Reprints, 1964), pp. 232-3 (Originally published in London, 1898). It is not irrelevant to note here that, as Titus Burckhardt says, the Christian "knightly attitude towards women is Islamic in origin" (*Moorish Culture in Spain* [London: Allen & Unwin, 1972], p. 93). Simonde de Sismondi, writing in the early 19th century, asserts that Arabic literature was the source of "that tenderness and delicacy of sentiment and that reverential awe of women which have operated so powerfully on our chivalrous feelings" (*Histoire de la littérature du Midi de l'Europe*, quoted in R. Boase, *The Origin and Meaning of Courtly Love* [Manchester: Manchester University Press, 1977], p. 20).

5 Lane-Poole, *op. cit.*, pp. 233-4.

6 Quoted in Thomas Arnold, *The Preaching of Islam* (London: Luzak, 1935), pp. 88-9.

7 Martin Lings, *Muḥammad: His Life According to the Earliest Sources* (London: Islamic Texts Society and George Allen & Unwin, 1983), pp. 297-8.

8 Arnold, *op. cit.*, pp. 81-2.

9 A copy of the document is displayed to this day in the monastery, which is the oldest continually inhabited convent in Christendom. See J. Bentley, *Secrets of Mount Sinai* (London: Orbis, 1985), pp. 18-19.

10 See their website: http://www.netureikarta.org.

11 Bernard Lewis, *The Jews of Islam* (Princeton: Princeton University Press, 1984), p. 8.

12 A. Schleifer, "Jews and Muslims: A Hidden History," in *The Spirit of Palestine* (Barcelona: Zed, 1994), p. 2.

13 Quoted in Schleifer, *op. cit.*, p. 5.

14 Burckhardt, *op. cit.*, pp. 27-28.

15 Despite the fact that Maimonides suffered at the hands of the Almohads, during a rare episode of persecution in Muslim Spain, the next stage of his career—as physician to Saladin—manifested his continuing loyalty to Muslim rule.

16 Quoted in Schleifer, *op. cit.*, p. 8.

[17] Mark Cohen, "Islam and the Jews: Myth, Counter-Myth, History," *Jerusalem Quarterly*, no. 38 (1986): 135.

[18] A *dhimmī* is a non-Muslim who enjoys the *dhimma*, or "protection" of the Muslim state.

[19] *Ibid.*, p. 137.

[20] For a full treatment of the nature of Muslim grievances see the chapter in this volume by Ejaz Akram entitled "The Muslim World and Globalization: Modernity and the Roots of Conflict."

[21] See Mohamed Chérif Sahli, *Abdelkader: Le Chevalier de la Foi* (Algiers: Entreprise algérienne de presse, 1967), pp. 131-2.

[22] *Ibid.*, pp. 136-7.

[23] Cited in Michel Chodkiewicz, *The Spiritual Writings of Amir ʿAbd al-Kader* (Albany: State University of New York, 1995), p. 2. This selection of texts from the Emir's *Mawāqif* reveals well the other side of the Emir: his inner spiritual life, lived out as a master of Sufism. In this work the Emir comments on Qur´ānic verses and hadiths, as well as upon Ibn ʿArabī's writings, doing so from a rigorously esoteric perspective. Indeed, the Emir was designated as the *wārith al-ʿulūm al-akbariyya*, inheritor of the Akbarī sciences, those sciences pertaining to the Shaykh al-Akbar ("the greatest master"), Ibn ʿArabī. See pp. 20-24 for this little known aspect of the Emir's function.

[24] See Churchill, *op. cit.*, p. 295. There are many testimonies to the Emir's kindness and fairness by French soldiers taken prisoner by him, one of the better known being that of Captain Morisot. See Sahli, *op. cit.*, p. 133.

[25] Churchill, *op. cit.*, p. 314.

[26] *Ibid.*, p. 318.

[27] Like the Emir, Imām Shāmil was regarded with awe not only by his own followers, but also by the Russians; when he was finally defeated and taken to Russia, he was fêted as a hero. Although occasionally embroidered with romanticism, Lesley Blanch's *Sabers of Paradise* (New York: Caroll and Graf, 1960) conveys well the heroic aspect of Shamil's resistance. For a more scholarly account, see Moshe Gammer, *Muslim Resistance to the Tsar: Shamil and the Conquest of Chechnia and Daghestan* (London: Frank Cass, 1994). Our own *Crisis in Chechnia: Russian Imperialism, Chechen Nationalism and Militant Sufism* (London: Islamic World Report, 1995) offers an overview of the Chechen quest for independence from the eighteenth century through to the war of the mid-1990s, with a particular stress on the role of the Sufi brotherhoods in this quest.

[28] See his article in this volume: "The Decline of Knowledge and the Rise of Ideology in the Modern Islamic World."

[29] That is, a *dhimmī*. See note 18 above.

[30] Quoted in Churchill, *op. cit.*, pp. 321-2.

[31] Abū Bakr Sirāj al-Dīn, *The Book of Certainty* (Cambridge: Islamic Texts Society, 1992), p. 80. See also the essay by S. H. Nasr, "The Spiritual Significance of Jihad," ch. 1 of *Traditional Islam in the Modern World* (London: Kegan Paul International, 1987); and also the excellent book by Charles Le Gai Eaton, *Remembering God: Reflections on Islam* (Chicago: ABC International, 2000), especially chs. 7 and 8, which eloquently reveal the anti-traditional spirit that motivates so much of what poses as *jihād* today.

32 This and several other sayings of similar import, together with Qur'ānic verses relating to *dhikr*, are quoted by al-Ghazālī in his *Invocations and Supplications*, trans. K. Nakamura (Cambridge: Islamic Texts Society, 1990), pp. 6-8. See also Ibn ʿAṭā'Allāh al-Iskandarī's remarkable work devoted entirely to the theme of *dhikr*, *The Key to Salvation: A Sufi Manual of Invocation*, trans. Mary Ann Danner (Cambridge: Islamic Texts Society, 1996).

33 Quoted by the Shaykh al-ʿArabī al-Darqāwī, founder of the Darqāwī branch of the Shādhiliyya Sufi order. See *Letters of a Sufi Master*, trans. Titus Burckhardt (Bedfont, Middlesex: Perennial Books, 1969), p. 9.

34 See the essay by Omar Benaissa, "Algerian Sufism in the Colonial Period," in *Algeria: Revolution Revisited*, ed. R. Shah-Kazemi (London: Islamic World Report, 1996), for details of this religious influence of the *ṭarīqa* of the Shaykh on Algerian society; and our own essay, "From Sufism to Terrorism: The Distortion of Islam in the Political Culture of Algeria," in which several points made in the present article are amplified.

35 Alexis de Tocqueville bitterly criticized the assimilationist policy of his government in Algeria. In a parliamentary report of 1847 he wrote that, "We should not at present push them along the path of our own European civilization, but in their own .... We have cut down the number of charities [i.e. religious *waqf* institutions], let schools fall into ruin, closed the colleges [i.e. *madrasas*] .... the recruitment of the men of religion and of the [*Sharīʿa*] law has ceased. We have, in other words, made Muslim society far more miserable, disorganized, barbaric and ignorant than ever it was before it knew us" (Quoted in Charles-Robert Ageron, *Modern Algeria*, trans. Michael Brett [London: Hurst, 1991], p. 21).

36 Léon Roche, *Dix Ans à travers l'Islam* (Paris, 1904), p.140-1. Cited in M. Chodkiewicz, *op. cit.*, p. 4.

37 Cited in Churchill, *op. cit.*, pp. 137-8.

38 Frithjof Schuon, *Islam and the Perennial Philosophy* (London: World of Islam Festival, 1976), p. 101. Schuon also refers to ʿAlī as the "representative *par excellence* of Islamic esotericism" in *The Transcendent Unity of Religions*, 1st ed. (London: Faber and Faber, 1953), p. 59.

39 Cf. the following verse in the Bhagavad-Gita: "Who thinks that he can be a slayer, who thinks that he is slain, both these have no [right] knowledge: He slays not, is not slain" (*Hindu Scriptures*, trans. R. C. Zaehner [London: Dent, 1966], p. 256).

40 *The Mathnawī of Jalāluddīn Rūmī*, trans. R. A. Nicholson (London: Luzac, 1926), Book 1, p. 205, lines 3787-3794. The parentheses are inserted by Nicholson. See Schleifer's comments on Rūmī's account of this episode in "Jihad and Traditional Islamic Consciousness," *op. cit.*, pp. 197-9.

41 As Rūmī says, continuing ʿAlī's discourse; see line 3800, p. 207.

42 We follow Muḥammad Asad's translation of these elliptical verses. See his *The Message of the Qur'ān* (Gibraltar: Dār al-Andalus, 1984), p. 942.

Chapter 5

Roots of Misconception: Euro-American Perceptions of Islam Before and After September 11

Ibrahim Kalin

In the aftermath of September 11, the long and checkered relationship between Islam and the West entered a new phase. The attacks were interpreted as the fulfillment of a prophecy that had been in the consciousness of the West for a long time, i.e., the coming of Islam as a menacing power with a clear intent to destroy Western civilization. Representations of Islam as a violent, militant, and oppressive religious ideology extended from television programs and state offices to schools and the internet. It was even suggested that Makka, the holiest city of Islam, be "nuked" to give a lasting lesson to all Muslims. Although one can look at the widespread sense of anger, hostility, and revenge as a normal human reaction to the abominable loss of innocent lives, the demonization of Muslims is the result of deeper philosophical and historical issues.

In many subtle ways, the long history of Islam and the West, from the theological polemics of Baghdad in the eighth and ninth centuries to the experience of *convivencia* in Andalusia in the twelfth and thirteenth centuries, informs the current perceptions and qualms of each civilization vis-à-vis the other. This paper will examine some of the salient features of this history and argue that the monolithic representations of Islam, created and sustained by a highly complex set of image-producers, think-tanks, academics, lobbyists, policy makers, and media, dominating the present Western conscience, have their roots in the West's long history with the Islamic world. It will also be argued that the deep-rooted misgivings about Islam and Muslims have led and continue to lead to fundamentally flawed and erroneous policy decisions that have a direct impact on the current relations of Islam and the West. The almost unequivocal identification of Islam with terrorism and extremism in the minds of many Americans after September 11 is an outcome generated by both historical misperceptions, which will be analyzed in some detail below, and the political agenda of certain interest groups that see confrontation as the only way to deal with the Islamic world. It is hoped that the following analysis will provide a historical context in which we can make sense of these tendencies and their repercussions for both worlds.

Two major attitudes can be discerned in Western perceptions of Islam. The first and by far the most common view is that of clash and confrontation. Its roots go back to the Christian rejection of Islam as a religion in the eighth century when Islam first arose on the historical scene and was quickly perceived to be a theological and political threat to Christendom. The medieval European view of Islam as a heresy and its Prophet as an impostor provided the religious foundations of the confrontationalist position which has survived up to our own day and gained a new dimension after September 11. In the modern period, the confrontationalist view has been articulated in both religious and non-religious terms, the most famous one being the "clash of civilizations" hypothesis, which envisions the strategic and political conflicts between the Western and Muslim countries in terms of deep religious and cultural differences between the two, and which is analyzed critically by Waleed El-Ansary and Ejaz Akram in this collection. The second view is that of co-existence and accommodation which has become a major alternative only in recent decades although it has important historical precedents in the examples of Emanuel Swedenborg, Goethe, Henry Stubbe, Carlyle, and others. Proponents of the accommodationist view consider Islam to be a sister religion and in fact part of the Abrahamic tradition and prove, in the case of Swedenborg and Goethe, the possibility of envisioning co-existence with Islam and Muslims while remaining true to the word and spirit of Christianity. This position, which will be analyzed very briefly at the end of the essay, marks a new and important chapter in the history of Islam and the West with implications for long-term civilizational co-existence and understanding.

The first part of the essay will look at how Islam was perceived to be a religious heresy first by Christian theologians in the East and then in Europe. Such common views of Islam as the religion of the sword, the Prophet Muḥammad as a violent person, and the Qur´ān as a book of theological gibberish have their roots in this period. The second part will focus on late medieval and Renaissance views of Islam as a world culture pitted against the intellectual and religious dominance of Christianity. Although some of the late medieval and Renaissance thinkers saw Islam under the same light as they saw all religions and thus derided it as irrational and superstitious, they had a sense of appreciation for the philosophical and scientific achievements of Islamic civilization. This rather new attitude towards Islam had a major role in the making of eighteenth and nineteenth century representations of Islam in Europe and paved the way for the rise of Orientalism as the official study of things Oriental and Islamic for the next two centuries. The third part of the essay will analyze Orientalism within the context of the Western perceptions of Islam and how it has determined the modern depiction of Islam in the Western hemisphere. Having provided this historical sketch, the last part of the essay will look in greater detail at how the modern language of violence, militancy, terrorism, and fundamentalism, used disproportionately to construct a belligerent image of Islam as the "other," goes back to the early medieval perceptions of Islam as the religion of the sword. It will be argued that the concepts of *jihād* and *dār al-islām* (the abode of Islam) versus *dār al-ḥarb* (the abode of war) have been grossly misinterpreted and militarized through the meta-narrative of fundamentalist Islam to preempt the possibility of crafting a discourse of dialogue and co-existence between Islam and the West.

From Theological Rivalry to Cultural Differentiation: Perceptions of Islam during the Middle Ages

As a new dispensation from Heaven which claimed to have completed the cycle of Abrahamic revelations, Islam was seen as a major challenge to Christianity from the outset. References to Jewish and Christian Prophets, stories and other themes in the Qur´ān and the Prophetic traditions (*ḥadīth*), sometimes concurring with and sometimes diverging from the Biblical accounts, contributed to both a sense of consternation and insecurity and an urgency in responding to the Islamic claims of authenticity. The earliest polemics between Muslim scholars and Christian theologians attest to the zeal of the two communities to defend their faiths against one another. Baghdad and Syria from the eighth through tenth centuries were the two main centers of intellectual exchange and theological polemics between Muslims and Christians. Even though theological rivalry is a constant of this period, many ideas were exchanged on philosophy, logic, and theology which went beyond theological bickering. In fact, Eastern Christian theologians posed a serious challenge to their Muslim counterparts because they were a step ahead in cultivating a full-fledged theological vocabulary by using the lore of ancient Greek and Hellenistic culture. The reception of Islam as a religious challenge for Christianity was not because Islam was different and claimed to be a new religion. On the contrary, the message of Islam was too similar to both Judaism and Christianity in its essential outlook, in spite of the Qur´ānic criticisms of certain Judaic and Christian beliefs.

The other important factor was the rapid spread of Islam into areas that had been previously under Christian rule. Within a century after the conquest of Mecca, Islam had already spread outside the Arabian peninsula, bringing with it the conversion of large numbers of people in areas extending from Egypt and Jerusalem to Syria, the Caspian Sea and North Africa. While Jews and Christians were granted religious freedom as the People of the Book (*ahl al-kitāb*) under Islamic law and did not face conversion by force, the unexpected pace with which Islam spread sent alarms to those living in Western Christendom. A few centuries later, this very fact would be used as a base for launching the Crusades against Muslims. Furthermore, the westward march of Muslim armies under the banner of the Umayyads, the Abbasids, and then the Ottomans added to the sense of urgency until the decline of the Ottoman Empire as a major political force in the Balkans and the Middle East. The spread of Islam, which was a riddle for many European Christians, was attributed to two main reasons: the spread of the religion by the sword and the Prophet's appealing to animal desires through polygamy and concubines. As we shall see below in the words of the seventeenth century traveler George Sandys, the simplicity of the Islamic faith was occasionally added to this list, referring, in a quasi-racist way, to the simple-mindedness of Muslim converts.[1]

The combination of Islam as a religion with its own theological premises and the expansion of Muslim borders in such a short period of time played a key role in shaping the anti-Islamic sentiment of the Middle Ages. No single figure can illustrate this situation better than St. John of Damascus (c. 675-749) known in Arabic as Yuhanna al-Dimashqī and in Latin as Johannes Damascenus. A court official of the Umayyad caliphate in Syria like his father Ibn Manṣūr, St. John was a crucial figure not only for the formation of Orthodox theology and the fight against the iconoclast movement of the eighth century, but also for the history of Christian polemics against the "Saracens." In all likelihood, this pejorative name, used for Muslims in most of the anti-Islamic polemics, goes back to St. John himself.[2] St. John's polemics, together with those of Bede (d. 735) and Theodore Abu-Qurrah (d. 820 or 830),[3] against Islam as an essentially Christian heresy or, to use St. John's own words, as the "heresy of the Ishmaelites," set the tone for medieval perceptions of Islam and continued to be a major factor until the end of the Renaissance.[4] In fact, most of the theological depictions concerning Islam as a "deceptive superstition of the Ishmaelites" and a "forerunner of the Antichrist"[5] go back to St. John. Moreover, St. John was also the first Christian polemicist to call the Prophet of Islam an imposter and a false prophet: "Muḥammad, the founder of Islam, is a false prophet who, by chance, came across the Old and New Testament and who, also, pretended that he encountered an Arian monk and thus he devised his own heresy."[6]

What is important about St. John's anti-Islamic polemics is that he had a direct knowledge of the language and ideas of Muslims which was radically absent among his followers in the West.[7] R. W. Southern has rightly called this the "historical problem of Christianity" vis-à-vis Islam in the Middle Ages, i.e., the lack of first-hand knowledge of Islamic beliefs and practices as a precaution or deliberate choice to dissuade and prevent Christians from contaminating themselves with a heretical offshoot of Christianity.[8] The absence of direct contact and reliable sources of knowledge led to a long history of spurious scholarship against Islam and the Prophet Muḥammad in Western Christianity, resulting in the forging of Islam as an eerie foe in the European consciousness for a good part of the Middle Ages. The problem was further compounded by the Byzantine opposition to Islam and the decidedly inimical literature produced by Byzantine theologians between the eighth and tenth centuries on mostly theological grounds. Even though the anti-Islamic Byzantine literature displays considerable first-hand knowledge of Islamic faith and practices,[9] including specific criticisms of some verses of the Qur´ān, the perception of Islam as a theological rival and heresy was its leitmotif and provided a solid historical and theological basis for later critiques of Islam.[10]

If deliberate ignorance was the cherished strategy of the period, the out-and-out rejection of Islam as a theological challenge was no less prevalent. The Qur´ānic assertion of Divine unity without the Trinity, the countenance of Jesus Christ as God's Prophet divested of divinity, and the presence of a religious community without clergy and a church-like authority were some of the challenges that did not go unnoticed in Western Christendom. Unlike Eastern Christianity, which had a presence in the midst of the Muslim world and better access to the Islamic faith, the image of Islam in the West was relegated to an unqualified heresy and regarded as no different than paganism or the Manicheanism from which St. Augustine had his historical conversion to Christianity. In contrast to Spain where the three Abrahamic faiths had a remarkable period of intellectual and cultural exchange, the vacuum created by the spatial and intellectual confinement of Western Christianity was filled in by folk tales about Islam and Muslims, paving the way for the new store of images, ideas, stories, myths, and tropes brought by the Crusaders. Paradoxically, the Crusades did not bring any new or more reliable knowledge about Islam, but instead reinforced its image as paganism and idolatry. There was, however, one very important consequence of the Crusades insofar as the medieval perceptions of Islam are concerned.

The Crusaders, it is to be noted, were the first Western Christians to go into Islamdom and witness Islamic culture with its cities, roads, bazaars, mosques, palaces and, most importantly, its inhabitants. With the Crusader came not only the legend of Saladin (Ṣalāḥ al-Dīn al-Ayyūbī), the conqueror of Jerusalem, but also the stories of Muslim life, its promiscuity, its wealth and luxury, and such goods and commodities as silk, paper, and incense. Combined with popular imagery, these stories and imported goods, presenting a world immersed in the luxuries of worldly life, confirmed the "wicked nature" of the heresy of the Ishmaelites. Although the subdued sense of admiration tacit in these stories did very little to correct the image of Islam, it opened a new door of perception for it as a culture and civilization. In this way, Islam, vilified on purely religious and theological grounds, came to possess a neutral value, if not possessing any importance in itself. The significance of this shift in perception cannot be overemphasized. After the fourteenth century, when Christianity began to lose its grip on the Western world, many lay people who did not bother themselves with Christian criticisms of Islam, or any other culture and religion for that matter, were more than happy to refer to Islamic culture as a world outside the theological and geographical confinements of Christianity. In a rather curious way, Islamic civilization, to the extent to which it was known in Western Europe, was pitted against Christianity to reject its exclusive claim to truth and universality. This explains, to a considerable extent, the double attitude of Renaissance Europe towards Islam: it hated Islam as a religion but admired its civilization.

During the passionate and bloody campaign of the Crusades, a most important and unexpected development took place for the written literature on Islam in the Middle Ages. This was the translation of the Qur´ān for the first time into Latin under the auspices of Peter the Venerable (d. c. 1156). The translation was done by the English scholar Robert of Ketton, who completed his rather free and incomplete rendition in July 1143.[11] As expected, the motive for the translation was not to gain a better understanding of Islam by reading its sacred scripture but to better know the enemy. In fact, Peter the Venerable explained his reasons for the undertaking of the translation of the Qur´ān as follows:

> If this work seems superfluous, since the enemy is not vulnerable to such weapons as these, I answer that in the Republic of the great King some things are for defense, others for decoration, and some for both. Solomon the Peaceful made arms for defense, which were not necessary in his own time. David made ornaments for the Temple though there was no means of using them in his day. So it is with this work. If the Moslems cannot be converted by it, at least it is right for the learned to support the weaker brethren in the Church, who are so easily scandalized by small things.[12]

Regardless of the intention behind it, the translation of the Qur´ān was a momentous event, since it shaped the scope and direction of the study of Islam in the Middle Ages and provided the critics of Islamic religion with a text on which to build many of their anticipated criticisms.[13] Parallel with this was an event that proved to be even more alarming: introduction of the Prophet of Islam into the Christian imagery of medieval Europe. Although St. John of Damascus was the first to call the Prophet of Islam a "false prophet," before the eleventh century there were hardly any references to "Mahomet" as a major figure in the anti-Islamic literature. With the induction of the Prophet into the picture, however, a new and eschatological dimension was added to the preordained case of Islam as a villain faith because the Prophet of Islam could now be identified as the anti-Christ heralding the end of time.

This portrayal of the Prophet of Islam suffered from the same historical problem of medieval Europe to which we have referred, namely the lack of knowledge of Islam based on original sources, texts, first-hand accounts and reliable histories. It is a notorious fact that there was not a single scholar among the Latin critics of Islam until the end of the thirteenth century who knew Arabic with any degree of proficiency. We may well remember Roger Bacon's complaint that Louis XI could not find a person to translate an Arabic letter of the Sultan of Egypt and write back to him in his language.[14] In fact, the official teaching of Arabic in a European university would not take place until the second part of the sixteenth century when Arabic began to be taught regularly at the Collège de France in Paris in 1587. Nevertheless, the first work ever to appear on the Prophet in Latin was Embrico of Mainz's (d. 1077) *Vita Mahumeti*, culled mostly from Byzantine sources and embellished with profligate details about the Prophet's personal and social life.[15] The picture that emerged out of such works largely corroborated the apocalyptic framework within which the Prophet of Islam and his discomforting success in spreading the new faith was seen as a fulfillment of the Biblical promise of the anti-Christ. As expected, the theological concerns of this period shunned any appeal to reliable scholarship for the next two centuries, preempting the creation of a less belligerent image of the Prophet.

Almost all of the Latin works that have survived on the Prophet's life had one clear goal: to show the impossibility of such a man as Muḥammad to be God's messenger. This is exceedingly clear in the picture with which we are presented. The Prophet's "this-worldly" qualities as opposed to the "other-worldly" nature of Jesus Christ was a constant theme. The Prophet, it was argued, was given to sex and political power, both of which he used, the Latins reasoned, to oppress his followers and destroy Christianity. He was merciless towards his enemies, especially towards Jews and Christians, and took pleasure in having his opponents tortured and killed. The only reasonable explanation for the enormous success of Muḥammad in religious and political fields was something as malicious as heresy, i.e., that he was a magician and used magical powers to convince and convert people. The focus on the psychological states of the Prophet was so persuasive for Europeans that as late as in the nineteenth century William Muir (1819-1905), a British official in India and later the principal of Edinburgh University, joined his medieval predecessors by calling the Prophet a "psychopath" in his extremely polemical *Life of Mohammed*. Many other details can be mentioned here including the Prophet's having a Christian background, that his dead body was eaten and desecrated by pigs, or that he was baptized secretly just before his death as a last attempt to save his soul.[16]

The foregoing image of the Prophet of Islam was an extension of the unwavering rejection of the Qur´ān as authentic revelation. In fact, once the Prophet had been portrayed as a possessed and hallucinatory spirit, it was more convincing in the eyes of the opponents for the Qur´ān to be attributed to such a man as Muḥammad. Having said that, there was also a deeper theological reason for focusing on the figure of the Prophet. Since Christianity is essentially a "Christic" religion and Jesus Christ the embodiment of the Word of God, the Latin critics accorded a similar role to Muḥammad in the religious universe of Islam: one could not understand and reject the message of Islam without its messenger. At any rate, the rejection of the Qur´ān as the word of God and the representation of the Prophet as a possessed spirit and magician immersed in the lusts of the inferior world stayed with the Western perception of Islam into the modern period. Perhaps the most disturbing outcome of this has been the exclusion of Islam from the family of monotheistic religions. Even in the modern period, where the interfaith trialogue between Judaism, Christianity, and Islam has come a long way thanks to the indefatigable work of such scholars as Seyyed Hossein Nasr, Ismail Raji al-Faruqi, and Kenneth Cragg,[17] we are still not prepared to speak with confidence of a Judeo-Christian-Islamic tradition by which Islam can be seen within the same religious universe as the other two Abrahamic faiths. The absence of such a discourse reinforces the medieval perceptions of Islam as a heretic and pagan faith, and thwarts the likelihood of generating a more inclusive picture of Islam on primarily religious grounds.

From the Middle Ages Through the Modern Period: The European Discovery of Islam as a World Culture

The Christian impression of Islam as a heretical religion was countered by the admiration of Islamic civilization in the works of some late medieval and Renaissance thinkers. The Islamic scientific and philosophical culture, *inter alia*, played a significant role in this process. Here we will mention only two examples, both of which show the extent to which Muslim philosophers were embraced with full enthusiasm. Our first example is Dante and his great work *The Divine Comedy*, an epitome of medieval Christian cosmology and eschatology in which everything is accorded a place proper to its rank in the Christian hierarchy of things. Writing in his purely Christian environment, Dante places the Prophet and ʿAlī, his son-in-law and the fourth caliph of Islam, in hell.[18] By contrast, he places Saladin, Avicenna, and Averroes in limbo, thus granting them the possibility of salvation. This positive attitude is further revealed by the fact that Siger de Brabant, the champion of Latin Averroism, is placed in paradise as a salute to the memories of Avicenna and Averroes. With this scheme, Dante points to a first step in coming to terms with Islam: if it is to be rejected as a faith, its intellectual heroes are to be accorded their proper place. This conclusion can also be regarded as a result of Dante's interest in Islamic philosophy and science and is corroborated by the fact that besides Avicenna and Averroes, he refers to some Muslim astronomers and philosophers in other writings. The influence of the nocturnal ascent or the night journey (*miʿrāj*) of the Prophet of Islam on the composition and structure of the *Divine Comedy* has been debated by a number of European scholars, pointing to Dante's overall interest in Semitic languages and Arabic-Islamic culture. The Spanish scholar Asin Palacios has claimed that the night journey served as a model for the *Divine Comedy*.[19] In spite of Dante's rejection of the Prophet for strictly Christian reasons, his appreciation of Islamic thought and culture is a remarkable example of how the two civilizations can co-exist and interact with one another on intellectual and cultural grounds.

Another closely associated case in which one can easily discern a different perception of Islamic culture is the rise of Latin Averroism in the West and its dominance of the intellectual scene of the Scholastics until its official ban in 1277 by Bishop Tempier. Even though Averroism was denounced as a heretical school, it remained to be a witness to the deep impact of Islamic thought on the West. Roger Bacon (1214-1294), one of the luminaries of thirteenth century Scholasticism, called for the study of the language of the Saracens so that they could be defeated on intellectual, if not religious, grounds. Albertus Magnus (c. 1208-1280), considered to be the founder of Latin scholasticism, was not shy in admitting the superiority of Islamic thought on a number of issues in philosophy. Even Raymond Lull (c. 1235-1316), one of the most important figures for the study of Islam in the Middle Ages, was in favor of the scholarly study of Islamic culture in tandem with his conviction that the Christian faith could be demonstrated to non-believers through rational means.[20] Finally St. Thomas Aquinas (1225-1274), who represents the pinnacle of Christian thought in the classical period, could not remain indifferent to the challenge of Islamic thought and especially that of Averroes since Averroism was no longer a distant threat but something right at home as represented by such Latin scholars as Siger de Brabant (c. 1240-1284), Boethius of Dacia, and other Averroists.[21]

It is pertinent to point out that this new intellectual attitude towards Islam came to fruition at a time when Western Europe, convinced of the nascent threat of Muslim power, was hoping for the conversion of the Mongols ("Tartars" as they were called by Latins) to Christianity for the final undoing of Islam. That the clergy saw conversion as a probable way of dealing with the problem of Islam was clear in the missionary activities of Bernard of Clairvaux (1090-1153), the founder of the Cistercian order and an instrumental figure for the dispatching of the second Crusade in the twelfth century, and Raymond Lull, the "first missionary to Muslims," despite the fact that neither of them conceived the goal of the Crusades to be one of proselytizing. In complaining about the absence of missionary work designed for the Gentiles, Bernard of Clairvaux implored his fellow Christians: "Are we waiting for faith to descend on them? Who [ever] came to believe through chance? How are they to believe without being preached to?"[22] With Mongols embracing Islam under the leadership of Oljaytu, the great grandson of Genghis Khan, however, these hopes were dashed[23] and the deployment of philosophical rather than purely theological methods of persuasion presented itself as the only reasonable way of dealing with the people of the Islamic faith. Interestingly enough, the attention paid by European scholars to Islamic culture minus its religion in the eleventh and twelfth centuries contributed to what C. H. Haskins has called the "Renaissance of the twelfth century."[24]

The experience of *convivencia* of the three Abrahamic religions in Andalusia is an important chapter in the European perceptions of Islam during the Middle Ages. The translation movement centered in Toledo, the rise of Mozarabs and Mudejars, and the flourishing of Islamic culture in southern Spain, are some of the indications of a different mode of interaction between Islam and medieval Europe with a strong tendency to see Islamic culture as superior. Already in the ninth century, Alvaro, a Spanish Christian, was complaining about the influence of Islamic culture on the Christian youth:

> My fellow Christians delight in the poems and romances of the Arabs; they study the works of Mohammedan theologians and philosophers, not in order to refute them, but to acquire a correct and elegant Arabic style. Where today can a layman be found who reads the Latin commentaries on Holy Scriptures? Who is there that studies the Gospels, the Prophets, the Apostles? Alas! The young Christians who are most conspicuous for their talents have no knowledge of any literature or language save the Arabic; they read and study with avidity Arabian books; they amass whole libraries of them at a vast cost, and they everywhere sing the praises of Arabian lore.[25]

Although the perception of Islam as a religion did not undergo any major change, the appreciation of the Muslim culture of Andalusia provided a framework in which important ideas were exchanged in the fields of philosophy, science, and art. Despite the expected tensions of power between various groups, Spain as a "frontier culture" became home to many new ideas and cultural products from the Beati miniatures and Flamenco music to Elipandus' revival of "adoptionism." Toledo, Seville, and Cordoba were hailed not simply as "Muslim" cities in the religious sense of the term but as places of opulence, elegance, and remarkable cultural exchange and interaction.[26] One can also mention here the deep impact of Islamic culture on Spanish literature and in particular the influence of Sufism on St. John of the Cross.

In spite of the esteemed memory of Andalusia, the belligerent attitude towards Islam as a heresy remained invariable even after the demise of the Christian Middle Ages when Western Europe set out to forge a new paradigm which would culminate in the rise of a new secular worldview. Pascal (1623-1662), perhaps the most passionate defender of the Christian faith in the seventeeth century, for instance, was as harsh and uncompromising as his predecessors in condemning the Prophet of Islam as an impostor and fraudulent prophet. The "fifteenth movement" of his *Les Pensées*, called "Contre Mahomet," voices an important sentiment of Pascal and his co-religionists on Islam and the Prophet Muḥammad: Muḥammad is in no way comparable to Jesus; Muḥammad speaks with no Divine authority; he brought no miracles; his coming has not been foretold; and what he did could be done by anyone whereas what Jesus did is supra-human and supra-historical.[27]

A similar attitude penetrates the work of George Sandys (1578-1644) entitled *Relation of a Journey begun An. Dom. 1610. Foure Books. Containing a description of the Turkish Empire, of Aegypt, of the Holy Land, of the Remote parts of Italy, and Ilands adioyning*, which is one of the earliest travel accounts of the Islamic world to reach Europe. Hailed as both a humanist and a Christian, Sandys saw Islam under the same light as did Pascal, and as a result had no intentions of placing his "humanist" outlook over his Christian prejudices against Islam. Sandys' book contains important observations on the Islamic world, highly polemical remarks about the Qur´ān and the Prophet, and finally some very edifying praises of Muslim philosophers. The dual attitude of rejecting Islam as a religion while admiring its cultural achievements is clearly exemplified in Sandys' work. Of "the Mahometan Religion," Sandys has the following to say:

> So that we may now conclude, that the *Mahometan* religion, being deriued from a person in life so wicked, so worldly in his projects, in his prosecutions of them so disloyall, treacherous & cruel; being grounded vpon fables and false reuelations, repugnant to sound reason, & that wisedome which the Diuine hand hath imprinted in his workes; alluring men with those inchantments of fleshly pleasures, permitted in this life and promised for the life ensuing; being also supported with tyranny and the sword (for it is death to speake there against it); and lastly, where it is planted rooting out all vertue, all wisedome and science, and in summe all liberty and ciuility; and laying the earth to waste, dispeopled and vninhabited, that neither it came from God (saue as a scourge by permission) neither can bring them to God that follow it.[28]

Having rejected the religious foundations of Islam, Sandys follows suit in pitting Muslim philosophers against Islam as a common strategy of the late

Middle Ages and the Renaissance. The assumption behind this, voiced by a figure no less prominent than Roger Bacon, was the secret conversion of Avicenna and Averroes to Christianity and/or their profession of the Muslim faith for fear of persecution. For many Europeans, this was the most plausible way of explaining the genius of Muslim philosophers and scientists against the backdrop of a religion that the medieval West abhorred, ignored, and rejected. Thus Sandys speaks of Avicenna (Ibn Sīnā) in terms of praise and vindication while discarding Islam as irrational on the basis of the celebrated "double-truth theory" attributed by St. Thomas Aquinas to Averroes:

> For although as a *Mahometan*, in his bookes *De Anima* and *De Almahad*, addressed particularly to a *Mahometan* Prince, he extolleth *Mahomet* highly, as being the *seale* of diuine *lawes* and the *last of the Prophets*.... But now this Auicen, laying downe for a while his outward person of a Mahometan, and putting on the habite of a Philosopher; in his Metaphysicks seemeth to make a flat opposition between the truth of their faith receiued from their Prophet, and the truth of vnderstanding by demonstrative argument.... And it is worthy obseruation, that in the judgment of Aucien one thing is true in their faith, & contrary in pure & demonstratiue reason. Wheras (to the honor of Christian Religion be it spoken) it is confessed by all, & enacted by a Councel, that it is an errour to say, one thing is true in Theology, & in Philosophy the contrary. For the truths of religion are many times aboue reason, but neuer against it.[29]

A similar line of thought is articulated in Peter Bayle's monumental *Dictionnaire historique et critique* (Historical and Critical Dictionary, 1697). Bayle (1647-1706) was one of the pioneers of the Enlightenment and his skeptical scholarship had a deep impact on the French Encyclopedists, championed by Diderot, and the rationalist philosophers of the eighteenth century. His *Dictionnaire*, which has been aptly called the "arsenal of the Enlightenment," devotes a generously lengthy twenty-three page entry to the Prophet of Islam under the name "Mahomet" as opposed to seven pages on Averroes and only half a page on al-Kindī ("Alchindus"). Bayle exercises caution in narrating the Christian bashings of Islam and the Prophet and rejects as simply foolish and baseless some of the legendary stories concerning the Prophet's tomb being in the air, his dead body having been eaten by dogs as a sign of Divine curse and punishment, and his being the anti-Christ. There is enough material, Bayle argues, with which to charge the Prophet of Islam:

> I will not deny, but, in some respects, the zeal of our own disputants is unjust; for if they make use of the extravagances of a Mahometan legendary, to make Mahomet himself odious or to ridicule him, they violate the equity, which is due to all the world, to wicked, as well as good men. We must not impute to any body what they never did, and consequently we must not argue against

> Mahomet from these idle fancies, which some of his followers have fabled of him, if he himself never published them. We have sufficient material against him, tho' we charge him only with his own faults, and do not make him answerable for the follies, which the indiscreet and romantic zeal of some of his disciples has prompted to write. (translation revised)[30]

Having stated this precaution, Bayle joins his fellow Europeans in describing the Prophet of Islam as a man of sensuality and bellicosity, an impostor and a "false teacher." In the *Dictionary*, the Prophet appears under the same light of medieval Christian polemics, and Bayle states, on Humphrey Prideaux's authority:

> Mahomet was an impostor, and that he made his imposture subservient to his lust.... what is related of his amours, is very strange. He was jealous to the highest degree, and yet he bore with patience the gallantries of that wife ["Aʿishah], which was the dearest to him" and that "... I choose to concur with the common opinion, That Mahomet was an impostor: for, besides what I shall say elsewhere his insinuating behavior, and dexterous address, in procuring friends, do plainly show, that he made use of religion only as an expedient to aggrandize himself." (translation revised)[31]

While Bayle's entry is hardly an improvement upon the gruesome picturing of the Prophet in the previous centuries, it does contain some important observations on Islamic culture, based mostly on the available travel accounts of the time. The modesty of Turkish women, for instance, is narrated in the context of stressing the "normalcy" of Muslim culture, which is contrasted to the common mores of Europe, indicating in a clear way the extent to which Europe's self-image was at work in various depictions of Islam and Muslims. Bayle also praises Muslim nations for their religious tolerance and admonishes the zeal of medieval Christians to persecute their own co-religionists. Like many of his predecessors and peers, Bayle pits Muslim history against the injunctions of the religion of Islam and explains the glory of Muslim history as a result of the deviation of Muslim nations from the principles of Islam rather an application of them. As he writes:

> The Mahometans, according to the principles of their faith, are obliged to employ violence, to destroy other religions, and yet they tolerate them now, and have done so for many ages. The Christians have no order, but to preach, and instruct; and yet, time out of mind, they destroy, with fire and sword, those who are not of their religion. "When you meet with Infidels," says Mahomet, "kill them, cut off their heads, or take them prisoners, and put them in chains, till they have paid their ransom, or you find it convenient to set them at liberty. Be not afraid to persecute them, till they have laid down their arms, and submitted to you." Nevertheless, it is true, that the Saracens quickly left off the ways of violence; and that the Greek churches, as well the orthodox as the schismatical, have continued to this day under the yoke of Mahomet. They have their Patriarchs, their Metropolitans, their Synods, their Discipline, their Monks.... It

may be affirmed for a certain truth, that if the western princes had been lords of Asia, instead of the Saracens and Turks, there would be now no remnant of the Greek church, and they would not have tolerated Mahometanism, as these Infidels have tolerated Christianity. (translation revised)[32]

Towards the end of his entry, Bayle refers his readers to the work of Humphrey Prideaux (d. 1724) of Westminster and Christ Church for further information about Islam, whose title leaves little need to explain its content: *The true nature of imposture fully display'd in the life of Mahomet: With a discourse annex'd for the vindication of Christianity from this charge. Offered to the considerations of the Deists of the present age.* Prideaux's book, published in 1697, was one of the most virulent and bitter attacks on Islam during the Enlightenment. That it became a best-seller in the eighteenth century and was reprinted many times into the nineteenth century tells much about the Enlightenment approach to Islam.[33] The robust rationalism and overt disdain for religion that characterized the Enlightenment was a major factor in the reinforcement of medieval perceptions of Islam as a religious worldview, and attacking Islam was an expedient way of deconstructing religion as such. This attitude is obvious in Voltaire (1694-1778), one of the most widely read celebrities of the Enlightenment, who took a less hostile position towards Islamic culture while maintaining the erstwhile Christian representations of the Prophet Muḥammad. In his famous tragedy *Fanatisme ou Mahomet le prophète*, Voltaire projects Muḥammad as a prototype of fanaticism, cruelty, imposture, and sensuality, which was nothing new to his readers except for the legends and stories that he himself had invented. In a letter to Frederick of Prussia, he states:

[That] a merchant of camels should excite a revolt in his townlet … that he should boast of being rapt to Heaven, and of having received there part of this unintelligible book which affronts common sense at every page; that he should put his own country to fire and the sword, to make this book respected; that he should cut the fathers' throats and ravish the daughters; that he should give the vanquished the choice between his religion and death; this certainly is what no man can excuse.[34]

The ambivalent attitude of the seventeenth and eighteenth centuries, torn between the received images of Islam and the Prophet from Christian polemics and the glory of Islamic civilization witnessed by many travelers and scholars, resulted in a different genre of writing concerning Islam. One important work to be mentioned here is Stubbe's defense of Islam. A typical Renaissance man, historian, librarian, theologian, and a doctor, Henry Stubbe (1632-1676), published an unusual book with the following title: *An account of the rise and progress of Mahometanism with the life of Mahomet and a vindication of him and his religion from the calumnies of the Christians.*[35] In fact, it was this book which had led Prideaux to write his attack on Islam mentioned above. Stubbe had no reservations about going against the grain and responding to the traditional charges of violence and sensuality associated with Muslims. More importantly, he openly defended Islamic faith as more proximate to man's reason and nature as a tacit way of criticizing Christian theology and the sacraments. A typical passage from his book reads:

> This is the sum of Mahometan Religion, on the one hand not clogging Men's Faith with the necessity of believing a number of abstruse Notions which they cannot comprehend, and which are often contrary to the dictates of Reason and common Sense; nor on the other hand loading them with the performance of many troublesome, expensive, and superstitious Ceremonies, yet enjoying a due observance of Religious Worship, as the surest Method to keep Men in the bounds of their Duty both to God and Man.[36]

In addition to the Islamic faith, the Prophet also receives a very fair treatment from Stubbe, who appears to be heralding the rise of a new class of European scholars of Islam in the eighteenth and nineteenth centuries. Another very important exception of this period is the famous Swiss theologian and mystic Emanuel Swedenborg (1688-1772) and his historical theology of the rise of Islam. Swedenborg, who is one of the most important figures of eighteenth century Christian thought, considered the spread of Islam to be part of Divine Providence. For him, the true goal of Islam and its Prophet was to destroy the rampant paganism of pre-Islamic Arabs and their neighbors because the Church was too weak and dispersed to fight against paganism. It was as a response to this historic moment that the Lord sent a religion "accommodated to the genius of the orientals." As Swedenborg writes:

> The Mahometan religion acknowledges the Lord as the Son of God, as the wisest of men, and as the greatest prophet … that religion was raised up by the Lord's Divine Providence to destroy the idolatries of many nations … that all these idolatries might be extirpated, it was brought to pass, by the Divine Providence of the Lord, that a new religion should arise, accommodated to the genius of the orientals, in which there should be something from both Testaments of the Word, and which should teach that the Lord came into the world, and that he was the greatest prophet, the wisest of all men, and the Son of God. This was accomplished through Mahomet.[37]

Although Swedenborg attributes the belief in the divinity of Jesus Christ to Muslims, which is unwarranted in the Islamic sources, he hastens to add that the reason why Islam accepted Jesus only as a prophet and not a divine being was because "the orientals acknowledged God the Creator of the universe, and could not comprehend that He came into the world and assumed the Human. So neither do Christians comprehend it."[38] By combining his theology of history with an anthropology of the "orientals," Swedenborg confronts Islam as a religion whose essential message is the same as that of Christianity. That such an inclusivist approach should be taken by a mystic theologian of the stature of Emanuel Swedenborg is extremely important considering the rising tide of conservative Christian attacks on Islam in recent decades and especially after September 11. The example of Swedenborg together with Goethe and others evinces the reality of a peaceful co-existence between Christians and Muslims on both social and, more importantly, religious and theological grounds.

In contradistinction to the radical opposition of Pascal, Bayle, Prideaux, and Voltaire to Muḥammad as a figure of religion, some of their contemporaries, including Stubbe, saw something different in the Prophet of Islam as a man of the world. Divested of his claims to have received God's word, the Prophet Muḥammad could be appreciated for what he had accomplished in history. This is an important shift from the strictly Christian assessments of Muḥammad as a false prophet, to putting increasingly more emphasis on his human qualities. This new attitude is also the beginning of the depiction of the Prophet and many other figures of the past as "heroes" and "geniuses," the ostensibly non-religious terms that the Enlightenment intellectuals were fond of using against the Christian conceptions of history.

The seventeenth and eighteenth centuries witnessed the rise of many scholars and intellectuals who looked at the Prophet of Islam under this new light, which eventually led to more liberal and less inimical appraisals of Islam and Muslims. In England, Edward Pococke (1604-1691), the first chair holder of Islamic studies at Oxford, published his *Specimen Historiae Arabum*, a medley of analyses and translations on the history of Islam, its basic tenets and practices, and a selective rendering of one of the works of al-Ghazālī. Judged by the standards of his time, Pococke's work was a major step in the scholarly study of Islam. Furthermore, Pococke was one of the first among the European scholars of Islam to spend time in the Islamic world collecting material for his studies. Of equal importance and prominence was George Sale (1697-1736), who produced the first English translation of the Qur´ān in 1734, making use of Lodovico Maracci's Latin translation[39] published at Padua in 1698, rather than that of Robert Ketton published in the twelfth century.

Sale had no intentions of granting Islam any authenticity as a religion, and he made this point very clear in his "Preliminary Discourse" written as a preface to his translation. His overall approach to Islam, which earned him the somewhat belittling title of "half-Mussulman," was to set the tone for the eighteenth and nineteenth century studies of Islam in Europe, and paved the way for the establishment of Orientalism as a discipline. Sale's translation was a huge improvement on an earlier rendering of the Qur´ān into English by Alexander Ross, which was based on Andre du Ryer's French translation published in 1647.[40] Like that of Sale, Ross' translation contained a short discourse on Islam and the Prophet in which Ross explained the *raison d'être* of the translation to his Christian readers and assured them that there was no danger in reading the Qur´ān because it was comprised of "contradictions, blasphemies, obscene speeches, and ridiculous fables...."[41] It is important to note that the Ross translation was the first edition of the Qur´ān in America, which came out in Massachusetts in 1806 and enjoyed a wide circulation until the Sale translation became the standard text. In any case, Sale's translation was the definitive text of the Qur´ān in the English language until the end of the nineteenth century and it was on the basis of this translation that Gibbon and Carlyle read and discarded the Qur´ān as "a wearisome confused jumble, crude, incondite; endless iterations, long-windedness, entanglement; most crude, incondite; —insupportable stupidity, in short! Nothing but a sense of duty could carry any European through the Qur´ān."[42]

While the Qur´ān and, by derivation, the religious foundations of Islam were invariably denied, the human qualities of the Prophet of Islam were invoked by the humanist intellectuals of the eighteenth and nineteenth centuries either to level subtle criticisms against Christianity or simply to cherish their secular humanist philosophy of history. The depiction of the Prophet as a genius and hero, with a piercing mind and perspicacity, remarkable powers of persuasion, sincerity, and dedication reached a climax with Carlyle and his heroic philosophy of history. In Carlyle's work, the Prophet is presented as a remarkable man of the world: a hero, a genius, a charismatic figure, a personality that the Christian spirit of the Middle Ages was incapable of seeing and appreciating. Although Carlyle had placed his analysis of the Prophet within a clearly secular framework and thus preempted any charges of heresy, he still felt obligated to apologize for his positive estimation of the Prophet: "as there is no danger of our becoming, any of us, Mahometans, I mean to say all the good of him I justly can. It is the way to get at his secret: let us try to understand what he meant with the world; what the world meant and means with him, will then be a more answerable question."[43]

A much more assertive voice of the time was that of Goethe (1749-1832), who was neither secretive nor apologetic about his admiration for things Islamic. His *West-oestlicher Diwan* was a loud celebration of Persian-Islamic culture and his interest in the Islamic world went certainly beyond the mere curiosity of a German poet when he said, as quoted by Carlyle, that "if this be *Islam*, do we not all live in *Islam*?"[44] In the nineteenth century, Goethe's call was taken up by a whole generation of European and American poets and men of literature, which included such celebrities as Emerson and Thoreau.[45]

Nineteenth Century Perceptions of Islam: From Pilgrim to Orientalist

Outside the world of theology, philosophy, and literature, there were many Europeans whose thirst and curiosity for the Orient was not to be quenched by reading books. So they went to the Islamic world and produced a sizeable literature of travel accounts about Muslim countries, their customs, cities, etc. These were the European travelers of the seventeenth, eighteenth, and nineteenth centuries whose ranks included such people as Burton, Scott, Kinglake, Disraeli, Curzon, Warburton, Nerval, Chardin, Chateaubriand, Flaubert, Lamartine, Pierre Loti, and Tavernier.[46] The wealth of information they brought back to Europe contributed to the popular, if not academic, perceptions of Islam and Muslims whereby the impenetrable world of the Saracens and Orientals was now disclosed for many Europeans through the imaginative discourse of the travelers. In some curious ways, these travel accounts had an impact similar to that of the Crusades almost seven centuries before: a first-hand experience of the Orient was made available for public consumption in Europe and it was entrenched not in the religious concerns and hostilities of Christian theologians, but in the new mission of the Occident to "civilize" the Orient—the celebrated *mission civilisatrice* of the colonial period.[47] Perhaps the most elegant and radical expression of this view came from André Gide, the famous French poet and writer and recipient of the Nobel Prize in literature in 1947. In his famous *Journals*, Gide gives an account of his journey to Turkey in 1914, which turns out to be an utter disappointment for him:

> Constantinople justifies all my prejudices and joins Venice in my personal hell. As soon as you admire some bit of architecture, the surface of a mosque, you learn (and you suspected already) that it is Albanian or Persian.... The Turkish costume is the ugliest you can imagine; and the race, to tell the truth, deserves it.... For too long I believed (out of love of exoticism, out of fear of chauvinistic self-satisfaction, and perhaps out of modesty), for too long I thought that there was more than one civilization, more than one culture that could rightfully claim our love and deserve our enthusiasm.... Now I know our Occidental (I was about to say French) civilization is not only the most beautiful; I believe, I know that it is the *only one*—yes, the very civilization of Greece, of which we are the only heirs.[48]

Like their intellectual peers in the seventeenth and eighteenth centuries, most of these travelers were interested in the "worldly" qualities of Islamdom, perhaps with a good intention of dispelling some long-standing misgivings about a world in which Europe had now a vital interest. Their narrations, ranging from recondite and arid inventories of names and places to spirited depictions and imaginary ruminations, were based not so much on a genuine interest in penetrating into the Islamic world as reflecting and constructing it through the eyes of an upper-class European writer. A somewhat crude indication of this is the fact that many of those travelers, notwithstanding such notable exceptions as Sir Richard Burton,[49] did not learn any of the Islamic languages or make any serious study of the beliefs and practices of Muslims other than what was available to them in Europe as common knowledge. In his celebrated travelogue, *Travels in Persia 1673-1677*, Sir John Chardin makes a number of observations on the Persians and displays a mixed feeling towards them. Speaking of the "temper, manners, and customs of the Persians," he says:

> They are courtly, civil, compliant, and well-bred; they have naturally an eager bent to Voluptuousness, Luxury, Extravagancy, and Profuseness; for which Reason, they are ignorant both of Frugality and Trade. In a Word, they are born with as good natural Parts as any other People, but few abuse them so much as they do ....
>
> ... [B]esides those Vices which the Persian are generally addicted to, they are Lyers in the highest Degree; they speak, swear, and make false Depositions upon the least Consideration; they borrow and pay not; and if they can Cheat, they seldom lose the Opportunity; they are not to be trusted in Service, nor in all other Engagements; without Honesty in their Trading, wherein they overreach one so ingeniously, that one cannot help but being bubbl'd; greedy of Riches, and of vain Glory, of Respect and Reputation, which they endeavor to gain by all Means possible.[50]

An important outcome of this literature is what Edward Said calls "Orientalizing the Orient,"[51] i.e., the further romanticizing and vilification of Muslim peoples. In its more artistic and literary manifestations, Orientalism reinforces the mystique of the Orient by evoking such fixed identities and stereotypes as the exotic harem, the sensuous East, the Oriental man and his concubines, city streets immersed in mystery, all of which are to be seen vividly in the naturalistic European paintings of the Orient in the nineteenth century. These images of the Orient are still alive in the European mind and continue to be an inexhaustible resource for Hollywood constructions of Islam and Muslims in America.

It would not be a stretch to say that the nineteenth century bore witness to the most extensive interaction between Islam and the West. It was in this century that the academic study of Islam exploded—more than anyone in Europe could have imagined before. The new interest in Islam was closely tied to the political, economic and, most importantly, colonial circumstances of the nineteenth century, during which time a handful of European countries had proceeded to occupy a good part of the Islamic world. As we can see from the long list of Orientalist scholars, the nineteenth century witnessed a sudden and dramatic rise in the study of Islam, surpassing both qualitatively and quantitatively the work of the last millennium over a period of seventy years: Silvestre de Sacy (1758-1838), the father of French Orientalism; E. W. Lane (1801-1876) whose *Arabic-English Lexicon* is still a classic;[52] Karl Pfander, a German missionary working in India and famous for his controversy with Indian Muslim scholars; J. von Hammer-Purgstall (1774-1856), known for his meticulous studies on Ottoman history and Arabic, Persian, and Turkish poetry; William Muir, mentioned earlier; F. D. Maurice (1805-1872), a prominent theologian of the Church of England and the author of *The Religions of the World and Their Relations with Christianity*, a key text for the understanding of Christian perspectives on Islam in the nineteenth century; Ernest Renan (1823-1892) whose famous lecture at the Sorbonne on Islam and science incited a long controversy and elicited the responses of a number of Muslim intellectuals of the time, including Jamal al-Din Afghani and Namik Kemal.[53]

These and many other figures writing on Islam and the Islamic world in the nineteenth century unearthed a new terrain for the study of Islam and crafted new modes of perception vis-à-vis the Islamic world. The contributions of these scholars to the shaping of the modern Western images of Islam were manifold. First, they were the direct conduits for satisfying the curiosity of the European populace about the Islamic world that was now, after centuries of menacing presence and bewildering success, under the political, military, and economic dominance of the West. In this limited sense, the concept of Islam articulated in the works of these scholars was intractably tied to the new colonial identity of Western Europe. Secondly, the torrent of information about the Muslim world, its history, beliefs, schools of thought, languages, geography, and ethnic texture served scholarship as much as power. It can hardly escape our attention that a good number of scholars, travelers, and translators of the nineteenth century, credited duly with relative expertise, were colonial officers sent to the Orient with clear and detailed job descriptions. The third and, for our purposes, the most important legacy of this period was the completion of the groundwork for the full-fledged establishment of what came to be known as Orientalism—a new set of categories, typologies, classifications, terminologies, and methods of coming to terms with things Oriental and Islamic.

Orientalism reached a climax in the second half of the nineteenth and the first part of the twentieth century,[54] and a truly impressive and ambitious venture was set in motion by a dozen or so European academics who were to mould the modern study of Islam in Western universities. With all of their ambitions, fervor, differences, scholastic diligence, and distinctly Western identities, such names as Ignaz Goldziher (1850-1921), Snouck Hurgronje (1857-1936), Duncan Black Macdonald (1863-1943), Carl Becker (1876-1933), David Samuel Margoliouth (1858-1940), Edward Granville

Browne (1862-1926), Reynold Alleyne Nicholson (1868-1945), Louis Massignon (1883-1962), and Sir Hamilton A. R. Gibb (1895-1971) became, *inter alia*, the towering figures of the Orientalist study of Islam.[55] By producing a massive body of books, journals, articles, translations, critical editions, reports, and academic posts for the study of Islam, the Orientalist scholars generated an enduring legacy that has shaped the parameters of the modern study of Islam and the Muslim world up to our own day.

The Orientalist journey in the path of representing Islam, however, contributed very little to the amelioration of the mystique of Islam and the Orient, which had been inherited from the pre-modern era. Some of the Western students of Islam were simply not interested in such an enterprise and focused their energies on their solitary work. In other cases, the dark image of Islam as a decadent and dying civilization, a backward, irrational, and sensual world was reinforced and made its way into popular culture through fiction, TV images, Hollywood productions, and media reporting. In this regard, Arberry's conciliatory remark that the seven British scholars of Islam, including Arberry himself, whom he analyzes in his *Oriental Essays*, "have striven, consciously or unconsciously, by the exercise of somewhat specialized skills to help build a bridge between the peoples and cultures of Asia and Europe"[56] appears to state no more than an unfinished project and unfullfilled will. Beyond the individual proclivities of Orientalist scholars, Orientalism was marred by a number of structural and methodological problems, some of which are still operative in the current representations of Islam. It is thus crucial to identify them in order to understand the ways in which Islam is constructed as the eerie "other" at best and as the enemy at worst. Without claiming to be exhaustive, we can briefly highlight some of these issues.

In its early stages, Orientalism functioned within the matrix of the nineteenth century European mindset. Currents of thought, from Romanticism and rationalism to historical criticism and hermeneutics, which had shaped Western humanities and the new colonial order, were at work in the remaking of the picture of Islam. Yet the Orientalists showed little interest in overcoming the limitations of studying another culture with categories that were patently Western. It was within this framework that the perennial search for "correspondences," homogenous structures, and orthodoxies in the Islamic tradition became a hallmark of the Orientalist tradition, whether one's field of study was popular Sufism, political history, science, or jurisprudence.[57] Inevitably, this has led to such grotesque generalizations as "Islamic orthodoxy," popular Islam versus high Islam, or Sufism versus religious law, often couched in the abstract language of academic parlance, that have been no less inhibiting and essentializing than the medieval conceptions of Islam—conceptions that continue to play out in popular images of Islam in the West today. Secondly, the Orientalist tendency was to analyze the Islamic world: as a decaying civilization whose only import, at least for the Western student of Islam, was either its obscure textual tradition or the variegated responses of Muslim intellectuals to the challenges of the modern world. All of the leading figures of classical Orientalism, for instance, were unanimous in presenting Islamic philosophy and sciences as no more than a port for the transmission of Greek lore to Europe. In reading such classical works of Orientalism as Solomon Munk's *Mélanges de philosophie juive et arabe* (1859) or De Boer's *Geschichte der Philosophie im Islam* (1903), one gets the impression that Islamic philosophy, if this name was allowed at all, was essentially a long commentary in Arabic on Greek and Hellenistic thought taking the forms of either Aristotelianism or neo-Platonism.[58] The best compliment one could accord the Islamic intellectual tradition was, in the words of von Grunebaum, "creative borrowing,"[59] and within this framework the obsessive search for "originality" in Islamic thought was destined to fail.

Thus Islam, having lost its universal appeal and vitality, was seen not as a living tradition with a human face but as an object of study to be historicized and relativized. At this point, it is important to note that the fascination of the nineteenth and early twentieth century scholars of Islam resulted in a number of studies on "modern Islam" dealing exclusively with figures and movements that had come into contact with the modern West on intellectual and political grounds, while neglecting or simply ignoring a large part of the Islamic world, namely the traditional *ʿulamāʾ*, Sufis, and their followers who had not felt a need to respond to the West in ways that would have attracted the attention of Western scholars. It was only after the 1960s and 1970s, when classical Orientalism was called into question, that we began to see works dealing with the traditional world of Islam in the eighteenth and nineteenth centuries. There remains, however, a long list of names yet to be studied including Shaykh ʿAbd al-Qādir al-Jazāʾirī, Shaykh Aḥmad al-ʿAlawī, Aḥmad ibn Idrīs, Ḥājjī Mullā Sabziwārī, Babanzade Aḥmed Hilmī, and Muṣṭafā Sabrī Efendi, the last Shaykh al-Islām of the Ottomans. In this sense, the Orientalist enterprise of mapping out the Islamic world has turned out to be an unfinished, if not failed, project.

The Legacy of Orientalism and the American Context: Islam as the "Other"?

In the modern period, by which I mean the twentieth and the present century, the relation between the Islamic world and the West continues to be screened through inherited images and stereotypes. The depiction of Islamic societies as sensual, despotic, backward, underdeveloped, tribal, promiscuous, aberrant, irrational, and mysterious collectivities have found its way into American popular culture. Such movies as *Navy SEALS* (1990), *Killing Streets* (1991), *The Human Shield* (1992), *The Son of the Pink Panther* (1993), *True Lies* (1994), and *Executive Decision* (1996), provide ample evidence for the persistence of monolithic and violent images of Arabs and Muslims. The uncontrolled use of stereotypes in the entertainment industry has a powerful impact on how ordinary movie-goers come to perceive hundreds of millions of people of Middle Eastern and Asian descent. Thinking through stereotypes and fixed identities creates the delusion of "seen one of 'em, seen 'em all," and uninformed or misinformed readers hastily associate these wild images with what they read in the print media about the Islamic world, the Middle East, and Muslims in general. To use Sam Keen's analogy, the vilification of Arabs, which in the eyes of many Americans represents quintessential Islam because a great majority of them cannot tell the difference between an Arab and non-Arab Muslim, becomes a free ride for portraying the other as villains and extremists: "You can hit an Arab free; they are free enemies, free villains—where you couldn't do it to a Jew or you can't do it to a black anymore."[60]

These violent images have too often become props for the construction of Islamophobic political discourses. The narrative of political, militant, and fundamentalist Islam, produced and sustained by an enormous network of writers, policy makers, journalists, and speakers, is no less damaging and insidious than their counterparts in the entertainment world. This narrative relegates the word "Islam" to political and military confrontation and has the debilitating effect of reducing the Muslim world to a subcategory of the Middle East conflict. Ironically, or perhaps we should say tragically, many people in Europe and America turn to Islam as a way of understanding the causes of the Middle East conflict. This approach, perpetuated in Western media on a daily basis, reinforces the image of Islam as a distant and foreign phenomenon, as a violent and militant faith, and as a monolithic world prone to extremism of all kinds.[61] According to a survey conducted by the National Conferences in 1994, forty-two percent of the 3000 Americans interviewed believe that "Muslims belong to a religion that condones or supports terrorism." Forty-seven percent accept the view that Muslims are "anti-Western and anti-American."[62] Until recently, this was the dominant view even among high school students in the US who have either never been exposed to Islam or have only been exposed to a distortion of it.[63] As became clear after September 11, political realities of the Islamic world are now seen through the lens of cultural stereotypes and amorphous collectivities, and this has become part of the public knowledge about Islam and Muslims. In presenting Bernard Lewis' book *What Went Wrong*, for instance, an anonymous reporter broached the subject by saying that "suddenly the world wants to understand the culture that produced those who one fine day chose to incinerate themselves along with some 3,000 innocent Americans." In fact, Lewis' epigraphic statement from his book sums up this sentiment in condescending language: "If the peoples of the Middle East continue on their present path, the suicide bomber may become a metaphor for the whole region, and there will be no escape from a downward spiral of hate and spite, rage and self-pity, poverty and oppression."[64]

The presumed confrontation between Islam and the West, already revitalized by Huntington's "clash of civilizations" hypothesis, was thrown into full relief after the tragic and deplorable attacks on New York and Washington. Two main attitudes towards Islam have crystallized in the aftermath of September 11. The first is the resurfacing of the medieval descriptions of Islam as the religion of the sword, the Prophet as a violent person, Muslim societies as monolithic, violent, and power-driven collectivities, etc. The second attitude is to identify Islam as a code of belief and action that is obstinately irrational, anti-modern, aberrant, rigid, religious, and traditional. As expected, all of these stereotypes and attitudes have been employed to account for the root causes of the current confrontation between the Islamic and Western worlds. The identification of Islam with violence and militancy on the one hand, and with intolerance and tyranny on the other, is now a powerful image by which Islamic societies are understood and judged in the Western hemisphere. A typical example is Paul Johnson's essay published in the *National Review* as a response to the September 11 attacks. Johnson, who cannot even claim to be a lay reader of Islam but sees himself entitled to speak as an authority on Islamic history, argues that "Islam is an imperialist religion.... Islam remains a religion of the Dark Ages.... mainstream Islam is essentially akin to the most extreme form of Biblical fundamentalism.... the history of Islam has been a history of conquest and reconquest...."[65] Johnson's militant language is indicative of the extent to which the narrative of political Islam and terrorism contributes to the antagonistic representations of Islam as the "other" of the West. In a similar spirit, Francis Fukuyama claimed that "Islam, by contrast, is the only cultural system that seems regularly to produce people like Osama bin Laden or the Taliban who reject modernity lock, stock and barrel. This raises the question of how representative such people are of the larger Muslim community, and whether this rejection is somehow inherent in Islam."[66]

In the decades leading up to September 11, many academics, policymakers, and the so-called terrorism experts have repeatedly portrayed Islam as a religion that condones and produces violence on a consistent basis. The images of suicide bombers, hijackings, assassinations, street riots and uprisings, which have a profound impact on the European and American perceptions of the Islamic world, inform the coded language of "militant Islam," and their *raison d' être* is attributed in an astonishingly simplistic way to the religion of Islam or Muslim culture rather than to the particular political circumstances that have given rise to them. In some cases, religious elements have been openly brought into the debate to explain the anti-Western and anti-American sentiments in the Islamic world. In an interview given to *Time* magazine after his 1980 election, President Reagan claimed that "Muslims were reverting to their belief that unless they killed a Christian or a Jew they would not go to heaven."[67] Twenty-some years later, the situation has not changed very much as we read in Pat Robertson's denouncement of Islam as "a violent religion bent on world domination" and Patrick J. Buchanan's defense of "America against Islam." In one of his messianic talks, Robertson took issue with President Bush's assertion that Islam is a peaceful religion. Instead, Robertson argued that Islam is "not a peaceful religion that wants to coexist. They want to coexist until they can control, dominate, and then, if need be, destroy."[68] Echoing Reagan's remarks, he added that "the Koran makes it very clear that if you see an infidel, you are to kill him," the "infidel" in the quotation being Jews and Christians. The same view was expressed in a more militant fashion by a certain Victor Tadros in an essay called "Islam Unveiled"–"unveiling" now becoming the buzzword for all those who have come to realize the "true nature of Islam." Presenting himself as "Arabic/English translator" on the internet pages of the Texas Christian University where the piece is posted, Tadros reveals his wisdom of unveiling by saying that:

> Most of the Western nations are unaware of the fact that the spirit of Islam is one of enmity, hostility, and Holy War (*jihād*) against both Jews and Christians. There is no other religion but Islam, that commands, in a crystal clear and emphatic way, its true-blue followers to kill both Jews and Christians and destroy their properties.[69]

One can easily discard such views as grossly exaggerated and fanatical, having no value and relevance for the mainstream views concerning Islam. It is, however, a strong indication of the widespread misconceptions of Islam, especially among conservative Christians in the US,[70] and does not appear to be confined to a few aberrant voices. After September 11, for instance, evangelist Rev. Franklin Graham, the son of Billy Graham, called Islam "a very evil and wicked religion" and Rev. Jerry Vines, the past president of the Southern Baptist Convention, called the Prophet of Islam "a demon obsessed pedophile."[71] The presumed conflict between Islam and Christianity on predominantly religious grounds is conceived to be a struggle of the "Cross over the Crescent," to use the title of Samuel Zwemer's famous book.[72] In a speech given on Dec 7, 2001, Patrick Buchanan, for instance, spoke on the "survival of Islam" as if speaking of an epidemic that needs to be eradicated. Upgrading Huntington's "clash of civilizations" to a "war of civilizations," Buchanan asked if

> ... a war of civilizations [is] coming? Clearly, not a few in the Islamic world and the West so believe, and ardently desire.... For no matter how many deaths or defeats we inflict, we cannot kill Islam as we did Nazism, Japanese militarism and Soviet Bolshevism [note the comparison between Islam and the evils of the twentieth century].... If belief is decisive, Islam is militant, Christianity milquetoast. In population, Islam is exploding, the West dying. Islamic warriors are willing to suffer defeat and death, the West recoils at casualties. They are full of grievance; we, full of guilt. Where Islam prevails, it asserts a right to impose its dogma, while the West preaches equality. Islam is assertive, the West apologetic—about its crusaders, conquerors and empires. Don't count Islam out. It is the fastest growing faith in Europe and has surpassed Catholicism worldwide as Christianity expires in the West and the churches empty out, the mosques are going up.[73]

While the title of another essay by Buchanan, "Why Does Islam Hate America," is a good summary of this kind of discourse,[74] the finest and most informed example of analyzing the contemporary Islamic world through essentialist categories and stereotypes on the one hand, and the narrative of confrontation on the other, has been given by Bernard Lewis in his famous article "The Roots of Muslim Rage," published almost ten years before September 11. Purporting to be an account of the contemporary Islamic world, Lewis' article sums up the main trait of Muslims with such words as rage, resentment, bitterness, revulsion, hatred, revenge, "holy war against the infidel enemy," struggles, attacks, hostility, and rejection. Lewis considers the "problem of the Islamic world:" i.e., extremism and fundamentalism, to be deeply rooted in its history and cultural preferences. Thus he locates the roots of what he labels as the "Muslim rage" in the cultural and civilizational realities of the Islamic world:

> Clearly, something deeper is involved than these specific grievances, numerous and important as they may be—something deeper that turns every disagreement into a problem and makes every problem insoluble.
>
> It should by now be clear that we are facing a mood and a movement far transcending the level of issues and policies and the governments that pursue them. This is no less than a clash of civilizations—the perhaps irrational but surely historic reaction of an ancient rival against our Judeo-Christian heritage, our secular present, and the worldwide expansion of both.[75]

Seen in this light, the history of Islam and the West becomes, in Lewis' words, "a long series of attacks and counterattacks, *jihāds* and crusades, conquests and reconquests." It is remarkable that such a prominent historian as Lewis should reduce at one stroke the 1400 years history of Islamic and Western worlds to "attacks and conquests" and contribute to the monolithic perception of Islam as a menacing power bent on destroying Western civilization. Lewis' attempt to summarize the present reality of the Islamic world in terms of rage and resentment against the West leads to gross generalizations and misrepresentations that one would normally expect only from an uninformed or deliberately misleading historian. Throughout this essay and his other works, Lewis looks at history through patterns and categories that culminate in his depiction of Islam and Muslims as immersed in rage, hatred, and a sense of revenge. This is not only to misunderstand the present conditions of the Muslim world but also to misinform and mislead the public at large into thinking that Muslims in the Muslim world, Europe, and America are part of a larger force directed against the foundations of Western civilization. Furthermore, Lewis, like many of his followers, uses the blanket term "Islamic fundamentalism" to discredit and categorize all of the socio-political organizations in the Islamic world as militarist and terrorist structures. This becomes poignantly clear and alarming when Lewis presents his modern version of *jihād* as the "holy war against the infidel West":

> The army is God's army and the enemy is God's enemy. The duty of God's soldiers is to dispatch God's enemies as quickly as possible to the place where God will chastise them—that is to say, the afterlife. In the classical Islamic view, to which many Muslims are beginning to return, the world and all mankind are divided into two: the House of Islam, where the Muslim law and faith prevail, and the rest, known as the House of Unbelief or the House of War, which it is the duty of Muslims ultimately to bring to Islam [Lewis does not explain where he derives this clause from]. But the greater part of the world is still outside Islam, and even inside the Islamic lands, according to the view of the Muslim radicals, the faith of Islam has been undermined and the law of Islam has been abrogated. The obligation of holy war therefore begins at home and continues abroad, against the same infidel enemy.[76]

In spite of his renowned scholarship, Lewis does not discuss the historical origination of the terms *dār al-islām* and *dār al-ḥarb*, nor does he mention the other geo-religious divisions, such as *dar al-ṣulḥ* or *dār al-ʿahd* ("the abode of peace and agreement" with which Muslim societies have an agreement of peace and where Muslim groups live as minorities under non-Muslim rule). By failing to observe these nuances, Lewis presents *dār al-ḥarb* as an Islamic missionary concept. But in reality these territorial divisions have entered Islamic law specifically to provide a blueprint for international relations and to regulate the legal and religious lives of Muslims living under non-Muslim rulers and sometimes as prisoners of war. In contrast to the Orientalist view that *dār al-ḥarb* means "abode of war," i.e., countries with which Muslims are in constant battle,[77] the classical sources of Islamic law use the term in the sense of what we call "foreign countries" today. War against such foreign countries is allowed only when the Muslim state is attacked and the bond of peace (*ṣulḥ* and *ʿahd*) is broken unilaterally.[78] Just as defining a country as "foreign" does not mean discord or conflict, the term *dār al-ḥarb*, which is a legacy of the imperial era, does not mean war or battle. Neither Lewis nor those who distort and misrepresent the concepts of *jihād* and *dār al-ḥarb*, however, make an earnest effort to present a fuller picture of these Islamic concepts. Thus their radicalized and militant readings are found not in the classical sources of Islam written in Arabic, Persian, or Turkish, but mostly in Western works written in English, German, or Dutch. It is not difficult to see how this skewed interpretation militarizes and demonizes the concept of *jihād*—an irresistible fashion before and especially after the September 11th attacks. The word *jihād* has now been equated with militancy and terrorism and is invariably translated as "holy war" in spite of the fact that the holy war tradition originates from the history of Christianity. *Jihād*, which is always mentioned with such words as fundamentalism, terrorism, hatred, and revenge, is used to create a mass hysteria that invigorates the monolithic considerations of Islam. This view was voiced by such a prominent figure of the French intellectual scene as Jacques Ellul. Shortly before his death, in his preface to Bat Ye'or's *The Dhimmi: Jews and Christians under Islam*, Ellul wrote:

> … it is most important to grasp that the *jihād* is an institution in itself; that is to say, an organic piece of Muslim society…. The world, as Bat Ye'or brilliantly shows, is divided into two regions: the *dar al-Islam* and the *dar al-harb*, the "domain of Islam" and "the domain of war." The world is no longer divided into nations, peoples, and tribes. Rather, they are all located en bloc in the world of war, where *war is the only possible relationship with the outside world* [emphasis added]. The earth belongs to Allāh and all its inhabitants must acknowledge this reality; to achieve this goal there is but one method: war. The Koran allows that there are times when war is not advisable, and a momentary pause is called for. But that changes nothing: war remains an institution, which means that it must resume as soon as circumstances permit.[79]

Examples can be multiplied almost *ad infinitum*. In a book written to "explain" the 1993 bombing of the World Trade Center in New York City, Yossef Bodansky, staff director of the Republican Task Force on Terrorism and Unconventional Warfare and the former technical editor of the *Israeli Air Force* magazine, defined *jihād* as the religious and social basis of an international terrorist infrastructure: "Islamic terrorism has embarked on a Holy War—*jihād*—against the West, especially the United States, which is being waged primarily through international terrorism."[80] A similar hysteria was expressed by Amos Perlmutter of American University in a more alarming and tantalizing way when he informed his readers about a "general Islamic war being waged against the West, Christianity, modern capitalism,

Zionism, and Communism all at once."[81] Lumping these divergent aspects of Western civilization into an essential whole, Perlmutter, with a remarkable flight of fancy, declares Islam as the "other" of the West and repeats what Ernest Renan had said in his 1862 inaugural lecture at the College de France: "The Muslim is in the profoundest contempt of education, science, [and] *everything that constitutes the European spirit*" (emphasis added).[82]

The campaign to discredit Islam and thus deliberately widen the gap between Muslims and the West is not limited to the Islamic world proper. It has now been carried to Muslim communities in the US with a clear intent to preempt the possibility of Islam having a human face in America. Steve Emerson's documentary called "*Jihād* in America: An Investigation of Islamic Extremists' Activities in the United States," broadcast in 1994, was a major blow to the public image of *jihād,* which means both inner struggle and fight for the good of the society, but is now equated with terrorism.[83] Instead, Emerson's film depicted a dark and renegade world of terrorists, extremists, fundamentalists, and all the other stereotypes of the narrative of political and fundamentalist Islam. Emerson's militant onslaught on Islam and confrontationist discourse implicated all Muslims in the US as potential criminals and his allegations carry clearly cultural and ideological biases against Islam and Muslims. To substantiate his imaginary scenario, Emerson, who became notorious for his bogus accusation that the Oklahoma City bombing on April 19, 1995 was an "Arab-Muslim terrorist attack," claimed that the so-called Islamic fundamentalists "use their mosques and their religious leaders to form the nucleus of their terrorist infrastructure."[84] In a more combative tone, Emerson declared his vision of the "Muslim hatred of the West": "The hatred of the West by militant Islamic fundamentalists is not tied to any particular act or event. Rather, fundamentalists equate the mere existence of the West—its economic, political, and cultural system—as an intrinsic attack on Islam."[85]

In a similar vein, Samuel Huntington presents the resistance of the Islamic world to secular globalization as being equal to the rejection of democracy, human rights, equality, and the rule of law—the very notions that the so-called Islamists have been struggling to bring to their own home countries: "Western ideas of individualism, liberalism, constitutionalism, human rights, equality, liberty, the rule of law, democracy, free markets, the separation of church and state, often have little resonance in Islamic [and other] ... cultures."[86] Huntington thus mistakes the lack of electoral democracy in present-day Muslim and primarily Middle Eastern countries for the absence of a democratic culture, grossly ignoring the political realities and power structures in those countries. As shown by the work of Norris and Inglehart, based on a huge survey conducted in 75 countries, nine of which are Muslim, between 1995 and 2001,[87] Huntington's assumption that the idea of democracy does not exist in the Islamic world is unsubstantiated by the perceptions and attestations of common people in Muslim countries. As Esposito points out, these remarks point not so much to a clash of cultures and societies that can be justified on social or civilizational grounds as to "a market for clash."[88]

The labeling of Islam as a religion that condones and begets violence and terrorism against Muslims or non-Muslims is a creation of the narrative of militant Islam which has been thoroughly deconstructed by David Dakake and Reza Shah-Kazemi in their contributions to this volume. Proponents of such distortion refuse to admit the ubiquitous reality of violence committed in the name of religion. A cursory look at recent history reveals that violent and terrorist acts have been carried out in the name of all the major world religions including Judaism, Christianity, and Hinduism. Reverend Michael Bray and the bombing of abortion clinics, Timothy McVeigh and the bombing of federal buildings in Oklahoma, David Koresh and the events that took place in Waco, Texas, the religio-political conflict between the Catholics and the Protestants in Northern Ireland, or the implication of the Serbian Orthodox Church in the genocidal killing and raping of more than 250,000 Muslims in Bosnia are but a few examples one can mention in relation to Christianity. Similarly, the killing of 38 Palestinians by Baruch Goldstein, a Brooklyn psychologist, upon entering the al-Khalīl mosque in Hebron in 1994, the assassination of Israel's Prime Minister Yitzhak Rabin by Yigal Amir, who belonged to an extremist Jewish organization, and Meir Kahane's justification of violence and terrorism in the name of Judaism are just a few examples that one can mention in relation to Judaism.[89]

Such examples underline an important facet of our modern predicament that goes beyond national and religious boundaries, namely the violent character of modern culture. It is obvious that none of these cases represent the majority view of Judaism or Christianity and expectedly no attempt is made to trace the origins of such violent acts to the religion itself or its history. The alarming fact is that the same procedure has not been followed in the case of Islam. Moreover, as Joseph E. B. Lumbard shows in his study of the decline of the Islamic intellectual tradition, the rise of militant views among certain groups in the Islamic world is closely tied to the degeneration of traditional Islamic values on the one hand, and the destructive forces of modernization on the other. Therefore, the commonly held view that Muslim societies need to be modernized more in order to overcome the problem of intolerance and extremism is to put the cart before the horse. It is not the traditional beliefs and practices of Islam but their distortions and misrepresentation that are the root of the problem and which require urgent attention.

The fact that Islam is singled out among other religions or religious groups against which charges of violence and extremism can easily be brought, demonstrates the extent to which we become captive to our own history. In spite of the colonial period, the golden age of Orientalism, and the massive body of information about Islam and the Muslim world in Western institutions of learning, Islam is still perceived as an alien phenomenon outside the religious and intellectual horizon of the Western world. The lack of knowledge and familiarity that had obstructed the study of Islam for centuries during the Middle Ages continues to be a stumbling block for the appreciation of the rich tapestry of Islamic culture and history. Furthermore, since the average Westerner is much more familiar with the Judeo-Christian tradition, he or she is in a better position to appreciate the diversity of that tradition and distinguish between the rule and the exception that proves it. In the case of Islam, we scarcely refer to a Judeo-Christian-Islamic tradition whereby the historical unknowing of Islam may be undone and a more realistic picture of Islam may be constructed.

In addition to the charges of militancy and terrorism, the current perceptions of Islam in Europe and the US are also paralyzed by the lack of democracy and secularism in Muslim countries. As we have seen in the above quotes from Lewis and Huntington, it is argued that the absence of a civic culture to promote democracy, freedom, and women's rights is attributed to traditional Islamic culture, which is portrayed as oppressive, backward, irrational, patriarchal, etc. Although Lewis envisions no essential clash between the principles of Islam and the ideals and procedures of democracy, he nevertheless blames "Islamic fundamentalists" for "exploit[ing] the opportunities that a self-proclaimed democratic system by its own logic is bound to offer them."[90] Gilles Kepel takes a more radical approach and argues for the essential incompatibility of Islam and democratic principles when he says that "the rejection of even a chimerical notion of democracy is actually inherent in Islamic religious doctrine."[91] It is remarkable that Western observers such as Kepel should present a narrow and minimalist reading of the debate over democracy in the Islamic world that has been going on for the last three or four decades, and relegate it to the views of few extremist religious figures. As Pippa Norris and Ronald Inglehart have demonstrated, most Muslims oppose the secular character of Western democracy, not the ideals of democracy itself. Although such criticisms do exist, they are mostly reactions to the way in which democracy is exploited in many Muslim countries to legitimate corrupt and oppressive regimes. Furthermore, the so-called anti-Western or anti-American sentiments arise from the open support given to these regimes by European countries and the US. As Michael Salla points out, "the West is likely to provide military and economic support to the governments in question in order to crush

Islamic militancy, while providing diplomatic cover for widespread political repression and human rights abuses."[92] A tragic example of Western double-standards on democracy in the Islamic world is Algeria where the US preferred, in the words of Robin Wright, a "police state" to an Islamic democracy.[93]

At this point, the question of democracy in the Islamic world assumes two important dimensions: intellectual and political. The intellectual nature of the democracy debate is self-evident as many Muslim intellectuals and leaders, including the so-called fundamentalists or Islamists, have been engaged in a critical and constructive dialogue with such issues as political participation, power-sharing, representation, governance, human rights, religious and cultural pluralism, minorities, etc. Looking at the debate in the last several decades, one can assuredly say that forging a non-secular definition of democracy and political rule that will not disenfranchise traditional Islamic values is more than a mere possibility and is taking place in various Muslim countries.[94]

As for the political aspect, it is obvious that both the presence and lack of democracy in the Islamic world has grave policy implications, and the European and American policies often make the issue even more complex and difficult. In some cases, the promotion of democracy, i.e., withholding support from "good allies-bad regimes," presents itself as a dichotomy because "pushing hard for political change might not only disrupt the effort to promote peace but could also work against vital US interests: stability in the oil-rich Persian Gulf and in strategically critical Egypt."[95] Seen from this angle, supporting oppressive regimes becomes a rule of thumb in foreign policy decisions whose ideological foundations are supplied by the narrative of fundamentalist Islam and terrorism as discussed above. All we are left with then is either the messianic threat of Islamic fundamentalism or the "political inability and immaturity" of the Arabs who are, in the words of the movie *Lawrence of Arabia* (1962), "a political naïf in need of tutelage from a wiser Westerner."[96] By the same token, the question of Palestine is attributed to the undemocratic nature of Arabs. It is claimed that the issue between Israel and the Palestinians "is not occupation, it is not settlements, and it certainly is not Israeli brutality and aggression. It is the Arabs' inability to live peacefully with others."[97] Such statements are nothing short of racism but do not bother us because the Arabs are the "free criminals" of the new world. They permeate the American public debate over democracy in the Islamic world and cloud, to say the least, the lingering political problems of Muslim countries that cannot be understood properly in isolation from the global network of governments, international organizations, and corporate business interests.

Debate over the absence of secularism in Muslim countries presents a case similar to the question of democracy. Islamic claims to political rule and the unexpected successes of the so-called Islamists in such countries as Turkey, Malaysia, Iran, and Algeria are usually explained as an anomaly that arises out of the lack of a secular tradition in the Islamic world. The Western-style separation between church and state does not have any historical precedence in Islam, and the attempts to reconcile religion and politics are considered to be cases of religious extremism and fanaticism. By the same token, the rise of Islamic fundamentalism in the Muslim world is attributed to the absence of secularism on the one hand, and the failure of secularist governments on the other. Turkey is mentioned as an exception to the rule due to its program of secularism and Westernization launched in 1923 under the leadership of Kemal Ataturk, the founder of the modern Turkish Republic. In recent years, this has led to a lively debate over the so-called "Turkish model" with its secularist, modern, and pro-Western predilections that can be exported to other Muslim countries. This view not only grossly simplifies the problem of secularism in the Islamic world but also presents a distorted picture in which any or all attempts to overcome the misdeeds of secularism are interpreted as turning the clocks back and obliterating the principles of democracy and human rights. As a result, the secularist regimes in the Islamic world are supported at all costs lest the threat of religious fundamentalism and fanaticism become a reality. This assumption, however, obscures the fact that the secular authority of the state in countries like Turkey is used as a shield against religion rather than guaranteeing the rights of various religious groups against each other and against the overwhelming power of the state. As Graham Fuller points out, Turkey is an example that merits consideration not because "Turkey is 'secular'; in fact, Turkish 'secularism' is actually based on total state control and even repression of religion. Turkey is becoming a model precisely because Turkish democracy is beating back rigid state ideology and slowly and reluctantly permitting the emergence of Islamist movements and parties that reflect tradition, a large segment of public opinion, and the country's developing democratic spirit."[98]

The power-driven and often crude application of secularism in such countries as Tunisia, Algeria, and Turkey has been instrumental in disenfranchising and radicalizing large segments of society in the Islamic world. Using secularism as a way of repressing Islamic norms and local traditions in the name of modernization, state-centered power elites have created chasms between the ruler and the ruled and further widened the gap between the forces of modernity and traditional beliefs and practices; for the project of modernization has been enforced by oppressive and often corrupt regimes whose legitimacy is derived not so much from their constituency as their strategic alliances with Western governments. It is obvious that secularism, as developed during the European Enlightenment, with its non-religious and profane view of the world and society, is not compatible with Islam or any religious tradition for that matter. Secularism as a philosophical project constructs the world in terms of a self-enclosed and immanent reality with a clear rejection of the transcendent. The humanist utopia that humanity will outgrow religion underlies much of the secularist discourse and criticism leveled against Islam and its revival in the twentieth century as we read in Lewis' presentation of "our Judeo-Christian heritage, our secular present" as a point of contention between Islam and the West. The triumph of secularism, however, has been called into question and now, as we see in the work of Peter Berger and others, there is a growing movement to de-secularize the world.[99]

True, the secular character of modern Western civilization is seen as a threat and an area of confrontation in the Muslim world, which remains by and large more religious and traditional than many other parts of the world. Exportation of modern consumerist culture, its popular icons, and the modes of behavior that come with them are perceived to have an eroding effect on the texture of traditional Muslim societies, and propel many to denounce the West as a materialist civilization. It should be pointed out, however, that this view of the West is not very different from that of a pious Christian living in Europe or in America who sees sex, drugs, violence, individualism, destruction of the family, school shootings, or the moral depravity of wanton consumerism under the same or similar light as a devout Muslim, Jew, or Hindu. The difference is the deep culture shock that accompanies a non-Westerner's perception of modern culture. It also needs to be emphasized that the primary target of anti-modernist and anti-Western discourse is not so much the West in and of itself but the West *in* the Islamic world, i.e., what some have referred to as the "McDonaldization" of the world, which poses a threat not only to people of the Islamic faith, but to local and indigenous traditions the world over. Tropes and commodities of modern Western culture become a source of contention when they are exported to traditional societies in the name of modernization, development, and globalization by regimes that lay claim to democracy and secularism. Paradoxically, when these criticisms are translated from the Islamic world back to the West, they are typically presented as bases for militant fundamentalism and anti-modernism while similar criticisms in the West are divested of any such militant or political connotations.

Finally, one should also evaluate such criticisms of modernism and Westernization against the backdrop of European colonialism and its enduring legacy in the Islamic world. A good part of the anti-Western discourse to be found in the Islamic world today has its roots in the eighteenth and nineteenth centuries when encounter with Europe and the modern world meant carrying the brunt of imperialism and colonialism. The fact that more than seventy percent of the Islamic world was under European colonial rule in the second half of the nineteenth century has had a profound impact on how the contemporary Islamic world came to perceive the West as a colonial and enslaving power.[100] We see this clearly in al-Jabarti's celebrated encounter with and testimony to the Napoleonic invasion of Egypt in 1798: for al-Jabarti and his fellow Egyptians, modern Europe was embodied not in new scientific discoveries or ideas of liberty and fraternity but in the violent reality of the invasion of Egypt—the cultural heartland of the Islamic world—by France, the seat of the French Revolution of 1789.[101] Furthermore, the defense of Muslim lands during the historic transition from the empire to the nation-states was undertaken by Muslim leaders and intellectuals who formulated their anti-colonialist struggle as *jihād* against the occupying countries of Europe and Russia.[102] Such concepts as *ummah*, *jihād*, and *dār al-ḥarb* assumed a new geo-political meaning and became part of the modern Islamic discourse during the colonial period. This fact should be kept in mind when analyzing their repercussions in the Islamic world today. For many of the so-called Islamist intellectuals and leaders, overcoming the socio-economic, political, and intellectual heritage of the colonial and post-colonial periods is an ongoing struggle for Muslim societies to reassert their identities in a day and age in which the secularizing effects of modernization and globalization are felt throughout the world.[103]

In spite of the widespread perceptions of Islam as the menacing "other" of the West, whether conceived as Judeo-Christian, secular, or both, there is an alternative view that considers Islam and the Islamic world as a sister civilization to the West and as part of the Abrahamic tradition which includes Judaism, Christianity, and Islam. Voiced by many European and American scholars and intellectuals, this view, whose full analysis we must leave for another study, takes the approach of accommodation, coexistence, and dialogue as its starting point and vehemently denies the demonization of Islam through the narrative of Islamic fundamentalism, radicalism, and terrorism. The proponents of this view, such as Edward Said, John Esposito, John Voll, Bruce Lawrence, James Piscatori, Graham Fuller, and Richard Bulliet, consider the Islamic world not as a monolithic unit but as a diverse, dynamic, and multi-faceted reality. Rather than looking through the mirror of fixed identities and stereotypes, they identify the problems of Muslim countries vis-à-vis themselves and the West within the context of their social and political circumstances. While admitting the existence of some radical voices in the Islamic world as a small minority, they see the Islamic vision of life as essentially tolerant, democratic, and not necessarily anti-Western and anti-American. Although they acknowledge that there are cultural differences between the Islamic world and the West, they do not conceive an essential(ist) clash between the two and see Islam as an intellectual and spiritual challenge rather than a military threat to the West.[104] They also stress the fact that most of the anti-American sentiment in the Islamic world emanates from American foreign policy, which adopts a double standard on the question of democracy in Muslim countries and especially in the Middle East, and provides unconditional and one-sided support to Israel.[105] They also recognize the experience of Muslim minorities in Europe and the US as a valuable chapter in the history of the two worlds with tremendous potentials for dialogue and co-existence between Islam and the West. It would not be a stretch to say that the sharp contrast between the confrontationalist and accommodationist perspectives represents a new chapter in the history of Islam and the West, both at the level of civilizational co-existence and policy decisions in the post-September 11 era.[106]

Conclusion

Western perceptions of Islam are more a reflection of the West's understanding of itself than of Islam. The same holds true for the Muslim perceptions of the West. Both worlds see one another through the eyes of their own self-understanding, as they strive to come to terms with their own identity and their views of the other. The Muslim perceptions of the West are inevitably encoded in Muslim modes of self-understanding that have undergone a number of changes throughout Islamic history, generating new modes of perception and understanding towards the West. A Muslim's view of Christianity or Greek philosophy in the ninth century is not the same as his approach to modern science and technology in the eighteenth or nineteenth centuries. When we speak of continuities and discontinuities in the history of Islam and the West, we can do so only within the context of the perseverance or waning of such modes of self-perception and self-understanding. In this sense, the encounter of the Muslim world with the modern West, its science and technology, its military and economic might, and its worldview is also an encounter with itself, in that the Muslim world's self-perception informs the ways in which the "West" as a term of contrast and comparison is constructed in the Islamic world. Such burning issues as tradition and modernity, religiosity and secularism, revival of Islamic civilization, economic and political development in Muslim countries, and modern science and technology and their socio-philosophical challenges cannot be properly discussed in today's Islamic world without taking into account the role played by the West in this process.

By the same token, the West's encounter with Islam is a coming to terms with its own self-image. Ethnocentrism, universalism versus particularism and locality, representations of the other, the legacy of colonialism, globalization, human rights, pluralism, and the limits of modernism are only a few among the many issues that define the West in its relation to the non-Western world. In a day and age in which national and cultural boundaries are crossed over in a myriad of media, none of these issues can be discussed without attending to their meanings and implications for cultures and identities beyond the precincts of the Western world. At this juncture, studying Islam and its Western constructions is an exercise in looking at ourselves and our modes of perception as they are reflected in the images and categories by which we understand the other. Whether Islam is conceived to be a religious heresy, a theological challenge, a sister civilization, or simply an alien culture, we can no longer fail to see its relevance and urgency for the West's self-understanding in the new millennium.

Notes

[1] These usual explanations for the spread of Islam were prevalent even among such American writers of the nineteenth century as Edward Forster, John Hayward, and George Bush, the first American biographer of the Prophet. See Fuad Sha´ban, *Islam and Arabs in Early American Thought: The Roots of Orientalism in America* (North Carolina: The Acorn Press, 1991), pp. 40-43.

[2] According to Oleg Grabar, the term "Saracen" comes from the word "Sarakenoi": "John of Damascus and others after him always insisted on the fact that the new masters of the Near East are Ishmaelites, that is, outcasts; and it is with this implication that the old term *Sarakenoi* is explained as meaning "empty (because of or away from?) of Sarah (*ek tes Sarras kenous*) and that the Arabs are often called *Agarenois*, obviously in a pejorative sense" (Oleg Grabar, "The Umayyad Dome of The Rock In Jerusalem," *Ars Orientalis* 3 (1959): 44).

[3] For Theodore Abu-Qurrah and extracts from his writings against Islam, see Adel-Theodore Khoury, *Les Théologiens Byzantins et L'Islam: Textes et Auteurs* (Louvain: Editions Nauwelaerts, 1969), pp. 83-105.

[4] Bede was the first theologian to label the Saracens as enemies of God in his biblical commentaries. This was important for finding a place for the Saracens in the Christian version of biblical history.

[5] Daniel J. Sahas, *John of Damascus on Islam: The "Heresy of the Ishmaelites"* (Leiden: E. J. Brill, 1972), p. 68.

[6] *De Hearesibus*, 764B, quoted in Sahas, *ibid.*, p. 73.

[7] For St. John's career in Syria under the Umayyad caliphate, see Sahas, pp. 32-48.

[8] R. W. Southern, *Western Views of Islam in the Middle Ages* (Cambridge: Harvard University Press, 1962), p. 3.

[9] As Kedar points out, this was a result of the daily interaction of Eastern Christians with Muslims. See his *Crusade and Mission: European Attitudes toward the Muslims* (Princeton: Princeton University Press, 1984), p. 35f.

[10] Some of the anti-Islamic texts produced by Byzantine theologians have been collected in Adel-Theodore Khoury, *Les Théologiens Byzantins et L'Islam*, where one can follow the representative texts of such theologians as St. John of Damascus, Theodore Abu-Kurra, Theophane the Confessor, Nicetas of Byzantium, and George Hamartolos.

[11] On Ketton's translation see Marie-Thérèse d'Alverny, "Deux Traductions Latines du Coran au Moyen Age" *Archives d'histoire doctrinale et littéraire du Moyen Age* 16 (Paris: Librairie J. Vrin, 1948) published in her *La connaissance de l'Islam dans l'Occident médiéval* (Great Britain: Variorum, 1994), I, pp. 69-131 where d'Alverny also analyzes Mark of Toledo's Latin translation completed shortly after that of Ketton. See also James Kritzeck, "Robert of Ketton's Translation of the Qur'an," *Islamic Quarterly* 2, no. 4 (1955): 309-312.

[12] Quoted in Southern, *ibid.*, pp. 38-9. In spite of his deliberate anti-Islamic campaign, Peter the Venerable ushered in a new era in the European studies of Islam in the Middle Ages. See James Kritzeck, *Peter the Venerable and Islam* (Princeton: Princeton University Press, 1964), pp. 24-36.

[13] Cf. Kenneth M. Setton, *Western Hostility to Islam and Prophecies of Turkish Doom* (Philadelphia: American Philosophical Society, 1991), pp. 47-53.

[14] Cf. James Windrow Sweetman, *Islam and Christian Theology*, part 2, vol. 1 (London: Lutterworth, 1955), pp. 98-99. Marie-Thérèse d'Alverny draws attention to the same problem in her important essay "La connaissance de l'Islam en Occident du IXe au milieu de XIIe siécle," *Settimane di studio del Centro italiano di studi sull'alto medioevo 12, L'Occidente e l'Islam nell'alto medioevo, Spoleto 2-8 aprile 1964, col. II Spoleto, 1965*, published in *La connaissance de l'Islam dans l'Occident medieval*, V, pp. 577-8.

[15] Southern mentions two other works of equal importance. The first is Walter of Compiegne's *Otia de Machomete* written between 1137 and 1155, and the second Guibert of Nogent's *Gesta Dei per Francos*, composed at the beginning of the twelfth century, which is an account of the Crusades with a chapter devoted to the Prophet of Islam. Cf. Southern, *ibid.*, p. 30.

[16] For more on the image of the Prophet of Islam in the West from the Middle Ages and the Renaissance up to the present, see Clinton Bennett, *In Search of Muḥammad* (Cassell: London & New York, 1998), pp. 69-92 and 93-135; and Norman Daniel, *Islam and the West: The Making of an Image* (Oxford: Oneworld, 1993; first published in 1960), pp. 100-130. For a critical evaluation of three Orientalist scholars on the Prophet of Islam, see Jabal Muḥammad Buaben, *Image of the Prophet Muḥammad in the West: A Study of Muir, Margoliouth and Watt* (Leicester: The Islamic Foundation, 1996).

[17] Cf. Seyyed Hossein Nasr, *Knowledge and the Sacred* (Albany, NY: State University New York Press, 1989), pp. 280-308; "Comments on a Few Theological Issues in Islamic-Christian Dialogue" in *Christian-Muslim Encounters*, Yvonne and Wadi Haddad (eds.), (Florida: Florida University Press, 1995), pp. 457-467; and "Islamic-Christian Dialogues: Problems and Obstacles to be Pondered and Overcome," *Muslim World* no. 3-4 (July-October 1998): 218-237; Kenneth Cragg, *The Call of the Minaret* (New York: Orbis Books, 1989, 2nd printing; first published in 1956) and *Muḥammad and the Qur'ān: A Question of Response* (New York: Orbis Books, 1984); Ismail Raji al-Faruqi (ed.), *Trialogue of the Abrahamic Faiths* (Herndon, VA: International Institute of Islamic Thought, 1982). See also Frithjof Schuon, *Christianity/Islam: Essays on Esoteric Ecumenism* (Bloomington, IN: World Wisdom Books, 1985).

[18] *Inferno*, Canto 28 where Dante describes the heretics in the eighth circle of hell. Dante puts the Prophet Muḥammad in the ninth bowge as a heretic responsible for schism and discord. We can see in this depiction the repercussions of the labeling of Islam as an Ishmaelite heresy by St. John of Damascus and Bede in the eighth century. For the spiritual significance of ʿAlī see Reza Shah-Kazemi's contribution to this volume: "Recollecting the Spirit of *Jihād*."

[19] Cf. Miguel Asin Palacios, *Islam and the Divine Comedy*, tr. with abridgment by Harold Sunderland (London: 1926), pp. 256-263.

[20] Lull's most important work *Ars Magna* provides ample material for his approach to Islam as a religious and cultural/philosophical challenge.

[21] Averroists were known for their distinctly heretical views and all of these views—attributed to Averroes and his Latin followers—were listed in the 1277 condemnation of Averroism. Among those, four are the most important: the eternity of the world; the claim that God does not know the particulars; monopsychism, i.e., the view that there is only one intellect for all human beings and this absolves individuals of their moral responsibility; and finally the all-too-famous double-truth theory, i.e., the view that

religion and philosophy hold different truths and that they should be kept separate. The third view on monopsychism was taken to be such a major challenge for Christian theology that St. Thomas Aquinas had to write a treatise called *On the Unity of the Intellect against the Averroists.* For the 219 propositions condemned by Bishop Tempier on the order of Pope John XXI, see *Philosophy in the Middle Ages: The Christian, Islamic, and Jewish Traditions,* ed. Arthur Hyman and James J. Walsh (Indianapolis: Hackett Publishing Company, 1973), pp. 584-591.

22 *De consideratione,* III, I, 3-4, quoted in Benjamin Z. Kedar, *Crusade and Mission,* p. 61.

23 Oljaytu's embracing of the Shiʿite branch of Islam instead of Buddhism or Christianity, the two religions he had studied before accepting Islam, is a momentous event in the history of Islam with repercussions both for Shiʿism and Muslim-Christian relations. For some of the Christian reactions to the historic Mongol conversion, see David Bundy, "The Syriac and Armenian Christian Responses to the Islamification of the Mongols" in John Victor Tolan (ed.), *Medieval Christian Perceptions of Islam* (New York/London: Garland Publishing, 1996), pp. 33-53.

24 Haskins attributes a considerable role to the interaction of Muslims and Christians in al-Andalus and especially in Toledo where many of the translations from Arabic into Latin were made for the flourishing of a new intellectual climate in the twelfth century. See his *The Renaissance of the Twelfth Century* (Cambridge: Harvard University Press, 1976; first published in 1927), especially pp. 278-367.

25 Alvaro, *Indiculus luminosus,* chap. 35, quoted in Grunebaum, *Medieval Islam* (Chicago/London: The University of Chicago Press, 1946), p. 57.

26 For a brief treatment of Andalusia in the history of Islam and the West, see Anwar Chejne, "The Role of al-Andalus in the Movements of Ideas Between Islam and the West" in Khalil I. Semaan (ed.), *Islam and the Medieval West: Aspects of Intercultural Relations* (Albany: SUNY Press, 1980), pp. 110-133. See also, Jane Smith, "Islam and Christendom," in *The Oxford History of Islam,* ed. by J. L. Esposito (Oxford: Oxford University Press, 1999), pp. 317-321.

27 *Les Pensées de Blaise Pascal* (Le club français du livre, 1957), pp. 200-1.

28 *Relation of a Journey begun An. Dom. 1610,* p. 60, quoted in Jonathan Haynes, *The Humanist as Traveler: George Sandys's Relation of a Journey begun An. Dom. 1610* (London/Toronto: Fairleigh Dickinson University Press, 1986), p. 71.

29 *Ibid.*, pp. 59-60, quoted in Haynes, p. 70.

30 *The Dictionary Historical and Critical of Mr. Peter Bayle* (New York/London: Garland Publishing, Inc., 1984), vol. IV, p. 29. All translations of Bayle have been slightly modified from medieval spellings to more modern spellings.

31 Bayle, *The Dictionary,* pp. 47 and 30.

32 Bayle, *The Dictionary,* p. 39.

33 On Prideaux's approach to Islamic history, see P. M. Holt, "The Treatment of Arab History by Prideaux, Oackley and Sale" in B. Lewis and P. M. Holt (eds.), *Historians of the Middle East* (London: Oxford University Press, 1962), pp. 290-302.

34 From the *Lettre au roi de Prusse* quoted in N. Daniel, *Islam and the West,* p. 311.

35 Stubbe's book remained in manuscript form until 1911 when it was edited and published for the first time by Hafiz Mahmud Khan Shairani (London: Luzac, 1911). A

second edition was printed in Lahore in 1954. For references to Stubbe's work, see P. M. Holt, *A Seventeenth-Century Defender of Islam: Henry Stubbe (1632-76) and His Book* (London: Dr. Williams' s Trust, 1972).

36 Quoted in Holt, *A Seventeenth-Century Defender of Islam*, pp. 22-23.

37 E. Swedenborg, "Divine Providence" in *A Compendium of Swedenborg's Theological Writings*, edited by Samuel M. Warren (New York: Swedenborg Foundation, Inc., 1974; first edition 1975), pp. 520-1.

38 *Ibid.*, p. 521.

39 In addition to his meticulous translation of the Qur´ān into Latin as late as the end of the seventeenth century, Maracci also wrote a number of polemics against Islam including his *Prodromus* and *Refutatio*, both of which have been added to his translation. Cf. N. Daniel, *Islam and the West*, p. 321.

40 There were other translations of the Qur´ān into the European languages in the eighteenth and nineteenth centuries. The works of Claude Etienne Savary (1750-1788), Garcin de Tassy (1794-1878), and Albert de Biberstein Kasimirski (1808-1887) contained partial translations of the Qur´ān into French. Several anonymous translations of the Qur´ān in English were in circulation in the nineteenth century but Sale's rendering remained to be the definitive text. In Germany, Martin Luther's (1483-1546) interest in the Qur´ān was already known and some have even attributed a selective translation to Luther. In 1659, Johann Andreas Endter and Wolfgang Endter published a German translation of the Qur´ān titled *al-Koranum Mahumedanum*. As a fashion of the late Middle Ages, the Qur´ān was called the "sacred book of the Turks" and sometimes the "Turkish Bible." This was followed by Johan Lange's version published in Hamburg in 1688. Theodor Arnold's *Der Koran*, based on the Arabic original and Sale's English translation, was published 1746 to be followed by David Friedrich Megerlin's *Die Turkische Bibel order des Koran* in 1772. A comprehensive list of Qur´ān translations can be found in Ismet Binark and Halit Eren, *World Bibliography of Translations of the Meanings of the Holy Quran: Printed Translations, 1515-1980*, edited with introduction by Ekmeleddin Ihsanoglu (Istanbul: Research Center for Islamic History, Art, and Culture [IRCICA], 1986). See also Muḥammad Hamidullah (trans.), *Le Saint Coran* (Paris: Club Francais du Livre, 1985), pp. LX-XC.

41 Quoted in Fuad Sha´ban, *Islam and Arabs in Early American Thought*, p. 31.

42 Thomas Carlyle, *On Heroes, Hero-Worship and the Heroic in History* (1840) ed. Carl Niemeyer (Lincoln/London: University of Nebraska Press, 1966), pp. 64-65. Carlyle mentions Sale's translation as a "very fair one."

43 Carlyle, *ibid.*, p. 43.

44 Carlyle, *ibid.*, p. 56.

45 Cf. John D. Yohannan, *Persian Poetry in England and America: A 200-Year History* (Delmar, N.Y.: Caravan Books, 1977).

46 Cf. Edward Said, *Orientalism* (New York: Vintage Books, 1979), pp. 166-197.

47 This is not to suggest that the inherited religious biases against Islam were absent in the narrations of the "humanist" travelers of Europe. George Sandys' *Relation of a Journey*, mentioned above, is a case in point. Sandys' accounts of Turkey, Egypt, the Holy Land, and Italy clearly reveal the extent to which the seventeenth century humanists of Europe were under the influence of Christian polemics against Islam. Cf. Jonathan Haynes, *The Humanist as Traveler: George Sandys's Relation of a Journey*, pp. 65-81.

48 André Gide, *Journals 1889-1949*, trans. Justin O'Brien (New York: Vintage Books, 1956), vol. I, pp. 177, 181.

49 Burton was so much engaged in assuming a local identity that he presented himself as a Muslim doctor of Indian descent. His *Personal Narrative of a Pilgrimage to al-Madinah and Meccah (1855-1856)* bears testimony to his knowledge of Arabic language and Islamic culture.

50 Sir John Chardin, *Travels in Persia 1673-1677* (New York: Dover Publications, Inc., 1988), pp. 184 and 187.

51 Edward Said, *Orientalism*, p. 49ff.

52 Lane's *An Account of the Manners and Customs of the Modern Egyptians*, published first in 1836, is even more important than his Lexicon in revealing his approach to the Arab-Islamic world.

53 Albert Hourani provides a very fine analysis of these and other minor figures in his *Islam in European Thought* (Cambridge: Cambridge University Press, 1991), pp. 18-34.

54 According to one estimate quoted by Said, close to 60,000 books about the New Orient were written between 1800 and 1950. Cf. E. Said, *Orientalism*, p. 204.

55 For I. Goldziher, C. S. Hurgronje, C. H. Becker, D. B. Macdonald, L. Massignon, see Jean Jacques Waardenburg, *L'Islam dans le miroir de l'Occident. Comment quelques orientalistes occidentaux se sont penchés sur l'Islam et se sont formé une image de cette religion* (Paris: Mouton, 1963). See also A. J. Arberry, *Oriental Essays: Portraits of Seven Scholars* (Surrey: Curzon Press, 1997; first published in 1960) and Maxime Rodinson, *Europe and the Mystique of Islam* (Seattle/London: University of Washington Press, 1987), pp. 83-129.

56 A. J. Arberry, *Oriental Essays* (Great Britain: Curzon Press, 1997; first published in 1960), p. 7.

57 A classical example of the Orientalist construction of an Islamic orthodoxy is I. Goldziher's "Stellung der alten islamichen Orthodoxie zu den antiken Wissenchaften," *Abhandlungen der Koniglich Preussischen Akademie der Wissenchaften*, Jahrgang, 1915 (Berlin: Verlag der Akademie, 1916) where Goldziher establishes the *kalam* (theology) and *fiqh* (jurisprudence) critiques of philosophy especially by the Ḥanbalite scholars as the official position of "Islamic orthodoxy" against the pre-Islamic traditions. This article has been translated into English by M. L. Swartz in his *Studies on Islam* (Oxford: Oxford University Press, 1981), pp. 185-215.

58 T. J. De Boer's work has been translated into English by E. R. Jones as *The History of Philosophy in Islam* (New York: Dover Publications, Inc., 1967).

59 Gustave E. von Grunebaum, *Medieval Islam*, p. 294. This theme is further articulated in a collection of essays edited by von Grunebaum as *Unity and Variety in Muslim Civilization* (Chicago: The University of Chicago Press, 1955).

60 Sam Keen, *Faces of the Enemy* (Cambridge: Harper and Row, 1986), pp. 29, 30, quoted in J. Shaheen, *Arab and Muslim Stereotyping in American Popular Culture* (Washington D. C.: Center for Muslim-Christian Understanding, Georgetown University, 1997), p. 12.

61 Cf. Jack Shaheen, *The TV Arab* (Ohio: The Popular Press, 1984) and *Arab and Muslim Stereotyping*. See also Michael Hudson and Ronald G. Wolfe (eds.), *The American Media*

and the Arabs (Washington D.C.: Center for Contemporary Arab Studies, Georgetown University, 1980).

62 J. Shaheen, *Arab and Muslim Stereotyping*, p. 3.

63 Michael Suleiman, *American Images of Middle East Peoples: Impact of the High Schools* (New York: Middle East Studies Association, 1977), quoted in Fred R. von. Der Mehden, "American Perceptions of Islam," in *Voices of Resurgent Islam*, ed. by John L. Esposito (Oxford: Oxford University Press, 1983), p. 21.

64 *Jerusalem Post*, April 7, 2002.

65 P. Johnson, "'Relentlessly and Thoroughly': The Only Way to Respond," *National Review*, October 15, 2001, p. 20.

66 F. Fukuyama, "The West Has Won," *The Guardian*, October 11, 2002.

67 Quoted in Fawaz A. Gerges, *America and Political Islam: Clash of Cultures or Clash of Interests?* (Cambridge: Cambridge University Press, 1999), pp. 69-70.

68 *The Washington Post*, February 22, 2002, A02. This is as if taken verbatim from Renan: "Islam was liberal [tolerant] when it was weak and was violent when it became strong" (*L'Islamisme et la science* [Paris: 1883], p. 18).

69 http://www.magazine.tcu.edu/forum/display_message.asp?mid=599

70 Another powerful myth often invoked to exclude Islam from the Judeo-Christian tradition is the stupendous idea that Muslims believe in a God other than what Jews and Christians believe. One may recall here the so-called "moon-god Allāh" story according to which Muslims worship the "Moon God," a pagan deity. This myth has been popularized by Dr. Robert Morey in his lectures and publications including *The Moon-god Allāh*, *Islam: the Religion of the Moon God*, *Behind the Veil: Unmasking Islam*, and *The Islamic Invasion: Confronting the World's Fastest Growing Religion*.

71 Nicholas D. Kristof, "Bigotry in Islam—And Here," *New York Times*, July 9, 2002.

72 For Zwemer, who founded and edited the *Muslim World* for nearly four decades, and other missionary views of Islam in the modern period, see Jane I. Smith, "Christian Missionary Views of Islam in the 19th-20th Centuries," in Zafar Ishaq Ansari and John L. Esposito (eds.), *Muslims and the West: Encounter and Dialogue* (Islamabad: Islamic Research Institute, 2001), pp. 146-177.

73 December 7, 2002 "Coming Clash of Civilizations?" at http://www.theamericancause .org/patcomingclashprint.htm.

74 March 5, 2002, at http://www.theamericancause.org/patwhydoesislam.htm.

75 Bernard Lewis, "The Roots of Muslim Rage," *The Atlantic Monthly* (September 1990): 47-60.

76 Lewis, *ibid.* See also Lewis' "Islam and Liberal Democracy," *The Atlantic Monthly* (February 1993): 93.

77 L. Massignon, *La Crise de l'autorité religieuse et le Califat en Islam* (Paris, 1925), pp. 80-81; E. Tyan, *Institutions du droit public musulman* (Paris, 1954) Vol. II, p. 302; Majid Khadduri, *War and Peace in the Law of Islam* (Baltimore: Johns Hopkins Press, 1955), pp. 53 and 170; *ibid.*, "International Law," in *Law in the Middle East*, M. Khadduri and H. J. Liebesny (eds.), (Washington D.C.: Middle East Institute, 1955), pp. 349-370. Cf. also the Encyclopedia of Islam entry "dar al-harb" reprinted in *Shorter Encyclopedia of Islam*, ed. by H. A. R. Gibb and J. H. Kramers (Ithaca: Cornell University Press, n.d.), pp. 68-69.

78 For some of the classical sources on the subject, see Ahmad al-Sarakhsi, *al-Mabsut* (Istanbul: Dar al-daʿwah, 1912), vol. 30, p. 33; Ibn al-Qayyim al Jawziyyah, *Ahkam ahl al-dhimmah* (Damascus, 1381 [A.H.]), vol. I, p. 5; and Ibn Abidin, *Radd al-mukhtar* (Beirut: Dār al-Kutub al-ʿIlmiyyah, 1415/1994), vol. III, pp. 247, 253. For an excellent survey of the classical sources, see Ahmet Ozel, *Islam Hukukunda Ulke Kavrami: Daru'l-islam, Daru'l-harb, Daru'l-sulh* (Istanbul: Iz Yayincilik, 1998).

79 Bat Ye'or's *The Dhimmi: Jews and Christians under Islam* (Rutherford: Fairleigh Dickinson University Press, 1985), from the Preface.

80 Quoted in Paul Findley, *Silent No More: Confronting America's False Images of Islam* (Beltsville, MD: Amana Publications, 2001), p. 65.

81 *The Wall Street Journal*, October 4, 1984.

82 Ernest Renan, *L'Islamisme et la science*, p. 3.

83 For a full analysis of the traditional Islamic interpretation of *jihād* see David Dakake's "The Myth of a Militant Islam" and Reza Shah-Kazemi's "Recollecting the Spirit of *Jihād*" in this volume.

84 The *Wall Street Journal*, June 25, 1993. After September 11, Emerson added a new item to his attacks and defamations with his book *American Jihad: The Terrorists Living Among Us* (New York: Free Press, 2002). For a similar approach, see Daniel Pipes, "Fighting Militant Islam, Without Bias," *City Journal* (Autumn 2001).

85 *San Diego Union Tribune*, June 8, 1993, quoted in P. Findley, p. 71.

86 Samuel P. Huntington, *The Clash of Civilizations and the Remaking of World Order* (New York: Simon & Schuster, 1997), p. 258 quoted in John Esposito, *Unholy War: Terror in the Name of Islam* (Oxford: Oxford University Press, 2002), p. 127.

87 Pippa Norris and Ronald Inglehart, "Islam and the West: Testing the Clash of Civilizations Thesis," John F. Kennedy School of Government, Harvard University, Working Paper Number RWP02-015, April 22, 2002.

88 Huntington, *The Clash of Civilizations*, p. 126.

89 Mark Juergensmeyer's work *Terror in the Mind of God: The Global Rise of Religious Violence* (Berkeley/London: University of California Press, 2000) contains much valuable material on modern justifications of the use of violence in the name of religion and shows the extent to which violence can take on various names and identities.

90 Lewis, "Islam and Liberal Democracy," p. 93.

91 Gilles Kepel, *The Revenge of God: The Resurgence of Islam, Christianity and Judaism in the Modern World* (University Park: Pennsylvania State University Press, 1994), p. 194.

92 Michael E. Salla, "Political Islam and the West: A New Cold War or Convergence?," *Third World Quarterly* 18, no. 4 (December 1997): 729-743.

93 Robin Wright, "Islam, Democracy and the West," *Foreign Affairs* (Summer 1992): 137-8 quoted in Gerges, *America and Political Islam*, pp. 29-30.

94 There is an ever-growing literature on Islam and democracy, pointing to the vibrancy of the debate in the Islamic world. For a brief discussion of the cases of Malaysia, Indonesia, and Iran, see John Esposito, *Unholy War: Terror in the Name of Islam* (Oxford: Oxford University Press, 2002), pp. 133-145. See also J. L. Esposito and John Voll, *Islam and Democracy* (Oxford/New York: Oxford University Press, 1996); A.

Soroush, *Reason, Freedom, & Democracy in Islam: Essential Writings of ʿAbdolkarim Soroush*, translated and edited with a critical introduction by Mahmoud Sadri, Ahmad Sadri (New York: Oxford University Press, 2000); Azzam S. Tamimi, *Rachid Ghannouchi: A Democrat within Islamism* (New York: Oxford University Press, 2001); and Fatima Mernissi, *Islam and Democracy: Fear of the Modern World* (Reading, Mass.: Addison-Wesley Pub. Co., 1992).

95 Martin Indyk, "Back to the Bazaar," *Foreign Affairs* 81, no. 1 (February 2002): 75-89.

96 Quoted in Ralph Braibanti, *The Nature and Structure of the Islamic World* (Chicago: International Strategy and Policy Institute, 1995), p. 6.

97 The columnist Mona Charen quoted in Robert Fisk, "Fear and Learning in America," *Independent*, April 17, 2002.

98 Graham Fuller, "The Future of Political Islam," *Foreign Affairs* 81, no. 2 (March/April 2002): 59.

99 Cf. Peter L. Berger (ed.), *The Desecularization of the World: Resurgent Religion and World Politics* (Washington, D.C.: Ethics and Public Policy Center, 1999). See also the essays by John Keane, P. Berger, Abdelwahab Elmessiri, and Ahmet Davutoglu in *Islam and Secularism in the Middle East*, ed. by J. L. Esposito and A. Tamimi (New York: New York University Press, 2000), and William E. Connolly, *Why I am Not a Secularist* (Minneapolis: University of Minnesota Press, 1999).

100 For a treatment of the eighteenth and nineteenth century Islamic movements within the context of European colonialism, see John Voll, "Foundations for Renewal and Reform" in *The Oxford History of Islam*, ed. by J. L. Esposito, pp. 509-547. See also John L. Esposito, *The Islamic Threat: Myth or Reality?*, pp. 168-212.

101 Cf. al-Jabarti's narration of the French invasion of Egypt and his cultural response to Napoleon in *Al-Jabarti's Chronicle of the French Occupation 1798: Napoleon in Egypt*, trans. Shmuel Moreh (Princeton: Markus Wiener Publishers, 1997, 3rd printing).

102 Cf. S. V. R. Nasr, "European Colonialism and the Emergence of Modern Muslim States," in *The Oxford History of Islam*, pp. 549-599.

103 Cf. Bruce B. Lawrence, *Shattering the Myth: Islam Beyond Violence* (Princeton: Princeton University Press, 1998), pp. 40-50 and Yvonne Yazbeck Haddad, "Islamism: A Designer Ideology for Resistance, Change and Empowerment," in *Muslims and the West: Encounter and Dialogue*, pp. 274-295.

104 Cf. my "Deconstructing Monolithic Perceptions: A Conversation with Professor John Esposito," *The Journal of Muslim Minority Affairs* (April 2001): 155-163.

105 For an analysis of these scholars from the point of view of US foreign policy decisions, see Mohommed A. Muqtedar Khan, "US Foreign Policy and Political Islam: Interests, Ideas, and Ideology," *Security Dialogue* 29, no. 4 (1998): 449-462.

106 For the policy recommendations of the accommodationist wing, see Gerges, *America and Political Islam*, pp. 28-36.

Part III

Political Dimensions

Chapter 6

The Economics of Terrorism: How bin Laden Is Changing the Rules of the Game

Waleed El-Ansary

At first glance, the actions of suicidal terrorists may not appear to be explicable in terms of game theory. Indeed, none of the key assumptions of game theory (which we explain in the course of the paper) seem to apply clearly in such a situation.[1] Game theory assumes, for example, that players must know the rules of the game, and that action must occur within those rules. But what could possibly be the rules of the current terrorist game involving suicide? Game theory also assumes that players have a way of selecting an action from those that are permitted. But what should we assume about what motivates terrorists in the current situation? Moreover, how does what a terrorist thinks we will do affect his own selection? To the extent that suicidal terrorism seems irrational, it will appear to rule out reliable answers to these three questions, and it is therefore no surprise if such terrorists are not thought of in game theoretic terms.

But we suggest that these questions have real answers, and one does not need to be a Nobel laureate and game theorist like John Nash to figure them out.[2] This paper attempts to demonstrate how tenets of game theory apply to current political situations and to draw out the implications for our strategy in dealing with terrorism. The answers, however, require understanding a host of complex issues. For starters, to properly answer these questions requires an understanding of different "types" of Muslims and how they view each other, how and why some groups have inverted Islamic values, and the history of various parts of the Islamic world, particularly the Middle East. And that is just the beginning, because "second-order" factors, such as the West's understanding of Islam, have influenced some of these "first-order" issues.[3] As we might expect, policymakers are divided over how to answer the three game theory questions, because an understanding of all the aforementioned issues is so difficult to achieve. To take a simple example related to the understanding of Islamic values, David Dakake points out that it is most difficult for many Westerners to understand the Qur´ān because, unlike the Bible, the verses rarely come with their historical context supplied.[4]

Addressing these game theory questions is therefore a daunting task. In the face of this complex situation, there are three possible groups into which policymakers may fall. Policymakers may be so puzzled by the overwhelming number and complexity of issues that they feel unable to answer any of the game theory questions, and doubt that game theory even applies to suicide attacks in the first place. For the sake of convenience, let us call this first hypothetical group our "puzzled policymakers." As a second possibility, policymakers may believe that they have the answers to these questions, but a close analysis of their proposed answers may prove them to be inconsistent with the self-understanding of the players on the other side. Such policymakers therefore do not really know the rules of the game, because they do not know the payoffs to the other players of different combinations of moves. Let us call this second hypothetical group our "mistaken policymakers." A third possibility is that policymakers actually have the right answers and know the rules of the game, in the sense that their answers are consistent with the self-understanding of the players on the other side. Only on the basis of this correct understanding could we determine to what extent the currently available options and payoffs in the game (i.e., the rules) are fixed or could be changed unilaterally. Let us call this third hypothetical group our "discerning policymakers."

Obviously, we all hope that actual policymakers setting strategy for the United States in the current crisis are among our discerning policymakers. We clearly would not want puzzled policymakers to determine strategy, as this hypothetical group would not have the right answers to the strategic questions. Fortunately, this group is not necessarily an obstacle to adopting the right strategy, because the group knows that it does not know the answers. Such "simple ignorance" usually does not interfere with the recommendations of discerning policymakers. The mistaken policymakers, however, may interfere, because this hypothetical group is not only ignorant, but is also unaware of this ignorance. Such a lethal combination makes for "complex ignorance" and inevitably leads to strategic errors.

The purpose of this paper is to help achieve an understanding of the strategic issues and a level of strategic thinking corresponding to our discerning policymakers.[5] To that end, we will combine game theory with the findings of the other papers in this collection and insightful works by leading scholars of Islamic studies, such as Seyyed Hossein Nasr, Victor Danner and others, which have examined many of the aforementioned issues in-depth.

Game theory was founded by the great mathematician John von Neumann in 1944 with the publication of *The Theory of Games and Economic Behavior* written in collaboration with the mathematical economist, Oskar Morgenstern.[6] As we shall see, game theory uses three questions to study "games" like poker and chess, as well as far more serious and deadly situations like the September 11th terrorist attacks. We use these three simple game theory questions to help clarify our subsequent analysis, examining different answers to them among our three groups of hypothetical policymakers. The first question regarding the "rules of the game," which specify available moves and the payoffs for different combinations of moves, is the "payoff question." The second, regarding what motivates a player to select one move over another, or whether they are "playing the game" aimlessly or playing to maximize some objective, is the "instrumental rationality" question. The third question of how what one thinks his opponent will do affects his selection is the "anticipation question." Of course, strategic thinking existed before the emergence of game theory and one can understand strategy without using its terminology. So we examine the strategic issues without this terminology before using it to help clarify the differences between the three groups of hypothetical policymakers.

Divided into seven sections, the paper applies these questions to the issues which have come to the fore in the wake of September 11th. The first section considers the concern our puzzled policymakers raise about whether game theory is applicable to the current situation at all, and argues that the planning behind the attacks in fact suggests the existence of an underlying strategy. The second section examines statements by bin Laden to understand his "publicly stated" strategy espousing terrorism. His arguments are useful for understanding the strategy of terrorists in general and are thus germane to this study even if bin Laden himself did not plan the September 11th attacks. The third section incorporates the findings of other papers in this collection to analyze this stated strategy according to Islamic principles, examining the necessary intellectual conditions underlying bin Laden's inversion of Islamic values. The fourth section analyzes his stated strategy according to game theory, and the fifth and sixth sections examine the ways, if any, in which bin Laden's statements should inform our own strategy. These latter sections consider alternative responses to our mistaken and discerning groups of hypothetical policymakers, respectively, and conclude that the current crisis is as much intellectual as it is political. The seventh section is a postlude to the paper.

I. Can Game Theory Really Apply?

Let us briefly turn to the concern raised by our puzzled policymakers on whether game theory applies to the current situation at all. Perhaps the most basic argument for this view is that any terrorist who volunteers for a suicide mission is insane and cannot have a coherent strategy in doing so. While this may apply to some terrorists, we do not believe it necessarily applies to them all. Indeed, the coordinated attacks of September 11th suggest a high degree of preparation and planning associated with some kind of underlying strategy. And if we examine the background of Mohammed Atta, the alleged leader of the September 11th attacks, we have further reason to doubt that there was no strategy. We recognize that this exercise is hypothetical since we are not certain as to who was involved in the attacks, but the point is to show that strategic thinking should not necessarily be ruled out simply because a suicide attack seems contrary to our notions of rational thought.

Atta came from a middle-class Egyptian family and completed his bachelor's degree in architectural engineering at Cairo University in 1990. To enter this engineering program, he had to score in the top five percent of high school graduates in annual entrance examinations during his final year of high school in Egypt.[7] After going to Germany in 1992, he enrolled in Hamburg Technical University to obtain the equivalent of a master's degree in urban planning. Ultimately, Atta earned the highest possible score on his master's thesis, which was described as "brilliant."[8] Is it plausible that a man as intelligent as Atta (or, if not him, whoever actually led the attack with such precision) would simply throw his life away purposely, without a final goal and a plan for achieving that goal in which such an extreme act would have its place?

In answering this question, we do not need to know whether or not Atta or whoever executed the attacks was pursuing the right end when he committed suicide, which involves "substantive rationality." We only need to know that the terrorists were pursuing some end in a consistent manner, which involves "instrumental rationality," meaning that they rank different options in a consistent manner within a means-end framework.[9] Moreover, we do not need to assume that terrorists are instrumentally rational in *everything* they do, but only that they are instrumentally rational in their terrorist activities.[10] In other words, they are not "playing the game" aimlessly, but are playing in order to maximize some objective, pursuing their perceived payoffs with the most effective means. Our puzzled policymakers therefore implicitly suggest that the terrorists are instrumentally *irrational*, in which case there is no need to search for an underlying strategy. Our other policymakers assume that the terrorists are instrumentally rational, in which case it is useful to dig deeper to discover what the underlying strategy might be. Given Atta's intelligence (or that of whoever led the attack), it seems reasonable to assume instrumental rationality, even if he may be substantively irrational in having the "wrong" end.[11] And instrumental rationality for the ringleader suggests the possibility of instrumental rationality for the group as well, which is (presumably) pursuing a common end.

II. Bin Laden's Statements: Implications for Terrorist Strategy

Although the mistaken and discerning groups of policymakers agree that the terrorists have a strategy, they disagree on how to interpret bin Laden's statements regarding terrorism and their implications for terrorist strategy. We therefore quote him extensively in this section using his interviews with reporters, responses to followers, and videotaped statements. Our main objective is to understand bin Laden's "publicly stated" strategy espousing terrorism, even though this might not necessarily be his "real" strategy. But as we shall see, the very fact that he uses these arguments publicly yields valuable insights. And even if he were not behind the September 11th attacks (since he only admits previous knowledge of them while denying involvement), his arguments espousing terrorism would certainly be useful for understanding the strategy of the terrorists, who would be aware of bin Laden's arguments.[12] In game theoretic terms, we shall see that bin Laden publicly indicates answers to the payoff and anticipation questions.

In one of bin Laden's most important interviews (with ABC's John Miller in 1998), he argues that United States foreign policy is unjust, that the US does not respond to moral arguments, and therefore calls for retaliation against the United States. He maintains that his "tit-for-tat" terrorism is "commendable" because it is based upon the principle of "reciprocity."[13] Bin Laden states:

> After World War II, the Americans grew more unfair and more oppressive towards people in general and Muslims in particular.... The Americans started it and retaliation and punishment should be carried out following the principle of reciprocity.... America has no religion that can deter her from exterminating whole peoples. Your position against Muslims in Palestine is despicable and disgraceful. America has no shame.... Nothing could stop you except perhaps retaliation in kind. We do not have to differentiate between military and civilian ...[14]

However, bin Laden also argues that conflict between Americans and the Islamic world is not necessary, and that the source of the problem is special interests influencing United States foreign policy. In response to Miller's question regarding a message for the American people, bin Laden answers:

> I say to them that they have put themselves at the mercy of a disloyal government ... [that] represents Israel inside America.... They [Israelis] make use of America to further their plans for the world, especially the Islamic world. American presence in the Gulf provides support to the Jews and protects their rear. And while millions of Americans are homeless and destitute and live in abject poverty, their government is busy occupying our land and building new settlements and helping Israel build new settlements in the point of departure

> for our Prophet's midnight journey to the seven heavens. America throws her own sons in the land of the two Holy Mosques for the sake of protecting Jewish interests.... We say to the Americans as people and to American mothers, if they cherish their lives and if they cherish their sons, they must elect an American patriotic government that caters to their interests not the interests of the Jews.... This is my message to the American people. I urge them to find a serious administration that acts in their interest and does not attack people and violate their honor and pilfer their wealth.[15]

Thus, bin Laden clearly distinguishes between the American people and the United States government. He views other foreign policy complaints in the context of Israeli special interests and a "war against Islam" waged by Western governments, espousing a tit-for-tat terrorism strategy against the United States to counteract the special interests, and criticizing other governments in the region for cooperating with the United States in the interests of Israel. As we shall see, the Israeli-Palestinian issue appears to "color" all of bin Laden's complaints against United States foreign policy.

Bin Laden repeats the same message to his followers, focusing on this issue by arguing that it is not in the self-interest of Western governments to pursue "anti-Islamic" foreign policies, but that Israeli special interests have dragged Western governments into the conflict and exposed their citizens to retaliation for "almost nothing." In responding to a question posed by some of his followers, bin Laden states that:

> ... it is not in the interest of Western governments to expose the interests of their people to all kinds of retaliation for almost nothing. It is hoped that people of those countries will initiate a positive move and force their governments not to act on behalf of other states and other sects. This is what we have to say and we pray to Allāh to preserve the nation of Islam and to help them drive their enemies out of their land.[16]

According to bin Laden, the media also has an important role to play in this "war against Islam" by portraying negative images of Islam, which he once again links to the Israeli-Palestinian issue. He concludes the 1998 interview with John Miller by stating: "Let not the West be taken in by those who say that Muslims choose nothing but slaughtering ... the European and the American people and some of the Arabs are under the influence of Jewish media."[17] And bin Laden explains to his followers that the media influences election outcomes, claiming: "If the people have elected those governments in the latest elections, it is because they have fallen prey to the Western media which portray things contrary to what they really are."[18]

This combination of special interest influence on government policymaking, the media, and election outcomes leads to a self-perpetuating cycle, according to bin Laden, mobilizing Western leaders and populations for a "war against Islam."

> The leaders in America and in other countries as well have fallen victim to Jewish Zionist blackmail. They have mobilized their people against Islam and against Muslims. These are portrayed in such a manner as to drive people to rally against them. The truth is that the whole Muslim world is the victim of international terrorism, engineered by America at the United Nations. We are a nation whose sacred symbols have been looted and whose wealth and resources have been plundered. It is normal for us to react against the forces that invade our land and occupy it ...[19]

Thus, bin Laden argues that a "Crusader-Zionist alliance" has formed against the Islamic world as a result of Israeli special interests and the media. But he articulates this argument to different degrees in various statements and interviews depending on the audience's background and familiarity with the issues. For example, when he is addressing an American or Western audience in an interview on CNN or ABC, bin Laden invariably mentions the role of Israeli special interests in the "war against Islam." But when he is addressing an Arab or Muslim audience, he sometimes explains how he views Israeli special interests and the media as the underlying cause of the "Crusader-Zionist" alliance, but often does not, perhaps because most Muslims are already familiar with such arguments. As Thomas Friedman observes, "Just go anywhere—Egypt, Saudi Arabia, Pakistan—and you'll hit your head against this wall.... You say America is a democracy; they will say it's a country whose media and politics are controlled by Jews."[20] Finally, when bin Laden is dealing with a mixed audience in broadcasts such as on al-Jazeera, his discussion of Israeli special interests and media varies depending on the intended audience and other circumstances.

In these statements bin Laden intensely opposes the presence of U.S. troops in Saudi Arabia and sanctions on Iraq. But he explains these in the context of an ongoing "Crusader-Zionist" war against Islam, the center of which is the Israeli-Palestinian issue, and this intensifies opposition to the later elements of United States foreign policy in the region. What bin Laden could otherwise explain as the pursuit of United States economic interests in the absence of the Israeli-Palestinian issue and special interests, he explains as part of a "Crusader-Zionist alliance" in light of these interests. Whereas the former view offers mitigating circumstances such as Saddam Hussein, the operation of world oil markets, and the Saudi government's request for military support, the latter view does not, making it far easier to "sell" a war against an "unjust" United States. The Israeli-Palestinian issue is therefore a natural integrating point of bin Laden's foreign policy complaints regardless of his real sentiments.

We illustrate this in Table 1 below, showing how the "intensity of opposition" to United States troops in Saudi Arabia and sanctions on Iraq increases in light of Israeli special interests and a "Crusader-Zionist alliance" war against Islam. Of course, the numbers are somewhat arbitrary, and we simply use them to illustrate the concept of a "multiplier effect," or how the Israeli-Palestinian issue multiplies the intensity of Muslim opposition to later elements of United States foreign policy.

Table 1. Intensity of Opposition to U.S. Foreign Policy

	No "Crusader-Zionist" Alliance	"Crusader-Zionist" Alliance
U.S. Troops in Saudi Arabia	12	120
Sanctions on Iraq	11	110

We shall refer to this increase in opposition to elements of United States foreign policy as the "Israeli multiplier," which bin Laden uses in his arguments to gain recruits and support. Although the Israeli multiplier may simply increase the attractiveness of bin Laden's espousal of terrorism for some individuals, the Israeli multiplier may also paradoxically increase the intensity of opposition to other foreign policy elements over the Israeli-Palestinian issue itself. This is because other elements of foreign policy such as troops in the Gulf or sanctions on Iraq are perceived as an "expansion" of aggression against Muslims, increasing the urgency of a response to the most recent developments. Consequently, the Israeli-Palestinian issue could take a back seat to the more recent threats. Thus, the Israeli multiplier can increase the intensity of opposition to the other issues and *may* increase their relative rankings, but not decrease them. We illustrate these various possibilities with the following example in Table 2, which adds an additional row and a middle column to Table 1, reflecting the Israeli-Palestinian issue and a lower Israeli multiplier, respectively. As in Table 1, the first column shows the intensity of opposition *without* the perception of a "Crusader-Zionist alliance," which we label as "separable issues."

Table 2. Intensity of Opposition to Elements of U.S. Foreign Policy

		"Crusader-Zionist" Alliance —Israeli Multiplier	
	"Separable" Issues	Lower Multiplier (Same Rankings)	Higher Multiplier (Rankings Change)
U.S. Troops in Saudi Arabia	12	24	120
Sanctions on Iraq	11	22	110
Israeli-Palestinian issue	100	100	100

The second and third columns show the intensity of opposition to United States foreign policy *with* the perception of a "Crusader-Zionist alliance," but the second has a lower Israeli multiplier than the third, generating different levels of opposition to the other foreign policy issues and different rankings. As we shall see, survey research is more consistent with the figures in the second column than those in the first and third columns.

Bin Laden's statements show that he believes that few (if any) Muslims are represented in the first column, and that the overwhelming majority of Muslims are represented in the second and third columns. Indeed, he always employs the Israeli multiplier when he addresses a Muslim audience, often without even attempting to prove the existence of a "Crusader-Zionist alliance," since most Muslims are already convinced of the power of Israeli special interests and media, as Thomas Friedman's earlier comment suggests.[21] Bin Laden's statements also reveal that he believes many more Muslims rank the Israeli-Palestinian issue first and are represented in the second rather than the third column. For example, in his October 2001 interview with the al-Jazeera television network, first made public by CNN in early 2002, bin Laden states: "Many Western and Eastern leaders have said that the true roots of terrorism should be dealt with; they meant the Palestinian cause. Then we have a righteous cause, but they couldn't admit this out loud for fear of America."[22] However, bin Laden clearly believes that some Muslims are represented by the third column, and he appears to fall into this category himself, stating:

> *Jihād* is a duty to liberate Al-Aqsa, and to help the powerless in Palestine, Iraq, and Lebanon and in every Muslim country. There is no doubt that the liberation of the Arabian Peninsula from infidels is a duty as well. But it is not right to say that Osama put the Palestinian issue first.... Sometimes we find the right elements to push for one cause more than the other. Last year's blessed *intifada* helped us to push more for the Palestinian issue. This push helps the other cause. Attacking America helps the cause of Palestine and vice versa. No conflict between the two; on the contrary, one serves the other.[23]

Thus, if an Egyptian ranks the Israeli-Palestinian issue first in importance, sanctions on Iraq second, and U.S. troops in Saudi Arabia third, whereas a Saudi reverses these priorities, both can work together to execute the same tit-for-tat strategy, and bin Laden appeals for them to do so. In fact, this may be exactly what happened on September 11th, regardless of whether or not bin Laden was involved in planning the attacks.

The Israeli multiplier is therefore essential to understand the logical consistency of bin Laden's statements, which simultaneously emphasize the presence of U.S. troops in Saudi Arabia on the one hand and the Israeli-Palestinian issue and "Crusader-Zionist alliance" on the other. Without the multiplier, his various statements seem highly inconsistent, generating confused conclusions (which we shall return to in section five). It is also important to understand how bin Laden argues that the U.S. troops in Saudi

Arabia simultaneously: 1) weaken the Saudi economy,[24] 2) provide a "staging post" for continuing aggression to destroy Iraq, the "strongest neighboring Arab state" which could threaten Israel,[25] and 3) increase United States influence in the region. Because all three are in Israeli interests, bin Laden argues that removing the U.S. troops in Saudi Arabia would contribute to several objectives with a single means. He also claims that United States influence interferes with the foreign policies of Middle Eastern governments in favor of Israeli interests.[26] Consequently, bin Laden links these issues in a way that suggests the U.S. troops in Saudi Arabia should have a higher Israeli multiplier than sanctions on Iraq since the former helps make the latter possible, and contributes to Israeli interests in multiple ways.[27] In any case, to understand the central role of the Israeli-Palestinian issue for bin Laden, it is not sufficient to simply know how he ranks different elements of United States foreign policy. One must also know the *reasons* he gives for his ranking. Otherwise, one could think that the numbers in the third column based on a high Israeli multiplier were in the first column with no Israeli multiplier. And this error would deny the fact that the Israeli-Palestinian issue increases opposition to other elements of foreign policy in the region. But without the Israeli multiplier, few Muslims would rank the Israeli-Palestinian issue third in importance and even more would rank it first since the multiplier may increase the urgency of other issues, but not the Israeli-Palestinian issue itself (which would be analogous to multiplying by one). As we shall see, it is strategically crucial not to overlook this point.

It is also significant to note that bin Laden claims that the "corrupt" domestic and foreign policies of Middle Eastern regimes exist *because* of United States influence, and he does not blame the regimes for having these policies *independent* of this influence. Although one could argue that this corruption has nothing to do with the United States, bin Laden does not make this argument. Moreover, he does not mention other issues upon which he opposes United States influence, and does not appear to view American support for the "corrupt Saudi regime" as a separate source of opposition relative to the three foreign policy issues in Table 2. The argument that the terrorists oppose the United States because of their support for corrupt regimes is therefore somewhat redundant with arguments regarding the three foreign policy issues themselves, and should not be viewed separately.[28] The same applies to bin Laden's opposition to the Saudi regime.[29]

In any case, bin Laden attempted to convey a similar message to the entire world in his first videotaped statement on al-Jazeera after September 11th, reiterating his tit-for-tat terrorism strategy in the context of the Israeli-Palestinian issue. He opened by saying that Americans are now experiencing the fear that Palestinians and others have suffered for 80 years, and closed by saying that Americans will not feel secure until Palestinians and others feel secure:

> And this is America filled with fear from the north to south and east to west, thank God. And what America is facing today is something very little of what we have tasted for decades. Our nation, for more than 80 years has tasted this humiliation.... And to America, I say to it and to its people this: I swear by God the Great, America will never dream nor those who live in America will never taste security and safety unless we feel security and safety in our land and in Palestine.[30]

As Bernard Lewis points out, the opening reference to 80 years[31] is apparently to 1918, when "the Ottoman sultanate, the last of the great Muslim empires, was finally defeated—its capital, Constantinople, occupied, its sovereign held captive, and much of its territory partitioned between the victorious French and British Empires."[32] Shortly afterwards in 1922, the League of Nations gave Britain supervisory control over Palestine and mandated the creation of a Jewish homeland there. The United States expressed its approval through a joint Congressional resolution signed by President Warren G. Harding on July 24, 1922, and provided subsequent support. From bin Laden's perspective, "the United States directly invited the Jews to enter a land occupied by Muslims and then prevented the Muslims from doing anything about it," for there was no organized Jewish presence in Palestine between 70 A.D. and 1922.[33] In a 1995 interview with a French journalist, bin Laden claims that "I did not fight against the communist threat (in Afghanistan) while forgetting the peril from the West.... The urgent thing was communism, but the next target was America."[34]

Of course, bin Laden's version of tit-for-tat is not an Islamic strategy, no matter how "effective" it might prove to be, as the papers by David Dakake and Reza Shah-Kazemi make abundantly clear.[35] Muslims generally criticize both bin Laden and United States foreign policy, and it is incorrect to limit one's choices to "liking" the latter and "disliking" the former, or vice-versa (although one cannot simultaneously "like" bin Laden and United States foreign policy). Although Islam does have rules defining a "just war" and rules of engagement, the murder of innocent civilians inflicts an injustice that no strategic results can ever make up for, even if we accept (for the sake of argument) that United States foreign policy may kill innocent civilians in Palestine and other places in the Islamic world. Islam is not a religion in which "the ends justify the means," and no Muslim is allowed to return one injustice with another injustice. Indeed, Islamic law even prohibits the use of fire against opponents in war, ruling out the type of attacks on September 11th as well as nuclear bombs ("dirty" or otherwise). Islamic law also prohibits poisoning the wells of opponents, ruling out chemical and biological warfare. Such weapons of mass destruction are products of secular thought, not Islamic science and technology. Bin Laden therefore argues for the need to "go beyond" traditional Islamic views because of United States foreign policy, and applauds the terrorists who executed the September 11th attacks for doing so.[36] He is not an authentic product of traditional Islamic thought, but combines elements of both Islamic and secular viewpoints in a lethal and syncretistic manner.

Bin Laden attempts to bypass traditional Islam and change the rules of a just war by arguing that the old rulings of Islamic law are no longer adequate and that new rulings are necessary based on *ijtihād*.[37] In Islam, this is a creative but disciplined effort to give fresh views on old issues or derive legal rulings for new situations, including warfare, from the accepted juridical sources of Islam. An ethical judgment such as *ijtihād* is not just one "religious" judgment among many, to be weighed against other judgments (political, economic, or social) in deciding how to act. It is itself an "all-things-considered" judgment based on spiritual principles, taking all other factors into account.

Bin Laden's Machiavellian strategy, which is ruthless and immoral, is the product of an erroneous *ijtihād* that is obviously inconsistent with the consequences of the fundamental Islamic doctrine of Unity (*tawḥīd*).[38] This doctrine is expressed in its most universal manner in the first testimony of the Islamic faith, *Lā ilāha illā Llāh* (There is no god but God). As William Chittick observes: "In all the different schools of thought that have appeared over Islamic history, one principle has been agreed by everyone ... the fact that God is one and that He is the only source of truth and reality.... To think Islamically is to recognize God's unity and draw the proper consequences from His unity. Differences of opinion arise concerning the consequences, not the fact that God is one."[39] In the next section, we shall examine how bin Laden's arguments are inconsistent with traditional Islam based on *tawḥīd*. Nevertheless, bin Laden attempts to break away from the traditional Islamic view by arguing for what he calls "commendable" terrorism, or terrorist attacks with spiritual rewards rather than penalties. He bases his argument on the "principle of reciprocity." In response to questions from followers on the moral status of terrorism, he argues that:

> ... terrorism can be commendable and it can be reprehensible. Terrifying an innocent person and terrorizing him is objectionable and unjust, also unjustly terrorizing people is not right. Whereas, terrorizing oppressors and criminals and thieves and robbers is necessary for the safety of people and for the protection of their property. There is no doubt in this. Every state and every civilization and culture has to resort to terrorism under certain circumstances for the purpose of abolishing tyranny and corruption. Every country in the world has its own security system and its own security forces, its own police and its own army. They are all designed to terrorize whoever even contemplates to attack that

country or its citizens. The terrorism we practice is of the commendable kind, for it is directed at the tyrants and the aggressors and the enemies of Allāh ....[40]

The reference to "terrorizing oppressors and criminals and thieves and robbers" relates to terrorizing those who commit crimes against others, not crimes against themselves. According to this argument, the United States is a terrorist target for its "Crusader-Zionist" foreign policy, which threatens "the safety of [our] people and protection of their property," not for its domestic policy, which is irrelevant to the tit-for-tat argument. It is past United States foreign policy in the context of a "Crusader-Zionist alliance" that determines whether terrorism is "commendable" or "reprehensible," whether there are spiritual payoffs or penalties from retaliatory attacks, not domestic policy. Bin Laden maintains that if the United States and Israel did not "start the war against Islam first," there could be spiritual penalties rather than rewards from terrorist attacks, in addition to the (possible or certain) loss of one's own life and external goods. There is clearly a foreign policy "trigger point" for "commendable" terrorism.

Obviously, perceived spiritual rewards from terrorism are essential to suicide attacks like September 11th and the self-understanding of those who execute them since there are no rewards of external goods for suicide terrorists. Although not all of the terrorists knew the targets and timing of the September 11th attacks far in advance, they all knew that the operation would become suicidal at some point, that this could be at any time, and that they might not be told very early because of the need for secrecy in the terrorist cells. This policy is stated quite clearly in the al-Qaeda terrorism manual, and bin Laden confirmed this in the videotape discovered in Qandahar.[41] By the time the terrorists were ready to board the planes, all of them knew they were about to die, and the pilots knew relatively far in advance.

Since bin Laden publicly claims that the United States bases its foreign policy on Israeli and other interests, like oil, rather than moral principles, and that "America worships money,"[42] he suggests that the United States will have an incentive to change its "Crusader-Zionist" foreign policy under the right combination of costs and benefits, and threatens the American people accordingly. He would certainly be familiar with cost-benefit analysis and the importance of "incentive systems" because he studied management and economics at King Abdul Aziz University in Saudi Arabia while obtaining degrees in public administration and civil engineering. He discusses the economic impact of military strikes against economic targets in his 1996 Declaration of War (although in a different context), as well as urging that the "economical [sic] boycotting of the American goods is a very effective weapon of hitting and weakening the enemy, and it is not under the control of the security forces of the regime."[43]

Therefore, his publicly declared tit-for-tat strategy espousing terrorist attacks until the United States stops its current foreign policy is a public threat to induce us to adopt a more cooperative foreign policy by changing the current policy's costs and benefits.[44] As bin Laden stated in his December 27, 2001 videotape release:

> They [the 19 terrorists] shook America's throne and struck the U.S. economy in the heart.... This is clear proof that this international usurious, damnable economy—which America uses along with its military power to impose infidelity and humiliation on weak people—can easily collapse.... (the attacks) have inflicted on New York and other markets more than a trillion dollars in losses.... If their economy is destroyed, they will be busy with their own affairs rather than enslaving the weak peoples.... The economic bleeding is continuing to date, but it requires further strikes. The young people should make an effort to look for the key pillars of the U.S. economy. The key pillars of the enemy should be struck, God willing.[45]

William Beeman points out the irony behind bin Laden's choice of strategy to influence United States foreign policy since it seems to "be drawn from the American foreign policy playbook."[46] He notes that:

> When the United States disapproves of the behavior of another nation, it "turns up the heat" on that nation through embargoes, economic sanctions, or withdrawal of diplomatic representation.... The State Department has theorized that if the people of a rogue nation experience enough suffering, they will overthrow their rulers, or compel them to adopt more sensible behavior. The terrorist actions in New York and Washington are a clear and ironic implementation of this strategy against the United States.[47]

Indeed, bin Laden claims to desire the "overthrow" of special interest groups that are creating the "war against Islam," urging the American people to elect a government "that acts in their interest."[48]

Given the potential economic impact of terrorism, tit-for-tat is an effective way to increase the costs to the United States of its current foreign policy. Because the number of vulnerabilities in a target as large as the United States is so great, the costs of defense against terrorism are extremely high, and the logistics behind the strategy are daunting. Defending against a single attack significantly raises enforcement and search costs throughout the entire economy, and these costs are ongoing. Senator John Warner and others have therefore argued that merely trying to defend against terrorism is simply not an option, and that the "best defense is a good offense."[49]

Similarly, there is no guarantee that terrorists will not be able to penetrate these defenses, and continued attacks could adversely affect the economy by reducing consumer sentiment and demand and creating additional volatility and potential losses in financial markets. Although the Federal Reserve and the Bush administration can introduce policies to limit the economic damage if terrorism stops now, significant economic damage would occur if comparable acts of terrorism were to recur.[50] Indeed, for every dollar the terrorists spent on the World Trade Center attacks, they created over one million dollars of economic damage. This ratio is based on estimates that the terrorists only spent $200,000 on the attacks, whereas the direct economic costs from damage, and on-going search and enforcement, and indirect costs, such as losses to the airline industry, decline in retail sales, the increase in unemployment, etc. are far in excess of $200,000,000,000. Given this dangerous asymmetry, the payoff to the United States of reducing the direct and indirect costs of terrorism by eliminating the terrorists is quite high.

Finally, bin Laden's publicly stated strategy may ultimately increase the price of oil and deny easy access to Saudi oil for the United States if the current Saudi regime is destabilized and replaced by a less cooperative one. The use of oil as a foreign policy weapon could have devastating economic costs, and recent *Frontline* interviews with James Baker and Brent Scowcroft clearly point out the degree of United States interests in this issue.[51] Bin Laden knows that this is a serious threat to combat Israeli special interests. As Vali Nasr points out, most Saudis believe that United States troops are the "Republican guards" of the Saudi regime, defending it from its own people, not from Saddam Hussein,[52] which also enhances Israeli interests, according to bin Laden.

In game theory terms, we can quickly summarize the results of this section by noting that bin Laden's statements provide publicly stated answers to the payoff question on the foreign policy trigger point for "commendable" terrorism and the anticipation question on how what terrorists think we will do affects their selection. Thus, bin Laden's strategy is quite clear to many Muslims, even though it may be quite mystifying to many Americans. Unfortunately, a small minority of Muslims actually agree with bin Laden's Machiavellian tactics, despite the fact that they are against Islamic principles and law.

III. Analyzing the Stated Strategy According to Islam

We must now raise the question as to why bin Laden claims that his strategy is Islamic, and why some Muslims respond favorably to it. Are we forced to conclude that it is an Islamic strategy, and that Islam is a "religion of the sword"? The other essays in this collection clearly demonstrate that it is erroneous to equate violent forms of Islamic fundamentalism with traditional Islam itself, and that the notion of necessary or inevitable conflict between Islam and the West is false. As we shall see in the coming sections, this has crucial implications for our strategic response, affecting our judgment on: 1) whether or not the terrorists were actually attacking our domestic policy, and 2) whether or not economic development in the Middle East will reduce terrorism.

Reza Shah-Kazemi's paper presents the stark contrast between bin Laden's view of *jihād* and the traditional Islamic view.[53] He draws upon historical evidence in the examples of Saladin and ʿAbd al-Qādir al-Jazāʾirī to demonstrate that both Western and Islamic sources recognize the profound chivalry present in the great Muslim warriors of the past, and how this is related to their inner struggle for spiritual realization (the "greater *jihād*"), which has been entirely dismissed by violent fundamentalists. Similarly, David Dakake's paper demonstrates that the Islamic tradition has always opposed extremism and vigilante militancy, examining in great detail the Qurʾānic verses that are usually quoted to prove that Islam preaches violence towards Jews and Christians, who are supposedly the "infidel." He demonstrates that such interpretations are fallacious, and examines how many modern "fundamentalists" employ Qurʾānic verses as prooftexts for wanton violence, taking them out of their historical and interpretive context to "apply them in ways which entail clear innovations from their generally accepted meanings."[54] In fact, traditional Islamic civilization easily accommodates other religions within its spiritual universe, because Islam teaches that there is one God but many prophets. As Seyyed Hossein Nasr writes:

> We live in a period in which the writing of revisionist history has become common. But no matter how one seeks to distort history for ideological and political ends, one cannot deny that for centuries Jews and Christians lived amidst Muslims in peace and security, even if they did not enjoy all the rights of the Muslim majority. In any case, however, Islamic history was not witness to any 1492s or 1992s [a reference to the expulsion of Muslims and Jews from Spain in 1492 and the massacre of Muslims in Bosnia in 1992].[55]

Unfortunately, erroneous conceptions of Islam persist in the West, and Ibrahim Kalin examines the historical roots behind them in his paper by examining how "the medieval European view of Islam as a heresy and its Prophet as an impostor provided the religious foundations of the confrontationalist position which has survived up to our own day and gained a new dimension after September 11."[56] He proposes an alternative to the confrontationalist position and the received categories of Orientalism, demonstrating how Western perceptions of Islam are "as much a reflection of its view of the Islamic world as it is of itself … [and how the] West's encounter with Islam is a coming to terms with its own self-image."[57] He discusses the most famous modern-day version of the confrontationalist view, namely Huntington's "clash of civilizations" thesis, arguing that it is fatally incomplete, since it abstracts from the essence of the problem it seeks to solve, confusing the relation between religion and civilization on one hand and their interconnections with conflict and peace on the other. These essays have important implications for placing bin Laden and others of his ilk in their proper context.

Several of the other essays also point to the unfortunate intellectual conditions in the Muslim world that underlie bin Laden's statements and which are crucial to a proper understanding and explanation of them. For example, Joseph E. B. Lumbard examines "the imbalance in the application of the traditional Islamic sciences which has allowed for the modern misinterpretations from both radical reformists and liberal secularists to persist and prevail."[58] He points out that bin Laden's arguments would not be possible and could not appeal to any Muslim without the decline of the traditional Islamic sciences and educational system (what he terms the "*iḥsānī* tradition"), which were greatly weakened in almost every part of the Islamic world by the imposition of secular modes of thought and institutions. This first occurred during the colonial era, which contributed to an intellectual "inferiority complex" among many Muslims vis-à-vis the West, particularly among the youth, who often associate power with truth.[59] This in turn led to the rise of modernism in the Islamic world, an attempt to reinterpret Islam in conformity with the secular sciences of nature. Fuad Naeem's paper provides an instructive case study of this phenomenon in the Indian Subcontinent, and a traditional Islamic intellectual response by Maulana Thanvī, who also opposed fundamentalism.[60] T. J. Winter also provides a first-hand account of the "poverty of fanaticism" and its relation to secular thought in his paper, explaining its lure for some Muslim youth and how it is completely inconsistent with traditional intellectual thought. As Ghazi bin Muḥammad observes:

> The rise of secularism has paradoxically contributed, by way of militant and ignorant reaction, to the rise of fundamentalism. For the banners of fundamentalism invariably contain slogans against atheism and secularism, and draw many simple believers to them on that account. Now it may well be asked how is this leading to "disequilibrium and upheaval" among traditional religious culture, if secularism only leads to "more religion"? The answer is that the religious fundamentalism which is waxing in the modern world is vastly and qualitatively different from the traditional religion which is waning, and that the difference between them is, precisely, that fundamentalism is opposed to all traditional "religious culture" as such (and therefore, in the end, bound to damage and impoverish religion as such).[61]

"Secular fundamentalism," or the intolerance of other world-views in modernist thought, breeds intolerant Islamic fundamentalism as a reaction, which actually combines elements of secular and religious thought.[62] This is a necessary intellectual condition for bin Laden's version of Islamic fundamentalism (not all types of Islamic "fundamentalism" are violent).[63] To clarify this, we must discuss: 1) the relationship between the traditional Islamic intellectual (*ʿaqlī*) heritage and Islamic civilization that excludes terrorism on the one hand, and 2) the relationship between secular fundamentalism and violent forms of Islamic fundamentalism that make terrorism possible on the other.[64] Several scholars have dealt masterfully with both issues, although we cannot review the literature in this paper.[65] Suffice it to say, there is an intimate link between work, spiritual education, and sacred ambiance in traditional Islamic civilization that is forged by the Islamic sciences, making terrorism unconscionable.[66] This is not to deny that *non-violent* forms of Islamic fundamentalism, which also reject essential aspects of the Islamic intellectual heritage, existed before the advent of modernist thought and led to some degree of decadence in the Islamic world. But such non-violent fundamentalism is simply a truncated approach to Islam that can operate within the broader context of traditional Islamic civilization since such fundamentalism does not substitute secular intellectual thought in place of the Islamic intellectual heritage. This involves decadence, but not deviation.[67] Whether or not a particular version of Islamic fundamentalism today would employ terrorist tactics depends on the extent to which secular sciences fill the vacuum created by the denial of the Islamic intellectual heritage and erosion of Islamic civilization. This does not deny the fact that a *violent* form of Islamic fundamentalism such as the Khārijite movement, which was directed against other members of the Muslim community (not non-Muslims), also existed well before the advent of modernism.[68] But current examples of violent fundamentalism are clearly more common than in the past because of secular fundamentalism, and much more dangerous given modern weapons of mass destruction and other products of secular science.

Unfortunately, Wahhābī fundamentalist thought is a relatively truncated approach to Islam that is particularly prone to erroneous and dangerous combinations of Islamic and secular ideas through *ijtihād* because Wahhābī thought is particularly harsh in discouraging the study of the Islamic intellectual heritage. It is not coincidental that bin Laden was raised in such an environment. This does *not* imply that Wahhābī thought necessarily inverts Islamic values or that the ideal Wahhābī is a terrorist engaging in erroneous forms of *ijtihād*, as bin Laden has done. Many Wahhābīs are pious Muslims who would not commit terrorist acts, and the introduction of secular thought into the Islamic world does not absolve bin Laden of moral responsibility for espousing terrorism. But the risk of the inversion of Islamic values is high in Wahhābī thought because secular philosophy often enters such a society through the "back door" with secular sciences of nature and ways of making and doing things, causing a break in the link between work and spiritual education.[69] We therefore suggest that this is the basis upon which bin Laden develops a Machiavellian tit-for-tat strategy.[70] In game theory terms, bin Laden clearly espouses the wrong answer to our payoff question since there are severe spiritual penalties for terrorist attacks on non-combatants.

Ironically, the United States encouraged Wahhābī fundamentalist thought during the war in Afghanistan against the Soviets in the 1980s and early 1990s as an anti-communist ideology. Vali Nasr points out that United States policymakers also liked this brand of "Sunnī Islamic fundamentalism" because it helped to isolate Iran, which is Shīʿite.[71] The terrorist attacks of September 11th are in part the unintended effects of this policy, and United States policymakers apparently did not understand the difference between traditional Islamic groups and their more dangerous fundamentalist counterparts. As Ibrahim Kalin points out, Western scholars' understanding of the Islamic intellectual heritage is by-and-large extremely poor, making it virtually impossible for policymakers to recognize the difference between these groups and to anticipate a "boomerang" effect from misguided policies.[72]

IV. Analyzing the Stated Strategy According to Game Theory

Although bin Laden's stated strategy is immoral from an Islamic point of view, it is ruthlessly clever from a strictly game theory point of view. This is because tit-for-tat is the "optimal strategy" in many common strategic situations. But the intuitive effectiveness of tit-for-tat in many situations is obvious since it has:

> four properties which tend to make a decision rule successful: avoidance of unnecessary conflict by cooperating as long as the other player does, provocability in the face of an uncalled for defection by the other, forgiveness after responding to a provocation, and clarity of behavior so that the other player can adapt to your pattern of action.[73]

In fact, both the U.S.-led coalition against terrorism and the terrorists themselves claim to be using tit-for-tat morally. The coalition claims it is attempting to bring to justice those who perpetrated the terrorist attacks, and many politicians have argued that inaction is more dangerous than action because retaliation against terrorists sends a signal that helps to discourage others from attempting similar acts. Not only does the coalition hope to eliminate current terrorists, it also hopes to force at least some would-be terrorists to adopt a more cooperative strategy in the future.

Unfortunately, bin Laden uses the same arguments. His statements indicate that he believes United States policymakers know that they "defected first" because he believes that they know they are influenced by Israeli special interests to pursue an unjust foreign policy. From his point of view, not retaliating against United States defection will encourage aggression against Muslims by sending the "wrong signal" to the United States. The ongoing nature of the "war against Islam" and the killing of Muslim civilians require corresponding attacks on American civilians according to bin Laden. Moreover, he claims that he has no incentive to attack American civilians first since this would be reprehensible terrorism.[74] All this has extremely important consequences for our strategic response.

V. Reactions to Tit-for-Tat

So how are we to react to bin Laden's publicly declared tit-for-tat strategy? There are several possible responses, and we shall focus on three major categories in this section. One is to deny that the terrorists' "real" strategy is tit-for-tat and claim that they would attack the United States regardless of our foreign policy because Islam is a "religion of the sword," is against freedom and democracy, preaches violence towards Jews and Christians, inherently leads to militant fundamentalism, etc. In other words, the terrorists are attacking us because of our values and our domestic policy rather than our foreign policy, suggesting that a military solution may be the most appropriate response.

A second possibility is to accept that the terrorists are responding to United States foreign policy with a tit-for-tat strategy, but to deny that the Israeli-Palestinian issue is a major foreign policy cause of the terrorist attacks. For example, some people argue that the United States' support of "corrupt regimes" in the Arab world is the real foreign policy cause of terrorist hatred of the United States, or that the presence of United States troops in Saudi Arabia or economic sanctions against Iraq are the real problems. The corresponding solutions are either to modify our foreign policy along the relevant dimensions, or simply use the military solution mentioned earlier with no change in foreign policy, or some combination of the two.

A third possible response is to argue that neither United States domestic nor foreign policy caused the terrorist attacks, but that Middle Eastern governments and domestic policies caused them. For example, one could argue that the terrorists are "jealous" of the freedom and material wealth of Americans, and attacked for irrational, subconscious reasons. Or one could argue for a rational analogy, and claim that the terrorists are engaged in a "civil war" to replace "puppet" governments in the Middle East that cooperate with the "infidels" of the West. Accordingly, the September 11th attacks were a desperate attempt to gain support for this ailing Islamic revolutionary movement, and "Americans ... have been drawn into somebody else's civil war."[75] In either case, the ultimate solution has little to do with United States foreign or domestic policy, but has everything to do with Middle East domestic policy. Therefore, an economic solution that reduces the attractiveness of Islamic fundamentalism combined with a military response and specific political changes in the Middle East may be the most appropriate response.

In the full-length monograph, we demonstrate that each of these possible responses, which deny the centrality of the Israeli-Palestinian issue in the terrorist attacks, involves a misunderstanding of the statements by bin Laden and ignores the Israeli multiplier. At best, some of these differing explanations may suggest foreign policy conditions necessary for the terrorist attacks, such as the presence of United States troops in Saudi Arabia, which is arguable. But none provide a complete account of the sufficient conditions for the attacks, which is what proponents of such views often claim. Such views belong to the mistaken policymakers. In game theory terms, these proposals are based on the wrong answers to our payoff and anticipation questions. Moreover, we suggest that some of the proposed solutions will not only fail to stop terrorism against the United States, but might even backfire. A full treatment of this issue requires philosophical judgments that we will address in the next section, although we will introduce them here. Finally, although we have presented these different responses in three mutually exclusive categories, elements of the three responses can be combined in a variety of ways.[76]

A. United States Domestic Policy

Turning to the first option, let us consider the view that the terrorists' real strategy is to attack the United States regardless of our foreign policy because Islam is a "religion of the sword," is against freedom and democracy, preaches violence towards Jews and Christians, inherently leads to militant fundamentalism, etc. As we noted earlier, the other essays in this collection demonstrate that such assertions regarding Islam are false. Although some Islamic fundamentalists oppose freedom of religion and democracy, bin Laden does not make these arguments to justify tit-for-tat terrorism, as several scholars point out.[77] Suffice it to say here that bin Laden urges Americans to elect a government that will be loyal to the American people's interests rather than special interest groups, which he claims have corrupted United States foreign policy. Such arguments hardly suggest that bin Laden espouses terrorism to defeat democracy and eliminate freedom of religion in the United States.

In fact, suicide attacks do not make much strategic sense if the terrorists' objective is to change our domestic policy rather than foreign policy. No amount of terrorist attacks could ever lead Americans to actually abandon freedom of religion and democracy. However, terrorism could theoretically affect the costs and benefits of foreign policy, and induce a change in it. Therefore, attacking the United States to induce foreign policy changes makes more sense strategically than attacking it to induce domestic policy changes. This is especially true for suicide attacks, because the lower the probability of achieving the desired policy changes, the more important it is to sustain the attacks in future rounds by conserving human resources using a non-suicidal approach, such as that of the Unabomber Ted Kaczynski. Consequently, suicide attacks would *not* be the "strategically optimal method" for terrorists attempting to influence United States domestic policy (assuming the terrorists would even want to try), but could be "optimal" for foreign policy, especially if terrorists believe that special interest groups drive it. Failure to recognize this gives the wrong answer to our anticipation question, suggesting terrorists expected us to change our democracy and way of life rather than our foreign policy.

This view also gives the wrong answer to our payoff question. As we noted earlier, it is past United States foreign policy—in the context of a "Crusader-Zionist alliance"—that, according to bin Laden, determines whether terrorism is "commendable" or "reprehensible," and whether there are spiritual payoffs or penalties from retaliatory attacks, not domestic policy. Indeed, focusing on United States domestic policy would lend support to the spiritual penalty argument and undermine bin Laden's position, for there are no demonstrations in the Islamic world against legislation in Oregon allowing women to go nude on public beaches, but there are demonstrations against United States foreign policy. Since bin Laden's tactics are spiritually unacceptable to the overwhelming majority of Muslims, despite United States foreign policy, such tactics would be even more unacceptable without it. Therefore bin Laden *must* focus on foreign policy in the context of a "Crusader-Zionist alliance" in order to change the rules of the game and blunt criticism from Muslim scholars that there are spiritual penalties rather than payoffs from terrorist attacks.

Somewhat similar arguments apply to the view that the terrorists were attacking modernism rather than foreign policy. For example, John Voll provides an insightful analysis of the al-Qaeda recruitment video, and argues that the "conflict as defined in this film is *not* simply a 'Jihad against McWorld,'" referring to McDonald's, Kentucky Fried Chicken, and other "symbols of the Americanizing forces of McWorld that have been attacked by anti-American demonstrators following the terrorist attacks on the World Trade Center and the American military response." In fact, he says:

> there are virtually no images of McWorld as the enemy in this recruitment video.... The conflict is presented not as a clash of cultures and lifestyles, or even of civilizations. It is presented as a conflict between righteous but weak peoples who are oppressed and subjugated by the tremendous physical power of an unbelieving enemy.[78]

Moreover, Voll points out that "the very format of a contemporary, well-produced video argues against seeing the movement that the video represents as 'anti-modern.'"[79] In fact, bin Laden's organization is a product of "globalizing modernity," utilizing modern communications technology and global networks. In short, "'modernity' is not so much an issue as is the power that modernity has given to people who are viewed as unbelievers."[80] If we accept that violent versions of Islamic fundamentalism are the other side of the coin of secular fundamentalism, then there is a great deal of consistency between fundamentalism and modernism (with the exception of some elements of Islamic law), and it is incorrect to maintain that the fundamentalists' hatred of modernism caused the September 11th attacks.[81] Non-violent Islamic fundamentalism may reject modernism, but violent versions of Islamic fundamentalism thrive on it because they share common principles with the secular intellectual sciences.

Moreover, if the objective of the terrorists is to attack modernism, how do suicide attacks make strategic sense since they cannot end modernism?[82] Why not attempt to live so as to continue the attacks (like the Unabomber)? Why not select targets in one's own country where it is not too late to stop modernism, rather than in the United States where it is too late? We suggest that these questions do not have satisfactory answers, and that the notion that the terrorists executed the suicide attacks to protest against modern skyscrapers, for example, rather than United States foreign policy, is absurd.

Unfortunately, the perception of Islam as a religion of the sword, combined with a lack of understanding of bin Laden's rejection of the Islamic intellectual heritage, makes it seem plausible to some policymakers that the terrorists were simply attacking our lifestyle and trying to impose a different way of life on Americans. This makes the terrorists' strategy appear to be ahistorical by denying the role of the United States' past foreign policy in the game, as if violent Islamic fundamentalism were something "essential" rather than the accidental result of historical contingencies.

The strategic response usually associated with this view is military. However, we argue that simply relying on a military solution rather than recognizing the terrorists' foreign policy complaints may backfire, because bin Laden announced his tit-for-tat strategy publicly. Would-be terrorists are now watching for a change in United States foreign policy, and the lack of any change will reinforce bin Laden's argument, making terrorism against American civilians "even more commendable" as well as strategically necessary in the minds of some misguided individuals, leading to a very unfortunate cycle of violence. This makes the answers to the payoff and anticipation questions "worse," not "better."

It is important to note that this reverses the claims of some policymakers who suggest that any change in foreign policy necessarily "sends the wrong signal" to current or would-be terrorists, encouraging more terrorism on the United States, just as negotiating with a bank robber holding hostages can encourage more bank robberies. This analogy does not apply to the current situation. In the case of a bank robber holding hostages, he knows that he initiated the conflict, and he wants to survive the conflict. But in the current case, we are dealing with terrorists who believe that the United States initiated the conflict, and that American policymakers know this, as well as the fact that the terrorists are willing to commit suicide in opposing our foreign policy. Sending "the wrong signal" in tit-for-tat only applies when the party who defects first "gets away with it," and both parties know who defected first. An exclusively military response sets the stage for a continuous cycle of violence. We will consider how to avoid this in the next section.

B. Other Elements of United States Foreign Policy

The second possible response is to accept that tit-for-tat is the terrorists' strategy and that the United States should consider changes in its foreign policy, but to deny that the Israeli-Palestinian issue is a major foreign policy cause of the terrorist attacks. For example, some people argue that United States' support of "corrupt regimes" in the Arab world is the real foreign policy cause for terrorist hatred of the United States. But we have already argued that bin Laden does not view such support as a separate source of opposition relative to the three foreign policy issues themselves, and we will not pursue this question further here.

Others maintain that the real cause of the attacks is the presence of United States troops in Saudi Arabia or economic sanctions against Iraq. Thus, Dore Gold, an adviser to Ariel Sharon and former Israeli ambassador to the United Nations, argues that:

> The "guarantee of Israel's survival" appears only as the *third* reason for criticizing U.S. policy (in bin Laden's 1998 edict).... Political pressure on Israel to make concessions under present-day Palestinian violence could easily compromise Israeli security, but would not address either the *primary* or even *secondary* reasons behind the rage of militant Islam toward America.[83]

However, any view that denies the central role of the Israeli-Palestinian issue on the basis of its ranking ignores the crucial role of the Israeli multiplier in increasing opposition to subsequent elements of United States foreign policy, confusing the ranking of foreign policy elements based on a high Israeli multiplier (the third column in Table 2) for the ranking *with no* Israeli multiplier (the first column). This ignores the reasons bin Laden gives for his ranking based on a "Crusader-Zionist war" and Israeli special interests. The "Israel is not the issue" argument therefore takes bin Laden's statements out of context and makes the Israeli-Palestinian issue appear to be less than a secondary concern for him. Such an argument is even less convincing when one considers that the Israeli-Palestinian issue has been a motivating concern for bin Laden for some time, as it was for his teachers and mentors.[84] Suffice it to say here that the background of the bin Laden family suggests a real, on-going concern with this issue, particularly Jerusalem.[85]

Survey research also undermines the plausibility of the "Israel is not the issue" argument. In a survey shortly before the September 11th attacks conducted in five Arab countries—Egypt, Saudi Arabia, the United Arab Emirates, Kuwait, and Lebanon—Shibley Telhami states:

> I asked people how important the Palestinian issue is to them personally. I can tell you that, in four of these countries, in Saudi Arabia, the United Arab Emirates, Lebanon, and Kuwait, nearly 60% of the people said that it is the single most important issue to them personally, and in Egypt 79% of the people said it's the single most important issue to them personally. That is astonishing ...[86]

Telhami's survey asks respondents how important the Palestinian issue is *personally*, not how important it is as a source of anti-American sentiment, which would be even greater. Moreover, he points out that his findings are not simply a product of anti-Israeli media in the Arab world:

> There are people who believe that this is all the doing of the media, you know, that this is a function of a new media in the region that is sensational.... But let me tell you this. My research shows that the "al-Jazeera phenomenon" has nothing to do with this. In Saudi Arabia, for example, those who didn't watch al-Jazeera ranked the Palestinian issue higher in their priorities than those who did watch al-Jazeera. And in Egypt, where only about 7% of the people have satellite television altogether, you have the largest share of the public, 79%, saying the Palestinian issue is most important to them.[87]

Indeed, Telhami suggests that "we have a misunderstanding of what this issue means in the region" and "think of it in very simplistic terms," pointing out that, "this issue is central to the collective consciousness in the region, to the collective Arab and Islamic identity."[88]

Seyyed Hossein Nasr's "The Spiritual Significance of Jerusalem: The Islamic Vision" is a seminal article to explain why this issue takes on such direct spiritual significance for Muslims.[89] Indeed, "Jerusalem is the heart of the holy land, a term in fact used in the Qur´ān and not explicitly in the Bible," and there are several reasons why "the attachment to Jerusalem is no less real for Muslims than for Jews and Christians."[90] He points out three main reasons which themselves lead to a fourth, which apply on both exoteric and esoteric levels. The first reason is that Jerusalem was the first *qibla*, or direction of prayer, for Muslims, and Nasr explains the "mystical" relationship between Jerusalem and Mecca, which is the second *qibla*.[91] The second reason is that the Prophet Muḥammad made his ascent (*mi'rāj*) to the Divine Presence from Jerusalem, and the Qur'an states, "Glorified be He who carried His servant by night from the Inviolable Place of Worship [Makkah] to the Far Distant Place of Worship [Jerusalem] the neighborhood whereof We have blessed, that We might show him of Our tokens! Lo! He, only He, is the Hearer, Seer" (17:1 [Pickthall translation]). Nasr points out that:

> ... there are numerous sayings of the Prophet (*ḥadīth*) and traditional commentaries which clarify the meaning of this verse and elucidate the significance of the *mi'rāj* which is associated with the inner meaning of the daily prayers and is the prototype of spiritual realization in Islam especially in its esoteric dimension associated with Sufism. There is in fact a famous Arabic adage according to which the daily canonical prayers (*ṣalāt*) are the nocturnal or spiritual ascent (*mi'rāj*) of the true believer (*mu'min*).[92]

This ascent is the basis of bin Laden's remark that "while millions of Americans are homeless and destitute and live in abject poverty, their government is busy occupying our land and building new settlements and helping Israel build new settlements in the point of departure for our Prophet's midnight journey to the seven heavens."[93] The third reason for the significance of Jerusalem for Muslims concerns Islamic eschatological teachings that "this historical cycle will come to an end with the return of Christ" to Jerusalem, for Muslims believe in the Second Coming of Christ as do Christians.[94] Finally, these three reasons together made Jerusalem a site of pilgrimage for Muslims. "For the past fourteen centuries and until the 1967 war which caused Jerusalem to cease to be controlled by Islamic authorities, most of those making the *ḥajj* (to Mecca) would also make pilgrimage to Jerusalem, as the third holy city to be visited (the time that the city was held by Crusaders being an exception)."[95] This is why bin Laden's father was so pleased to be able to make pilgrimage to all three mosques in a single day using his private helicopter. Indeed, there is a *ḥadīth*, or saying of the Prophet, according to which, "Allāh, may He be praised and exalted, said of Jerusalem: You are my Garden of Eden, My hallowed and chosen land. Whoever lives here does so because I had mercy upon him, and whoever leaves this place does so because I am angry with him."[96]

Because of the spiritual significance of Jerusalem, no Muslim has the right (or ability) to negotiate with it, which in the minds of Muslims would be like betraying God and the Prophet. Nasr observes that:

> Not all the Palestinians nor all the Arabs nor even all the over one billion and two hundred million Muslims now living in the world could give Jerusalem

> away for no matter what amount of wealth, power, land or any other worldly compensation. The attachment of Muslims to Jerusalem is permanent and will last as long as human history itself.[97]

Indeed, the Israeli-Palestinian issue would not take on such direct spiritual significance if Israel were located in some part of Syria, for example, and did not involve Jerusalem (although most Muslims would of course sympathize with other displaced Muslims). While the occupied territories are certainly not an insignificant issue, particularly for Palestinians, the spiritual significance of Jerusalem is essential for understanding the recent suicide attacks against the United States. In short, the hypothetical group of policymakers who deny the centrality of the Israeli-Palestinian issue do not understand the rules of the game (our payoff question) because of an incorrect understanding of the spiritual significance of Jerusalem for Muslims, and how this colors their perception of United States foreign policy. Changes in foreign policy based on an incorrect understanding of the rules of the game may reduce some anti-American sentiment in the region, but this alone is unlikely to stop terrorist attacks as long as the Israeli-Palestinian issue, the center of which is the question of Jerusalem, remains outstanding. A simple military solution is also likely to backfire, as discussed earlier.

C. Middle Eastern Domestic Policy

Turning to our third possible reaction to bin Laden's public strategy, one could argue that domestic policy changes in the Middle East—an American "wish list" of political changes in the Arab and Muslim world—could stop terrorism against the United States. In the full-length monograph, we examine different versions of this argument, particularly Michael Doran's argument that the United States was "drawn into somebody else's civil war."[98] Bin Laden actually reverses this argument, accusing United States foreign policy of *leading to* a civil war in Saudi Arabia and other countries.[99] Indeed, changing the domestic policies of the Saudi regime in the way bin Laden espouses involves rejecting United States foreign policy, since he provides the same reasons for opposing both, as we pointed out earlier. And if the Saudi regime completely rejected United States foreign policy and removed the troops from Saudi Arabia, the Israeli-Palestinian issue and sanctions on Iraq would still be outstanding. This returns us to the question of whether or not the terrorists would attack if their only foreign policy complaint was the Israeli-Palestinian issue; and we already know that bin Laden states that they would.

At best, Middle Eastern domestic policy is a necessary rather than a sufficient condition for the September 11th attacks. Indeed, granting all of the items on an American "wish list" of political changes in the Arab and

Muslim world might still not stop terrorism against the United States. In fact, the economic solutions usually proposed by those who wish to change Middle Eastern domestic policies ignore the role of spiritual payoffs in bin Laden's new rules espousing "commendable terrorism," and could actually backfire. Daniel Pipes argues that Islamic fundamentalism is not a product of poverty, and can even result from wealth (although for very different reasons than we do).[100] Unfortunately, Pipes does not make the causal connection between secular fundamentalism and Islamic fundamentalism to explain this fact. Once again, it is no coincidence that bin Laden was raised in a modernized economic environment that weakened traditional Islam, creating the necessary intellectual conditions for bin Laden's tit-for-tat strategy and the positive response of some Muslims to it, which we discussed earlier. Typical economic development solutions could actually increase Islamic fundamentalism and the risk of terrorism because such solutions destroy the link between the economy and the Islamic intellectual heritage. As we pointed out in the previous section, there is an intimate connection, on the one hand, between spiritual education and work in a traditional Islamic economy that prevents terrorism, and on the other hand, between dangerous combinations of Islamic and secular thought in modernist approaches to economic development that make terrorism possible. This analysis raises important philosophical questions that we briefly note in the next section.

The third reason for doubting the wisdom of a modernist economic solution is that there are environmental effects of economic development to consider, and nobody knows the long-run consequences of the environmental damage we have already done, let alone the impact of increased industrialization.[101] Indeed, if the entire world had industrialized in the same way as the United States and Western Europe, an environmental catastrophe would have occurred even greater than the problems we already face. The modernist economic development solution may be substituting one problem with another (worse) environmental one.

Of course, military and economic approaches have a role to play in the overall solution, but they will not work alone and without modification, unless we are to try and convince every Muslim that U.S. foreign policy is just, and that Islamic values on the connection between the spiritual significance of nature, art, and production are false. We must also hope to avert an environmental catastrophe. In the next section, we will suggest a more appropriate economic solution that effectively responds to Islamic fundamentalism while respecting nature.

VI. Understanding the Rules of the Game: The Current Intellectual Crisis

In light of the previous analysis, the discerning policymakers with an accurate understanding of the rules of the game will recognize that the suicide attacks of September 11th are part of a tit-for-tat strategy directed against United States foreign policy, not an ahistorical response against United States domestic policy. These policymakers will also recognize that the Israeli-Palestinian issue is the central foreign policy complaint of the terrorists, around which they integrate other issues as part of an ongoing "war against Islam" motivated by Israeli special interests. This perception of a "Crusader-Zionist alliance" increases the intensity of terrorist opposition to subsequent United States foreign policy in the region. This "Israeli multiplier" is the key to understanding the logical consistency of bin Laden's statements, which simultaneously emphasize the presence of U.S. troops in Saudi Arabia on the one hand and the Israeli-Palestinian issue on the other. The discerning policymakers do not confuse rankings based on a high Israeli multiplier for rankings *without* it, which could make the Israeli-Palestinian issue appear to be less than a secondary concern for some terrorists. Although variations in the Israeli multiplier can generate different rankings of elements of United States foreign policy, terrorists with different rankings can cooperate on the same tit-for-tat strategy. We can determine this much by simply examining bin Laden's statements, as we have seen in the previous sections.

This suggests that the Israeli-Palestinian issue may be a necessary and sufficient foreign policy condition for the September 11th attacks when combined with the necessary intellectual conditions mixing secular and Islamic thought. If we eliminate all other foreign policy complaints, terrorists could still have attacked, given the fact that the Israeli-Palestinian issue generates more anti-American sentiment in the region than all other factors combined. Subsequent elements of United States foreign policy do not appear to generate enough opposition without the Israeli multiplier to trigger the attacks, even if the multiplier sometimes changes the rankings of the issues. The risk of future attacks certainly comes more from this foreign policy issue than any other.

Because the terrorists believe that tit-for-tat is the optimal strategy, and believe that United States policymakers know that the United States "defected first" under the influence of Israeli special interests to pursue an unjust foreign policy, a purely military response will backfire. The current situation is not analogous to dealing with a bank robber holding hostages, as our mistaken policymakers believe. There are only three ways to stop terrorism based on a tit-for-tat strategy in this instance: 1) convince terrorists that the United States did not defect first, 2) convince terrorists that terrorism on American civilians is not an acceptable tit-for-tat response even if the United States did defect first, or 3) address the foreign policy complaints of the terrorists. The discerning policymakers know that the correct strategic choice between these three options depends on a correct moral choice. If the United States policy on the Israeli-Palestinian issue has been fair historically, then the first option is preferable because we did not defect (by committing an injustice) first and must retaliate against terrorist defection while explaining the fairness and justice of our foreign policy towards the Palestinians.[102] But if the United States has not pursued a fair policy on the Israeli-Palestinian issue by favoring Israel, then the discerning policymakers recognize that we must pursue the third option because in this case the first and second will certainly fail in moral and strategic terms. In either scenario, the morally correct choice determines the strategically correct choice.

Some policymakers may object that the United States cannot afford the negative "reputation effects" of changing foreign policy now, regardless of whether or not this is "moral." This is because other threats loom on the horizon that are not of an Islamic stripe, and we cannot compromise in one area without compromising in others. Joshua Brockwell explains this point of view as follows:

> To capitulate to the demands of terrorists (i.e., those who wish to maximize the social cost of maintaining the status quo) is tantamount to veering off the road during a game of "chicken." That is to say, realism as a political ideology thinks in terms of prestige, honor, and the like. The willingness on the part of political elites to acquiesce to the demands of a rag-tag minority in Islam (and I think we would agree that al-Qaeda is just that), would show to the international community the weak face of the sole hegemonic stabilizer in today's post-Cold War environment. Simply put, for the realists in D.C., this cannot and will not happen.[103]

This suggests a "one-size-fits-all" approach to international affairs rather than a "mix-and-match" approach. But we argue that our discerning policymakers adopt different strategies for different game structures, since one cannot use the same strategy to play poker as to play blackjack. Although the "game of chicken," in which both sides face disaster from lack of co-operation, may apply to other strategic situations, it does not apply here, since there is nothing we can threaten suicide terrorists with, given the expectation of spiritual rewards of "commendable terrorism." Terrorists will therefore drive ahead, even if it involves crashing, and the spiritual rewards change the structure of the game.[104] Although we sympathize with the concern that any change in foreign policy will "send the wrong signal" to other countries for other aspects of our foreign policy, entire countries have different incentives than terrorists. We examine this issue in detail in the full-length monograph, and argue that there are many ways to position a "mix-and-match" foreign policy to reduce the possibility of negative spillover effects of a foreign policy change.[105] Suffice it to say here that although there may be situations in which moral considerations diverge from material interests, this is not one of them.

But judging the fairness of our historical policy on the Israel-Palestinian issue involves assessing: 1) the history of actions of the Israelis and Palestinians in the conflict, and 2) the distribution of land between them. And the ethical assessment of both issues is affected by theological arguments about the correct interpretation of the sacred texts and their political implications. For example, Christian Zionists believe that they should help the Jews return to their homeland to "accelerate" the Second Coming of Christ, as Victor Danner points out in a brilliant essay on traditional, modernist, and fundamentalist eschatological doctrines in the Abrahamic faiths.[106] Other Christians disagree with this fundamentalist view. Although we cannot enter the details of this debate here, it bears emphasizing that this debate largely determines how many Christians view the moral standing of the actions of the Israelis and Palestinians in this conflict. Obviously, if one side is "doing the will of God," that side cannot have committed an injustice by starting the conflict first.[107] The same theological argument affects one's view of the distribution of land. If someone from Mars came to earth and saw two peoples with claims to the same land, one might expect half the land to be given to one party and the other half to the other party. But this is obviously not the case currently since 78% of the land is for Israelis and 22% is for Palestinians, not including the Israeli settlements, which reduce this to around 19%.

In the full-length monograph, we examine the relationship between secular thought and various forms of religious fundamentalism as they relate to this issue. As Ghazi bin Muḥammad points out, "This is a blight that has afflicted more or less all the world's traditional populous religions: Judaism, Christianity, Islam, and even, recently, Hinduism—as evinced by Bharata Janatra Party (B.J.P) for example—and Buddhism (as seen in Burma, for instance)."[108] On the one hand, secular thought contributes to contemporary religious fundamentalism by obscuring the religious sapiential perspective that penetrates the inner meaning of revelation. But on the other hand, secular thought is not strong enough to convert fundamentalists into "good" secularists or religious modernists. Thus, secular thought is both unable to solve the Israeli-Palestinian political crisis and has contributed to it. We therefore maintain that our discerning policymakers should look for a political solution to the Israeli-Palestinian conflict—the primary impetus to Islamic fundamentalist terrorism around the world—based upon the sapiential perspective within each of the Abrahamic religions. The key is to identify those within each of the Abrahamic religions with the gift of a sapiential perspective, and to empower them to engage the primary issues of this conflict. This requires men and women with insight into the very source of peace and harmony and with sufficient sanctity to become instruments of God's mercy. This is not a matter of "uniformity" between the religions that is often proposed by religious modernists and "new age" groups, as Seyyed Hossein Nasr so eloquently points out, but of recovering the sapiential perspective that can produce a political solution to the Israeli-Palestinian issue that is beyond the scope of Jewish and Christian fundamentalists.[109] As we shall argue in the postlude, only the sapiential perspective can completely solve the question of Jerusalem by providing the understanding of the depth of meanings of revelation necessary to live in a multi-religious world. Similarly, Ibrahim Kalin and Ejaz Akram clear the ground by exposing the fatal flaws inherent in the work of both Samuel Huntington and Francis Fukuyama in light of the sapiential perspective. This prepares the way for discerning policymakers to develop a sound theoretical framework for analyzing the interconnections between religion, conflict, and peace.[110] Analogous arguments apply to the economic solution. Indeed, both revelation and nature have an inner meaning that is the subject of the esoteric intellectual sciences of all religions, which are necessary in order to address the current environmental and political crises. Secular thought obscures one's ability to penetrate these inner meanings, and we examine an appropriate economic solution based on the traditional intellectual perspective, such as is beautifully articulated by Titus Burckhardt, in the full-length monograph.[111]

Unfortunately, current policymakers do not appear to be pursuing the appropriate political and economic solutions based on the intellectual perspective of our discerning policymakers, and appear to be dominated by secular, modernist-religious, and fundamentalist perspectives. There seems to be little political will to reconsider our foreign policy on the Israeli-Palestinian issue. Few scholars in the West even understand the Islamic intellectual heritage (or any other traditional intellectual heritage) and therefore usually undermine it (directly or indirectly); and few, if any, economists know of the writings of Titus Burckhardt, which are essential to an economic solution based on Islamic or other spiritual values, instead, approaching economic development from a modernist point of view. Indeed, many policymakers deny that game theory even applies to terrorist attacks. Moreover, the majority of the remaining policymakers either seek conventional military and economic solutions, which do not recognize that tit-for-tat is the terrorists' strategy, or do not recognize the centrality of the Israeli-Palestinian issue if they recognize tit-for-tat. And even if policymakers recognize the need to address the latter, how can they implement a solution among the variety of Jewish, Christian, and Muslim fundamentalists without a traditional intellectual perspective? Indeed, if the Orientalists and economists do not have the correct intellectual and economic solutions—and they are supposed to be the "experts"—how can the policymakers know? In short, the current crisis is intellectual at least as much as it is political—it suggests a lack of knowledge of spiritual principles. But it is only a matter of time before political and environmental problems will force us to reconsider our foreign and domestic policies in light of these spiritual principles.[112] We conclude that without a change in our understanding of the rules of the game in light of spiritual principles and without adopting appropriate political, intellectual, and economic solutions to the problems that prompt terrorist attacks against the United States, such attacks are likely to continue, even while we fervently pray they do not. And if they occur, the cause will not be that the United States wrongly pressured Israel to restrain its use of force against Palestinians, as Benjamin Netanyahu claims. The attacks will be the result of the moral and intellectual failure of all parties involved in the conflict.

VII. Postlude

We conclude with a suggestion to apply traditional spiritual principles to resolve the issue of Jerusalem.[113] Israeli-Palestinian peace talks always postpone the subject of Jerusalem's status to the end, on the theory that it is the most difficult issue to resolve. However, it is not as difficult if one is aware of the traditional intellectual heritage in the three Abrahamic religions. One can actually begin with the issue of Jerusalem by focusing on the interests, as opposed to the positions, of the three religions in access to the holy sites, specifically the Dome of the Rock, the Noble Sanctuary or Temple Mount as the Jews call it, the Western or Wailing Wall, and the Church of the Holy Sepulcher. In fact, the religious authorities worked out practical solutions to these issues long ago. For example, Jews and Christians can visit the Dome of the Rock, and Muslims can visit the Wailing Wall and the Church of the Holy Sepulcher without performing overtly visible rites of their own there. If believers of different faiths pray silently and without visible gestures in one another's sanctuaries, most would not object.

The issues become difficult when we address who should have sovereignty over, or political control of, the sites. This was what the Crusades were fought over, as well as the war of 1967 and the current *intifada*, although there are many other issues too, of course. For example, why should Palestinians not be allowed to repair their homes or to build new homes in East Jerusalem? Why should Jews be allowed to build in the occupied territories?

These and other issues on the treatment of Palestinians are important and they receive much sympathy from Arabs and Muslims around the world. But the bedrock issue for Muslims everywhere is the Dome of the Rock, the Axis of the World along which Muḥammad ascended to the Throne of God. This is why many Muslims were outraged when Ariel Sharon took an entourage of 1000 Jews, including many soldiers, to the Temple Mount, flaunting Israel's political and military control over the Temple Mount and exacerbating the situation prior to the attacks of September 11th.

Perhaps the only way to achieve peace in the Middle East would be for Jerusalem to be depoliticized. It should not be a political capital of either Israel or Palestine, but be given a unique status as a spiritually sovereign entity under a theocracy of the traditional representatives of the three Abrahamic religions; not an "international" city under the auspices of the United Nations, as some have suggested, but a spiritual polity under the auspices of God. Obviously, establishing such a polity will not be easy, and would require assistance from those within each religion who are best able to recognize those truths that all three religions proclaim in common. But we believe that if this, the most difficult issue of all, the "control" of the Temple Mount and Old Jerusalem, could be resolved, and peace could be established at this spiritual center of the Abrahamic religions, the Presence (*sakīna* in Arabic and *shekinah* in Hebrew) of God Almighty could flow down through that center and bring peace throughout the Middle East—"*wa Llāhu aʿlam*—and God knows best."

Notes

[1] For an excellent and highly readable introduction to game theory, see Shaun Hargreaves Heap and Yanis Varoufakis, *Game Theory: A Critical Introduction* (London: Routledge, 1995). This introduction examines the philosophical underpinnings of game theory, and provides an interesting critique, although not from a religious point of view.

[2] John Nash was one of the pioneers of game theory, for which he won the Nobel Prize in economics, and was the subject of the highly acclaimed film *A Beautiful Mind.*

[3] Second-order does not necessarily mean secondary.

[4] See David Dakake, "The Myth of a Militant Islam," in this volume.

[5] This paper is an abridged version of a monograph of the same title which is forthcoming.

[6] John von Neumann and Oskar Morgenstern, *The Theory of Games and Economic Behavior* (New York: Wiley, 1964 [c1944]).

[7] The university admissions system in Egypt works quite differently than in the United States. In Egypt, scores on national examinations determine which field a person may select to major in, not the university one can go to. In the United States, the situation is the reverse: students compete to get into universities in which they may then select any field as a major.

[8] John Hooper, "The Shy, Caring, Deadly Fanatic: The Double Life of a Suicide Pilot," *The Observer*, September 23, 2001.

[9] See Shaun Hargreaves Heap, *et al.*, *The Theory of Choice: A Critical Guide* (Cambridge, MA: Blackwell, 1992). Instrumental rationality implies that the terrorists can rank different options in a consistent manner within a means-end framework. For example, if a terrorist had three options, A, B, and C, and preferred A to B, B to C, and A to C, he would have consistent, or instrumentally rational, preferences. In this case, we should not rule out the applicability of game theory just because we disagree with the end that is the basis of his rankings. However, if he preferred A to B, B to C, and C to A instead of A to C, this would be inconsistent and "go in circles," in which case there is no stable end that he is pursuing, and game theory does not apply. With such "circular preferences," efficiency has no meaning because there is no single goal that is the object of efficiency.

[10] Using game theory does not require terrorists to be "globally consistent"; it only requires them to be either consistent in a *specific range* of choices that are relevant to playing the game, or to be "locally consistent."

[11] In game theory terms, this answers the second, instrumental rationality question about the motivation of the terrorists. A complete answer on exactly *what* objective the terrorists are maximizing relates to the payoff question based on the rules of the game that shows the payoffs for the players of different combinations of moves, which we shall examine shortly. The usual order of the three game theory questions begins with the instrumental rationality question on whether or not the players are maximizing anything, and ends with the payoff question based on the rules of the game. But we changed the usual order for ease of presentation.

[12] In this case, his recent calls for *jihād* against the United States by all Muslims would simply continue the strategy activated by the actual terrorists that he had already incited with his earlier statements.

13 Tit-for-tat is the strategy of starting with cooperation, and thereafter doing what the other player did on the previous move.

14 See transcripts of the John Miller interview, available online at the PBS website: http://www.pbs.org/wgbh/pages/frontline/shows/binladen/who/interview.html.

15 *Ibid.*

16 See transcripts of responses to questions on the *Frontline* special, "Hunting Bin Laden" at http://www.pbs.org/wgbh/pages/frontline/shows/binladen/who/interview.html.

17 John Miller interview (1998).

18 See transcripts of responses to questions from followers on the *Frontline* special "Hunting Bin Laden."

19 *Ibid.*

20 Thomas Friedman, "Another Wall Must Come Down," *New York Times*, March 3, 2002.

21 Bin Laden's argument is clearly "path dependent" in that earlier events exert important influences upon the eventual outcome. If the Israeli-Palestinian issue occurred last historically among the three issues rather than first, explaining United States foreign policy in terms of Israeli special interests and media would be much more difficult. In this case, the view that the elements of our foreign policy are "separable" (the first column in our tables) might then be more relevant. But because the Israeli-Palestinian issue comes first historically, the argument that Israeli special interests and media shape United States foreign policy in the region is common among many Arabs and Muslims. Since this colors the perception of subsequent United States foreign policy in the minds of many Muslims, bin Laden can use it in marketing and recruitment.

22 For a transcript of the interview see http://www.cnn.com/2002/WORLD/asiapcf/south/02/05/binladen.transcript/index.html.

23 *Ibid.*

24 Specifically, bin Laden links the problems in the Saudi economy to the enormous cost of maintaining U.S. troops in Saudi Arabia, U.S. influence on Saudi oil production and prices, and the unnecessary award of extravagant contracts to American corporations after Desert Storm. In his "Declaration of War Against the Americans Occupying the Land of the Two Holy Places," bin Laden argues that:

> The crusader forces became the main cause of our disastrous condition, particularly in the economic aspect of it, due to the unjustified heavy spending on these forces [U.S. troops in Saudi Arabia]. As a result of the policy imposed on the country, especially in the field of the oil industry where production is restricted or expanded and prices are fixed to suit the American economy ignoring the economy of the country [sic]. Expensive deals were imposed on the country to purchase arms. People are asking what is the justification for the very existence of the regime then? (p. 6).

Bin Laden claims that Saudi officials admit this in the exchange of accusations between the Saudi and United States governments after the Khobar Towers attack on U.S. residences in Dhahran:

> So we have the Americans stating that the causes of the explosions are the bad policies of the regime and the corruption of members of the ruling family, and the regime is accusing the Americans of exceeding their authority by taking

> advantage of the regime and forcing it to enter into military and civil contracts which are beyond its means, which led to great economic slide which has affected the people [sic].

See "The New Powder Keg in the Middle East," *Nida´ul Islam* (October-November 1996). Available online at http://www.newyorker.com/fact/content/?011119fa_FACT2.

25 World Islamic Front Statement, "*Jihad* against Jews and Christians," February 22, 1998. See http://www.newyorker.com/fact/content/?011119fa_FACT2.

26 For example, in the1996 interview in *Nidau´ul Islam*, bin Laden links the Israeli-Palestinian issue and United States foreign policy against Muslims to the "corrupt" foreign policy of the Saudi regime in the following manner:

> The external policy of the Saudi regime towards Islamic issues is a policy which is tied to the British outlook from the establishment of Saudi Arabia until 1364 A.H. [1945 A.D.], then it became attached to the American outlook after America gained prominence as a major power in the world after the second World War. It is well-known that the policies of these two countries bear the greatest enmity towards the Islamic world. To be taken out of this category is the final phase of the rule of King Faisal, as there was a clear interest in Muslim issues, in particular *Quds* (Jerusalem) and Palestine.

In fact, bin Laden argues that the "Zionist-Crusader alliance resorted to killing and arresting the truthful *ʿulamā´* (religious scholars) and the working *daʿees* (preachers for Islam)" to suppress efforts to change the foreign policies of the Saudi and other Middle Eastern regimes ("Declaration of War," p. 4). The Saudi regime is "apostate" in bin Laden's eyes since "to support infidels against the Muslims is one of the ten 'voiders' that would strip a person from his Islamic status" ("Declaration of War," p. 7).

27 In this case, one could combine a higher Israeli multiplier on U.S. troops in Saudi Arabia with a lower multiplier on sanctions against Iraq. This combination would imply a ranking of U.S. troops in Saudi Arabia first, the Israeli-Palestinian issue second, and sanctions on Iraq third. But for ease of presentation and to simplify the analysis, we do not present this in Table 2, which assumes that a single multiplier (whether lower or higher) applies to all the elements equally (within the second and third columns). The central role of the Israeli-Palestinian issue does not change whether we use the same or different Israeli multipliers for different elements. But we recognize that there are linkages between the various foreign policy elements that could justify higher multipliers for some elements than for others.

28 We say "somewhat" rather than "completely" redundant because the terrorists could oppose, for example, the loss of Saudi control over Saudi foreign and domestic policies as a separate source of opposition to the United States. But since opposition to the three elements of foreign policy is the basis of the opposition to United States influence on Saudi foreign and domestic policy to begin with, we must avoid "double-counting" the former by inflating the latter, which is a relatively residual issue in this context.

29 Bin Laden opposes the Saudi regime for the same reasons he opposes United States foreign policy. Indeed, the Israeli multiplier increases the intensity of opposition to both governments, and Saudi cooperation with the United States in military and other efforts takes on a very different "color" with the Israeli-Palestinian issue than without it. In fact, he accuses the Israeli-American alliance of *leading to* civil war in Saudi Arabia and other countries. Consequently, policy changes by the Saudi regime unrelated to the three issues in Table 2 would not (significantly) reduce his opposition to it. And even

if it removed U.S. troops from Saudi Arabia, the Israeli-Palestinian issue and sanctions on Iraq would still be outstanding, leaving open the question of whether or not the terrorists would still attack American civilians (which we shall return to).

30 Translation of al-Jazeera tape, October 7, 2001. Available online at http://www.newyorker.com/fact/content /?011119fa_FACT2.

31 There is some discrepancy between various translations of bin Laden's statement. Some translations read "since nearly 80 years" (such as CNN and ABC) whereas others read "more than 80 years" (such as the Associated Press). For a comparison of the translations, see http://www.september11news.com/OsamaSpeeches.htm. The correct translation is "more than 80 years." The difference between them can influence the date one looks for to understand bin Laden's reference, either starting with the end of the Ottoman sultanate in 1918 or the League of Nations mandate in 1922. The Israeli-Palestinian issue has its roots in both dates, as we point out below.

32 Bernard Lewis, "The Revolt of Islam," *The New Yorker*, November 19, 2001. Available online at http://www.newyorker.com/fact/content/?011119fa_FACT2.

33 Eric Fleischauer, "Tracing Hatred: Bin Laden's Ill Will Rooted in Centuries of Conflict," *Decatur Daily*, October 15, 2001.

34 *Frontline* special "Hunting Bin Laden," bin Laden's edicts and statements.

35 David Dakake, "The Myth of a Militant Islam," and Reza Shah-Kazemi, "Recollecting the Spirit of *Jihād*."

36 Bin Laden suggests this in the videotape discovered in Qandahar that was released by the United States government on December 13, 2001.

37 "Traditional" Islam (as we use the term here) is not simply inherited convention, but is "that single tree of Divine Origin whose roots are the Qur´ān and the *Ḥadith*, and whose trunk and branches constitute that body of tradition that has grown from those roots over some fourteen centuries in nearly every inhabited quarter of the globe" (Seyyed Hossein Nasr, *Traditional Islam in the Modern World* [London and New York: Kegan Paul International, 1987]), pp. 11-12. This remarkable book also deals with many misconceptions about traditional Islam, such as the spiritual significance of *jihād*, and the male and female in the Islamic perspective.

38 In fact, the spiritual and intellectual qualifications necessary for proper *ijtihād* are so enormous that there is a debate over whether anyone today has the qualifications necessary to perform it, particularly since it requires in-depth knowledge of the Islamic intellectual heritage as well as the transmitted sciences. Regardless of whether or not one believes the "gate of *ijtihād* is closed" to contemporary Muslims, the overwhelming majority of them reject bin Laden's "innovative" *ijtihād* and Machiavellian tactics, even if many Muslims are critical of United States foreign policy in the Middle East.

39 William Chittick, "Recovering the Islamic Intellectual Heritage," p. 2.

40 See transcripts of responses to questions from followers from the *Frontline* special, "Hunting Bin Laden."

41 See the al-Qaeda terrorism manual and the videotape mentioned in the previous footnote.

42 As quoted by Daniel Pipes, "God and Mammon: Does Poverty Cause Militant Islam?," *The National Interest* (Winter 2002).

43 Interestingly, bin Laden discusses the potential targeting of economic sites in Saudi

Arabia by the United States. See his "Declaration of War" at http://www.danielpipes.org/article/104.

44 For an excellent analysis of the role of special interests in influencing policy-makers in a democracy, see Mancur Olson's *The Rise and Decline of Nations* (New Haven: Yale University Press, 1984). The application of Olson's arguments to the terrorist attacks is beyond the scope of the current paper, but is an important topic for future research.

45 Transcripts of bin Laden's December 27, 2001 videotaped statement on al-Jazeera. Available online at http://www.fas.org/irp/world/para/ladin_122701.pdf.

46 William Beeman, "Understanding Osama Bin Laden," September 12, 2001. Available online at http://www.alternet.org/print.html?StoryID=11487.

47 *Ibid.*

48 John Miller interview (1998).

49 Interview with Senator John Warner on *Larry King Live*, October 2001.

50 Some economists like Paul Krugman argue that there is an economic "silver-lining" to the attacks in the sense that the Federal Reserve will act more aggressively to increase the money supply, shortening the recession that the economy was already entering. However, this argument assumes that the terrorist attacks will not continue. Moreover, the attacks increase on-going search and enforcement costs, regardless of the Federal Reserve's response. The same argument applies to William Baumol's article, "Long Run Consequences of the Terrorist Acts—Possible Stimulating Effects," (forthcoming).

51 See transcripts of *Frontline* interviews with James Baker and Brent Scowcroft, "Saudi Arabia: A Time Bomb?" Available online at http://www.pbs.org/wgbh/pages/frontline/shows/saudi/interviews/.

52 *Ibid.*, interview with Vali Nasr. This is also consistent with bin Laden's repeated assertions that the United States gets back the money it pays for Saudi oil by selling the Saudi regime things the country does not need.

53 See Reza Shah-Kazemi's, "Recollecting the Spirit of *Jihād*," in this volume.

54 See David Dakake, "The Myth of a Militant Islam," in this volume.

55 Seyyed Hossein Nasr, "The Spiritual Significance of Jerusalem: The Islamic Vision," *Islamic Quarterly* no. 4 (1998): 233-242.

56 See Ibrahim Kalin's "Roots of Misconception: Euro-American Perceptions of Islam Before and After September 11," in this volume.

57 *Ibid.*, p. 31.

58 Joseph E. B. Lumbard, "The Decline of Knowledge and the Rise of Ideology in the Modern Islamic World."

59 "The conquered imitate the conquerors," as Ibn Khaldūn, the renowned fourteenth century Muslim scholar of history and society, suggested. This is particularly true among young people, to whom nothing is more humiliating than colonization, and who therefore embrace secular sciences and technology for power and independence.

> ... it must not be overlooked that, apart from any question of aesthetics or spirituality, people have in all ages imitated those who were strongest; before having strength people want to have at least the appearance of strength, and

the ugly things of the modern world have become synonymous with power and independence. The essence of artistic beauty is spiritual, whereas material strength is "worldly," and, since the worldly regard strength as synonymous with intelligence, the beauty of the tradition becomes synonymous not merely with weakness, but also with stupidity, illusion, and the ridiculous; being ashamed of weakness is almost always accompanied by hatred of what is looked on as the cause of this apparent inferiority—in this case, tradition, contemplation, truth (Frithjof Schuon, *Castes and Races* [Middlesex: Perennial Books, 1982], p. 79).

60 See Fuad Naeem's, "A Traditional Islamic Response to the Rise of Modernism," in this volume.

61 Ghazi bin Muḥammad, *The Sacred Origin of Sports and Culture* (Louisville, Kentucky: Fons Vitae, 1998), pp. 36-37. He provides a concise, but penetrating analysis of these issues in the section, "What is Culture?"

62 We do not limit the term secularism to the political "separation of Church and state" and the term modernism to the application of secular thought to other aspects of society (as Bernard Lewis seems to do in "The Roots of Muslim Rage," *The Atlantic Monthly* [September 1990]). Modernism, in the sense that we use the term here, is contrasted with tradition, which we discussed earlier, and "implies all that is merely human and now ever more increasingly subhuman, and all that is cut off from the Divine source," failing to draw the consequences of the fundamental doctrine of Unity. Modernism and secularism, as we use these terms, are almost the same, but not identical since Islamic (and other "religious") modernists differ from secular modernists on (some) elements of Islamic (or religious) law, not the intellectual sciences. See Seyyed Hossein Nasr, *Traditional Islam in the Modern World*, p. 98.

63 On the different types of Islamic fundamentalism and a masterful treatment of the issues dealt with in this section, see Seyyed Hossein Nasr, *Traditional Islam in the Modern World*. For a comparison of traditional and fundamentalist conceptions of *jihād* and the latter's relation to secular thought, see the remarkable series of essays by Abdullah Schleifer on *jihād* in the journal *Islamic Quarterly*. Part 1 is in vol. 23, no. 2 (1979); part 2, in vol. 27, no. 4 (1983); part 3, in vol. 28, no. 1 (1984); part 4, in vol. 28, no. 2 (1984); and part 5, in vol. 28, no. 3 (1984).

64 As regards civilization, we define it in terms of the application of theoretical sciences such as philosophy and sciences of nature to practical and productive sciences that determine what men do and make, respectively. Civilization is therefore intimately connected with Revelation in that metaphysics and the traditional sciences of nature are related to the inner meaning of Revelation.

65 In addition to the references already cited in this section, see Victor Danner, *The Islamic Tradition: An Introduction* (Amity, New York: Amity House, 1988), p. 210. The final chapter, "The Contemporary Muslim World," provides an exceptional analysis of the arguments discussed in this portion of the paper. Although some scholars claim that religion is compatible with modernism, in the full-length monograph of this paper we argue that this is an unsustainable middle position.

66 For example see Titus Burckhardt, "The Role of Fine Arts in Muslim Education," and Jean-Louis Michon "Education in the Traditional Arts and Crafts and the Cultural Heritage of Islam," in *Philosophy, Literature, and Fine Arts*, ed. Seyyed Hossein Nasr (Dunton Green, Sevenoaks, Kent: Hodder and Stoughton; Jeddah: King Abdulaziz University, 1982). Burckhardt's works on traditional economic institutions in Morocco hold the key

to the economic solutions proposed by our discerning policy-makers.

67 For an in-depth analysis of intellectual decadence versus deviation in the Islamic world, see Seyyed Hossein Nasr, *Islam and the Plight of Modern Man* (Chicago: Kazi Publications, 2000). For examples of how to explain this shift from decadence to deviation, or how the "micromotives" of a few can trigger enormous shifts in "macrobehavior" because of "domino effects," see Thomas C. Schelling, *Micromotives and Macrobehavior* (New York: Norton, 1978).

68 As David Dakake observes in his contribution to this volume:

> We should not have the impression that modern fundamentalists represent the first time that the traditional Islamic limits of warfare have been disregarded. The Khārijite movement, whose roots go back to a religio-political dispute in the first Islamic century, represent one of the most famous examples of just such transgression. The Khārijites were perfectly willing to attack "civilians," although their dispute was essentially with other members of the Muslim community, rather than with non-Muslims.... It is important to mention that throughout the early history of Islam the Khārijite position was condemned and even physically opposed by every major Muslim group, Sunnī and Shīʿite.

69 On the subject of secular philosophy being taught through the secular natural sciences in the Islamic world, see Seyyed Hossein Nasr's article, "The Teaching of Philosophy," in *Philosophy, Literature, and Fine Arts*, ed. Seyyed Hossein Nasr. On how non-violent fundamentalism prepares the way for violent fundamentalism under certain circumstances, such as the introduction of secular thought into the Islamic world after the invasion of colonial powers, see *Traditional Islam in the Modern World*. As Nasr points out:

> [W]hen those thinkers affected by this fideism confronted the West, they did so mostly from a perspective which was helpless before the specifically intellectual and rational challenges of the modern world and which had to have recourse to either an opposition based on fanaticism or refuge in the emotional aspect of faith alone. The result could not have but been catastrophic because the main challenge of the modern West to Islam ... [concerns] the domain of the mind and requires a response suitable to its nature.... (p. 308).

70 As we shall argue further on, secular sciences deny an ontological basis for values, reducing them to tastes (such as the preference for an apple as opposed to a pear) and setting the stage for a Machiavellian approach to strategy.

71 *Frontline* interview with Vali Nasr, "Saudi Arabia: A Time Bomb?"

72 Ibrahim Kalin, "Roots of Misconception: Euro-American Perceptions of Islam Before and After September 11."

73 Robert Axelrod, *The Evolution of Cooperation* (New York: Basic Books, 1984), p. 20. Axelrod performed an experiment to find a good strategy to use in repeated "Prisoner's Dilemma" situations, in which players are better off cooperating than mutually attempting to exploit each other, but are also tempted to resort to exploitation because of higher payoffs if the other player is a "sucker" who cooperates. According to Axelrod, he "invited experts in game theory to submit programs for a Computer Prisoner's Dilemma Tournament—much like a computer chess tournament.... To my considerable surprise, the winner was the simplest of all the programs submitted, TIT

FOR TAT." Axelrod circulated the results and requested entries for a second tournament, receiving sixty-two entries from six countries with contestants from an even broader range of fields including "professors of evolutionary biology, physics, and computer science, as well as the five disciplines represented in the first round." Some "very elaborate" programs were submitted, as were a number of attempts to improve on tit-for-tat itself. "TIT FOR TAT was again sent in by the winner of the first round, Anatol Rapoport of the University of Toronto. Again it won" (*Ibid.*, pp. vii-viii). Unfortunately, we cannot analyze how the structure of the current conflict is a variation of the well-known Prisoner's Dilemma game in this paper. We examine it in detail in the full-length monograph, arguing that fundamental changes in the neoclassical theory of choice are necessary to model spiritual values and their inversion.

74 This introduces interesting variations into the standard Prisoner's Dilemma game, as does the corresponding coalition claim, which we examine in the full-length monograph.

75 Michael Doran, "Somebody Else's Civil War," *Foreign Affairs* (January-February 2002): 23.

76 This is thoroughly examined in the full length monograph.

77 For example, John Voll provides an insightful analysis of the al-Qaeda recruitment video, pointing out that it does not engage in the "Islam and democracy debate," and that "in the minds of those who created this video, the conflict is not about attacking or defending Western style democracy and freedom, it is about responding with force to the seemingly overwhelming military power of the West" (See John Voll, "Bin Laden and the Logic of Power," Columbia International Affairs Online. Available at http://www.ciaonet.org/cbr/cbr00/video/cbr_v/cbr_v_2c.html. Moreover, Seyyed Hossein Nasr points out that the entire debate on the relationship between Islam and democracy is meaningless unless one specifies what type of democracy one is talking about. He draws an instructive analogy between Islamic views on ownership of private property and rule by the people. See Seyyed Hossein Nasr, *The Heart of Islam* (San Francisco: Harper Collins, 2002). Bin Laden himself rejects the argument that terrorists are reacting to United States domestic policy. In the December 27, 2001 videotaped statement, he argues, "What happened on 11 September is nothing but a reaction to the continuing injustice being done to our children in Palestine, Iraq, Somalia, southern Sudan, and elsewhere. Those who condemned these operations looked at the event as an isolated one. They did not link it with the previous events and the reasons behind it." See transcripts of bin Laden's December 27, 2001 videotaped statement on al-Jazeera.

78 John Voll, "Bin Laden and the Logic of Power."

79 *Ibid.*

80 *Ibid.*

81 As we suggested earlier, bin Laden has adopted secular tactics and technologies, and argued for the need to "go beyond" traditional Islamic views. If he was really against modernism, for example, why not object to the building of roads throughout Mecca (or something of that sort) as traditional scholars have in the past? The fact is that bin Laden and the alleged terrorists do not even have the necessary educational background in Islamic philosophy and metaphysics to understand the Islamic sciences of nature and the applied sciences to make such objections. For an in-depth analysis of this relation, see Seyyed Hossein Nasr, *Science and Civilization in Islam* (Cambridge, UK: Islamic Texts Society, 1987).

82 This does not necessarily mean that none of the terrorists involved in the September 11th attacks opposed any single element of modernism. But we suggest that any potential opposition was among a small minority of the terrorists, and could only play an incidental role in the attacks for that minority, perhaps adding to hatred of the United States or affecting target selection. For example, Mohammed Atta was concerned with issues of social and political justice such as the Israeli-Palestinian conflict on the one hand, and about the eclipse of traditional urban planning by its modern counterpart on the other. (His master's thesis on traditional versus modern approaches to urban planning at Hamburg Technical University earned the highest possible marks and was apparently brilliant.) We suggest that the former concern led to his participation in the September 11th attacks, whereas the latter concern may have increased his disdain for skyscrapers and his satisfaction in targeting the World Trade Center.

83 Dore Gold, "Israel is not the Issue: Militant Islam and America," *Jerusalem Letter/ Viewpoints*, October 1, 2001 (http://www.jcpa.org/jl/vp463.html). Similarly, Judith Miller argues that bin Laden's "three-page call-to-arms, published in February 1998, focused first on the plight of Muslims in the Arabian peninsula, second on the Iraqi people, and finally, not on Palestinians, but on the 'occupation' of holy Jerusalem." Regarding his 1996 "Declaration of War," she admits that bin Laden "cited the oppression of Palestinians by Israel," but she argues that "the condemnation was buried in an endless list of Muslim grievances against the United States" (Judith Miller, "Bin Laden's Media Savvy: Expert Timing of Threats," *New York Times (On the Web)*, October 9, 2001). Available online at http://www.nytimes.com/2001/10/09/international/middleeast/09OSAM.html.

84 See Peter Bergen, *Holy War, Inc.: Inside the Secret World of Osama bin Laden* (New York: The Free Press, 2001).

85 For example, see bin Laden's account of his father's love for Jerusalem in an interview by Jamal Isma'il at http://www.terrorism.com/terrorism/BinLadinTranscripts.html.

86 Shibley Telhami, "MEI Perspective: Professor Shibley Telhami's Keynote Speech at the Middle East Institute's 55th Annual Conference," October 19, 2001. Available online at http://www.mideasti.org/html/b-telhami101901.html.

87 *Ibid.*

88 *Ibid.*

89 Seyyed Hossein Nasr, "The Spiritual Significance of Jerusalem: The Islamic Vision," *Islamic Quarterly* no. 4 (1998): 233-242.

90 *Ibid.*, p. 234.

91 This view indirectly repudiates Orientalists' "political" accounts. Political explanations are based on the assumption that Islam is not a revelation from God, that no spiritual explanation for the direction of prayer is valid, and that the Prophet therefore changed the direction of prayer for political advantage.

92 *Ibid.*, p. 235.

93 See transcripts of interview by John Miller.

94 Seyyed Hossein Nasr, "The Spiritual Significance of Jerusalem: The Islamic Vision," p. 236.

95 *Ibid.*, p. 237.

96 *Ibid.*, p. 241.

97 *Ibid.*, p. 234.

98 Michael Doran, "Somebody Else's Civil War," *Foreign Affairs* (January-February 2002): 23. We maintain that Doran's version of the "Israel is not the issue" argument provides the wrong answers to all three of our game theory questions, suggesting the wrong payoffs to the rules of the game (ignoring their "collective" nature regardless of bin Laden's sentiments), implying instrumental irrationality for the terrorists (on pain of lending support to the opposite argument), and making the assumption that the terrorists assumed the United States would make an obvious strategic mistake (also on pain of supporting the opposite argument).

99 For example, see the "Declaration of War."

100 Daniel Pipes, "God and Mammon: Does Poverty Cause Militant Islam?," *The National Interest* (Winter 2002). He observes that, "not only are Bangladesh and Iraq not hotbeds of militant Islam, but militant Islam has often surged in countries experiencing rapid economic growth." Bin Laden certainly did not come from a poverty-stricken family and neither did the other suspects in the September 11th attacks.

101 For remarkable analyses of the intellectual and spiritual roots of the environmental crisis, see Seyyed Hossein Nasr, *Man and Nature* (Chicago: Kazi Publications, 1997), and Theodore Roszak, *Where the Wasteland Ends: Politics and Transcendence in Post Industrial Society* (Garden City, N.Y.: Doubleday, 1973).

102 The alternatives to this are moral and strategic errors in this case.

103 Joshua A. Brockwell, unpublished personal correspondence with author. This does not necessarily reflect his opinion, but is his summary of this point of view.

104 On the material level alone, the current situation may be a game of chicken, but the terrorists obviously do not limit themselves to this point of view, although they invert Islamic values.

105 Indeed, in the early days of the crisis, the Bush Administration declared that the then-recent talk of a Palestinian state was part of its foreign policy objectives "all along," citing the Mitchell Plan among others.

106 Victor Danner, "The Last Days in Judaism, Christianity, and Islam," in Arvind Sharma (ed.), *Fragments of Infinity: Essays in Religion and Philosophy, A Festschrift in Honor of Professor Huston Smith* (Garden City Park, New York: Avery Publishing Group, 1991), pp. 63-86.

107 Bin Laden may be aware of the role of Christian Zionism (as opposed to Jewish Zionism) in the formation of Israel, given his comments on British and American foreign policy before and after the Second World War in relation to Saudi Arabia, which we discuss further in the full-length version of the paper. But he clearly does not believe that the majority of Americans are Zionists (whether Jewish or Christian) because he maintains that Israeli special interests instigated the "war against Islam," not the American people.

108 Ghazi bin Muḥammad, *The Sacred Origin of Sports and Culture*, p. 38.

109 For a profound discussion of issues involved in comparative religion and the sapiential perspective in relation to the intellectual heritage of different religions, see Seyyed Hossein Nasr, *Religion and the Order of Nature* (Oxford: Oxford University Press, 1996).

110 For a further analysis of these arguments see my "An Analysis of the Interconnections

between Religion, Conflict, and Peace from a Traditional Point of View," Islamic Research Institute Working Paper, August 2002.

111 His approach, based as it is on the spiritual significance of production, allows for an environmentally sound economic solution since it is established upon the spiritual significance of nature, and responds to the intellectual errors of Islamic fundamentalism by integrating work and a spiritual education in a most profound manner, while yet alleviating poverty. In addition to the references cited earlier, see Burckhardt's article "Fez: Yesterday and Today," in *The Islamic City: Selected Papers From the Colloquium Held at the Middle East Center, Faculty of Oriental Studies in Cambridge, United Kingdom*, R.B. Serjeant (ed.) (Paris: UNESCO, 1980), and his book *Fez: City of Islam* (Cambridge, UK: Islamic Texts Society, 1992). See also the article by Jean-Louis Michon on Burckhardt in the Winter 1999 issue of *Sophia*, "Titus Burckhardt and the Sense of Beauty: Why and How He Loved and Served Morocco." This article has remarkable excerpts from Burckhardt's unpublished lectures on traditional economic institutions in Morocco. There is presently an urgent need to publish these lectures. The writings of E. F. Schumacher are also relevant in this regard, but Burckhardt's arguments on the relation between metaphysics, art, and the economy are more clear and precise than Schumacher's, whose economic writings have unfortunately been detached from their spiritual foundation by many later proponents of his view of economic development.

112 Consistency and the centrality of the traditional intellectual solution to the current problems demand it. We examine these issues and the current crisis in secular thought in the full-length monograph.

113 We owe the observations in this section to friends and colleagues who are remarkable representatives of traditional intellectual thought, though all errors and shortcomings are our own.

Chapter 7

The Muslim World and Globalization: Modernity and the Roots of Conflict

Ejaz Akram

Definitions of globalization abound, as they are the product of ideological and political leanings.[1] The subject of globalization has been addressed by philosophers, social scientists, and policymakers, but their views range from enthusiastic advocates to those who reprimand it as an effect of an odious cause. The goal of this paper is to address this phenomenon and its ramifications for the Muslim world. We will attempt to provide an explanation of why we should not expect that Muslims would simply want to emulate the modern industrial West. In the process we will demonstrate how globalization leads to the worsening of relations between the West[2] and the world of Islam, not to mention other areas of less developed Asia, Africa, and South America. Moreover, we will analyze the social, economic, and political impact of globalization, particularly on Muslim countries, a process which has unfortunately led to an adversarial image of the West in the minds of many Muslims. Finally, we shall analyze the challenges[3] to modernity,[4] and the assumption that the modern world is the best option among all options of social, economic, and political organization.

The earliest origins of globalization coincide with the beginning of modernity, which emerged with the secular humanism of the Renaissance and the Enlightenment, ushering in a gradual decline of religion and morality. The eighteenth and the early nineteenth centuries in European civilization were a period for the incubation and growth of modernism in the West, a time when Christianity was removed from the public square and yet Christian morality was still alive. This period can be classified as the *early modern period*, while the late nineteenth and early twentieth centuries represent the celebration of modernity with programs of modernization as prescriptive advice for the rest of the globe. This period may be called the *high modern* period. Finally, the post-War period may be classified as the *late modern period*, which, according to Oswald Spengler, is pregnant with the visible signs of the decline of the modern world.[5]

Globalization, the Non-West, and Islam

I. The Momentary Triumph of Ideology

Pro-globalization scholars such as Francis Fukuyama have argued that the world has progressed from primitive and traditional to advanced and modern conditions, and that liberal democracy constitutes the endpoint of mankind's evolution, the final form of human government.[6] Fukuyama said this soon after the demise of the Soviet Union, and made the claim that liberal democracy is universal and suitable for all because it triumphed over monarchism, fascism, and communism. This has become a fashionable thesis among those scholars and policy makers who feel that liberal democracy is universal. This, however, is an ideological viewpoint and a poor guide to any understanding of what constitutes the truly "universal."

In his article "The West has Won: Radical Islam Can't Beat Democracy and Capitalism," Fukuyama proclaims:

> We remain at the end of history because there is only one system that will continue to dominate world politics, that of the liberal-democratic West.... The clash consists of a series of rearguard actions from societies whose traditional existence is indeed threatened by modernization. The strength of the backlash reflects the severity of this threat. But time is on the side of modernity, and I see no lack of US will to prevail.[7]

In the same article Fukuyama argues that the September 11 attacks on New York and Washington were attacks on the center of global capitalism, which were evidently perpetrated by Islamic extremists unhappy with the very existence of Western civilization.[8] Fukuyama claims that the Islamic fundamentalists are the only group that has resisted modernism, which is essential to the condition that produces modernity. Fukuyama's thought might lead one to think that the challenge to modernism is the very function of Islamic fundamentalism's existence. This is a rather misleading conclusion. The reality is the *exact opposite*. Most scholars of Islamic fundamentalism have noted that it is by and large a modern phenomenon. That fundamentalism has a non-modern referent does not qualify its adherents as traditional people, as is discussed in Joseph E. B. Lumbard's contribution to this collection.[9] One of the profound agendas of the fundamentalists is the *thorough technological modernization* of Islamic societies. Fundamentalist Muslims are not only modernist Muslims, they are also the byproducts of the process of globalization.[10]

The assumptions of Fukuyama's thought have other important policy implications: if the conditions that have led to the formation of liberal democracies of the West are replicated, they will produce a similar set of results and thus make the world a better place. To achieve these conditions, a society must be reformed along social, economic, and political lines.

The proposal of political reforms—which purportedly lead to such an outcome—are often suggested by governments or through non-government agencies. In much of the social science literature, the latter have often been identified as the propellants of globalization.

The analytical shortcoming of Fukuyama's thesis is that he employs two elusive concepts with multiple meanings—"liberal" and "democracy"—to produce a single ideological meaning. But both "democracy" and "liberal" have a wide spectrum of meanings. A person of liberal social disposition may be politically and economically conservative or non-liberal, while a politically liberal person may be conservative and religious in his private life. When we speak of "liberal" in a democratic sense, it is important to realize that the liberal democracies of the Western world became liberal *first* and democratic *later.*

It may not be possible for the whole world to become liberal, let alone the West, given the antagonistic relationship between liberalism and religion. Ghazi Bin Muḥammad argues that the Fukuyaman perspective is purely a "worldly perspective" on what constitutes the perfect form of human organization.[11] Those sections of humanity that uphold religious worldviews do not regard the achievement of liberal democracy as the teleological moment in man's history. Even in Western societies, several social and political segments seem ambivalent about both liberalism and democracy, as is apparent from the Western world's recent shift to the right.[12] To expect the non-Western world to liberalize may be too naïve;[13] however, prospects for a democratic form of rule are a different question. In his *End of History*, Fukuyama argues that Islamic fundamentalism bears resemblance to European fascism, and therefore it constitutes a threat to liberal democracy:[14]

> Islam ... is very hard to reconcile with liberalism and the recognition of universal rights, particularly freedom of conscience and religion. It is perhaps not surprising that the only liberal democracy in the contemporary Muslim world is Turkey, which was the only country to have stuck with an explicit rejection of its Islamic heritage in favor of a secular society early in the twentieth century.[15]

Such misleading generalizations about Islam percolate widely in the pro-globalization policy circles where scholars such as Fukuyama are taken seriously. Although several governments of the modern Islamic world have displayed tyrannical tendencies, such governments derive no legitimacy from their past and are not representative of their people. Islam and a vast majority of Muslims recognize universal rights, particularly freedom of conscience and religion. In contrast, the Kemalist state of Turkey, which rejected its Islamic heritage in favor of a secular society, continues to impede human rights and subjugate the freedom of conscience and religion of its own citizens. Moreover, modern Turkey cannot be classified as liberal in any sense of the term, whether social, political, or economic. Socially, Turkey is a religious society, where an overwhelming majority of people are observant Muslims. Politically, its state ideology suppresses its Islamic heritage and persecutes its own people if they choose to use religious dress or symbols in the public arena. This does not qualify Turkey as a tolerant and liberal state. In the quest of economic protectionism from the liberal economics of globalization, Turkey aspires to enter the European Union and is a member of two other regional organizations, D-8 and the Economic Cooperation Organization (ECO). Thus the only example chosen by Fukuyama from the Muslim world as a model to be emulated by Muslims through the process of globalization is seriously flawed. If democracy means distributive justice, consensus, and the collective rule of people in order to safeguard their own interests (be they political, cultural, or spiritual), it remains very much the ideal of contemporary Muslim societies.

There are, however, obstacles to the attainment of democracy in this sense, which cannot be explained away merely on the basis of the incompatibility of democracy with Islam, as is done by Fukuyama. We shall take up the problem of Islam and democracy in the section that deals with the political aspects of globalization. But it is important to determine how the views of the pro-globalization forces, characterized by the thought of Francis Fukuyama, have important ramifications for the Muslim world. This mode of thought has arisen only lately because between 1945 and 1989 we lived in a bipolar world political system in which the Soviet Union was a serious challenger to the world system.[16] After 1989, however, many pro-globalization policymakers in the West began to perceive that the Muslim world presented a similar challenge to the world system. To counter the normative challenges of Islam to modernism, modernization was prescribed via globalization, a process that increased its pace in the 1990s.

II. Homogeny and Hegemony of Globalization

The agents of globalization, who are the beneficiaries of this development, are ever ready to present their ideas and the cultural forms they assume as universal, through all the technological means at their disposal. Helena Norberg-Hodge, in her article, "The Pressure to Modernize and Globalize" has cautioned that today's economic development models have deleterious effects on traditional societies and local cultures.[17] Norberg-Hodge, a Swedish philosopher and activist, has analyzed the effects of globalization on non-Western cultures by scrutinizing the negative aspects of tourism, media images, Western-style education, and the global economy's eclipse of local markets. She demonstrates how it has divided the local people, created artificial needs, broken down the bonds between the old and the young, and led to violence.[18] Henry Munson argues that in order to stop this violence, anger, and resentment against the West, the West must take the necessary steps to dilute that rage.[19] This would entail the removal of discriminatory trade barriers, cessation of the suppression of true democracy, and most of all a just and equitable solution to the Palestinian-Israeli conflict along the lines discussed by Waleed El-Ansary in his article in this volume entitled, "The Economics of Terrorism: How bin Laden is Changing the Rules of the Game."

The movement of people, ideas, and goods has been a universal process, and has always taken place historically across civilizations. Because of this, some people assume that "globalization" as we understand it in its current context has always existed. This is hardly true, because what we currently understand as "globalization" is not universal, but particular. Victor Segesvary argues that the recent form of globalization that was born out of the womb of modernity is not universal because it is a "drive toward conquering other cultural worlds by the worldview, forms of life, and styles of reasoning developed within Western civilization."[20] Segesvary views the current form of globalization in contradistinction to the "universal" type of contact between Islam and the West, citing how the European mind opened for the first time toward other civilizations as a consequence of the first Latin translation of the Qur´ān in 1543.[21] The "globalization" of the modern world, however, is particular because its foundational principles lie embedded in a constellation of historical events restricted to European history alone. Globalization is the *intensification* of the human condition we identify as modernity, which came about due to a gradual weakening of religion in Europe along with a concomitant disdain for tradition.[22] Ali Mazrui has demonstrated that globalization is a serious obstacle to such inter-civilizational understanding, because it aims at homogenizing different cultures and traditions around the world by establishing its own hegemony over them.[23]

For much of the non-European world, globalization started with colonialism.[24] Many parts of the Muslim lands were also directly or indirectly colonized, which was accompanied by a systematic destruction of the traditional institutions of earning, learning, and governing. If one looks at colonial India, one sees how the *madrasas* (religious institutions of learning), spiritual guilds of artisans, and the system of *panchayat* (grassroots democracy at the village level) were systematically broken down by British colonial policies. Later waves of globalization entailed a less direct but equally coercive relationship with the Muslim world. Even at the present time, despite formal independence, much of the third world is enmeshed in a net of financial and diplomatic dependency.[25] Many Muslims see the current form of globalization as a new process of colonialism which will increase their dependence on the West. Arnold Toynbee argues in "The World and the West" that as a consequence of

> Western civilization's assaults [on the non-West] … we saw that, on the first occasion, the West tried to induce the Far Eastern peoples to adopt the Western way of life in its entirety, including its religion as well as its technology, and that this attempt did not succeed. And then we saw that, in the second act of the play, the West offered to the same Far Eastern peoples a secularized excerpt from the Western civilization in which religion had been left out and technology, instead of religion, had been made the central feature; and we observed that this technological splinter, which had been flaked off from the religious core of our civilization towards the end of the seventeenth century, did succeed in pushing its way into the life of a Far Eastern society that had previously repulsed an attempt to introduce the Western way of life *en bloc*—technology and all, including religion.[26]

The debate over whether the conditions of modernity are good or bad for the human predicament aside, Toynbee demonstrates how ferociously modernity reached the non-West. The first contact of the non-Western traditional world with the modern industrial West was coercive in nature because it started with the subjugation of traditional societies. Since the beginning of modernity's arrival in the non-West, it has disturbed the balance of the non-West, particularly the Muslim world. Mark Levine argues, in "Muslim Responses to Globalization," that the Muslim world is ambivalent and suspicious about globalization. Globalization has created a fear of an "'invasion' of American culture to Muslim societies that will 'hollow us out from the inside and domesticate our identity.'"[27] Levine corroborates Toynbee's position, arguing:

> The consensus seems to be that globalization marks a continuation of the basic dynamic of Western domination and hegemony dating back hundreds of years, in which today America is utilizing globalization to overthrow existing political, economic, and cultural norms. In this context, globalization's cultural/ideological foundations provide it with the 'fire power' to realize its imperialist aims without causing classic revolutionary reactions to it, as did Western imperialism before it.[28]

The imperialist aspect of globalization is not only responsible for upsetting the non-West, but the West as well. Most experts of globalization agree that many of its effects on local economies, income distribution, and environment are essentially negative.[29] The welfare state is still functional in the advanced industrial societies, which has offset its effects for the time being. However, its harmful effects on the Third World are more discernible. Non-sustainability of agricultural practices, depletion of fisheries, export of hazardous materials from the West to the Third World, and detrimental impact of the applications of biotechnology are some of the negative aspects to which Martin Khor has drawn attention.[30]

In this brief essay, it is not possible to give an exhaustive account of all the adverse effects of globalization. Here we shall discuss the most obvious social, economic, and political consequences of globalization in relation to the Muslim world. In the socio-cultural domains, modernity entails a secularization of attitudes. This in turn results in the rejection of religious principles concerning the maintenance of the social order, which are then viewed as a backward form of human consciousness, impeding the march of "progress." It presupposes that literacy is an absolute good that creates enlightened masses capable of choosing the right people to run the state of affairs. In the economic arena, no matter which form of modernization is pursued, it is invariably aimed at breaking the small organizational unit, like the village, in favor of larger economic units that are directed from a remote center. Its economic practices are based on the logic of excessive production and consumption, which leads to waste and environmental degradation. In the political arena modernism requires that allegiance to spiritual or religious principles be set aside, and in their place adherence to historically European concepts such as the "nation" be created to define a political organization. To achieve this type of world, programs of modernization are directed to the underdeveloped world via epistemic authorities such as the IBRD, IMF, and multinational corporations, which have become the envoys of globalization.

The political, economic, and socio-religious aspects are discussed below to see how the globalization of modernism affects the Third World in general and the Muslim world in particular. Political aspects are most visible, economic aspects are intermediate, while those social aspects that have arisen due to the rupture of the religious core are properly causal in nature.

Political Aspects of Modernity and Globalization

Political aspects of globalization relate to the destruction of traditional forms of political organization and the fragmentation of the *umma* (Islamic community), the desacralization and amoralization of the political process, the evolution of the nation-state and its threat to the security of the Muslim world, and the problem of democracy in the Muslim world.

I. The Political Fragmentation of the Umma

In most pre-modern societies, the matrix of *God-king-country* was a way of connecting the tribe, the nation, or the empire with a higher and permanent reality in an ever-changing world, which was gradually replaced by *state-citizen* conditions. In the modern political landscape the belief in the absolute power of the Divinity was jettisoned and the idea of an absolute terrestrial power was cast upon the earthly king or parliament.[31]

Spiritual authority in empires and traditional states protected subjects against disruptive and immoral changes that may have been introduced by the king or a comparable political authority. The God-king-country milieu was embedded in the political culture of most medieval civilizations. According to certain interpretations of Islam, its justification can be found in the Muslim *sharīʿa,* or the sacred law of Islam, even though these interpretations are refuted by some in the modern Islamic world who favor a democratic form of rule. Given the sweeping social, cultural, and technological changes throughout the world, a resurrection of the old political arrangement is not possible. The Muslim world is rapidly transforming into mass societies which necessitates the creation of new forms of political arrangement that may be suitable for them. It must also be noted that most contemporary Muslim political scientists agree that the nation-state model, as represented by the *status quo,* is an inadequate form of governance for Muslim societies. Since the onset of modernity in the Muslim world, many Muslims feel that the dissolution of empires and the fragmentation of the Muslim world in various nation states—whose ideologies are often alien to Islamic consciousness—has led to a loss of spiritual unity among them.

According to Muslim teachings, unity resides in its perfection in the Divine, but its realization remains an ideal for Muslims in all walks of life. Whether realizable or not, the spirit of economic and political accord among the *umma* still exists in the hearts and minds of many Muslims.[32] Seyyed Hossein Nasr, in his "Islamic Unity: The Ideal and Obstacles in the Way of its Realization," has argued that Western colonialism is often seen by Muslims as the biggest obstacle to the realization of such unity because its policy prescriptions are often antagonistic to the *sharīʿa* and to the institutions inspired by it.[33] This has foiled the spirit of mutual cooperation among Muslims, insuring that most geographically contiguous Islamic lands of not able to integrate. This political accord for which traditional Muslims yearn is not possible so long as the nation-state remains strongly entrenched in the Muslim world, for the foundations of its legitimacy remain aspiritual and anti-religious, deriving support from human ideologies rather than transcendent realities.

II. The Desacralization of the Political Process

Muslims fear the desacralization of their way of life. In Europe this process occurred with society first and then the polity, but the Muslim world is threatened by it in reverse. The polity is more easily corruptible than the society, because the *sharīʿa* places prohibitions against the endorsement of desacralized behavior that is not cognizant of a higher reality. Practicing Muslims remain indisposed to the process of desacralized politics as evident from the fate of Christianity. As Emil Brunner laments: "Christianity destroyed ancient religion and mythology; then modern idealistic humanism grew out of the Christian tradition; but humanism following its rational tendency finally detached itself from its Christian foundation."[34] It is that detachment from the root which resulted in the emergence of the modern world from which Christian morality itself now suffers.

The desacralized view of political power is the result of a modern, secular view of the world, which is radically different from the traditional and sacred one, wherein all rule derives from the Supreme Ruler.[35] The idea of popular sovereignty and democratic representation intensifies this fragmentation because the principle of legitimation derives from man and not from God.[36] Thomas Molnar has argued that even though the modern political systems have presumably shed the burden of religion as "superstition," they have also undertaken a radical demythologization whose burden on their political systems is greater than that of the discarded sacred.[37]

III. The Nation-State and its Threat to Peace

The loss of the sacred in the realm of society and politics has led directly to a cycle of violence. Champions of modernism pose it as a pacifist and civilized ideology, which they juxtapose with traditional civilizations, seen as cruel and uncivilized. A cursory glance at the history of industrialism will reveal its relation to organized violence and gradual proclivity toward war among modern polities. War in conjunction with "economic progress" is also increasing rapidly in both frequency and destructive power. The birth of modern science and its technological application by modern industry and the modern polity in waging violence is unprecedented in history. The history of the modern nation-state is replete with cases where a state wages a war either for profit or to stimulate its industry. War has thus become a profitable industry and an instrument for further economic gains at the expense of human life and dignity. The militarized and industrialized nation-state has a special mission to accomplish and establish its particular economic system as well as its particular form of government through a coercive armed establishment.[38] It is the same state that has contributed to the decline of the human mind by devoting all its energy to empowering itself internally and externally.[39]

Despite the fact that the modern nation-state vies to offset such ills by talking of welfare, its pursuit of internal and external "security" has led to a situation where the attainment of enlightened life has rapidly faded. The concept of "security" in such a milieu has become absolute rather than remaining in its properly relative domain. Modern nations, particularly the industrial Western ones, have come a long and mistaken way in defining their security. The mainstream statesmen have ended up with a conception of security that has metamorphosed from military or external security of the state alone, to a blurred distinction of external and internal security of the state, precisely because globalization has enabled them to do so. However, internal security, which was heretofore the job of internal security agencies, police, civic patrols, and ministries of home affairs, is now being done by agencies whose level of militarization is no different than those of army regulars. The pretext of this militarization is that the "enemy" is now more sophisticated than the police. Ironically it is also legal to sell guns to these "enemies" for the sake of running the economy! It is equally ironic that the states that are militarily securest of all, talk of the erosion of security. It is beyond the understanding of such statesmen that there is no such thing as absolute security in this world. Life presents insecurity and adversity to all humanity, which is an inescapable "social fact" in the Durkheimian sense. Absolute security would mean the evasion of death and acquisition of eternal happiness, which is not a possibility for earthly humans. The statesmen of the contemporary world then proceed on yet another path of confusion to equate security with welfare. The latter is not approached from a relative perspective either, but with a certain imaginary and absolute standard. This standard of welfare informs the citizens and routinizes a culture of welfarism domestically that is totally blind to the needs of poorer societies, which more or less continue to provide for the welfare of these few. Justification for war in industrial societies thus comes around to defending such a culture and its material comfort. It is a war that is non-defensive and aims to destroy other cultures and traditional societies for the sake of its worldly luxuries.[40]

To situate this process historically, John Nef's periodization of Western civilization since the Renaissance is quite instructive. In understanding the incipient link between industrialism and war in his book *Western Civilization Since the Renaissance: Peace, War, Industry, and the Arts*, Nef locates the connection between the new type of warfare at the birth of Industrialism between 1494–1640. This degenerative process continued for another century in its second phase between 1640–1740, and finally entered its most destructive and bloody phase, in which industrialism is related to total war, between 1740 and the present.[41] According to Nef's periodization we now live in the last phase of industrialism in which the Industrial Revolution has enabled the Enlightenment's dark side to prevail.[42] This triumph is primarily responsible for the gradual transformation of a subject of an empire into a citizen soldier whose worldview is evolutionist and who has a mechanical conception of nature. It is the triumph of scientific materialism that has contributed to the destructive power of arms, the growth in the destructive powers of society, the gradual weakening of moral and aesthetic values, a decline of intellectuality, and a cult of violence leading eventually to a state of total war.[43]

Nef was not alone in pointing out that modern scientific progress and war have mutually reinforced each other. In the same vein, Martin Lings has pointed out how deviance from the middle path has led to the formation of opposite and opposing ideological extremes, which have given rise to more extremism. Lings' description of the total extremes leading to a self-destructive end corroborates Nef's views.[44] The future of industrialism in Nef's thought depends less on the success of industrialism inside the states and more upon the eventual integration of industrialism in the global arena with its concomitant control of the world's resources.[45] For the world industry and economy to integrate, several states must join hands, confer legitimacy through the auspices of their own consensus-making bodies (such as the UN and WTO), and declare all those who rise to protect what is legitimately theirs a security threat. War in traditional civilizations was a separate problem resulting from a political, economic, or religious clash, and which had only to come to an end for a return to normalcy. In the modern world, however, war is a total problem because it may stimulate economic growth and lead to more industrialism, while the latter may lead to more of the former. Nef has argued that this vicious circle is a result of national concerns that are immediate and particular, and not concerns that are far-reaching and universal.[46] The same modern tendency is an unnatural move "toward the special, toward the prosaic, toward the measurable and matter of-fact, toward material quantity, toward fear, hatred, and division."[47]

Although much of the Western world is moving toward overcoming the nineteenth-century fragmentation of nation states (as in the case of the European Union), most of its influential security pundits remain opposed to such movements of integration within the Muslim world. The theorists of integration in the European world uphold that certain conditions are necessary for any integration to occur.[48] Most of such conditions stipulated by them are present in the geographically and historically contiguous regions of Muslims, yet there is no such integration. Those who champion such logical geographical arrangement are de-legitimized and declared political adversaries, while arch-nationalist/arch-secularist dictators, such as Saddam Hussein and the Shah of Iran, who try to rewrite the history and geography of their own civilizations, have been supported by many Western states. The Western critics of Muslim regimes have often stated that tensions within the Muslim world are indigenous in nature, and that modernization or westernization would lead to less friction. James Piscatori, in his *Islam in the World of Nation States*, argues that there is no essential contention between Shīʿite and Sunnī Muslims or between Arabs and non-Arab Muslims and that most Muslims agree that Islam's decline is chiefly due to the adoption of Western ideas and culture. This, according to Piscatori, necessitates a political restructuring of their world order.[49] The political disorganization and dictatorship in the Muslim world is to a significant extent attributable to the existence of nation states. Since the nation-state is an outgrowth of secular European ideologies it has no referent in Muslim history. The imposition of nation states upon the Islamic world thus contributes to the cultural disorientation, social destructuring, and negative impact of Western influence on the Muslim world.[50]

Although the political life that the colonial West imposed upon the Muslim world started during the early modern period, its current form represents the politics introduced during half a century of power rivalry between the United States and the Soviet Union. During the early modern period, Europeans divided Muslim lands according to their own interests and thus stifled an organic and true global set of relations that had existed among and outside Muslim lands. The nation-state model, which even today remains alien to the Islamic political consciousness, locked the Muslim lands into economic and political units too small to be of any significance on a systemic level. More somber was the choice of regimes that was offered via reigning ideologies of modernism: Muslims were pressured either to accept the irreligious communist system, or embrace the "free world" on the other side of the Iron Curtain. The former system denied the existence of God outright, while the latter still belonged to the formerly Christian but now fully secular world. In the post-independence history of Muslim states, militarily powerful Western states have constantly dictated the type of regime they would like to see in many parts of the Muslim world. The latest American involvement in South Asia demonstrates this fact. Leaders such as the Egyptian and Pakistani presidents, Hosni Mubarak and Pervez Musharraf, are time and again reminded that their countries must become secular states like Turkey, rather than states with strong Islamic identities.[51] Such directives are more than mere suggestions. They carry with them a credible military threat that forces Muslim societies to bring about changes that are totally alien to their nature, and thus to accept cultural alienation and political humiliation. As yet, Muslims have neither had the option to select a form of political organization (nation-state, city states, confederation etc.), nor have they had the option to select what type of government they want (democracy, theocracy, monarchy etc.).

IV. The Problem of Democracy and the Islamic World

Martin Ling's exposition of the Platonic conception of types of rule is instructive here. According to Lings, aristocracy, i.e. rule by the best, was ideal for Plato (this would correspond in traditional Hindu terms to the rule of the *brahmin*, the priestly caste), followed by timocracy (or rule by the *kshatriya*, the warriors), then plutocracy (or rule by the *vaishya*, the merchants) and finally democracy (or rule by the *shudra*, the plebian).[52]

Beyond democracy lie tyranny and the breakup of political order after which society needs principled re-structuring once again. This traditional typology of regimes is distinctively different from the modern conception and its rules of legitimation. It has happened in the pre-modern era that types of rule have fallen from the ideal *brahamanic* (philosopher-kings), to *kshatriyic* (warrior-kings), to *vaishya* (the merchant rulers), but the *brahmanic* principles were nevertheless still revered. In contrast, the modern world is distinct in celebrating a form of rule which, according to Plato, constitutes a decidedly lower form. It is also considered the only legitimate form of rule, even though "true democracy" as it is commonly understood may not exist in a real sense in the modern Western world.

One of the seminal works on the current state of democracy in the West is Claes Ryn's *The New Jacobinism: Can Democracy Survive?* He argues that democracy in the Western states is on the decline due to the recession of moral and spiritual values that was once of central importance for the West. Ryn argues that the changes brought about by modernity have led to grave moral decline:

> the gradual disappearance from Western society of the type of moral self-control and discrimination on which constitutional democracy depends has produced increasingly blatant partisanship and general socio-political fragmentation.[53]

The general lack of the old system of ethics has led to a loss of critical detachment that was responsible for the democratic spirit.[54] Self-interest and re-election takes precedence over the risk of political unpopularity, which can be a consequence of stating uncomfortable truths. Ryn asserts that "successful politicians tend to be individuals lacking in deeper insight and conviction. The need to appeal to the great mass of people on virtually all issues pushes political discussion to ever lower levels of sloganeering and pandering."[55] This turns elections into "embarrassing displays of simplistic demagoguery in which advertising and media consultants play central roles."[56] Further, if one judges election candidates based on appeals they make to the voters, "the public is assumed to have a simplistic, almost infantile view of the world."[57] Another reason why democratic justice is receding from the Western world is because of the way issues are framed. Issues of immediate relevance are pushed aside in favor of distant political issues that often have little relevance in voters' day-to-day lives. According to Plato, the general loss of morality in a democratic form of government can bring a society to the brink of tyranny.[58] Ryn has identified how the loss of traditional Christian values has led to the loss of democracy. Culture plays a crucial role in this development. He argues that "entertainment forms an increasingly prominent part of Western culture and plays a central role in breaking down lingering traditional tastes and inhibitions."[59]

Ryn ascribes the fragmentation of today's democracies to relativism, nihilism, and a Fukuyaman type of liberal pluralism.[60] The reason democratic governance is leading to social fragmentation is because of the "self-assertion of groups and individuals that recognize no obligation beyond their partisan causes and are therefore approaching each other as belligerents."[61] According to him, *moral universality* does not abolish *particularity*, but it is important for the public of a democratic state to transcend their merely private interests and find common ground with the rest of society.[62] Since globalization is accelerating the effects of modernity, today's democracies are more likely to precipitate into anarchies precisely because of a gradual loss of moral principles. With the ethical fetters gone and technological means enhanced, the state becomes more controlling and intrusive, thereby eroding its citizen's rights. Because of this, some of the prominent features of today's industrialized Western societies are conformity and thought-control, which is dispensed through government propaganda, mass media, education, and forms of entertainment.[63] As Ryn observes, "De Tocqueville comes close to Plato in capturing this feature of modern democracy in his warnings about 'soft' democratic despotism. Unlike older, non-democratic despotism, de Toqueville writes, the new despotism 'would degrade without tormenting them'."[64]

In the light of the contemporary experience of Western states with democracy and their selective appeal to disenfranchised masses of the global political economy, the global democratization of the world order has its problems. As the famous international relations theoretician E. H. Carr argues, any sound political thought is based upon elements that are not only real but also Utopian, which sheds light on the problem of the globalization of democracy.[65] Even though the realization of democracy is *possible* in the Muslim world, this democracy is of a different type. Seyyed Hossein Nasr, in his *Ideals and Realities of Islam*, conceptualizes this possibility in the Muslim world as a "democracy of married monks, that is, a society in which equality exists in the religious sense in that all men are priests and stand equally before God as vice-gerents on earth."[66] Experimentation with the concept of "Islamic democracy," however, has been a rough ride for Muslims. The demand for democracy is evident throughout much of the Muslim world, but commitment to Westernization is no guarantee of democracy.[67] In their Book *Islam and Democracy*, John L. Esposito and John O. Voll present the following argument:

> The policy failures evident in American and European responses toward the subversion of the electoral process and indiscriminate repression of the FIS (Islamic Salvation Front) in Algeria and of the Renaissance party in Tunisia, like their impotence in the face of the genocide of Muslims in Bosnia or seeming indifference to the plight of Muslims in Chechnya and Kashmir, discredit in the

> eyes of Islamists and many other Muslims, the democratic commitment of the West. They reinforce the perception and charge that the U.S. and European governments are guilty of employing a "double standard," a democratic one for the West and selected allies and another for the Middle East and Islamist movements. Respect and support of the democratic process and human rights must be seen as truly universal and consistent.[68]

As this indicates, the cognitive elite in the West has several sets of double standards that especially ridicule the Muslim world. It champions democracy overseas, yet this ruling elite is ambivalent about democracy as good government for themselves in the long run. Within the Western world, due to changing demographics, it is now realized that if democracy truly reigned, the predominantly Caucasian establishment and the vanguards of the secular political system might lose power to those who do not share their values. In the United States, for example, non-whites may outnumber the white ruling elite in another generation. If the country is truly democratic, will heroes of the country still be white slave owners, like Washington and Jefferson, or will they be replaced by non-white national heroes such as Martin Luther King Jr. or Malcolm X? Europe has similar concerns. There are right-wing movements in such nations that want to revise the existing "liberal" political arrangement. Between 1999 and 2002, governments of Austria, Italy, Denmark, Norway, Portugal, the Netherlands, France, and Germany have all experienced a political and ideological shift to the right, which has also threatened European Union elections and its enlargement prospects.[69]

The connection between money and politics, which the Lobbying Disclosure Act of 1995 has sought to remedy, has plagued even the democratic system of the United States. It is a well-known feature of contemporary democratic politics that success in elections is more or less tied to the financial resources of political parties and their candidates. As Ryn has demonstrated, this is a problem even in institutionally more advanced countries whose democratic institutions provide some checks and balances against money's impact on electoral success. In the case of developing states with weak institutions of democratic representation, or with none at all, it is even easier to influence the electoral outcome with money. Desired changes can be made in small countries' political systems by strengthening one's favorite candidate's campaign through the infusion of money from the outside. Therefore, those states whose political process becomes a democratic one without a strong domestic system of checks and balances can easily be swayed from the outside, at the cost of national sovereignty.

When prescribing democracy overseas, a power like the United States does so only selectively and whenever it suits its own interests. First, many states and agencies in the modern Western world cherish and give legitimation to the democratic form of rule over other types of rule. Secondly, the same groups are becoming domestically ambivalent about democracy for themselves, given the sweeping demographic changes. Thirdly, these groups champion alien political forms to the Third World through globalization of political reforms; and finally, they deny them this type of rule at the same time, as is evident from the Algerian case.[70] This is just a glimpse of the double standards of Western policymaking groups when it comes to suggesting "reform" to the Muslim world. Anti-Western resentment in the minds of many Muslims is precisely due to such Western foreign policies.

Lings' interpretation of the Platonic ideal government is also a traditional Islamic critique of the modern mindset when it comes to the question of ideal government. According to him, since all that is brought into existence is doomed to decay, even the best will eventually deteriorate, but they will at least realize this condition of the fall. Even if the form of rule degenerates from plutocracy to anarchy, it is important that it be replaced by traditional principles or a principled autocracy for the sake of a residual link with an independent but accountable spiritual authority.[71] "The form of government in question," he states, "is clearly less principled than the highest form of government, it nonetheless belongs to the 'old order of things' and is definitely on the side of tradition, though it is liable to end by bringing tradition into disrepute."[72] In the eyes of many Muslims, a system of democracy without spiritual ethics seems unacceptable, because it is not aware of the fall—it even celebrates the conditions of the fall.

According to Lings, at a historical juncture like this, if a principled autocracy does not come to the rescue of a society, it will be at risk of falling into unprincipled demagogy. Democratic rule may, therefore, signify the beginning of the decline of a principled rule. But it is still better than anarchy, which is the lack of rule. Lings argues:

> The French Revolution in this sense was democratic in its original intention—witness the slogan *Liberté, Égalité, Fraternité*.... but in fact it was too precipitous to stop at democracy, so that the change from principled autocracy to unprincipled demagogy was almost direct [only to be] superseded by Napoleon's relatively principled autocracy.... It is not, however, a lower form of government which inaugurates rejection of principles. To pave the way for unprincipled dictatorship, the principles have first of all to be rejected by democracy in the name of liberty.[73]

Since degeneration takes place in all that is created, it is inevitable that any system of human governance, whether modern or traditional, will face that process. However, the process of renewal also exists within the spiritual center of mankind, which arrests the degenerative process for some time to come, thus preserving momentarily man's primordial heritage. Lings asserts that most religious communities, especially the traditional Islamic ones, see the modern world as an "organized system of subversion and degeneration" that has no inborn capacity for renewal because it is bereft of its transcendental core.[74] Along the same lines, Ryn states that "the evidence of decline in today's Western democracies could be balanced against more encouraging signs, but these cannot remove the impression that a civilization is disintegrating, and not just at the periphery—but at its moral core."[75] A form of rule that accommodates spiritual principles is a strong possibility in the Muslim world where religious ideals are still cherished. This, according to the Islamic spiritual perspective, can halt the degenerative process for some time to come. However, due to political weakness, the Muslim world at this point is not strong enough to choose this type of rule. This is compounded by Western influence on most political and economic matters in the Muslim world. Lings states that the impact of the West on the Islamic world is "to accelerate greatly a process of degeneration which was already taking place, and to give them as it were, a sideway push to ensure that they went downhill by a steeper and somewhat different course from the one they were following."[76] The reason that a vast majority of Muslims in the Muslim world are still governable by spiritual principles is because the process of desacralization of power has been only partial and unsuccessful.

Finally, there is an interesting question that is seldom asked among the scholars and practitioners of politics: why is there so much political theory in the history of the modern West and not in other civilizations such as Islam? Apparently, the modernist's answer is usually linear and simplistic: political theory could not *develop* in other places as much as it did in the West. If this be true, has all that development led us any closer to an ideal form of government? Perhaps traditional civilizations, including Islamic civilization, do not have as much political theory because they did not need it as much. If abuse of power and violation of citizen rights become a norm as a result of a general loss of ethics, one cannot help but think more and more of how to achieve a suitable form of government that is free of power abuse. This has been the *raison d' être* of political theory. The reason it mushroomed so much in secular Europe and not in other civilizations is precisely the loss of religious ethics in the West, which led to the decline of morality in the public square. Since the question of who has the ultimate power was resolved in principle in the traditional world, there was no need for superfluous guesses as to who did, and who should, wield power. If power was abused, it was difficult for the king to provide a legitimate cover for it because society, as well as the body politic, knew that he was in violation, even though he still continued to hold the reigns of power. The choice between a "secular but free world" or a "secular but communist" world could never become a basis from which suitable political theory could be expounded in a religious world such as the Islamic one.

Economic Aspects of Modernity and Globalization

Modernism has transformed the way we look at economy. The conception of modern economics has become divorced from ethics due to its faulty philosophical assumptions. Further, modern economics has changed because of the transformation in the notion of modern systems of law; the replacement of the *sharīʿa* based laws in favor of secular laws has led to a state of economic disequilibrium in the Muslim world. This disequilibrium is manifesting itself in a demand for excessive economic growth and development, which has an inverse relationship with a livable environment.

I. The Problem of Modern Economics

In the world of mass media and journalism, globalization is employed as a euphemistic term to hide those aspects that have affected our life adversely in the economic arena. In the "nomenclature" of globalization, "economic efficiency" means replacing workers with machines; the notion of "competitiveness" implies lowering of wages in the industrial states to match low wage foreign competitors; and "flattening the corporate structure" is another name for eliminating middle managers.[77] The mainstream media does little to address the malefic aspects of globalization, which threaten the economic well-being of society. Instead economic globalization is looked upon favorably, as if it will bring jobs and create more prosperity. When its negative aspects are acknowledged, this is often tempered with portrayals of anti-globalizationists as extremists and ne'er-do-wells. Jerry Mander and Edward Goldsmith have made a case against the global economy by arguing that people in the advanced industrial societies are trained to believe that our economic system operates on a "rational basis," and that the people who are in charge have benevolent motives.[78] Mander ascribes a host of problems to pro-globalization economic policies. He argues that the problems of

> overcrowded cities, unusual new weather patterns, the growth of global poverty, the lowering of wages while the stock prices soar, the elimination of local social services, the destruction of wilderness, even the disappearance of songbirds—are the products of same global policies. They are all but one piece, a fabric of connections that are ecological, social, and political in nature. They are reactions to the world's economic-political restructuring in the name of accelerated global development. This restructuring has been designed by economists and corporations and encouraged by subservient governments.[79]

The root of many of these problematic policies lies in the modern conception of economics. Modern economics is based upon the philosophy of scarcity of resources.[80] It presents a situation in which the needs and wants of an individual or a group exceed the resources available to satisfy them.[81]

Such a definition does not suppose a fundamental analytical difference between needs and wants. Everything is supposedly scarce and difficult to get, not because humanity's needs have exceeded the resources, but due to our unlimited wants and expectations. Items of daily need, services, and even human relations, have become *commodified* in a consumerist world. A value is put on them that is often understood in quantitative terms alone, and corresponds to either time or money, and eventually only money, because time, too, is reduced to potential money. There often comes a time when wage workers of the industrial society must decide whether it would be "profitable" to see their loved ones because it will "cost," at least in terms of time, if not money.

The quantification of time and its perceived scarcity has led to a general deterioration of human relations. This consciousness of scarcity is new, not comparable to the economic parsimony of traditional civilizations. Ibn Khaldūn, the fourteenth century Muslim philosopher, notes in his *Muqaddimah* how nature has unevenly distributed resources to humanity. Some live in abundance, some in scarcity. However, he argues that abundance is not in and of itself good; those who live in conditions of scarcity not only live longer but they are spiritually better off than those who live in abundance and luxury.[82] Compared to the traditional world, the modern world, which has actually led to more quantitative production than ever before, has more of everything. It is ironic that despite the fact that we have more of everything, we perceive that we live in conditions of scarcity. It is also interesting to note that the perceived scarcity is more in the rich industrial countries than in rural agrarian ones. It is equally ironic to note the increase in contemporary people's patterns of consumption, particularly food. The people in advanced industrial societies consume much more, proportionately, than the other societies. This is paradoxical, because if things are truly scarce, we should consume parsimoniously, but evidence indicates otherwise. In this sense the modern world is the exact opposite of the Khaldunian world. Ibn Khaldūn argues that even if resources are plenty, one must consume parsimoniously for reasons that are spiritual and physiological.[83] In the modern world, however, we perceive that things are scarce but we consume more and more! The comparative scarcity of resources in the Third World, on the other hand, has recently turned into destitution. Martin Khor has argued that globalization has led to economic colonialism, which is the cause of this destitution. As he writes: "... the countries whose economies have fallen under the control of foreign corporations, [their] resources are raided and shipped north to the wealthiest industrial nations."[84] As a consequence of this, argues Irfan Ul Haq, "mass poverty [that] has developed in the recent years is also being witnessed today, [which] is by and large a modern phenomenon and [is] persisting in spite of the availability of tremendous resources."[85]

The Islamic understanding of economics, in contrast to the prevalent secularist paradigm of economics, is not based upon "scarcity" but "plenty." According to this logic, if things have become too dear for some individuals despite their best efforts and intentions, then there must be a profound *disequilibrium* in the economy. This disequilibrium is most likely to be the result of a deviation from spiritual principles of justice that involves someone else consuming more than their fair share. Islam is a rival to the modern world system because of the opposition of its economic philosophy to that of the prevalent paradigms of economics. Steve Keen has shown that arguments by the neo-classical economists on the subject of market equilibrium rest on shaky ground because of their erroneous assumptions.[86] The neo-classical theory of economics *excludes* the spiritual values that constitute a necessary starting point of equilibrium analysis.[87] From an Islamic point of view, Keen's critique of neo-classical economics is consistent with the metaphysical assertion that the only way to achieve equilibrium in any domain on any level of reality is through conformity to the Truth. In the case of Islamic economics therefore, it means a *sharīʿa*-compliant economy.

Islamic economic values challenge the lack of economic values in the modern world. An economic system whose practices are devoid of ethics will continue to clash with the ideals that Muslims hold important. Economic aspects of modernity and globalization related to the modern world are still linked to the Muslim world in a colonial pattern. In this pattern, now called post-colonialism or neo-colonialism, the Muslim world is not subjugated directly through military means as it was during the nineteenth century. However, the Muslim world, like much of the underdeveloped world, is ruled indirectly but constantly subjugated economically and often militarily by the neo-colonial powers. Muslims gained relative independence from the West after World War II, but the nationalist ideologies that rallied the Muslim nations against colonialism also divided Muslim lands into economic units too weak to bring about welfare and security in their new regional environments. This lack of welfare is often ascribed to traditionalism and backwardness rather than modernity.[88] As Norberg-Hodge argues:

> It is easy to understand why people lay the blame at the feet of tradition rather than modernity. Certainly, ethnic friction is a phenomenon that predates colonialism, modernization, and globalization. But after nearly two decades of firsthand experience on the Indian subcontinent, I am convinced that "development" not only exacerbates tensions but actually creates them. As I have pointed out, development causes *artificial scarcity*, which inevitably leads to greater competition.[89]

During European colonialism, many Muslim institutions that were part and parcel of Islamic civilization were destroyed. Economic institutions such as the guilds, had a spiritual master who was *au fait* with things at the work place, such as conscience, ethics, and morality, which were jettisoned to accommodate a supposedly "free" market environment.[90] The free market is not really "free" from structural constraints imposed by governments and regional unions, and it no longer has a link with the transcendental system of ethics. The free market is theoretically silent on normative and political issues, but in reality, the free market is quite political. As James Caporaso and David Levine have noted, it is difficult to isolate the political aspect of economies, because to study them in isolation from politics can lead to economic determinism,[91] which is a poor way of understanding the free market. Similarly, Mander argues that the free market is only free "about the freedom it provides [to the] corporate players to deprive everyone of their freedoms, including the freedom hitherto enjoyed by democratic nations to protect their domestic economies, their communities, their culture, and their natural environment."[92] Claes Ryn's analysis of the free market and ethics is central to understanding the evolution of the free market. He points out how concepts such as the "free market," "capitalism," and "democracy" have multiple and often contradictory meanings. The evolution of the "free market" is indeed interesting according to Ryn's account:

> It should not be forgotten that among the impulses behind the French Revolution was a desire among the middle classes to [get] rid of various old restrictions on commerce. In today's Western society, the wish for economic freedom has been taken to an extreme by various radical "libertarians." It should be carefully noted that there is a sense in which a free market would become really free only when movement of goods and services is wholly unrestricted, unfettered not only by "external," legal, or institutional checks but by the inhibitions and tastes of civilized persons. A Rousseauistic, Jacobin desire to destroy traditional ethical and cultural restraints and socio-political structures can thus be said to aid in the creation of a truly free market.[93]

The entities that sponsor this type of "free market ethics" are not concerned with how income is generated but remain interested in how it is distributed:

> [The U.S.] economy is marked by a very uneven distribution of wealth and income .... It is estimated that 28% of the total net wealth is held by the richest 2% of families in the U.S. The top 10% holds 57% of the net wealth. If homes and other real estate are excluded, the concentration of ownership of financial wealth is even more glaring. In 1983, 54% of the total net financial assets were held by 2% of all families, those whose annual income is over $125,000. Eighty-six percent of these assets were held by the top 10% of all families.[94]

As implied by such statistics, the proponents of globalization and free trade control the global political economy by allowing its beneficiaries to acquire more and more, while the poor become poorer.

II. Law and Economics

The medieval Christian Church once had an active say in the economic affairs of Christians. The observations of theologians such as Thomas Aquinas held sway in matters related to work, work ethic, profit, usury, alms, and exploitation on both a micro and macro level. Now the Church and theologians play no central role in the public economic life of the West. The modern economy in this sense is free of ethical fetters of a transcendental nature when it comes to engaging in any type of commercial activity. As Ryn observes, this type of economy only recognizes external constraints, such as law, until a way is found to circumvent even these.[95]

Law is fundamental to understanding how the modern economic system and the traditional Islamic economic system are incompatible. Islam accommodates the idea of positive laws, or man-made laws to run a country, as long as these do not breach the sacred law.[96] Generally, law is understood in Islam as Divine *Nomos*, i.e., law by an Authority that is above all creation. However, in Islam most man-made laws can be judged from the point of view of Supreme law, the word of God, which according to Muslim belief has not changed and never will change. In the modern West, however, some aspects of religious law remain, but they have become disconnected from their transcendental source. In contemporary legal theory, the concept of law has shifted towards interpreting law as a *command* backed up by a set of relevant sanctions mandated by the coercive apparatus of the state. The legitimacy of such laws do not reside in their moral content but in their procedural aspects and enforceability by the state. This leaves no room for a standard in relation to which these laws can be judged. When it comes to the laws of property, property rights, transmission of property etc., Anglo-Saxon law is at loggerheads with the religious systems of law. Such a form of law is unacceptable to many Muslims both because it is completely divorced from immutable principles and because of the overformalization and secularization of the legal process in the West.

To know the type of law that is responsible for the legitimacy of any system is crucial. The modern system has devolved from a religious to a secular understanding of law. If the secular political system runs into crisis, the economic system which receives legitimacy from this law will also encounter a legitimation crisis. To establish universal legitimacy the proponents of modern economics must therefore claim that there are universal principles deriving from the ineluctable laws of nature upon which economics is based. This is a great paradox. First they deny transcendent and universal principles in order to clear the ground for secular-humanist systems. Then they re-establish some claim to universality in order to establish the legitimacy of the systems they wish to impose. This attempt to replace vertical principles deriving from revelation with horizontal universals, which in fact derive from the whims of human beings is the hallmark of secularism. Islam and other religious traditions do not deny natural laws, but they are always seen as being secondary in relation to their divine source.

It is not our intention to compare the ideals of Islam with the realities of the modern world, but with ideals as realized in Muslim history. Their continued practice even today in many parts of the Muslim world provides substantial evidence that for Muslims business was closely tied to Islamic ethics. This can be said not only of Islamic civilization but of other traditional civilizations which followed a transcendental system of ethics. In the Muslim world, occupational associations had a religious character that communicated the skills of a trade by means of formal apprenticeship that involved character as much as it involved skill. These bodies were either fraternal or corporate, but their occupational activities could not violate the law of *sharīʿa* that is held sacred by all Muslims. Occupations such as selling alcohol or running industries of fornication (such as pornography and prostitution), which are permissible in many parts of the modern world, cannot be a legitimate option for Muslims, even though they remain lucrative businesses.

III. The Limits of Economic Growth

Since the interpellation of the ideology of modern economism[97] takes place as a social process through the coercive arm of globalization, it gives people a certain identity that is distinct from their primordial identity because it is reductionist. What one does for work may impact one's consciousness. But escaping or resisting this ideological interpellation becomes difficult for the average person dwelling in the modern condition.

The ideological economism of the modern world can only be globalized through coercion because there is no room for mutual accommodation between it and Islamic economics. Since political independence is not viable without economic independence, suggestions of economic independence through more modernization are always made to the Muslim world. This process does not lead to more independence, but more dependence because of surmounting foreign debt, stringent conditions on loans, lack of an industrial base and lack of Import Substitution and Industrialization policies.[98] Economic modernization brings about technological development and a culture of technicalism promoted by globalization. However, it is important to realize that technology in and of itself is *not* neutral. Technology does not simply give rise to the conditions of modernity and its globalist ideology; it is simultaneously the servant and the master of hegemonic power interests, and therefore in and of itself disruptive and hegemonic.[99] Even during the incipient stages of technological production, its physical organization necessitates disruption in the traditional social setup, identity, and socio-economic ethos. In testing the waters of new technological developments, they find themselves engulfed in the sea of modernity. Norberg-Hodge has emphasized that this technological gap is much wider between the industrial West and the global South, which has a severe psychological impact on the latter.[100] But to attempt to reduce this gap has equally devastating long-term consequences.

Since globalization is not universal in its spirit or form, it can never give humanity what it needs. *That which is universal can only be universal after transcending the particular.* The origin of the capitalist economic system, which is the precursor of economic modernity, is embedded in certain particular historical circumstances, the exact replication of which is neither possible nor desirable for other societies. The East Asian world has managed to produce economic modernity in terms of production and consumption, but it too remains an experiment in process which is already proving costly in environmental terms. The predicament for prospective development for the undeveloped world is truly dismal. Edward Goldsmith has summed up the effect of global trade on the environment:

> Expanded economic growth and global development cannot be achieved without an immense overuse of resources, a fierce assault on remaining species of flora and fauna, the creation of toxic wastelands (and seas), and the degradation of the planet's natural ability to function in a healthy way. The idea, promoted in the corporate circles, that first we must make countries wealthy through development and then take care of the environment is high cynicism, since development does not produce wealth, save for a few people; the wealth that is produced is rarely spent on environmental programs; and anyway, by the time the theoretical wealth is generated, life will be unlivable.[101]

Take the example of China: during the initial stages of its industrialization process it was somewhat harmonious and livable. People bicycled to work and could breathe clean air, even in the larger cities. Today, as China has managed to industrialize to the extent of becoming a world economic power, it is becoming increasingly unlivable. Bicycles have rapidly disappeared from the streets of Beijing, thanks to the newly found wealth, and the automobiles have increased the noise and air pollution. Environmental degradation is the highest in the Western world, followed only by the East Asian Giants, while the non-industrial world (which includes most of the Muslim world and parts of Africa) is arguably least dangerous to the environment.[102] If the Muslim world were to follow the same path of modernization as the East Asians did, this planet would race toward destruction much faster. Thus, from an environmental perspective, the sensible thing to do would be the exact opposite of modernization. As Segesvary argues:

> … globalization and the coexistence of different civilizations is antithetical. Our future will be determined by this antithesis because globalization represents

> nothing but the worldwide domination of certain ways of life and certain ways of Western civilization ... worldwide conquest of consumerism, of the perpetual quest for always more of everything, and a certain lifestyle prioritizing material goods at the expense of spirituality and intellectual enrichment.[103]

To sum up: in the economic arena, globalization is a process that offers a "value free" and non-political system of economics but which does not accommodate transcendent laws, in contrast to Muslim economic ideals and practices which are grounded in religion. To ask Muslims to live by Western economic standards is not simply to ask them to adopt a different economic system; it is to ask them to adopt a different value system, one which contradicts several fundamental teachings of Islam.

Social Aspects of Modernity and Globalization

Segesvary argues that globalization is the ideological vehicle for a secular conception of the world, with a disappearance of genuine morality, an atomized conception of human relations, social dissent, an idolization of democracy, and destructive carelessness towards the environment.[104] He has identified some of the aspects that extend the social logic of the modern world to the rest of the non-Western world, which, he argues, "are nothing but extensions of principal features of late modern Western civilization to the whole world."[105] In this section we discuss some of the most obvious aspects of globalization. Among many such aspects of globalization, we isolate those that have an almost subliminal effect due to their omnipresence in the modern mass media: the gospel of equality (among people and between sexes); the substitution of the secular for the religious worldview; the myth of evolutionism, leading to an "ever-evolving" story of human origin; and the myth of progress whose utopian elements continue to shape the modern worldview.

I. The Modern Dream of Equality

The type of social change that is sought in the Muslim world by the pro-globalization governmental and non-governmental agencies frequently tends to be in conflict with the norms and ethics of Islam. Even if Islam does not negate those ideas or policy proposals made by the Western agencies, the latter do little to corroborate those principles from within the Islamic tradition, thereby alienating Muslim societies and also hurting their own cause. Take, for example, the overarching fixation of the West with "gender equality" in the Muslim world while ignoring the egregious violence against women in their own society. Agencies like the United Nations Development Program (UNDP), for instance, have done little to commission an inquiry into how Islam promises justice and fairness for women, but works with an *a priori* assumption that women belonging to religious communities are treated worse than women in secular societies. Since their bureaucratic version of reality is contingent upon statistics, and upon the inclusion of a certain number of females in the work force, they simply assume that the liberation of women has come about in the West, even though through this practice the institution of family as a whole may suffer more. Quantitative statistical data are not only a poor reflection of women's emancipation, they can also lead to insecurity for women.[106] Norberg-Hodge has evaluated the conditions of Ladakhi women of India as a consequence of state modernization programs, as well as the effect of globalization from overseas. She argues:

> ... women have become invisible shadows. They do not earn money for their work, so they are no longer seen as "productive." Their work is not included as part of the Gross National Product. In government statistics, the 10 percent or so Ladakhis who work in the modern sector are listed according to their occupation; the other 90 percent—housewives and traditional farmers—are lumped together as non-workers. Farmers and women are coming to be viewed as inferior, and they themselves are developing feelings of insecurity and inadequacy.[107]

In modern industrial societies equality-driven rhetoric has eclipsed the discourse of social justice because the modernist discourse is more concerned about the "dream of equality" than achieving justice. The social effects of the ideology of development and the harm it has done to the institution of the family are quite obvious, as documented by Germaine Greer, author of *The Female Eunuch*:

> The sexual liberation that accompanied the gender revolution has in most cases harmed *women* more than men. "The sexuality that has been freed ... is male sexuality." Promiscuity harms women more than men: women continue to experience the momentous consequences of pregnancy, while the male body is unaffected. When the USS *Acadia* returned from the Gulf War, a tenth of her female crewmembers had already been returned to America because of pregnancy aboard what became known as the *Love Boat*. The number of men returned was zero.[108]

The sexual revolution has not emancipated women in any meaningful sense. On the contrary, it has led to their subjugation in the name of freedom. As a result of the Industrial Revolution, it is estimated that over 80,000 women became prostitutes on the streets of London while one third of children born were illegitimate.[109] As things have progressed along a similar social direction, and despite the intervention of the welfare state to create laws to protect women from abuse, there is no significant improvement in the condition of women in the West:

> In 1971, one in twelve British families was headed by a single parent, in 1986 one in seven, and by 1992 one in five. Another consequence has been the pain of solitude. By the year 2020 a third of all British households will be occupied by a single individual, and the majority of those individuals will be female. One of the most persistent legends of the sexual revolution, that "testing the waters" before marriage helps to determine compatibility, seems to have been definitively refuted. Some of the briefest marriages are those that follow a long period of cohabitation.[110]

Despite such evidence, the industrial nations and their development agencies ask Muslim societies to adopt a path similar to that which has led Western societies to the breakdown of the family and the loss of meaning in life. In the modern imagination patriarchy is considered unequal, oppressive, and backwards, whereas a family's chances of survival diminish significantly due to the absence of a judicious and caring patriarch. The late Ivan Illich, one of the foremost Catholic philosophers of the late twentieth century, argues that open traditional patriarchy was much more benign than the covert economic sexism of the modern world.[111] In his critique of modern sexism in *Gender*, he says:

> The literature dealing with this economic sexism has recently turned into a flood. It documents sexist exploitation, denounces it as an injustice, usually describes it as a new version of an age-old evil, and proposes explanatory theories with remedial strategies built in.... The industrial society creates two myths: one about the sexual ancestry of this society and the other about its movement toward equality.... I know of no industrial society where women are the economic equals of men.[112]

Illich argues that modern industrial mass society cannot logically exist unless it imposes the assumption that both of the sexes are made for the same type of work, have the same needs, or perceive reality in a similar way.[113] Some of the cardinal pieces of advice given out by the development and globalization experts are economic growth, social and sexual equality, and equal female representation in the workforce. Illich's work on development has demonstrated that both economic growth and gender equality ideologies are attendant. He argues that economic growth will logically lead to more inequity and distributive injustice, which renders the gospel of equality complete nonsense. Because modern economics is the economics of scarcity, modern institutions from family to school to courtroom incorporate this assumption of scarcity.[114] Similarly education itself first became a commodity and then a scarce commodity. Now it has become a commodity without which one cannot grow up and be mature:

> In traditional societies [men and women] matured without the conditions for growth being perceived as scarce. Now, educational institutions teach them that desirable competence and learning are scarce goods for which men and

> women must compete.... [modern education therefore] assumes the scarcity of a genderless value; it teaches that he or she who experiences its process is primarily a human being in need of genderless education.... and economic institutions cannot exist without the abolition of gender and the social construction of sex.[115]

A supposedly neuter work force for the modern workplace is intrinsically gender destructive and sexist, and as such this phenomenon can only become exaggerated by more economic growth. According to Illich's judgment, to recover from this malady we should economically shrink and not expand, or else it will enhance the sexist exploitation, which has become a social characteristic of industrial society.[116] In the quest for good social relations, the subsistence economy as opposed to a growth-based economy is more likely to be sustainable and peaceful. While comparing traditional with modern cultures from a social and ecological point of view, Norberg-Hodge argues that "the old culture reflected fundamental human needs while respecting the natural limits. And it worked. It worked for nature and it worked for people."[117]

A vast majority of social activists subscribe to the view that gender is socially constructed. This position arises out of a belief in the "progress" and evolution of the human species, which itself is based on the assumption that religion is a backward form of human consciousness. From such a perspective, sex is a biologically determined phenomenon whereas gender is socially constructed. Further, it is a reaction to the nineteenth century medical view that a woman's personality is a function of her anatomy and reproductive function. In other words we have moved from one reductionist position to another. Along similar lines, social psychologists would argue that gender construction is purely a process of child development, while Marxist feminists would define the place of women entirely in relation to the means of production. Such studies of gender were criticized during the high modern period by anthropologists such as Margaret Mead, who demonstrated the differentiation of gender roles across societies and the lack of a singular pattern of gender development upon which the modern philosophy of gender is usually built. The globalization experts consider "gender-equality policies" as necessary for the Muslim world, caring little how gender and sex are perceived in traditional religious societies.

From Islamic philosophers to illiterate Muslims, anyone who professes the religion of Islam agrees that human beings are, first and foremost, spiritual beings.[118] Therefore, that which precedes the "form," identified with the female body, must have its spiritual essence above and beyond its material reality. Also, if the source of all life is God then the spiritual nature of both the male and female must issue from the Divine Reality itself. Muslims do not negate societal effects or biological realities, but they view them as realities contingent upon a higher reality. They can only be real insofar as they are integrated into the Real.[119] Social constructivist views of society—with or without evolutionist ideology—conflict with the Muslim conception of the human being and of gender. For a vast majority of Muslims, the nature, needs, and functions of the sexes are understood via the law of Islam, not through humanistic ideologies. If the inequalities and abuses which persist in several Muslim countries are to be ameliorated, they must be neutralized on the basis of Islamic principles, not through transient modern ideologies imported, or worse, imposed from outside.

Sachiko Murata has criticized mainstream feminism for its Eurocentricity and naïveté when it comes to understanding the predicament of the feminine. She remarks:

> It seems to me that feminists who have criticized various aspects of Islam or Islamic society base their positions upon a worldview radically alien to the Islamic worldview. Their critique typically takes a moral stance. They ask for reform, whether explicitly or implicitly. The reform they have in view is of the standard modern Western type.[120]

For Murata the conception of the role of women in Islam has a deep-seated prejudice in the West.[121] She argues that just as in Chinese cosmology, which views male and female principles of existence in *yang* and *yin* (or active and receptive), Islamic cosmology is based upon the complementarity or polarity of active and receptive principles.[122] This principle of duality can only make sense in relation to the principle of unity, whose perfect expression in the Islamic tradition is God Himself. Looking at female and male as inner and outer leads to a view that considers them as a single and intertwined unit in the light of unity. This view of women is only accepted by those who show preference for a spiritual over a material worldview. Modern ideas of women stand in contrast to views of women as outlined by Murata. The modern view of women, which has reached the Muslim world through the process of globalization, has created confusion of gender roles and made Muslim women unsure about themselves. The "fundamentalist" policies of several Muslim countries further aggravate the problem, but these are not so different from those of the West, for they too are based upon a denial of the spiritual and a reduction to the material. The continuing effort to impose "solutions" which deny the complimentary that Islam sees between men and women will only serve to foment the reactionary policies of puritanical literalists.

II. Secularism and the Muslim World

Another socio-cultural aspect of globalization is the spread of secularism to the Muslim world. Secularism is a social condition in which religion, its institutions, and its worldview stop being of central significance to society. Such changes often accompany what Tonnies called a shift from *Gemeinschaft* to *Gesellschaft*, or when a community loses its primordial association and becomes a modern mass society. Ironically, despite the fact that many Muslim societies are rapidly transforming into mass societies due to the pressures of modernization and globalization, they are becoming not less but more religious. Lamin Sanneh has argued that modernity is not impervious to the challenges of the "sacred."[123] In his thought-provoking article "Sacred and Secular in Islam," he demonstrates how sacred and secular are one for the Muslims, only because the latter is viewed in the shadow of the former. In the context of the surge in religious fundamentalism around the world, he argues that the West has reduced religion to individual piety and subjective dispositions by

> … giving the sacred little or no public merit. The Enlightenment and the inter-religious wars of Europe [led its] people to establish the state on a non-religious basis. Religion survived as personal habit and subjective preference, framed by emotions, feelings, and states of mind appropriate to the phenomenon, as Rudolph Otto describes in his classic work, *The Idea of the Holy*. This point expresses well the spirit of individualism. From the fundamentalist point of view, however, this notion of religion is offensive because religion is the revealed will of God for the public order, and for the individual as a member of the community.[124]

In the context of September 11, Sanneh argues that a secular West reacted with stunned surprise. After all, how could anyone want to harm people of a secular order that represent social progress? Given the long history of Muslims' grievances against the West, he asks, "is not the West's surprise itself surprising?"[125] He argues:

> The events of 11 September have breached the walls of secular invincibility, and also the logic of secular claims as neutral and normative. The modern religious resurgence has revealed the dogma of secular primacy to be vulnerable to rude surprises, making it imperative that we recognize the role of religion in people's lives for what it is.[126]

With regards to secularism, Sanneh's remedial advice for the affairs of the state is that "religion is too important for the state to ignore, and equally too important for the state to co-opt."[127] Western military adventures and the promotion of secular values will only fan more fundamentalism in the Muslim world, because most Muslims find few benefits in secularism to win their confidence.[128]

According to Islamic doctrine, the idea of God is built into human nature. From the Islamic perspective, therefore, it seems that modern man's soul is forever in search of the Divine. However, if humans are not open to the idea of the Divine, their soul can and must find objects of worship at a lower plane, hence the emergence of pseudo-spiritual cults that sometimes parade as authentic religious traditions. According to the spiritual principles of Islam, in the absence of human submission to the Divine Will, the nostalgia of the human soul for worship can manifest itself in other ways. This nostalgia's referent may be religious, but if it discounts the rituals of religion, it discounts the spirit of the entire religion. This symptom of the secularist condition amounts to the total denial of religion. The religious fanaticism exhibited by India's *Rashtriya Swayamsevak Sangh* (RSS) and *Sangh Parivar*, for example, have a religious referent, but their violent behavior with regards to the non-Hindus in India has demonstrated that the sacrosanct nature of other religious forms is not a consideration anymore. Similarly, Israeli Zionism has a religious referent, but has been reduced to a secular state ideology.[129] As noted earlier, pressures of secularism have also produced reactionary movements within the Muslim world. Muslim extremists are preoccupied more with the militant combat of the West than with preserving and presenting the spiritual message of Islam.

Mircea Eliade's *The Sacred and the Profane* is a great tool for understanding the nature of the sacred in opposition to the secular. He argues that "the modern Occidental experiences a certain uneasiness before many manifestations of the sacred,"[130] and this uneasiness is a result of the West's transition to a secular domain. Eliade argues that if we compare the men of modern societies with the religious men who lived in a sacralized cosmos, we find that the former dwell in a desacralized cosmos.[131]

The profusion of pseudo-spiritual religious cults gives evidence that religion in the modern world has become reduced to the "shopping mall approach," where one "shops" and "practices" a suitable religion, which is only a matter of personal choice (like a hobby). And as pointed out by Sanneh, it has nothing to do with one's life in public. Although the process of modernization and its concatenation with secularism is itself variable, it is certain that the globalization of the modern value system has produced exogenous pressures for secularism in the Muslim world. Muslim law does not classify life into two unconnected halves, one sacred and the other profane; the sacred law influences all walks of life, leaving none to a realm that is not cognizant of the transcendental Reality. Suggestions for the secularization of the Muslim world can only be expected to produce more violent reactions against modernism and globalization. As noted by Levine, what perpetuates the exacerbation of hostilities between the West and the Muslim world is the secularizing effect of globalization on the Muslim world. Moreover, the social effects of secularism in the modern Western world are too well known to ignore. Scholars such as Frithjof Schuon, René Guénon, and Seyyed Hossein Nasr have pointed out that it is imperative for the modern world to return to its primordial path and resuscitate its spiritual ethics; for the spiritual health of the Muslim world depends upon more Islam, not less Islam.[132] From this perspective, a resurgence of the fundamental values of Islam would be the only true antidote to the extremist reactions to globalization.

III. Evolutionism and the Myth of Progress

Other mythical elements that are causal to the social moorings of the modern world are the theory of evolution and the idea of progress. Initially the theory of evolution was an outcome of biology and natural science, but its gradual impact on philosophy, humanities, and social sciences has been tremendous because of the radical change in worldview it necessitated. Also, it is noteworthy that evolution is closely linked to the idea of progress. It is therefore important to take a critical look at this theory—so fundamental to the modern worldview—which is taught at the schools not as *theory* but as *fact*.

In its initial Darwinian form the theory of human evolution embraces a gradual, linear, and progressive view of change, in contrast to the later theorists, such as Stephen Jay Gould, who posit massive jumps in the evolutionary process. Now, the theory of evolution is the exact opposite of the creationist worldview as taught by the various traditional religions of the world. The latter believe that man, as well as other creatures, did not evolve from below but were created from above by the Creator, who is higher than all creation. For the evolutionists, if there is any example of human perfection at all, it must lie in some imaginary moment in the future because man is supposedly progressing from a lower to a higher and better form. According to this logic, the evolutionist perspective is bereft of an ethical standard because we continue to be backward compared to our improved future version that is still expected to come. The traditional religious worldview is the opposite, because it is not based on evolution but devolution. In the religious world, therefore, examples of human perfection abound, as regarded by the adherents of figures like Buddha, Christ, and Muḥammad. For the traditional people the moment of perfection is in the tangible knowledge of the Origin and not in an imaginary moment in the future. Even if modern man speaks of a gradual perfection, observation supports the fact that his ethics have consistently degenerated from the early modern to the late modern period. The religious world, in contrast, acknowledges that moral standards gradually depreciate only to be resuscitated by spiritual leaders or saints, who cure degeneration through a re-infusion of the transcendental ideals in man. In such a world, one is presented with a paragon of perfection and an ideal to be approximated as best one can. In contradistinction, the ethos of modernity is based upon negation and destruction of that which is the quintessential archetype, indispensable for maintaining the moral standards of society.

Traditional writers such as Ananda Coomaraswamy, René Guénon, Frithjof Schuon, Martin Lings, Seyyed Hossein Nasr, Titus Burckhardt, and Wolfgang Smith have repeatedly admonished the attentive academic elite of the world that the theory of evolution is pseudo-scientific, anti-spiritual, and dangerous for the future of humanity.[133] As the renowned economist E. F. Schumacher has observed in his *Guide to the Perplexed*:

> Evolutionism is not a science; it is science fiction, even a kind of hoax. It is far better to believe that the earth is a disc supported by a tortoise and flanked by four elephants than to believe in the name of "evolutionism" in the coming of some "superhuman" monster.[134]

Nasr has pointed out that those Muslims who are the products of educational systems of those states that have had the longest Western colonial rule (such as the Muslim states of the Indian Subcontinent) subscribe to the theory of evolution more than those Muslim lands where colonial education has made less impact.[135] Modernism and globalization continue to threaten educational institutions of non-Western societies, and the theory of evolution plays an important part in that process. It continues to mislead more people, only to be challenged by those who understand its social implications. It leads to changes in social attitudes toward religion, and as Norberg-Hodge has pointed out, the new system of education leads to the alienation of the youth from the older generation.[136] Moreover, this theory does not only reside in books and print media, but continues to impact the worldview of even those who are illiterate. It constantly affects average people's thinking on the origin of life, and the "nature" of human beings in that it presents human "nature" as essentially animal. Television stations such as the National Geographic, Discovery, and The Learning Channel constantly propagate the evolutionist perspective. The assumption of evolutionary thought is present in most media that deal with the "nature" of living things, especially humans and animals. More than just entertainment, these programs constitute the "gospel hours" of globalization whose impact is anti-spiritual and destructive for the world.

The social science counterpart of the theory of evolution is called social Darwinism. This theory claims that the law of "natural forces" (without defining either "nature" or "force") determines survival in human beings, analogous to the "laws of nature" in the animal kingdom. This theory has produced a view of the world where "might is right" because only the strong survive. Its economic counterpart was conceived in laissez-faire terms as in the philosophy of Herbert Spencer, while other Social Darwinists such as Glumpowicz and Sumner have argued that some races (i.e., the Europeans) are innately superior to others. According to them, the superior races have the "natural right" to dominate the inferior races. Decades later we find the communists, who argue from the opposite extreme, and insist on a Utopian equality of opportunity and conditions. Both of these world systems are at opposite extremes from the spiritual center, which, according to Muslims, is the source of balance in the world. The capitalist free market system is extreme because the winner can take all and there is no real compassion for the weak and the poor; in the socialist extreme, for the sake of the poor, one must have no choice but to submit to the supreme will of the state in its quest for achieving equality. But the social aspects that give rise to these ideologies, I argue, have failed to take root in the Muslim consciousness during the high modern period. Islam remains a way of life for Muslims, their need and also their world system, in theory and practice.

Just as the theory of evolution is linear and simplistic, so is the ideology of *progress*. The idea of progress is essentially materialist and utopian. It rests upon the logic of "today being better than yesterday, therefore tomorrow will be better than today," and hence a justification for a linear cumulative progress of humanity. Lord Northbourne has asserted that:

> ... the ideology of progress envisages the perfectibility of man in terms of his terrestrial development, and relegates it to a hypothetical future, whereas tradition envisages the perfectibility of man in terms of salvation or sanctification, and proclaims that it is realizable here and now.[137]

As early as the First and Second World Wars, people had developed a pessimistic view of the ideology of progress; they sensed that these wars were just a foretaste of the path of destruction that the modern world was taking. The idea of civilization, which was equated with social progress, the rise of rationalism over religion, the decline of local customs and social diversity, the advent of scientism and greater cultural uniformity among nations, all now seem highly suspect. To ask Muslims to conform to this chimerical view could thus be nothing but hubris.

Nineteenth-century science was based on the assumption that progress was contingent upon industrialism, while industry itself was technology-dependent. This technological advancement, according to the new view, gave birth to material welfare, better life standards, and growth in the rights of citizens due to high literacy. These were grand assumptions. Serious setbacks to these notions, however, came about with the rise of fascism in Europe where technology was primarily responsible for a vast number of deaths, while the citizens' rights swiftly vanished in Germany and Italy, despite education and high literacy rates. Gradually, confidence in the progressive nature of industrial society has disappeared, and there are intellectual groups inside the West as well as the Muslim world that are beginning to be aware of the social contradictions of modernity. As Levine has stated, globalization of such ideas has led to a general fear in Muslim societies of being culturally invaded by the forces of modernism.[138]

On the social level, therefore, the process of globalization has given birth to attitudes that have led to a new consciousness. The new social mooring and its concomitant loss of social ethics is due to the ideological impact of secularism, evolutionism, and a misleading view of human nature.

Conclusion

Globalization represents at once a certain condition, a process, as well as an ideology. As a condition, it is responsible for the impoverishment of a large number of people in the world. As a process, it has enabled us to shorten distance and time, which superficially seems fascinating, but its concomitant price is high in socio-economic terms. As an ideology, it continues to delude the masses into giving in to more control, and undermines the democratic spirit.

Nasr has argued that the loss of the traditional religious worldview and the induction of the ideological worldview has confined man's intellectual potential to humanism and dragged him down to the level of the infra-human.[139] Ideologies are by their very nature ephemeral and transient. Recent history has demonstrated that ideologies are the work of ideologues and marginal intellectuals, and are based upon the reduction of truth to whim, conjecture, and passional proclivities. Ideologies purport to have knowledge about science and religion but they are actually based on a distorted view of human nature. Since ideologies are evanescent, they have no answer to the existential dilemmas of humankind and cannot deliver the spiritual nourishment that is absolutely vital for a healthy human life. In contrast, religion is universal and it is the primordial tradition of humanity. Due to the perennial nature of the revealed religious teachings, they are the logical opponents of ideologies. So long as people who truly identify with any revealed faith, such as Islam, Judaism, Christianity, Hinduism, Buddhism and all the other divine dispensations that live in this world, they will not give up religion for an ephemeral ideology.

Inasmuch as globalization is an ideology of development, it threatens to overrun the sustainability of the planet.[140] Its origins lie in the early modern period, which intensified in Europe with the gradual relegation of religion to a backward element in human history. This relegation of man to a mere terrestrial being and the absolutization of the human state has led humanity on the course of environmental degradation.[141] Modernity seeks to destroy the power of religion over the human soul and questions the categories of sin and evil, whereas religions have always taught humanity to cultivate virtue and avoid evil.[142] The roots of modernity lie in rebellion against nature whereas in traditional civilizations, nature is understood as a reflection of the Divine, and is therefore sacred. But the fruits of modernity are seductive and in the quest for their acquisition the world is edging toward the brink of ecological and human disaster. From antiquity until the dawn of modern history, man lived harmoniously with nature; since then modern man has attempted to dominate and control it. It is not at all fortuitous that the historical origins of the domination and the rape of nature coincide with the historical rebellion of modern man against God. For a long period in world history the traditional world could not threaten the environment as compared to the threat posed by the modern world to the biosphere.

The poisoning of water, air, and soil by industry, the expansive system of urban growth, and the proliferation of an unnatural and mechanistic way of life is rapidly making the planet unlivable. Natural beauty in the pre-modern world reminded humanity of the splendor and majesty of the Heavens. Whatever is left is at risk of being destroyed by the military marvels of modern science such as atomic bombs. Peccei and Ikeda have estimated that ninety percent of all scientists employed today are employed by the defense industry.[143] The scientific community of the modern world seems to be doing little to avert this danger because it suffers from over-quantification, while it consistently ignores the qualitative aspects of human life due to its professed silence on ethical issues. The worldview modern science imparts to its adherents is based upon unexamined assumptions that are believed to be highly normative in nature and which govern the system of "truth" in modern society. Modern ideologies often corroborate their views from such "truths" of modern science.

The tribulations of the modern world, which are responsible for bringing the world to the brink of ecological disaster, are being coercively imposed upon the Muslim world and other parts of the traditional world with little regard for potential moral and environmental deterioration. "It might be said that the environmental crisis, as well as the psychological imbalance of so many men and women in the West, the ugliness of the urban environment and the like are the result of the attempt of man to live by bread alone, to 'kill all gods' and announce his independence of Heaven. But he cannot escape the effect of his actions, which are themselves the fruit of his present state of being."[144] The foundations of the modern world are built upon inherently contradictory aspects which have led humanity into a condition of ecological and social adversity. Religious ethics offer a viable alternative for re-infusing transcendental ethics and morality into human society; and this is essential for the resuscitation of a life grounded in principles.

Notes

[1] I wish to thank Dr. Mohammad Faghfoory, whose meticulous comments have always been insightful and instructive in projects I have recently undertaken.

[2] The West can be defined as the formerly Christian (but now secular) societies of Western Europe and its geographical extension to North America, South Africa, and Australasia. But the modern West, besides still being a geographical entity, is a non-geographical, ideological entity that dwells at the outposts of the geographical and ideological West in the geographical non-West. In this sense modernization and westernization are interchangeable.

[3] From amongst the several groups that are critical of modernity, the challenge of the traditionalist scholars is analytically most sound, precisely because tradition opposes modernism from its roots to its shoots. The traditional viewpoint appears menacing to modernity because it implicates the breakdown of the organizational principle of the modern world.

[4] Those changes, which started with the Reformation, leading on to the Enlightenment, and which shaped European attitudes toward religion as a backward form of human consciousness, are here referred to as "modernity." The triumph of reason over revelation, seventeenth-century scientism, evolution, intellectual relativism, secularism, and devaluation of religion are some of the traits that characterize modernity.

[5] Oswald Spengler, *The Decline of the West* (New York: Alfred Knopf, 1939), p. 3.

[6] Francis Fukuyama, *End of History and the Last Man* (New York: Avon Books, 1992), p. xi.

[7] http://www.guardian.co.uk.

[8] *Ibid.*

[9] See Joseph E. B. Lumbard, "The Decline of Knowledge and the Rise of Ideology in the Modern Islamic World."

[10] The label of "Islamic fundamentalism" is itself problematic because its direct counterpart in Arabic language, *uṣūliyya* or the "fundamentals of religion" denotes a positive element in the Muslim imagination. However, what makes the fundamentalists distinctively *modernist* is, among other things, their instrumental use of secular science and technology for their political ends that have a religious referent. As noted above (footnote 2), the terms "tradition" and "traditional" reject those elements of modernism that portray revealed religious traditions as inherently cruel and backward, and whose loss has rendered the modern world morally and spiritually bankrupt.

[11] Ghazi Bin Muḥammad, *The Crisis of the Islamic World* (Aman: Islamic World Report-Turab, 1995), p. 38.

[12] Judy Dumpsey, "Far Right Poses Risk to EU Enlargement" in *Financial Times*, UK, May 28, 2002.

[13] Bin Muḥammad, *The Crisis of the Islamic World*, p. 38.

[14] Fukuyama, *End of History and the Last Man*, p. 236.

[15] *Ibid.*, p. 217.

[16] World system theory rests upon the observation that the economic organization of the modern world is based globally and not nationally. The system is composed of

core regions which are the industrialized centers, and the periphery, the raw material-supplying underdeveloped world. The latter is in a state of perpetual impoverishment. This system has its origin in a capitalist agriculture that coincides with the beginning of secular morality. In traditional societies there was one political-bureaucratic system, i.e., the empires and several diverse economic structures, which preserved the diversity of cultures, whereas in the modern world, there is one economic world system and several political-bureaucratic systems. The singularity of economic system imposed upon the world through processes of modernization and globalization and their ideologies of modernism and globalism threaten to overrun diversity and make the world uniform.

17 Helena Norberg-Hodge, "The Pressure to Modernize and Globalize," in *The Case Against the Global Economy: And for a Turn Toward the Local* (San Francisco: Sierra Club Books, 1996), p. 33.

18 *Ibid.*, pp. 33-47.

19 Henry Munson, "Between Pipes and Esposito," *International Institute for the Study of Islam in the Muslim World*, ISIM # 10:02, p. 8.

20 Victor Segesvary, *From Illusion to Delusion: Globalization and the Contradictions of Late Modernity* (Bethesda: International Scholars Publication, 1999), p. xiv-xv.

21 *Ibid.*, p. xiv.

22 For an understanding of the term "tradition" see Joseph E. B. Lumbard's introduction to this volume.

23 Ali Mazrui, "Globalization, Islam, and the West: Between Homogenization and Hegemonization," *American Journal of Islamic Social Sciences* 15, no. 3 (Fall 1998): 2.

24 Ronald Chilcote, *Theories of Comparative Politics: The Search for a Paradigm* (Boulder: Westview Publications, 1981), p. 296-299.

25 *Ibid.*, p. 296.

26 Arnold Toynbee, "The World and the West," in Vera Micheles Dean and Harry D. Harootunian, *West and Non-West: New Perspectives* (New York: Holt, Rinehart and Winston, 1963), p. 420.

27 Mark Levine, "Muslim Responses to Globalization," *International Institute for the Study of Islam in the Muslim World*, ISIM # 10:02, p. 1.

28 *Ibid.*, p. 1.

29 See for example the works of E. F. Schumacher, *Small is Beautiful* and *This I Believe.*

30 Martin Khor, "Global Economy and the Third World," in *The Case Against the Global Economy: And for a Turn Toward the Local* (San Francisco: Sierra Club Books, 1996), pp. 47-59.

31 Power conferred upon a human free from Divine constraints is referred to here as absolute power, because of an intentional dislocation of the Divine from the understanding of what constitutes power.

32 By "political accord" I do not mean a large "nation-state" comprised of all historical Muslim lands; but instead, a regional order with representative states. This is to be distinguished from the haphazard demarcation of territories as they were carved up by the European colonial powers with the subsequent installment of corrupt puppet regimes by their neo-colonial successors.

[33] Seyyed Hossein Nasr, "Islamic Unity: The Ideal and Obstacles in the Way of its Realization," *Iqbal Review* 40, no. 1 (1999): 5.

[34] Emil Brunner, *Christianity and Civilization* (New York: Scribner, 1948), p. 87.

[35] Thomas Molnar, *Twin Powers: Politics, and the Sacred* (Grand Rapids, MI: William B. Eerdmans Publishing Company, 1988), p. 89.

[36] *Ibid.*, p. 89.

[37] *Ibid.*, p. 91.

[38] John U. Nef, *Western Civilization Since the Renaissance: Peace, War, Industry, and the Arts* (New York: Harper & Row, 1963), p. 411.

[39] *Ibid.*, p. 411.

[40] *Ibid.*, p. 412.

[41] *Ibid.*, pp. xv-xvi.

[42] *Ibid.*, p. xv.

[43] *Ibid.*, p. xvi.

[44] See the chapter "The Political Extreme," in Martin Lings, *The Eleventh Hour: The Spiritual Crisis of the Modern World in the Light of Tradition and Prophecy* (Lahore: Suhail Academy, 1988), pp. 45-59.

[45] Nef, *Western Civilization Since the Renaissance*, p. 412.

[46] *Ibid.*, p. 414.

[47] *Ibid.*, p. 415.

[48] Amalgamated security community according to Karl Deutsch can come about when "the integrating territories must share a common set of values and that the communication and transactions between them must expand in numerous ways .... successful integration requires a sense of community of a 'we feeling' among the populations of the integrating communities" (pp. 115-116). The geographically contiguous parts of most of the Muslim world, I shall argue, possess through the concept of *umma*, a spiritual solidarity that is much larger than such a feeling. Ernst Haas argues for that process "whereby the actors in several distinct national settings are persuaded to shift their loyalties, expectations and political activities toward a new center, whose institutions possess or demand jurisdiction over the pre-existing national states." He also says that "key groups that make the 'new' pluralistic society ... do not require absolute majority" (pp. 140-141). It is true that this process has occurred historically, but never in the history of the modern Muslim nation state, especially those areas that were direct colonies and retained the post-colonial states, with the exception of the United Arab Republic (UAR), which only lasted for two years before it fell apart. Stanley Hoffman's realism has challenged Haas' neo-functionalism by the theory of inter-governmentalism, stating that nation states will cooperate and integrate only in the area of "low politics," but that this will be less likely in "high politics," (pp. 157-158) an observation that ECO union corroborates, minus the disturbance factors such as nature of origins of the states in question, external influence in their international relations, integration in the world system, and the dependency factor. Finally, Bela Balassa's assumption that "functional integration is less useful but more politically expedient as opposed to the simultaneous integration of all sectors" (pp. 173-174) is only plausible as long as dependency theory reigns supreme. All of the above references in Brent F. Nelsen & Alexander C-G. Stubb,

The European Union: Readings on the Theory and Practice of European Integration, 2nd edition (Lynne Reinner Publishers, 1998).

49 James Piscatori, *Islam in the World of Nation States* (Melbourne: Royal Institute of International Affairs, 1986), p. 145.

50 Segesvary, p. 36.

51 Regarding Pakistan see *The Economist*, "The Saving of Pakistan," January 19, 2002, p. 9 (international edition).

52 Martin Lings, *The Eleventh Hour*, p. 47.

53 Claes Ryn, *The New Jacobinism: Can Democracy Survive?* (Washington, DC: National Humanities Institute, 1991), p. 55.

54 *Ibid.*, p. 56.

55 *Ibid.*, p. 57.

56 *Ibid.*, p. 57.

57 *Ibid.*, p. 57.

58 *Ibid.*, p. 58.

59 *Ibid.*, p. 59.

60 *Ibid.*, p. 62.

61 *Ibid.*, p. 62.

62 *Ibid.*, p. 63.

63 *Ibid.*, p. 65.

64 *Ibid.*, p. 66.

65 Anthony McGrew, "Democracy Beyond Borders? Globalization and Reconstruction of Democratic Theory and Politics" in *Transformation of Democracy* (Cambridge: Polity Press, 1997), p. 233.

66 Seyyed Hossein Nasr, *Ideals and Realities of Islam* (New York: Praeger, 1967), p. 110.

67 John Esposito and John Voll, *Islam and Democracy* (Oxford: Oxford University Press, 1996) pp. 193, 198.

68 *Ibid.*, p. 201.

69 Judy Dempsy, "Far Right Poses Risk to EU Enlargement," *Financial Times*, London, May 28, 2002. See also "Europe's Swing Back to the Right," *Financial Times*, London, June 17, 2002.

70 For a balanced account of the Algerian situation see, *Algeria, Revolution Revisited* (Islamic World Report, 1997).

71 Lings, *The Eleventh Hour*, pp. 47-48.

72 *Ibid.*, p. 48.

73 *Ibid.*, p. 48.

74 *Ibid.*, p. 54.

75 Ryn, *The New Jacobinism*, p. 60.

[76] Lings, *The Eleventh Hour*, p. 55.

[77] Jerry Mander and Edward Goldsmith, "Facing the Rising Tide," in *The Case Against the Global Economy: And for a Turn Toward the Local* (San Francisco: Sierra Club Books, 1996), p. 10.

[78] *Ibid.*, p. 11.

[79] *Ibid.*, pp. 10-11.

[80] Modern economics in its variant forms works with the assumption that available resources must be rationed either through price regulation or some central system of distribution. This assumption implies that resources are scarce or else they would not need to be rationed. In the absence of scarcity, no difficult choices would need to be made and no prices should be affixed on things that are abundant anyway. The idea of abundance would render the study of modern economics totally unnecessary. See Graham Bannock, R.E. Baxter, and Evan Davis, *Penguin Dictionary of Economics* (Auckland: Penguin, 1998), p. 371.

[81] *Ibid.*, p. 371.

[82] Ibn Khaldūn, *Muqaddimah: An Introduction to History*, trans. Franz Rosenthal (Princeton: Princeton University Press, 1967), pp. 65-69.

[83] *Ibid.*, p. 65.

[84] Martin Khor, "Global Economy and the Third World," p. 47.

[85] Irfan Ul Haq, *Economic Doctrines of Islam: A Study in the Doctrines of Islam and Their Implications for Poverty, Employment, and Economic Growth* (Herndon: International Institute of Islamic Thought, 1996), p. 211.

[86] See Steve Keen, *Debunking Economics: The Naked Emperor of the Social Sciences* (London: Zed Books, 2001).

[87] For further elaboration on this aspect of the neo-classical theory of economics, see Waleed El-Ansary's "The Economics of Terrorism," in this volume.

[88] Norberg-Hodge, "The Pressure to Modernize and Globalize," p. 45.

[89] *Ibid.*, p. 45.

[90] Seyyed Hossein Nasr, *Islam and the Plight of Modern Man* (London: Longman, 1975), p. 111.

[91] James Caporaso and David Levine, *Theories of Political Economy* (Cambridge: Cambridge University Press, 1992), p. 31.

[92] Mander, "Facing the Rising Tide," p. 12.

[93] Ryn, *The New Jacobinism*, p. 79.

[94] "Growing Income Disparity and the Middle Class Squeeze," http://www.justpeace.org/structures/squeeze.htm.

[95] Ryn, *The New Jacobinism*, p. 79.

[96] Sometimes certain special laws *can* be made that seemingly go against one of the aspects of Islamic tradition, but these are very special instances in which a decision has been made to promulgate a law because of pressing circumstances.

[97] The concept of *economism* is used to denote the ideological reduction of all walks of life—social, cultural, religious, and political—to a single economic base which serves

as a causal reservoir ready to supply materialist explanations for the symbolic and non-material.

98 Import Substitution and Industrialization (ISI) policies can only protect the economy if the nascent industrial sector becomes internationally competitive and nationally self-sufficient. In some states which used ISI, like those in Latin America and India, economic conditions remain distressed.

99 Segesvary, *From Illusion to Delusion*, p. 31.

100 Norberg-Hodge, "The Pressure to Modernize and Globalize," p. 45.

101 Edward Goldsmith, "Global Trade and the Environment," in Mander and Goldsmith, p. 78.

102 Ejaz Akram, "Environment, World System, and the Muslim Scholar" (Editorial), *American Journal of Islamic Social Sciences* 18, no. 2 (Summer 2001): i-iv.

103 Segesvary, *From Illusion to Delusion*, pp. 305-307.

104 Segesvary, *From Illusion to Delusion*, pp. 11-12.

105 *Ibid.*, p. 12.

106 Norberg-Hodge, "The Pressure to Modernize and Globalize," p. 42.

107 *Ibid.*, p. 42.

108 Abdal Hakim Murad, *Boys Will be Boys: Gender Identity Issues*, http://www.masud.co.uk.

109 Mortimer Chambers *et al* (eds.), *The Western Experience* (Boston: McGraw-Hill, 1999), vol. 2, p. 818.

110 Abdal Hakim Murad, *Boys Will be Boys.*

111 Ivan Illich, *Gender* (New York: Pantheon Books, 1982), p. 3.

112 *Ibid.*, pp. 3-4.

113 *Ibid.*, p. 9.

114 *Ibid.*, p. 11.

115 *Ibid.*, pp. 11, 13.

116 *Ibid.*, p. 16.

117 Norberg-Hodge, "The Pressure to Modernize and Globalize," p. 46.

118 Qur´ān: 51:58.

119 For a further explanation of this idea, see Joseph E. B. Lumbard, "The Decline of Knowledge and the Rise of Ideology in the Modern Islamic World," in this volume.

120 Sachiko Murata, *The Tao of Islam: A Sourcebook on Gender Relationships in Islamic Thought* (Albany: SUNY Press, 1992), p. 4.

121 *Ibid.*, p. 6.

122 *Ibid.*, pp. 6-7.

123 Lamin Sanneh, "Sacred and Secular in Islam," *International Institute for the Study of Islam in the Muslim World*, ISIM # 10:02, p. 6.

124 *Ibid.*, p. 6.

[125] *Ibid.*, p. 6.

[126] *Ibid.*, 6.

[127] *Ibid.*, p. 6.

[128] *Ibid.*, p. 6.

[129] For a traditional Jewish critique of the secularization of Israel see http://www.netureikarta.org/.

[130] Mircea Eliade, *The Sacred and the Profane: The Nature of Religion* (Orlando: Harcourt Brace, 1987), pp. 10-11.

[131] *Ibid.*, p. 17.

[132] See the essays of Reza Shah-Kazemi and Joseph E. B. Lumbard in this volume.

[133] John Herlihy, *Modern Man at Crossroads: The Search for the Knowledge of First Origins and Final Ends* (Lahore: Suhail Academy, 1999), p. 93.

[134] *Ibid.*, p. 93.

[135] Class lectures on the Perennial Philosophy.

[136] Norberg-Hodge, "The Pressure to Modernize and Globalize," p. 36.

[137] Lord Northbourne, *Looking Back on Progress* (London: Perennial Books, 1970), p. 22.

[138] Levine, "Muslim Responses to Globalization," p. 1.

[139] Seyyed Hossein Nasr, *Islam and the Plight of Modern Man*, p. 13.

[140] Goldsmith, "Global Trade and the Environment," p. 98.

[141] Seyyed Hossein Nasr, *Man and Nature* (London: Mandala, 1968), p. 6.

[142] *Ibid.*, p. 13.

[143] Aurelio Peccei and Daisaku Ikeda, in *Before Its Too Late*, ed. Richard Cage (New York: Kodansha International Ltd., 1984), p. 25.

[144] Nasr, *Man and Nature*, p. 13.

EPILOGUE

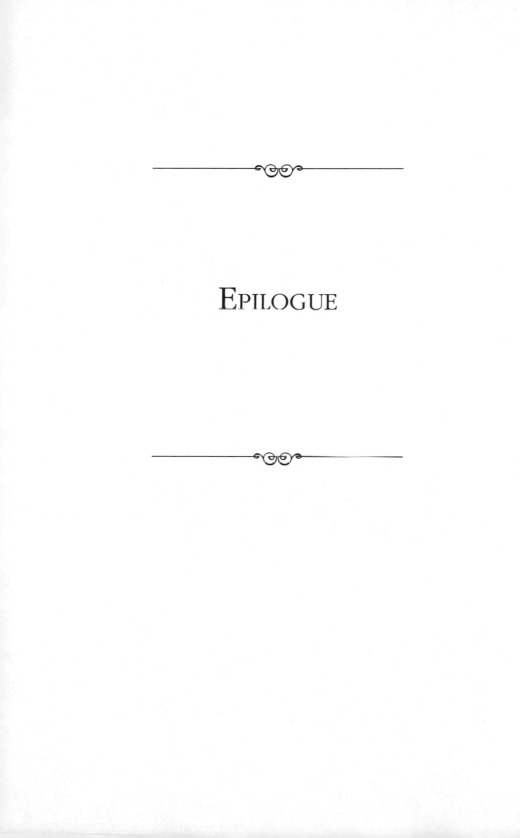

CHAPTER 8

THE POVERTY OF FANATICISM

T. J. WINTER

"Blood is no argument," as Shakespeare observed. Sadly, Muslim ranks are today swollen with those who disagree. The World Trade Center, yesterday's symbol of global finance, has today become a monument to the failure of global Islam to control those who believe that the West can be bullied into changing its wayward ways towards the East. There is no real excuse at hand. It is simply not enough to clamor, as many have done, about "chickens coming home to roost," and to protest that Washington's acquiescence in Israeli policies towards Palestine is the inevitable generator of such hate. It is of course true—as Shabbir Akhtar has noted—that powerlessness can corrupt as insistently as does power. But to comprehend is not to sanction or even to empathize. To take innocent life to achieve a goal is the hallmark of the most extreme secular utilitarian ethic, and stands at the opposite pole of the absolute moral constraints required by religion.

There was a time, not long ago, when the "ultras" were few, forming only a tiny wart on the face of the worldwide attempt to revivify Islam. Sadly, we can no longer enjoy the luxury of ignoring them. The extreme has broadened, and the middle ground, giving way, is everywhere dislocated and confused. And this enfeeblement of the middle ground, of the moderation enjoined by the Prophetic example, is in turn accelerated by the opprobrium which the extremists bring not simply upon themselves, but upon committed Muslims everywhere. For here, as elsewhere, the preferences of the media work firmly against us. David Koresh could broadcast his fringe Biblical message from Ranch Apocalypse without the image of Christianity, or even its Adventist wing, being in any way besmirched. But when a fringe Islamic group bombs Swedish tourists in Cairo, the stain is instantly spread over "militant Muslims" everywhere.

If these things go on, the Islamic movement will cease to form an authentic summons to cultural and spiritual renewal, and will exist as little more than a splintered array of maniacal factions. The prospect of such an appalling and humiliating end to the story of a religion which once surpassed all others in its capacity for tolerating debate and dissent now seems a real possibility. The entire experience of Islamic work over the past fifteen years has been one of increasing radicalization, driven by the perceived failure of the traditional Islamic institutions and the older Muslim movements to lead the Muslim peoples into the worthy but so far chimerical promised land of the "Islamic State."

If this final catastrophe is to be averted, the mainstream will have to regain the initiative. But for this to happen, it must begin by confessing that the radical critique of moderation has its force. The Islamic movement has so far been remarkably unsuccessful. We must ask ourselves how it is that a man like Nasser, a butcher, a failed soldier, and a cynical demagogue, could have taken over a country as pivotal as Egypt, despite the vacuity of his beliefs, while the Muslim Brotherhood, with its pullulating millions of members, should have failed, and failed continuously, for six decades. The radical accusation of a failure in methodology cannot fail to strike home in such a context of dismal and prolonged inadequacy.

It is in this context—startlingly, perhaps, but inescapably—that we must present our case for the revival of the spiritual life within Islam. If it is ever to prosper, the "Islamic revival" must be made to see that it is in crisis, and that its mental resources are proving insufficient to meet contemporary needs. The response to this must be grounded in an act of collective *muḥāsaba*, of self-examination, in terms that transcend the ideologized neo-Islam of the revivalists, and return to a more classical and indigenously Muslim dialectic.

Symptomatic of the disease is the fact that among all the explanations offered for the crisis of the Islamic movement, the only authentically Muslim interpretation, namely, that God should not be lending it His support, is conspicuously absent. It is true that we frequently hear the Qur´ānic verse which states that "God does not change the condition of a people until they change the condition of their own selves" (13:11). But never, it seems, is this principle intelligently grasped. It is assumed that the sacred text is here doing no more than to enjoin individual moral reform as a precondition for collective societal success. Nothing could be more hazardous, however, than to measure such moral reform against the yardstick of the *fiqh* (jurisprudence) without giving concern to whether the virtues gained have been acquired through conformity (a relatively simple task), or proceed spontaneously from a genuine realignment of the soul. The verse is speaking of a spiritual change, specifically, a transformation of the *nafs* (soul or self) of the believers—not a moral one. And as the Blessed Prophet never tired of reminding us, there is little value in outward conformity to the rules unless this conformity is mirrored and engendered by an authentically righteous disposition of the heart. "No one shall enter the Garden by his works," as he expressed it. Meanwhile, the profoundly judgmental and works-oriented tenor of modern revivalist Islam (we must shun the problematic buzzword "fundamentalism"), fixated on visible manifestations of morality, has failed to address the underlying question of what revelation is *for*. For it is theological nonsense to suggest that God's final concern is with our ability to conform to a complex set of rules. His concern is rather that we should be restored, through our labors and His grace, to that state of purity and equilibrium with which we were born. The rules are a vital means to that end, and are facilitated by it. But they do not take its place.

To make this point, the Holy Qur´ān deploys a striking metaphor. In Sūra *Ibrāhīm*, verses 24 to 26, we read:

> Have you not seen how God coineth a likeness: a goodly word is like a goodly tree, the root whereof is set firm, its branch in the heaven? It bringeth forth its fruit at every time, by the leave of its Lord. Thus doth God coin likenesses for men, that perhaps they may reflect. And the likeness of an evil word is that of an evil tree that hath been torn up by the root from upon the earth, possessed of no stability.

According to the scholars of *tafsīr* (exegesis), the reference here is to the "words" (*kalima*) of faith and unfaith. The former is illustrated as a natural growth, whose florescence of moral and intellectual achievement is nourished by firm roots, which in turn denote the basis of faith: the quality of the proofs one has received, and the certainty and sound awareness of God which alone signify that one is firmly grounded in the reality of existence. The fruits thus yielded—the palpable benefits of the religious life—are permanent ("at every time"), and are not man's own accomplishment, for they only come "by the leave of its Lord." Thus is the sound life of faith. The contrast is then drawn with the only alternative: *kufr*, which is not grounded in reality but in illusion, and is hence "possessed of no stability."[1]

This passage, reminiscent of some of the binary categorizations of human types presented early on in Sūra *al-Baqara*, precisely encapsulates the relationship between faith and works, the hierarchy which exists between them, and the sustainable balance between nourishment and fructition, between taking and giving, which true faith must maintain.

It is against this criterion that we must judge the quality of contemporary "activist" styles of faith. Is the young "ultra," with his intense rage which can sometimes render him liable to nervous disorders, and his fixation on a relatively narrow range of issues and concerns, really firmly rooted, and fruitful, in the sense described by this Qur´ānic image? Let me point to the answer with an example drawn from my own experience. I used to know, quite well, a leader of the radical "Islamic" group, the *Jamā ͑āt Islāmiyya*, at the Egyptian university of Assiut. His name was Ḥamdī. He grew a luxuriant beard, was constantly scrubbing his teeth with his traditional toothstick, and spent his time preaching hatred of the Coptic Christians, a number of whom were actually attacked and beaten up as a result of his sermons. He had hundreds of followers; in fact, Assiut today remains a citadel of hardline, Wahhābī-style activism.

The moral of the story is that some five years after this acquaintance, providence again brought me face to face with Shaykh Ḥamdī. This time, chancing to see him on a Cairo street, I almost failed to recognize him. The beard was gone. He was in trousers and a sweater. More astonishing still was that he was walking with a young Western girl who turned out to be an Australian, whom, as he sheepishly explained to me, he was intending to marry. I talked to him, and it became clear that he was no longer even a minimally observant Muslim, no longer prayed, and that his ambition in life was to leave Egypt, live in Australia, and make money. What was extraordinary was that his experiences in Islamic activism had made no impression on him—he was once again the same distracted, ordinary Egyptian youth he had been before his conversion to "radical Islam."

This phenomenon, which we might label "*salafi* burnout," is a recognized feature of many modern Muslim cultures. An initial enthusiasm, gained usually in one's early twenties, loses steam some seven to ten years later. Prison and torture—the frequent lot of the Islamic radical—may serve to prolong commitment, but ultimately, a majority of these neo-Muslims relapse, seemingly no better or worse for their experience in the cult-like universe of the *salafi* mindset.

This ephemerality of extremist activism should be as suspicious as its content. Authentic Muslim faith is simply not supposed to be this fragile; as the Qur´ān says, its root is meant to be "set firm." One has to conclude that of the two trees depicted in the Qur´ānic image, *salafi* extremism resembles the second rather than the first. After all, the Companions of the religion's founder were not known for a transient commitment: their devotion and piety remained incomparably pure until they died.

What attracts young Muslims to this type of ephemeral but ferocious activism? One does not have to subscribe to determinist social theories to realize the importance of the almost universal condition of insecurity which Muslim societies are now experiencing. The Islamic world is passing through a most devastating period of transition. A history of economic and scientific change which in Europe took five hundred years, is, in the Muslim world, being squeezed into a couple of generations. For instance, only thirty-five years ago the capital of Saudi Arabia was a cluster of mud huts, as it had been for thousands of years. Today's Riyadh is a hi-tech megacity of glass towers, Coke machines, and gliding Cadillacs. This is an extreme case, but to some extent the dislocations of modernity are common to every Muslim society, excepting, perhaps, a handful of the most remote tribal peoples.

Such a transition period, with its centrifugal forces which allow nothing to remain constant, makes human beings very insecure. They look around for something to hold onto, something that will give them an identity. In our case, that something is usually Islam. And because they are being propelled into it by this psychic sense of insecurity, rather than by the more normal processes of conversion and faith, they lack some of the natural religious virtues, which are acquired by contact with a continuous tradition, and can never be learned from a book.

One easily visualizes how this works. A young Arab, part of an oversized family, competing for scarce jobs, unable to marry because he is poor, perhaps a migrant to a rapidly expanding city, feels like a man lost in a desert without signposts. One morning he picks up a copy of the fundamentalist writer Sayyid Quṭb from a newsstand, and is "born-again" on the spot. This is what he needed: instant certainty, a framework in which to interpret the landscape before him, to resolve the problems and tensions of his life, and, even more deliciously, a way of feeling superior and in control. He joins a group, and, anxious to retain his newfound certainty, accepts the usual proposition that all the other groups are mistaken.

This, of course, is not how Muslim religious conversion is supposed to work. It is meant to be a process of intellectual maturation, triggered by the presence of a very holy person or place. Repentance (*tawba*), in its traditional form, yields an outlook of joy, contentment, and a deep affection for others. The modern type of *tawba*, however, born of insecurity, often makes Muslims narrow, intolerant, and exclusivist. Even more noticeably, it produces people whose faith is, despite its apparent intensity, liable to vanish as suddenly as it came. Deprived of real nourishment, the activist's soul can only grow hungry and emaciated, until at last it dies.

The Activism Within

How should we respond to this disorder? We must begin by remembering what Islam is for. As we noted earlier, our religion is not, ultimately, a manual of rules which, when meticulously followed, becomes a passport to paradise. Instead, it is a package of social, intellectual, and spiritual technologies whose purpose is to cleanse the human heart. In the Qur´ān, the Lord says that on the Day of Judgment, nothing will be of any use to us, except a sound heart (*qalbun salīm*).[2] And in a famous *ḥadīth*, the Prophet, upon whom be blessings and peace, says: "Verily in the body there is a piece of flesh. If it is sound, the body is all sound. If it is corrupt, the body is all corrupt. Verily, it is the heart."[3] Mindful of this commandment, under which all the other commandments of Islam are subsumed, and which alone gives them meaning, the Islamic scholars have worked out a science, an *ʿilm*, of analyzing the "states" of the heart, and the methods of bringing it into this condition of soundness. In the fullness of time, this science acquired the name *taṣawwuf*, in English "Sufism"—a traditional label for what we might nowadays roughly but more intelligibly call "Islamic psychology."

At this point, many hackles are raised and well-rehearsed objections voiced. It is vital to understand that mainstream Sufism is not, and never has been, a doctrinal system, or a school of thought—a *madhhab*. It is, instead, a set of insights and practices which operate within the various Islamic *madhhabs*; in other words, it is not a *madhhab*, it is an *ʿilm*, a science. And like most of the other Islamic sciences, it was not known by name, or in its later developed form, in the age of the Prophet (upon him be blessings and peace) or his Companions. This does not make it less legitimate. There are many Islamic sciences which only took shape many years after the Prophetic age: jurisprudence (*uṣūl al-fiqh*), for instance, or logic (*manṭiq*), or the innumerable technical disciplines of *ḥadīth*.

Now this, of course, leads us into the often misunderstood area of *sunna* (Prophetic custom) and *bidʿa* (innovation), two notions which are wielded as blunt instruments by many contemporary activists, but which are often grossly misunderstood. The classical Orientalist thesis was of course that Islam, as an "arid Semitic legalism," failed to incorporate mechanisms for its own development, and that it petrified upon the death of its founder. This, however, is an antisemitic nonsense rooted in the ethnic determinism of the nineteenth-century historians who had shaped the views of the early Orientalist synthesizers (Muir, Le Bon, Renan, Caetani). Islam, as the religion designed for the end of time, has in fact proved itself eminently adaptable to the rapidly changing conditions which characterize this latest and most "entropic" stage of history.

What is a *bidʿa*, according to the classical definitions of Islamic law? Many are familiar with the famous *ḥadīth*: "Beware of matters newly begun, for every matter newly begun is innovation, every innovation is misguidance, and every misguidance is in Hell."[4] Does this mean that everything introduced into Islam that was not known to the first generation of Muslims is to be rejected? The classical *ʿulamāʾ* do not accept such a literalistic interpretation. Let us take a definition from Imām al-Shāfiʿī, an authority universally accepted in Sunnī Islam. Imām al-Shāfiʿī writes:

> There are two kinds of introduced matters (*muḥdathāt*). One is that which contradicts a text of the Qurʾān, or the *sunna*, or a report from the early Muslims (*athar*), or the consensus (*ijmāʿ*) of the Muslims: this is an "innovation of misguidance" (*bidʿat ḍalāla*). The second kind is that which is in itself good and entails no contradiction of any of these authorities: this is a "non-reprehensible innovation" (*bidʿa ghayr madhmūma*).[5]

This basic distinction between acceptable and unacceptable forms of *bidʿa* is recognized by the overwhelming majority of classical *ʿulamāʾ*. Among some, for instance al-ʿIzz ibn ʿAbd al-Salām (one of the half-dozen or so great *mujtahids* of Islamic history), innovations fall under the five axiological headings of the *sharīʿa*: the obligatory (*wājib*), the recommended (*mandūb*), the permissible (*mubāḥ*), the offensive (*makrūh*), and the forbidden (*ḥarām*).[6]

Under the category of "obligatory innovation," Ibn ʿAbd al-Salām gives the following examples: recording the Qur´ān and the laws of Islam in writing at a time when it was feared that they would be lost, studying Arabic grammar in order to resolve controversies over the Qur´ān, and developing philosophical theology (*kalām*) to refute the claims of the Muʿtazilites. Category two is "recommended innovation." Under this heading the *ʿulamā´* list such activities as building *madrasas*, writing books on beneficial Islamic subjects, and in-depth studies of Arabic linguistics. Category three is "permissible," or "neutral innovation," including worldly activities such as sifting flour, and constructing houses in various styles not known in Medina. Category four is the "reprehensible innovation." This includes such misdemeanors as overdecorating mosques or the Qur´ān. Category five is the "forbidden innovation." This includes unlawful taxes, giving judgeships to those unqualified to hold them, and sectarian beliefs and practices that explicitly contravene the known principles of the Qur´ān and the *sunna*.

The above classification of *bidʿa* types is normal in classical *sharīʿa* literature, being accepted by the four schools of orthodox *fiqh*. There have been only two significant exceptions to this understanding in the history of Islamic thought: the Ẓāhirī school as articulated by Ibn Ḥazm, and one wing of the Ḥanbalī *madhhab*, represented by Ibn Taymiyya, who goes against the classical *ijmāʿ* on this issue, and claims that all forms of innovation, good or bad, are un-Islamic.

Why is it, then, that so many Muslims now believe that innovation in any form is unacceptable in Islam? One factor has already been touched on: the mental complexes thrown up by insecurity, which incline people to find comfort in absolutist and literalist interpretations. Another lies in the influence of the well-financed neo-Ḥanbalī *madhhab* called Wahhābism, whose leaders are famous for their rejection of all possibility of development. In any case, armed with this more sophisticated and classical awareness of Islam's ability to acknowledge and assimilate novelty, we can understand how Muslim civilization was able so quickly to produce novel academic disciplines to deal with new problems as these arose.

Islamic psychology is characteristic of the new *ʿulūm* which, although present in latent and implicit form in the Qur´ān, were first systematized in Islamic culture during the early Abbasid period (750-945). Given the importance that the Qur´ān attaches to obtaining a "sound heart," we are not surprised to find that the influence of Islamic psychology has been massive and all-pervasive. In the formative first four centuries of Islam, the time when the great works of *tafsīr, hadīth,* grammar, and so forth were laid down, the *ʿulamāʾ* also applied their minds to this problem of *al-qalb al-salīm*. This was first visible when, following the example of the second generation of Muslims, many of the early ascetics, such as Sufyān ibn ʿUyayna, Sufyān al-Thawrī, and ʿAbdallāh ibn al-Mubārak, had focused their concerns explicitly on the art of purifying the heart. The methods they recommended were frequent fasting and night prayer, periodic retreats, and a preoccupation with *murābaṭa*: service as volunteer fighters to defend the border castles of north Syria. This type of pietist orientation was not in the least systematic during this period. It was a loose category embracing all Muslims who sought salvation through the Prophetic virtues of renunciation, sincerity, and deep devotion to the revelation. These men and women were variously referred to as *al-bakkaʾūn*: "the weepers," because of their fear of the Day of Judgement, or as *zuhhād*, ascetics, or *ʿubbād*, "unceasing worshipers."

By the third century, however, we start to find writings which can be understood as belonging to a distinct devotional path. The increasing luxury and materialism of Abbasid urban society spurred many Muslims to campaign for a restoration of the simplicity of the Prophetic age. Purity of heart, compassion for others, and a constant recollection of God were the defining features of this trend. We find references to the method of *muḥāsaba*: self-examination to detect impurities of intention. Also stressed was *riyāḍa*: self-discipline.

By this time, too, the main outlines of Qurʾānic psychology had been worked out. The human creature, it was realized, was made up of four constituent parts: the body (*jism*), the mind (*ʿaql*), the spirit (*rūḥ*), and the self (*nafs*). The first two need little comment. Less familiar (at least to people of a modern education) are the third and fourth categories.

The spirit is the *rūḥ*, that underlying essence of the human individual which survives death. It is hard to comprehend rationally, being in part of Divine inspiration, as the Qurʾān says: "And they ask you about the spirit; say, the spirit is of the command of my Lord. And you have been given of knowledge only a little" (17:85). According to the early Islamic psychologists, the *rūḥ* is a non-material reality which pervades the entire human body, but is centered on the heart, the *qalb*. It represents that part of man which is not of this world, and which connects him with his Creator, and which, if he is fortunate, enables him to see God in the next world. When we are born, this *rūḥ* is intact and pure. As we are initiated into the distractions of the world, however, it is covered over with the "rust" (*rān*) of which the Qurʾān speaks.[7] This rust is made up of two things: sin and distraction. When these are banished through the process of self-discipline, so that the worshiper is preserved from sin and is focusing entirely on the immediate presence and reality of God, the rust is dissolved, and the *rūḥ* once again is free. The heart is sound; and salvation, and closeness to God, are achieved.

This sounds simple enough. However, the early Muslims taught that such precious things come only at an appropriate price. Cleaning up the Augean stables of the heart is a most excruciating challenge. Outward conformity to the rules of religion is simple enough; but it is only the first step. Much more demanding is the policy known as *mujāhada*: the daily combat against the lower self, the *nafs*. As the Qur´ān says: "As for him that fears the standing before his Lord, and forbids his *nafs* its desires, for him, Heaven shall be his place of resort" (79:40). Hence the Sufi commandment: "Slaughter your ego with the knives of *mujāhada*."[8] Once the *nafs* is controlled, then the heart is clear, and the virtues proceed from it easily and naturally.

Because its objective is nothing less than salvation, this vital Islamic science has been consistently expounded by the great scholars of classical Islam. While today there are many Muslims, influenced by either Wahhābī or Orientalist agendas, who believe that Sufism has always led a somewhat marginal existence in Islam, the reality is that the overwhelming majority of the classical scholars were actively involved in Sufism. The early Shāfiʿī scholars of Khurāsān: al-Ḥākim al-Nīsābūrī, Ibn Fūrak, al-Qushayrī, and al-Bayhaqī, were all Sufis, who formed links in the richest academic tradition of Abbasid Islam which culminated in the achievement of Imām Ḥujjat al-Islām al-Ghazālī. Ghazālī himself, author of some three hundred books, including the definitive rebuttals of Arab philosophy and the Ismāʿīlīs, three large textbooks of Shāfiʿī *fiqh*, the best-known tract of *uṣūl al-fiqh*, two works on logic, and several theological treatises, also left us with the classic statement of orthodox Sufism: the *Iḥyā´ ʿulūm al-dīn* (*The Revivification of the Religious Sciences*), a book of which Imām Nawawī remarked: "Were the books of Islam all to be lost, excepting only the *Iḥyā´*, it would suffice to replace them all."[9]

Imām Nawawī himself wrote two books which record his debt to Sufism, one called the *Bustān al-ʿārifīn* (*Garden of the Gnostics*), and another called *al-Maqāṣid*.[10] Among the Mālikīs, too, Sufism was the almost universally followed style of spirituality. Al-Ṣāwī, al-Dardīr, al-Laqqānī and ʿAbd al-Wahhāb al-Baghdādī were all exponents of Sufism. The great Mālikī jurist of Cairo, ʿAbd al-Wahhāb al-Shaʿrānī, defines Sufism as follows:

> The path of the Sufis is built on the Qur´ān and the *sunna*, and is based on living according to the morals of the prophets and the purified ones. It may not be blamed, unless it violates an explicit statement from the Qur´ān, *sunna*, or *ijmāʿ*. If it does not contravene any of these sources, then no pretext remains for condemning it, except one's own low opinion of others, or interpreting what

> they do as ostentation, which is unlawful. No-one denies the states of the Sufis except someone ignorant of the way they are.[11]

For Ḥanbalī Sufism one has to look no further than the revered figures of ʿAbdallāh Anṣārī, ʿAbd al-Qādir al-Jīlānī, Ibn al-Jawzī, and Ibn Rajab.

In fact, virtually all the great luminaries of medieval Islam: al-Suyūṭī, Ibn Ḥajar al-ʿAsqalānī, al-ʿAynī, Ibn Khaldūn, al-Subkī, Ibn Ḥajar al-Haytamī; *tafsīr* writers like Bayḍāwī, al-Ṣāwī, Abu'l-Suʿūd, al-Baghawī, and Ibn Kathīr;[12] doctrine specialists such as al-Taftazānī, al-Nasafī, al-Rāzī: all wrote in support of Sufism. Many, indeed, composed independent works of Sufi inspiration. The *ʿulamā'* of the great dynasties of Islamic history, including the Ottomans and the Moghuls, were deeply infused with the Sufi outlook, regarding it as one of the most central and indispensable of Islamic sciences.

Further confirmation of the Islamic legitimacy of Sufism is supplied by the enthusiasm of its exponents for carrying Islam beyond the boundaries of the Islamic world. The Islamization process in India, black Africa, and Southeast Asia was carried out largely at the hands of wandering Sufi teachers. Likewise, the Islamic obligation of *jihād* has been borne with especial zeal by the Sufi orders. All the great nineteenth century jihādists: ʿUthman dan Fodio (Hausaland), al-Sanūsī (Libya), ʿAbd al-Qādir al-Jazā'irī (Algeria), Imām Shāmil (Daghestan) and the leaders of the Padre Rebellion (Sumatra) were active practitioners of Sufism, writing extensively on it while on their campaigns. Nothing is further from reality, in fact, than the claim that Sufism represents a quietist and non-militant form of Islam. However, it has always been utterly different from modern, wild extremism, in that it is rooted in mercy and justice, forbidding the targeting of civilians, and conforming to the ethical ideal of the just war. Sufism forms no part of modern terroristic radicalism.

With all this, we confront a paradox. Why is it, if Sufism has been so respected a part of Muslim intellectual and political life throughout our history, that there are, nowadays, angry voices raised against it? There are two fundamental reasons here. Firstly, there is again the pervasive influence of Orientalist scholarship, which, at least before 1922 when Louis Massignon wrote his *Essai sur les origines de la lexique technique*,[13] was of the opinion that something so fertile and profound as Sufism could never have grown from the essentially "barren and legalistic" soil of Islam. Orientalist works translated into Muslim languages were influential upon key Muslim modernists—such as Muḥammad ʿAbduh in his later writings—who began to question the centrality, or even the legitimacy, of Sufi discourse in Islam. Secondly, there is the emergence of the Wahhābī *daʿwa*. When Muḥammad ibn ʿAbd al-Wahhāb, some two hundred years ago, teamed up with the Saudi tribe and attacked the neighboring clans, he was doing so under the sign of an essentially neo-Khārijite version of Islam. Although he invoked Ibn Taymiyya, he had reservations even about him. For Ibn Taymiyya himself, although critical of the excesses of certain Sufi groups, had been committed to a branch of mainstream Sufism. This is clear, for instance, in Ibn Taymiyya's work *Sharḥ futūḥ al-ghayb*, a commentary on some technical points in the *Revelations of the Unseen*, a key work by the sixth-century saint of Baghdad, ʿAbd al-Qādir al-Jīlānī.[14] Throughout the work Ibn Taymiyya shows himself to be a loyal disciple of al-Jīlānī, whom he always refers to as *shaykhunā* ("our teacher"). This Qādirī affiliation is confirmed in the later literature of the Qādirī *ṭarīqa* (order), which records Ibn Taymiyya as a key link in the *silsila*, the chain of transmission of Qādirī teachings.[15]

Ibn ʿAbd al-Wahhāb, however, went far beyond this. Raised in the wastelands of Najd in Central Arabia, he had inadequate access to mainstream Muslim scholarship. In fact, when his *daʿwa* appeared and became notorious, the scholars and *muftīs* (judges) of the day applied to it the famous *ḥadīth* of Najd:

> Ibn ʿUmar reported the Prophet (upon whom be blessings and peace) as saying: "Oh God, bless us in our Syria: O God, bless us in our Yemen." Those present said: "And in our Najd, messenger of God," but he said, "O God, bless us in our Syria; O God, bless us in our Yemen." Those present said, "And in our Najd, messenger of God." Ibn ʿUmar told that he thought he said on the third occasion: "Earthquakes and dissensions (*fitna*) are there, and the horn of the devil shall arise in it."[16]

And it is significant that almost uniquely among the lands of Islam, Najd has never produced scholars of any repute.

The Najd-based *daʿwa* of the Wahhabis, however, began to be heard more loudly following the explosion of Saudi oil wealth. Many, even most, Islamic publishing houses in Cairo and Beirut are now subsidized by Wahhābī organisations, which prevent them from publishing traditional works on Sufism, and remove passages in other works considered unacceptable to Wahhābist doctrine.

The neo-Khārijite nature of Wahhābism makes it intolerant of all other forms of Islamic expression. However, because it has no coherent *fiqh* of its own—it rejects the orthodox *madhhabs*—and has only the most basic and primitively anthropomorphic theology, it has a fluid, amoeba-like tendency to produce divisions and subdivisions among those who profess it. No longer are the Islamic groups essentially united by a consistent *madhhab* and the Ashʿarī or Māturīdī doctrine. Instead, they are all trying to derive the *sharīʿa* and doctrine from the Qur'ān and the *sunna* by themselves. The result is the appalling state of division and conflict which disfigures the modern Wahhābī condition.

At this critical moment in our history, the *umma* has only one realistic hope for survival, and that is to restore the "middle way," defined by that sophisticated classical consensus which was worked out over painful centuries of debate and scholarship. That consensus alone has the demonstrable ability to provide a basis for unity. But it can only be retrieved when we improve the state of our hearts, and fill them with the Islamic virtues of affection, respect, tolerance, and reconciliation. This inner reform, which is the traditional competence of Sufism, is a precondition for the restoration of unity and decency in the Islamic movement. The alternative is likely to be continued, and agonizing, failure.

Notes

1 For a further analysis of this passage, see Habib Ahmad Mashhur al-Haddad, *Key to the Garden* (London: Quilliam Press, 1990), pp. 78-81.

2 Sūra 26:89. The archetype is Abrahamic: see Sūra 37:84.

3 Bukhārī, *Kitāb al-īmān*, p. 39.

4 This *ḥadīth* is in fact an instance of *takhṣīṣ al-ʿamm*: a frequent procedure of *uṣūl al-fiqh* by which an apparently unqualified statement is qualified to avoid the contradiction of another necessary principle. See Aḥmad ibn Naqīb al-Miṣrī, *Reliance of the Traveler*, trans. Nuh Ha Mim Keller (Abu Dhabi, 1991), pp. 907-8, for some further examples.

5 Ibn ʿAsākir, *Tabyīn Kadhib al-Muftarī* (Damascus, 1347), p. 97.

6 Cited in Muḥammad al-Jurdānī, *al-Jawāhir al-luʾluʾiyya fī sharḥ al-Arbaʿīn al-Nawawiyya* (Damascus, 1328), pp. 220-1.

7 83:14: "No indeed; but what they were earning has rusted upon their hearts."

8 al-Qushayrī, *al-Risāla* (Cairo, n.d.), p. 393.

9 al-Zabīdī, *Itḥāf al-sāda al-muttaqīn* (Cairo, 1311), I, 27.

10 Translated by Nuh Keller (Evanston, 1994).

11 ʿAbd al-Wahhāb al-Shaʿrānī, *al-Ṭabaqāt al-Kubrā* (Cairo, 1374), vol. 1, p. 4.

12 It is true that Ibn Kathīr in his *Bidāya* is critical of some later Sufis. Nonetheless, in his *Mawlid*, which he asked his pupils to recite on the occasion of the Blessed Prophet's birthday each year, he makes his personal debt to a conservative and sober Sufism quite clear.

13 This work infuriated the traditional Orientalist orthodoxy by using superior scholarship to document the Qurʾānic roots of the great categories of Sufi method and theory. See the English translation by Benjamin Clark (Notre Dame, 1997).

14 Taqī al-Dīn Ibn Taymiyya, *Sharḥ futūḥ al-ghayb liʾl-Imām al-Rabbānī ʿAbd al-Qādir al-Jīlānī* (Damascus, 1995).

15 See G. Makdisi's article "Ibn Taymiyya: A Sufi of the Qadiriya Order," *American Journal of Arabic Studies* (1973).

16 Narrated by Bukhārī. The translation is from J. Robson, *Mishkāt al-Maṣābīḥ* (Lahore, 1970), II, 1380.

Select Glossary of Foreign and Technical Terms

ahl al-ḥadīth: One of the first communities of scholars in Islam which arose in the second Islamic century. They were committed to preserving the teachings of the Prophet Muḥammad in both word and deed.

ahl al-kitāb: "People of the Book"; a Qur'ānic term referring to those communities of non-Muslim peoples—particularly Jews and Christians—who have been given a sacred scripture by God. These peoples were granted special status and protection under Islamic law provided they paid a tax to the Islamic state or were willing to participate in *jihād* along with the Muslims.

ʿālim (pl. *ʿulamāʾ*): A learned scholar of Islam; the word usually refers to a jurist (*faqīh*, pl. *fuqahāʾ*), an expert in Islamic jurisprudence, but all learned people in any of the Islamic sciences—such as Qur'ān commentary, *ḥadīth*, *kalām*, philosophy, and Sufism—are *ʿulamā'*. In some Muslim countries they are referred to as *mullahs*.

anṣār: "Helpers"; an honorific term referring to the people of the town of Yathrib (later known as Madīna) who willingly accepted the message of Islam, invited the Prophet to reside in their city, and offered him refuge and support against the pagan Meccans.

ʿaqīdah (pl. *ʿaqā'id*): Creedal statements that summarize the basic tenets of faith in Islam.

ʿaqlī sciences: The philosophical and intellectual sciences such as can be learned naturally through the use of innate reason and intelligence. These include logic, natural science, metaphysics, and mathematics. One cannot learn any of these sciences solely on the basis of authority since they require understanding, unlike the transmitted (*naqlī*) sciences.

bidʿa: Innovation. A heavily debated term in contemporary Islam; many strident puritans claim that all innovation is forbidden (*ḥarām*) in Islam. Innovation actually falls under the five axiological headings of the *sharīʿa*: the obligatory (*wājib*), the recommended (*mandūb*), the permissible (*mubāh*), the offensive (*makrūh*), and the forbidden (*ḥarām*).

convivencia: Coexistence and co-habitation; it refers to the historical experience of religious-cultural tolerance and coexistence between

Jews, Christians, and Muslims in medieval Spain during the eleventh and fourteenth centuries C. E.

dār al-ʿahd: "The abode of agreement"; another term for "the abode of peace" (*dār al-islām*) with minor differences between the two.

dār al-ḥarb: "The abode of war"; denotes the opposite of *dār al-islām*. In the second and third Islamic centuries, when Muslim states expanded their borders in a relatively short period of time, the jurists considered all lands under non-Muslim rule as belonging to *dār al-ḥarb*. This designation lost its meaning as the territorial expansion of Muslim states came to an end in later centuries.

dār al-islām: "The abode of Islam"; indicates a place or country where Muslims live as a majority and can practice their religion freely.

dar al-ṣulḥ: "The abode of peace"; refers to lands or countries with which Muslim states have a formal agreement of peace. According to Islamic law, the agreement in question is for five or ten years but can be extended indefinitely.

Deoband: An influential seminary founded in 1867 at Deoband, India by *ʿulamāʾ* in order to preserve traditional Islamic teachings and educate Indian Muslims in the face of British colonial rule and the resulting breakdown of traditional and religious authority.

dhimmī: "One who is protected"; refers to non-Muslims living within the borders of the Islamic state, who, by virtue of their participation in the maintenance of the Islamic state (either through paying the *jizya* tax or by participating in *jihād* along with the Muslim armies), were afforded the protection of the empire, freedom of trade, and the right to their own legal courts to judge their internal disputes.

double-truth theory: A famous debate in medieval philosophy according to which there are two distinct sets of truth: religious and philosophical. Erroneously attributed to Ibn Rushd (Averroes), the theory implies the superiority of the philosopher and philosophical arguments over the prophet and religious dogmas.

fatwā (pl. *fatāwa*): A legal opinion issued by a scholar of Islamic law. Such opinions usually involve the application of Islamic law to new and varied circumstances that arise in the Islamic community. Technically, these opinions have no absolute authority over Muslims except to the extent that they willingly accept a particular opinion on a certain matter. *Fatwās* are often accorded a great deal of respect within the Islamic tradition, although their impact and the extent of their acceptance are often dependent upon the perceived legal knowledge of the issuer.

fiqh: The science or discipline of Islamic law whereby legal opinions (*fatwās*) are derived from the Qur´ān and the sayings of the Prophet Muḥammad (*ḥadīth*).

fiṭra: The original, unblemished state of human nature where one inclines naturally to *tawḥīd* and sees things "as they are in themselves."

Five Pillars of Islam: The foundations of the religion of Islam. They are: 1. attesting to the Divine unity (*la ilāha illā Llāh*, "There is no god but God"); 2. performing the ritual prayer (*ṣalat*) five times daily; 3. paying the annual tithe (*zakāt*) on one's wealth and possessions; 4. fasting (*ṣawm*) during the month of Ramadan; and 5. performing the pilgrimage (*ḥājj*) to Mecca, if health and wealth permit.

fundamentalism: An umbrella term used primarily for modern Muslim movements that are characterized by a call to return to the Qur´ān and *sunna*, involving a rejection of the Islamic tradition as it has developed in the last thirteen centuries, especially in its intellectual and Sufi dimensions. It entails a literalist and exclusivist methodology, and an emphasis on the political and social dimension of religion.

game theory: A theory of rational behavior for interaction between agents in a given situation that is governed by a set of rules specifying the possible moves for each participant and a set of outcomes for each possible combination of moves.

ḥadīth: The collected sayings of the Prophet of Islam. The *ḥadīth*, which comprise the Prophet's sayings, actions and tacit approvals, constitute the second most important source for Islamic teachings after the Qur´ān, though in volume they far exceed the Qur´ān.

ḥājj: The rite of pilgrimage to Mecca; the fifth of the "five pillars" of Islam. It is required that all Muslims perform this rite once in their life, so long as they possess the health and wealth to complete the journey.

al-ḥaqq: "The Truth" or "the Real"; one of the names of God. It also refers to the rights of all things in that all things are said to be truths which derive their reality from the Absolute Truth. They thus exist through It and cannot be understood except in relation to It.

ḥikma: Literally, "wisdom." In the Islamic intellectual tradition it came to denote that form of theosophy which was a synthesis of philosophy, mysticism (or Sufism), and the religious sciences.

humanism: The intellectual viewpoint increasingly prevalent in the West since the time of the Renaissance; it replaced the traditional Christian view of God as the center of all things by a belief in man as the measure of all things.

iḥsān: "Making beautiful" or "doing beautifully." According to the Prophet Muḥammad "doing beautifully (*iḥsān*) is to worship God as if you see Him, for if you do not see Him, He nonetheless sees you." It is thus considered by many to be the essence of worship in Islam.

ijmāʿ: Consensus of the Muslim community on a particular legal issue. It is seen in most schools of Islamic law as one of the four primary sources of the *sharīʿa*, along with the Qur´ān, *sunna*, and *qiyās*.

ijtihād: A creative but disciplined intellectual effort to derive legal rulings for new situations from the accepted juridical sources of Islam. *Ijtihād* is not just one "religious" judgment among many, to be weighed against economic, political, and other judgments in deciding how to act; it is itself an "all-things-considered" ethical judgment based on spiritual principles, taking all other factors into account.

ʿilm al-kalām al-jadīd: A new dialectical theology. As a result of the introduction of modern Western ideas into the Islamic world, Muslim modernists have called for a new dialectical theology that will engage and incorporate these new ideas.

īmān: "Faith" or "belief"; its objects are God, the angels, the revealed books, the prophets, the Last Day of Judgment, and God's measuring out (*qadar*). Typically, these are summarized in creedal statements (*ʿaqā´id*) and rigorously defined in *kalām*.

instrumental rationality: A "means-end" view of rationality that ranks actions in terms of their likelihood to satisfy a given set of objectives, not an assessment of the ends themselves (which involves substantive rationality).

ʿirfān (also *maʿrifa*): Gnosis; knowledge of things as they are in themselves; it derives directly from unveiling (*kashf*), without the intermediary of instruction.

jahl al-murakkab: Compound ignorance; when one thinks one knows what one does not know and is thus prevented from knowing.

jihād: Literally, "exertion" or "struggle"; used in Islam for every form of struggle—from the battle against one's inner vices to military warfare. *Jihād* is usually divided into two parts: "lesser *jihād*" (*jihād aṣghar*), meaning defensive war against aggression, oppression and/or occupation to defend one's life, family, property, religion, and country; and "greater *jihād*" (*jihād akbar*), meaning spiritual struggle against one's desires and temptations so as to improve oneself morally and spiritually.

jizya: The tax levied upon non-Muslims living within the borders of the Islamic state. This tax is mentioned in the Qur´ān (9:29) and was understood as a right of the state in relation to its non-Muslim subjects for the sake of the protection afforded them by the Islamic armies, as well as the economic and legal freedoms guaranteed them as subjects of the Islamic state. Non-Muslims who paid the *jizya* were known as *dhimmīs*, literally, "those who are protected."

Kaʿba: The primordial house of worship in Mecca that, according to Islamic tradition, was built originally by Adam as a temple to God and was later reconstructed by Abraham and his son, Ishmael. In the period immediately preceding the advent of Islam, the Kaʿba had become the center of several idolatrous cults throughout the Arabian peninsula and idols were to be found in, around, and on top of, the sanctuary. With the conquest of Mecca by the Muslims, the Prophet of Islam destroyed all of these idols and rededicated the Kaʿba to the worship of God alone. All Muslims, no matter where they are on the earth, turn to face this primordial temple to God in performing their daily prayers. It is considered the holiest site in Islam.

kāfir (pl. *kāfirūn*): Often translated as "unbeliever"; literally, "one who covers over," the implication being, "one who covers over *truth*" in some way or another. It is used in the Qur´ān to refer to those who either deny, or have forgotten, some essential aspect of their religion. From the Qur´ānic perspective, such people are not necessarily "atheists," but may lack a correct understanding of one or more aspects of their faith.

kalām: Dialectical theology based upon reason and rational investigation.

Kalām seeks to define the articles of faith, but is mostly a polemical and at times apologetic discipline.

khalīfa: Vicegerent or representative of God. The Qur´ān teaches that human beings were created to be God's vicegerents on earth. For many this refers to the proper role of the human being in relation to creation. In Islamic political thought, the *khalīfas* or Caliphs are the vicegerents or the successors of the Prophet.

khānqah (Arabic, *ribāt*): A Persian term for a Sufi retreat or cloister where Sufis devote themselves to spiritual exercises and the learning of both the inward and outward religious sciences of Islam.

kufr: "Ungrateful," "truth-covering"; usually translated as "unbelief" or "infidelity." In the Qur´ān it is opposed to both faith (*īmān*) and thankfulness (*shukr*).

madhhab: A school of jurisprudence. There are four in Sunnī Islam: the Hanafī, Hanbalī, Malakī, and Shāfiᶜī schools of law. The majority of Shīᶜi Muslims follow the Jaḥfarī school of law.

madrasa: Literally, "a place of study." From the third Islamic century it has referred to places set aside for religious learning. In the modern period it has come to mean any type of school.

maᶜrifa: see *ᶜirfān*

miᶜrāj: "The Night Journey" of the Prophet Muḥammad. Also called the "nocturnal ascent," a miraculous event that took place in 619 or 620 C. E. when the Prophet of Islam was taken by God from Mecca to Jerusalem and then through the seven heavens to the Divine Throne. It was after the *miᶜrāj* that the Muslims were required to perform prayers five times daily. In the Sufi tradition, the *miᶜrāj* also signifies the spiritual journey of the soul towards God.

modernism: The predominant post-Renaissance and post-Enlightenment worldview of Western civilization marked by rationalism, scientism, and humanism. In the Muslim world, it refers to those individuals and movements who have sought to adopt Western ideas and values from the nineteenth century onwards in response to Western domination and imperialism.

muḥaddith: A scholar of the sciences of the sayings of the Prophet Muḥammad.

muhājir (pl. *muhājirūn*): Literally "one who migrates"; an honorific term referring to those Muslims in Mecca who made the *hijra* (migration) with the Prophet from Mecca to Madīna in 622 C. E. (from which time the Muslim calendar begins its dating). It is often juxtaposed with the term *anṣār* ("helpers").

muḥaqqiq: Verifier; one who sees things as they are in themselves, without obfuscations.

mujāhid (pl. *mujāhidūn*): Literally "one who exerts himself"; refers to those who participate in *jihād*, as both an inward and outward exertion for the realization of religious objectives.

munāfiq (pl. *munāfiqūn*): "Hypocrite." In early Islamic history it refers to a fairly specific group of "Muslims" in Madīna who nominally accepted the authority of the Prophet of Islam, whilst working in various covert and overt ways to hinder his mission.

mushrik (pl. *mushrikūn*): A polytheist; literally, "one who falsely associates (something) with God," considering it to be likewise divine. It is most often used in the Qur´ān to refer to the Meccans and other Arabs who refused to accept the monotheistic vision of Islam.

mutakallim: A scholar of dialectical theology.

nafs: "Soul" or "self." Though used in different ways by Muslims, in general it refers to the human self which lies between the spirit (*rūḥ*) and the body (*jism*). This is the corruptible dimension of the human being which must be reformed.

naqlī sciences: Sciences such as can be learned only through transmission, going back ultimately to the founder of the science in question, and, in the case of the religious sciences, to the Revelation itself. These include the recitation of Qur´ān, *ḥadīth*, and grammar among others. One can learn such sciences on the basis of authority and imitation, unlike the philosophical and intellectual (*ʿaqlī*) sciences.

qiyās: Analogical reasoning as used in Islamic jurisprudence. It is understood in most schools of Islamic law to be one of the four primary sources of the *sharīʿa*, along with the Qur´ān, *sunna*, and *ijmāʿ*.

Quraysh: The dominant tribal group in Mecca. The Prophet of Islam was a member of this tribe, as were most of his early followers.

rasūlallāh: "Messenger of God"; the most common appellation for the Prophet Muḥammad. A messenger, or *rasūl*, is a prophet (*nabī*) who establishes a new religion, or a new religious law. Moses and Jesus are counted amongst their number.

rationalism: The philosophical position that sees reason as the ultimate arbiter of truth. Its origin lies in Descartes' famous *cogito ergo sum*, "I think, therefore I am."

ribāt: see *khānqah*

Rightly-guided Caliphs: The first four leaders of the Islamic community after the death of the Prophet of Islam in 632 C.E.: Abū Bakr, ʿUmar, ʿUthmān, and ʿAlī. They were all close companions of the Prophet during his lifetime, who succeeded him only in terms of his temporal, administrative functions (e.g., in collecting and distributing tax money, leading the Muslim armies in battle, upholding Islamic law in society, appointing regional governors, etc.), and not in his spiritual function as bringer of the revelation.

rūḥ: "Spirit"; the Divine Breath blown into Adam's body. It is a non-material reality which pervades the entire human body, but is centered on the heart (*qalb*). It represents that part of the human which is not of this world, and which connects the human with the Divine.

salaf: "The pious forbears"; refers to the early Islamic community that existed at the time of the Prophet and the immediate generations that followed him. The *salaf* are believed to have demonstrated the principal norms for what constitutes properly Islamic behavior. In modern Islamic discourse certain groups are referred to, or speak of themselves as, "*salafī*," i.e., looking to the example of the pious forbears.

secularism: The worldview that seeks to maintain religion and the sacred in the private domain; the predominant view in the West since the time of the French Revolution of 1789 C. E.

sharīʿa: The body of beliefs, practices, and laws which have their origin in the Islamic Revelation. It is generally labeled "Islamic law" in Western scholarship.

Shaykh al-Azhar: The Rector of al-Azhar, one of the oldest Islamic universities in the world, founded in Cairo over one thousand years ago. It is perhaps the foremost institution for the training of Islamic religious scholars of the majority Sunnī perspective. Although the Shaykh al-Azhar is today an appointee of the Egyptian government, the position still wields a great deal of religious and legal influence among Sunnī Muslims worldwide.

Shīʿism: The smaller of the two major branches of Islam, comprising about fifteen percent of Muslims. Shīʿites are distinguished from Sunnīs by their dedication to certain descendants of the Prophet called Imams.

soul: see *nafs*

spirit: see *rūḥ*

sunna: Wont; the model established by the Prophet Muḥammad, as transmitted in the *ḥadīth*.

Sunnism: The larger of the two main branches of Islam, comprising about eighty-five percent of Muslims, as contrasted with Shīʿism.

tafsīr: Commentary, interpretation; refers to the fourteen hundred year tradition of Qur'ānic commentary in Islam. It is said that the first commentary upon the Qur'ān is the *ḥadīth*.

taḥqīq: Verification; seeing things as they are in themselves through immediate perception without intermediaries.

tarbiya: The process of training and disciplining the soul (*nafs*).

tawḥīd: Literally "making one" or "asserting unity"; the cardinal Islamic doctrine of the unity of God.

tazkiya: Purification of the heart; often referred to in conjunction with *tarbiya*.

tit-for-tat: The strategy of starting with cooperation, and thereafter proceeding to do what the other player did on the previous move.

Tradition: Divine Revelation and the unfolding and development of its sacred content, in time and space, such that the forms of society and civilization maintain a "vertical" connection to the meta-historical, transcendental substance from which revelation itself derives.

umma: "Community," or "people." A Qur´ānic term used to refer to the various peoples and nations of the earth. The Qur´ān speaks of the fact that God has sent a prophet to every *umma*, and it is understood in Islam that each prophet has his own *umma*, who follows his message.

uṣūl al-fiqh: Principles of jurisprudence; the technical science of deriving legal rulings from the Qur´ān and *ḥadīth*.

waḥy: "Divine Revelation," received by a prophet from God; applies especially to the Qur´ān and other sacred scriptures such as the Torah and the Gospel.

Yathrib: The original name for the city of Madīna.

zakāt: The third of the "five pillars" of Islam. The *zakāt* is a tithe levied upon the wealth and property of Muslims which is distributed to the poorer members of society. It is not obligatory for non-Muslims living in Islamic societies.

For a glossary of all key foreign words used in books published by World Wisdom, including metaphysical terms in English, consult:
www.DictionaryofSpiritualTerms.org.
This on-line Dictionary of Spiritual Terms provides extensive definitions, examples and related terms in other languages.

Notes on Contributors

Joseph E. B. Lumbard is an American Muslim who now works as Assistant Professor of Islamic Studies at the American University in Cairo. A native of Washington, D.C., he is the founder and first director of the Islamic Research Institute. He received a Ph.D. and M.Phil. in Islamic Studies from Yale University and an M.A. in Religious Studies from the George Washington University. In order to complement his Western university training, he studied Qur´ān, Ḥadīth, Sufism, and Islamic philosophy with traditional teachers in Morocco, Egypt, Yemen, and Iran. He is conversant with a broad range of Islamic intellectual disciplines, and has first-hand experience of several oral and cultural traditions. An avid proponent of cross-cultural understanding, Dr. Lumbard has published several articles on comparative mysticism, Sufism, and Islamic philosophy, has lectured in academic arenas around the world, participated in inter-faith dialogue in Jewish and Christian forums, and appeared on several radio and television programs. He is the author of *"No god but God is my Fortress ...": Aḥmad al-Ghazālī on Dhikr* (forthcoming, Fons Vitae) and is currently working on *Aḥmad al-Ghazālī and the Metaphysics of Love*, the first extensive study of the life and work of the renowned Sufi in a European language.

Seyyed Hossein Nasr was born in Tehran, Iran in 1933. He received his advanced education at M.I.T. and Harvard University in the USA, before he returned to teach at Tehran University from 1958-1979. He founded the Iranian Imperial Academy of Philosophy and served as its first president, and was also president of Aryamehr University for several years. Since 1984 he has been University Professor of Islamic Studies at the George Washington University and president of the Foundation for Traditional Studies, publisher of the journal *Sophia*. He is a world-renowned scholar on Islam and the perennial philosophy and is the author of over fifty books and five hundred articles on topics ranging from comparative religion to traditional Islamic philosophy, cosmology, art, ecology, politics, and mysticism. Among his most notable works are *Ideals and Realities of Islam, Islam and the Plight of Modern Man, Knowledge and the Sacred* (the 1981 Gifford Lectures), *Traditional Islam in the Modern World, Religion and the Order of Nature,* and *The Heart of Islam.* His *The Philosophy of Seyyed Hossein Nasr* recently appeared as a volume in the prestigious Library of Living Philosophers series. The Seyyed Hossein Nasr Foundation is dedicated to the propagation of traditional teachings in general, and the various facets of traditional Islam and other religions in particular.

EJAZ AKRAM is Assistant Professor of Political Science at the American University in Cairo. A Pakistani-American scholar specializing in the interface between religion and the transnational politics of the Muslim world, he has an M.A. in Comparative and Regional Studies from the School of International Service at American University, as well as an M.A. in World Politics and a Ph.D. in International Relations from the Catholic University of America. He has lectured in several forums around the world and served as Managing Editor for *The American Journal of Islamic Social Sciences* from 2000-2002. Dr. Akram is currently editing *The Handbook of Islam* with Sage Publications (forthcoming).

WALEED EL-ANSARY is an Egyptian American with a Ph.D. in the human sciences from the George Washington University and an M.A. in Economics from the University of Maryland. He is currently an adjunct professor of Islamic Economics at the Graduate School of Islamic and Social Sciences, as well as a research scholar at the Islamic Research Institute, a think-tank based in Washington, D.C. His research focuses on Islamic and neoclassical economic theories and their implications for law and policy. His publications include "The Spiritual Significance of Jihād in the Islamic Approach to Markets and the Environment" (forthcoming), "Linking Ethics and Economics: The Role of Ijtihād in the Regulation and Correction of Capital Markets" (co-authored), and "Recovering the Islamic Economic Intellectual Heritage: Problems and Possibilities." He has lectured widely on topics relating to economics, philosophy, and policy.

DAVID DAKAKE is an American Muslim specializing in comparative religion and Islamic philosophy. He has an M.A. in Religious Studies from Temple University and is currently a Ph.D. candidate in their Department of Religion. He has also studied extensively in Egypt and Iran. His dissertation is entitled, "Defining Ambiguity: Early and Classical *Tafsīr* on the *Mutashābih* Verses of the Qur´ān." He has published articles on Islamic history and philosophy, taught courses at the university level on Judaism, Christianity, and Islam and Islamic mysticism, and delivered academic papers in the Middle East, Europe, and North America. Formerly a consultant for the Islamic Research Institute in Washington D.C., he is currently employed as a researcher in Islamic Studies at the George Washington University in Washington, D.C.

IBRAHIM KALIN is Assistant Professor of Islamic Studies at the College of the Holy Cross where he teaches courses on Islam, Islamic philosophy and theology, Sufism, Islam and the West, and Islam in the modern world. His field of interest is post-Avicennan Islamic philosophy and Mulla Ṣadra, with research interests in Islam and science, comparative and mystical philosophy, Islam and the West, and intellectual movements in the contemporary Muslim world. Dr. Kalin is the associate editor of *Resources on Islam and Science*, a web-based project of the Center for Islam and Science (http://www.cis-ca.net), which provides a comprehensive database on Islam and science. He is a recipient of the Center for Theology and Natural Sciences (CTNS) Science and Religion Course Program Award, 2002. His publications include articles on Islamic philosophy, Islamic science, and Western perceptions of Islam, and he has translated a number of Islamic philosophical texts from Arabic into English.

FUAD S. NAEEM is a Pakistani scholar now residing in the U.S. where he is pursuing a Ph.D. in the Islamic Studies program at Duke University. He has an M.A. in Hinduism and Islam from the George Washington University and is a specialist in the Islamic intellectual trends of the Indian Subcontinent. His fields of interest include later Islamic philosophy and Sufism, and the encounter between Islam and modernity.

REZA SHAH-KAZEMI is a Research Associate at the Institute of Ismāʿīlī Studies in London. His major work is *Paths to Transcendence: Spiritual Realization according to Shankara, Ibn ʿArabī, and Meister Eckhart* (forthcoming). His contributions to the traditionalist journals *Sophia* and *Sacred Web* deal with themes relating to the perennial philosophy, tradition, beauty, and prayer. He is currently preparing a new English translation of the Imam ʿAlī's *Nahj al-Balāgha.*

T. J. WINTER is the Sheikh Zayed Lecturer in Islamic Studies at the Divinity School, University of Cambridge, and the Director of the Muslim Academic Trust. He studied for many years in the Middle East and has published several translations of Arabic texts. Among them are Abū Ḥāmid al-Ghazālī's *The Remembrance of Death and the Afterlife (Kitāb dhikr al-mawt wa mā baʿdahu): Book XL of The Revival of the Religious Sciences (Iḥyā ʿulūm al-dīn)*, and *On Disciplining the Soul (Kitāb Riyāḍat al-nafs) and On Breaking the Two Desires (Kitāb Kasr al-shahwatayn): Books XXII and XXIII of The Revival of the Religious Sciences (Iḥyā ʿulūm al-dīn).*

Index

Abbasids, 146
ABC, 141, 195, 197, 228
ʿAbd al-Halīm Maḥmūd, 40
Abraham, 7, 129
absolute existence (*al-wājib al-wujūd*), 44, 58
Absolute Existence, 44, 58
Abū Bakr al-Ṣiddīq, 10, 16
Abū ʾl-Ḥuṣayn, 15, 32
Abu ʾl-Suʿūd, 292
Abū Maryam (Metropolitan of Miṣr), 19
Abū Saʿīd b. Abi ʾl-Khayr, 70
Abū Sufyān, 10, 125
Abū Thawr, 50
Abū ʿUbaydah ibn al-Jarrāh, 17
account of the rise and progress of Mahometanism, An (Stubbe), 156
Adam (prophet), 58, 65, 89, 99, 109
Ādharbayjān, people of, 19
Afghānī, Jamāl ad-Dīn, 40, 68, 72
Afghanistan, *vii*, 72, 138, 201, 209
Afghanistan, invasion of, *vii*
Africa, 13-14, 39, 68, 93, 95, 129, 145, 237, 260, 273, 292
Ahl al-ḥadīth, 45-46, 49-51, 66, 73, 297
ahl al-kitāb ("People of the Book"), 10, 145
Ahl-i-ḥadīth, 92
Aḥmad ibn Idrīs, 164
Aḥmad Rezā Shāh, 92
aḥwāl, 52
akhlāq, 52, 55
Akhtar, Shabbir, 283
Akram, Ejaz, *xviii*, 39, 113, 141, 144, 222, 237, 278, 307
ʿālam al-arwāḥ, 108
ʿAlawī, Shaykh Aḥmad al-, *xiii*, 134-135, 164
Albertus Magnus, 151
Aleppo, Christian population of, 17
Alexander the Great, 101
Algeria, 48, 68, 132, 134-135, 142, 174-175, 250, 276, 292
Algeria, French occupation of, 48
ʿAlī al-Jamal, Mulay, 135
ʿAlī, Chirāgh, *xvi*, 41, 89-90, 105-106
ʿAlī, Sayyid Amīr, 85
ʿAlī ibn Abī Ṭālib,137
Aligarh (college), 85-86, 89, 91, 96
Aligarh Movement, 86, 91
Allāh, 17-18, 20, 31-32, 48, 83, 93-95, 97, 103-104, 106, 109, 111, 113-114, 125, 134, 142, 170, 185, 196, 203, 216
Allāhabādī, Akbar, 87
Allāhu Akbar, 122
ʿālim, 82, 87, 93, 109, 113, 297
almsgiving (*zakāt*), 106
Alvaro, 152, 182
America (United States of), *vii-viii*, *xi*, *xv*, *xxi*, 26-27, 39-40, 72, 159, 161, 165, 167-169, 171, 176, 180, 183, 185-187, 195-197, 199, 201, 203-204, 214, 227, 233, 237, 242, 262, 273, 278, 298
Americans, 24, 27, 143, 165-166, 195-196, 200-201, 205, 210-211, 213, 216, 226, 234
Amir, Yigal, 141, 172
ʿAmr ibn al-ʿĀṣ, 19
Andalusia, *xii*, 143, 152-153, 182
angelology, 87
Anglo-Muḥammadan law, 83-84
Anglo-Saxon law, 258
Anṣār, 21, 34-35, 297
Anṣārī, ʿAbdallāh, 292
Ansary, Waleed El-, 48, 113, 144, 241, 277, 307
Answer to Modernism (Thanvī), 95-96, 114-116
anti-Christ, the, *xii*, 146, 149, 154
anticipation question, 193, 205, 212
anti-globalizationists, 254
anti-Israeli media, 215
anti-modernism, 176
Antioch, 17, 23
anti-Semitism, 127-128, 130
Apostles, 5, 152
ʿaqāʾid, 87, 94, 98, 297
Arabic-English Lexicon (Lane), 162
Arabs, *xii*, 22, 25, 31-32, 85, 107, 126, 152, 157, 165, 174, 180, 183, 185, 196, 216, 224, 226, 247
Arberry, A. J., 30, 163, 184
Arian, 20, 146
Aristotelianism, 164

Titles in The Perennial Philosophy Series by World Wisdom

A Buddhist Spectrum by Marco Pallis, 2003

The Essential Ananda K. Coomaraswamy, edited by Rama P. Coomaraswamy, 2004

The Essential Titus Burckhardt: Reflections on Sacred Art, Faiths, and Civilizations, edited by William Stoddart, 2003

Every Branch in Me: Essays on the Meaning of Man, edited by Barry McDonald, 2002

Islam, Fundamentalism, and the Betrayal of Tradition: Essays by Western Muslim Scholars, edited by Joseph E. B. Lumbard, 2004

Journeys East: 20th Century Western Encounters with Eastern Religious Traditions by Harry Oldmeadow, 2004

Living in Amida's Universal Vow: Essays in Shin Buddhism, edited by Alfred Bloom, 2004

Paths to the Heart: Sufism and the Christian East, edited by James S. Cutsinger, 2002

Returning to the Essential: Selected Writings of Jean Biès, translated by Deborah Weiss-Dutilh, 2004

Science and the Myth of Progress, edited by Mehrdad M. Zarandi, 2003

Seeing God Everywhere: Essays on Nature and the Sacred, edited by Barry McDonald, 2003

IHUMW 297
.0905
1
I82